The Life and Times of

# Hengest

Bryan Evans

Published 2014 by

Anglo-Saxon Books
www.asbooks.co.uk

Hereward, Black Bank Business Centre
Little Downham, Ely,
Cambridgeshire, England

PL



ISBN 978 1 898281740

# Contents

**Maps and illustrations by Bryan Evans ©**

# Foreword

## *A deadly onset*

A knot of men stood peering out from the doorway of the hall. It was the middle of the night, but one on watch had called the others to come and look. Outside, moonlight fell fitfully as clouds drifted across the night sky, and they could see light flickering in and out of the shadows under the eaves of buildings – but flickering on what? The men spoke under their breath. It was not the first glimmer of the dawn, for that was hours away. There was no crackling of fire, no billowing smoke, so it was not the gables of another hall burning. And it was surely not a dragon on the rampage! No, that flickering must be moonlight glinting on spearheads, on shields, and on war-helms. They were about to be attacked! (So spoke their leader, a young king named Hnæf.) The young warrior bade his friends rouse the others: let every man take his weapons and steel himself for the fight!

Even as warriors hastened to the doors of the hall, they heard voices outside, as their foes understood that they had been seen. Above the rest they caught the gruff tones of an older man urging a youth (Garulf he named him) not to risk his life in the first onslaught. But the youth paid no heed, and, next breath, they heard his bold words as he asked who held the door. Sigeferth was there, with Eaha. (Ordlaf and Guthlaf held the other door.) That war-lord gave answer, 'One hardened in battle, Sigeferth by name. And the death you would deal to me shall fall on you!' Then, all at once, there was uproar! Swords hissed as they were drawn from the sheaths, spear-butts were thrust against the window-shutters, warriors in ring-mail heaved their shoulders against the doors, and within the hall the floorboards groaned under the tread of warriors rushing to meet first one threat, then another. And in that first onset the youth, Garulf, fell. Dawn came at last (though it was gloomy enough within the shuttered hall), and in a short lull they heard the croaking of ravens as they wheeled overhead.

All day they fought, and the day after, with both sides snatching a few hours of wary sleep as night fell. For five days this went on, the dead piling up outside, while within all sixty men yet stood upon their feet. Then on the fifth day one bloodied defender staggered from his post, his mail-shirt rent, his war-helm buckled by hammer blows. And young Hnæf, seeing him fall, shook his head. How could they go on like this? Who would be next?

## *Inklings of a tale*

From the middle years of the fifth century AD there have come down to us inklings of a tale from the southern fringes of the North Sea. It is a tale of untroth, of a night onset on a hall, of a grim fight against high odds. It is a tale of lives blighted by hatred and revenge, of men rent by tangled loyalties, a tale of chance and mischance, and half-chance grasped with both hands. We have the tale in two short pieces of Anglo-Saxon poetry, the *Finnsburg Fragment* and an episode in the poem *Beowulf.* It is a tale of men and women caught up in unfolding deeds which they cannot master – yet they themselves help shape those deeds. This is the tale of Finn Folkwielder of the Frisians and his stronghold of Finnsburg, of his wife the lady Hildeburh, of Hnæf Halfdane her brother, and of a certain Hengest, a key figure in the drama. Now, in the chronicles of these times, this is the name of the historical (or legendary?) founder of the kingdom of Kent. Is the Hengest of the poems the same man as the Hengest of the history books? And was he a real person? The aim of this book is to find out what may be known about the players in this drama, and the background of this tangled tale.

We begin with an overview of the wider stage in this time of 'the breaking of nations': the Western Roman Empire threatened by Attila and his Huns; Britain, the restless 'north-west frontier' province, and the measures for its defence (the 'Saxon Shore' network, the use of *foederati* and *laeti*); the folkdoms of the North Sea southern rim, unsettled by the growing weakness of the Roman empire, the 'ripple effects' of the Hunnish threat, the rising Danish folkdom, and changing sea levels.

Next, we look at the witnesses for this period of our history: Gildas, Bede, the *Anglo-Saxon Chronicle*, and the *Historia Brittonum.* What story do they tell? Are they trustworthy? Has late material been interpolated into Gildas? Is the *Anglo-Saxon Chronicle* merely Wessex dynastic propaganda compiled long after the events described? The *Chronicle* says that the Wessex founders, Cerdic and Cynric, landed on the Hampshire coast, then, little by little, made their way inland. But archaeology points to the middle Thames as the cradle of the West Saxon kingdom. What are to make of this? Do the *Chronicle* and the *Historia Brittonum* tell different tales of the warring in Kent? Is it true that there are fictional characters and events in the *Chronicle*, and that the chronology is not to be taken seriously?

The question whether the tale of Hengest is history or legend is looked at. The critics point to a number of features of the story which they see as legendary: the three cries to Rome, the three ships, the leadership of two brothers with alliterating names (and animal names at that), Horsa's monument, and the treacherous massacre of three hundred British elders. The fact that the sons of the royal house of Kent were the 'Oiscingas' (from the name of Oisc, Hengest's supposed son) and not 'Hengestingas' is said by some to undermine the place of Hengest in the story. Was he perhaps added to the kinship list as the father of Oisc, to make a link with the legendary Germanic past? We have sought to offer reasonable answers to these points. It is noted that when the tale of Hengest and Horsa is compared with that of Lombard origins (as written down in the seventh century work, *The Origin of the Lombard Nation*) the Lombard story comes across as rather fanciful, but the record of Hengest and Horsa is seen to be very plain and matter-of-fact.

After a look at the place of kinlore (genealogy) among the Anglo-Saxons, and a weighing of the worth of oral tradition, we take a brief look at Anglo-Saxon seacraft, before going on to consider three 'models' of the Anglo-Saxon settlement: the 'going concern' model, the pirate base model, and folk migration. This is followed by a brief look at a number of early Anglo-Saxon kingdoms, to see if a particular model can be seen in these cases. There follows a much more detailed look at what may have happened in the Jutish lands of Kent, the Isle of Wight, and the Hampshire coastlands.

Two asides follow, one looking at the question whether the ethnic labels we have long been used to (Angle, Saxon, Jute) are in fact 'constructed', and the other looking at modern genetic studies.

Part one ends with a 'stock-take' of the Hengest tale. It is held that certain conclusions can be drawn which, though not provable, are defensible. As regards sources, it is held that Gildas's *De Excidio*, and the *Historia Brittonum*, are not to be wholly written off (though they must be used with care), but that Bede and the *Chronicle* are to be taken seriously. It is held that Hengest was a real historical figure, a mid-fifth century outlaw-adventurer, but that he was perhaps not blood kin to Oisc. Further, it is argued that a good case can be made for holding that the Hengest of the *Chronicle* was one and the same man with the Hengest of the poetry (of the *Finnsburg Fragment* and of the 'Episode' in the *Beowulf* poem). It is also held that the picture of Hengest and his war-band as disgruntled and rebellious *foederati* is credible.

In part two we look at the Hengest saga in its setting. The scene is set with notes on the warcraft and weapons of the Heroic Age, and on the warlord and his followers – seated in hall, feasting and glorying after warlike deeds wrought. Some of the matter of Anglo-Saxon heathenism is looked at: the fraught figures of Woden and Freya, the runes and their use for divination, and otherworld beings. The importance that the early English attached to wisdom, and to 'wyrd' or fate, is discussed. There follows some account of early English poetry, and outlines of some of the tales that formed part of the matter of the poet: the tales of Offa of Angeln, Heoden and Hild, Welund, Waldere. Then we look at the *Finnsburg Fragment*, that leaf of forty-eight lines of Anglo-Saxon poetry found, copied, and almost straightway lost, by George Hickes, about 1700. The tangles of this one sheet of verse are untangled as best as may be, drawing on Alan Bliss's editing of JRR Tolkien.

Part two closes with a look at two questions: what manner of man was the Hengest of the *Finnsburg Fragment* and the 'Episode'? And what shape did his career take? (The account offered here is a prose summary of the tale of Hengest as told in the poems in Part Three.)

# Maps

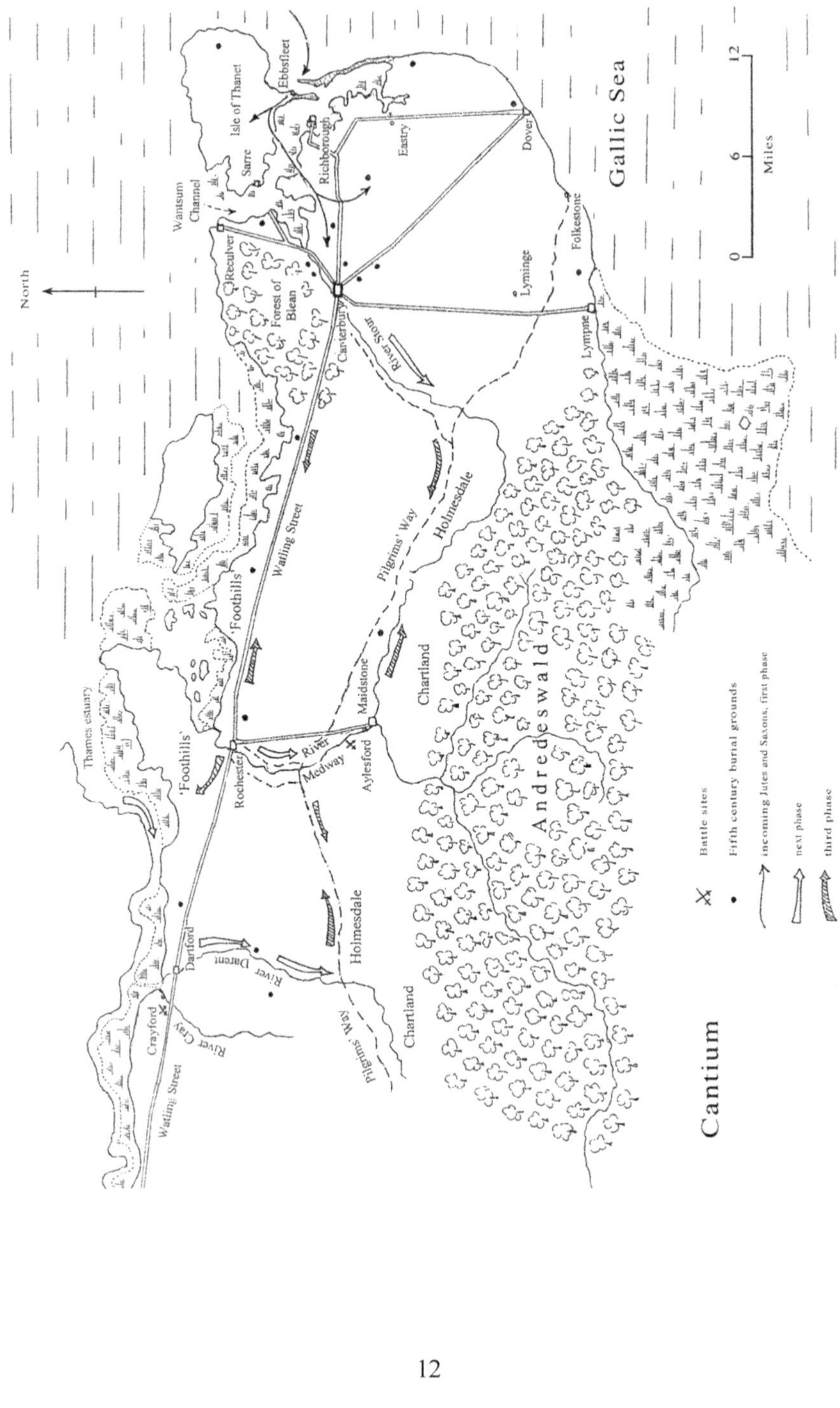
Cantium
North
Thames estuary
Wantsum Channel
Isle of Thanet
Ebbsfleet
Sarre
Richborough
Reculver
Forest of Blean
Canterbury
Eastry
Dover
Folkestone
Lyminge
Lympne
River Stour
Gallic Sea
'Foothills'
Watling Street
Rochester
River Medway
Aylesford
Maidstone
Chartland
Holmesdale
Pilgrims' Way
Andredeswald
Dartford
River Darent
Crayford
River Cray
0
6
12
Miles
Battle sites
Fifth century burial grounds
incoming Jutes and Saxons, first phase
next phase
third phase

**Durovernum Cantiacorum/Cantwaraburh**

Canterbury, c. 400-450

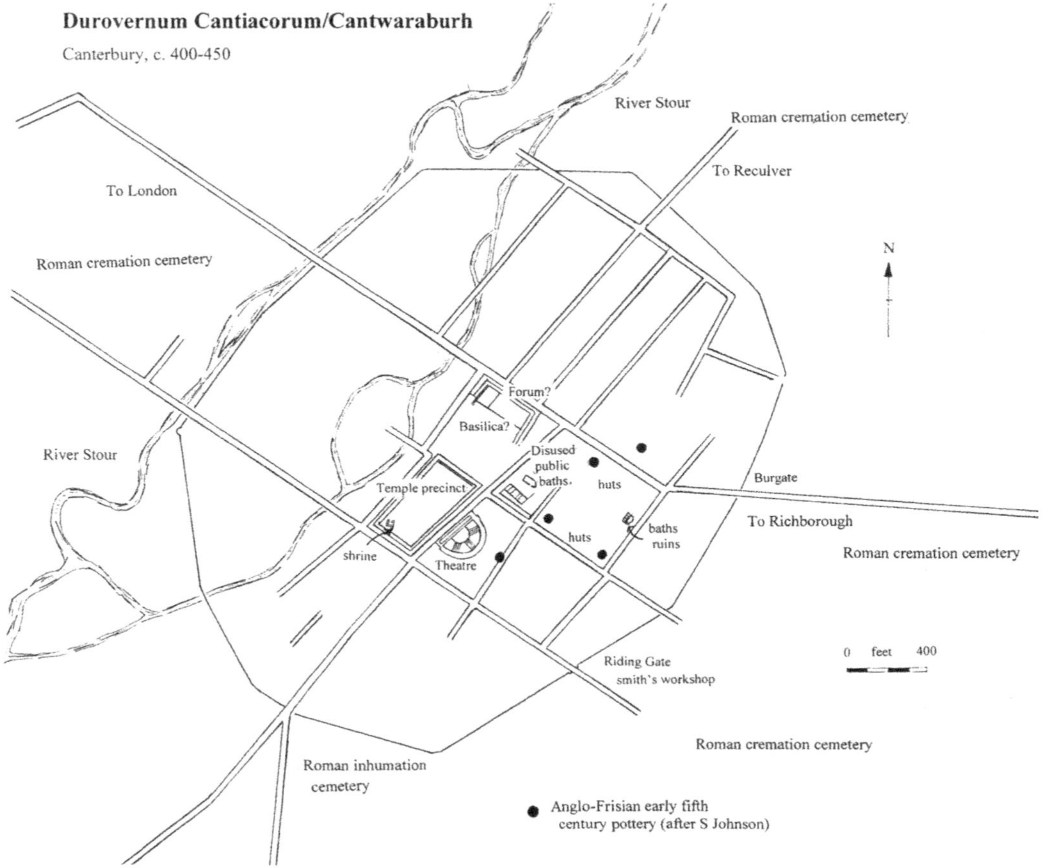

Roman Britain
and the Saxon Shore
Boundary lines of
the Provinces
(as near as may be)
N
Hadrian's Wall
Britannia Secunda
York
Lincoln
Flavia
Caesariensis
Brancaster
Burgh Castle
Britannia Prima
Walton Castle
Cirencester
Maxima
Caesariensis
Bradwell
Reculver
London
Richborough
Dover
Lympne
Marcae?
Portchester
Pevensey
Bononia
0
50
100
miles

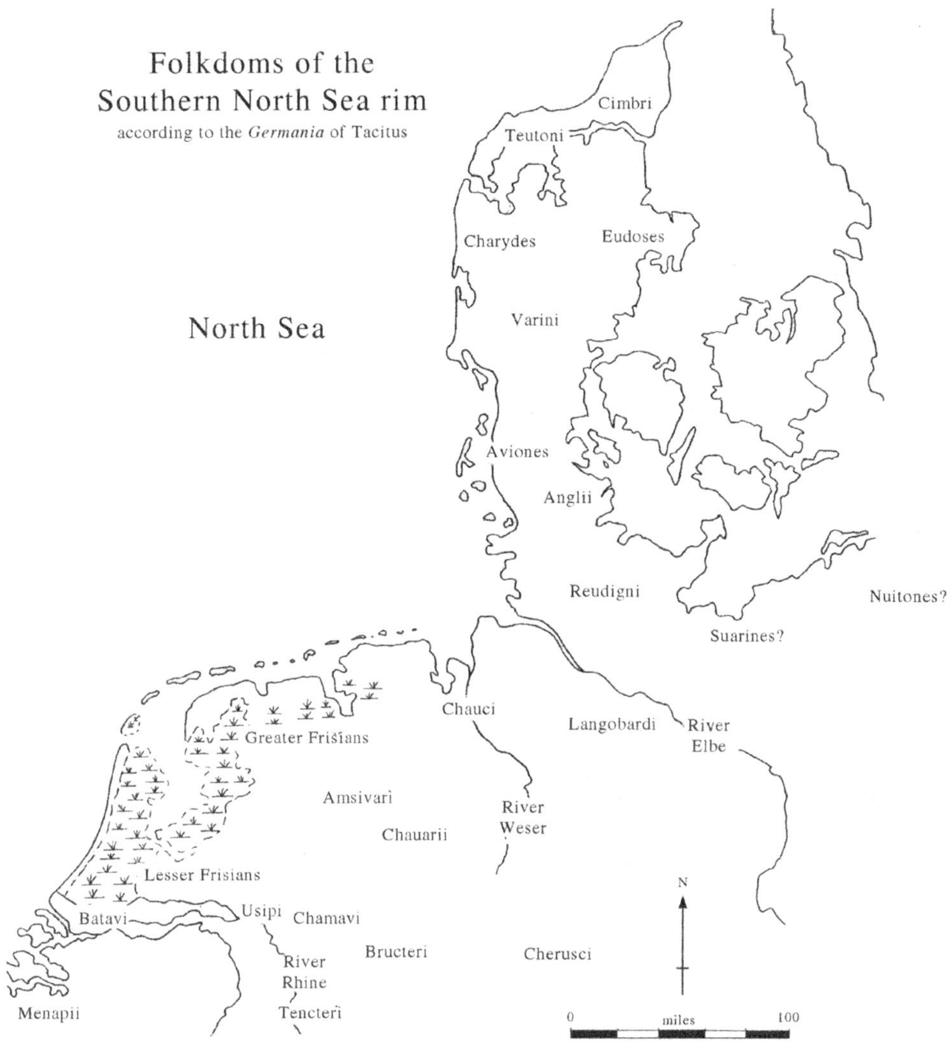
Folkdoms of the
Southern North Sea rim
according to the *Germania* of Tacitus
North Sea
Cimbri
Teutoni
Charydes
Eudoses
Varini
Aviones
Anglii
Reudigni
Nuitones?
Suarines?
Chauci
Langobardi
River
Elbe
Greater Frisians
Amsivari
Chauarii
River
Weser
Lesser Frisians
Batavi
Usipi
Chamavi
Bructeri
Cherusci
River
Rhine
Tencteri
Menapii
N
0
miles
100

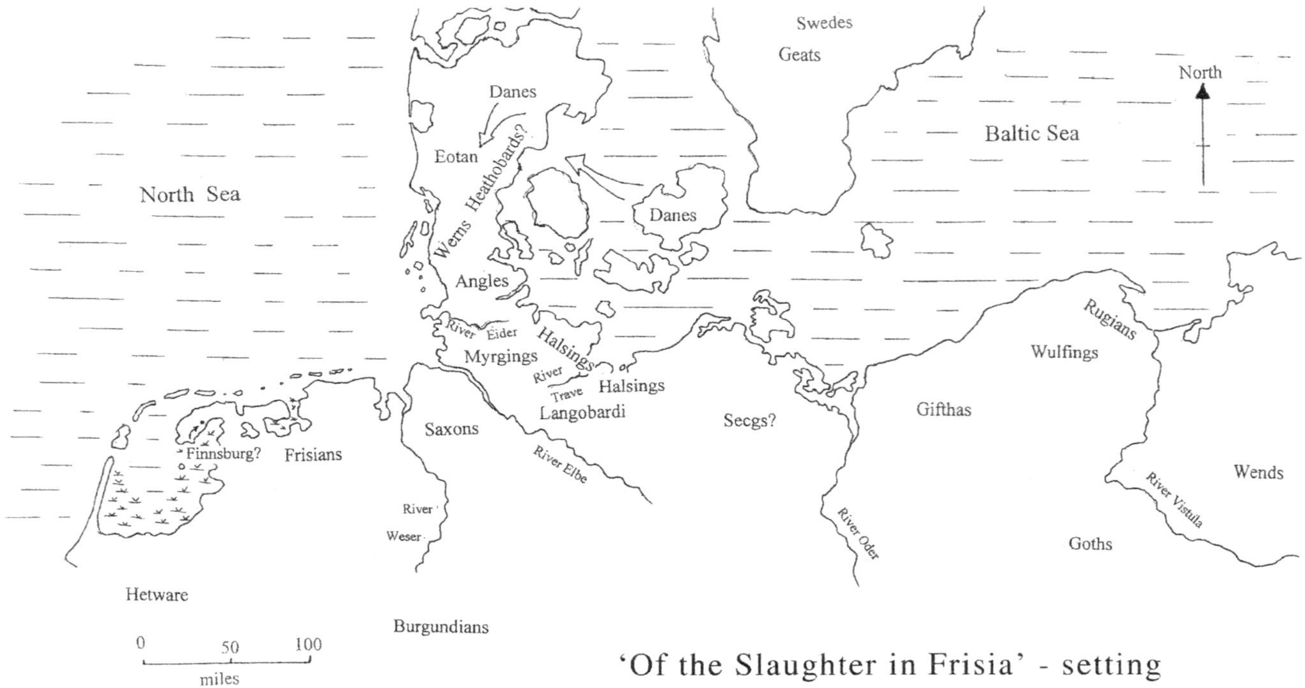


'Of the Slaughter in Frisia' - setting

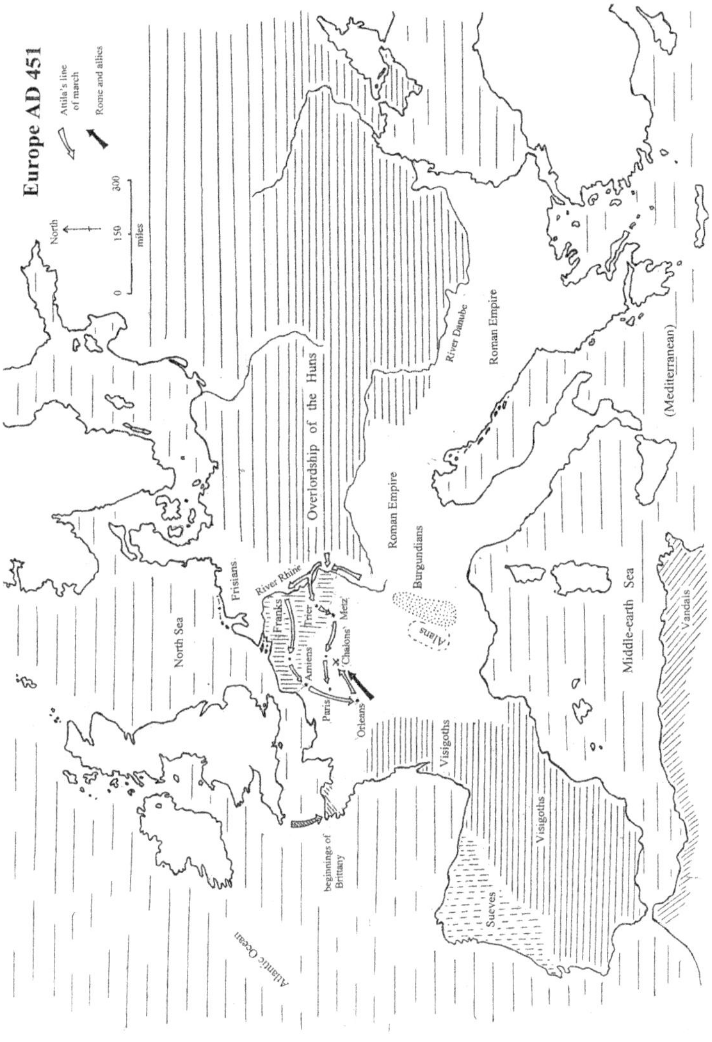
Europe AD 451
North
0 150 300
miles
Attila's line of march
Rome and allies
North Sea
Frisians
River Rhine
Franks
Trier
Amiens
Metz
Chalons
Paris
Orleans
Overlordship of the Huns
Roman Empire
Burgundians
Alans
River Danube
Roman Empire
Visigoths
beginnings of Brittany
Atlantic Ocean
Sueves
Visigoths
Middle-earth Sea
(Mediterranean)
Vandals

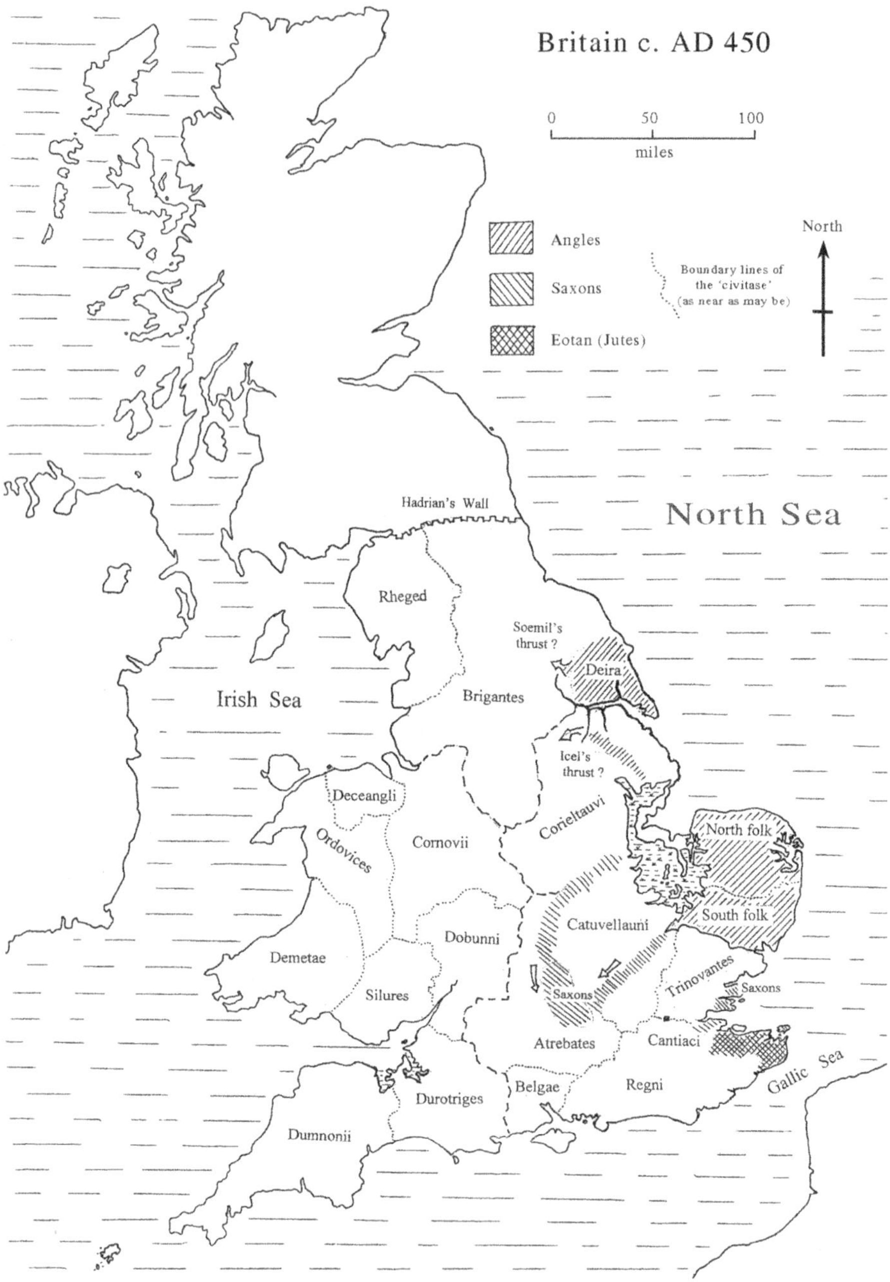
Britain c. AD 450
0 50 100
miles
Angles
Saxons
Eotan (Jutes)
Boundary lines of
the 'civitase'
(as near as may be)
North
North Sea
Hadrian's Wall
Rheged
Soemil's thrust ?
Deira
Brigantes
Irish Sea
Icel's thrust ?
Deceangli
Corieltauvi
North folk
Ordovices
Cornovii
Catuvellauni
South folk
Dobunni
Demetae
Trinovantes
Saxons
Silures
Saxons
Atrebates
Cantiaci
Gallic Sea
Belgae
Regni
Durotriges
Dumnonii

# Part 1: In time of 'the breaking of nations'

## *The battle of the Catalaunian Fields*

About the same time as that night onset against the hall of Finnsburg, war-hosts from half the folkdoms of western Europe gathered for battle on the flat plains of the Catalaunian fields, near Orleans, in Gaul (now France). How did this come about? To understand the answer we must go back some hundred years or so.

About the middle of the fourth century AD the Huns, moving westwards from their Central Asian homeland, crossed the Volga. They not only unsettled the folkdoms in their path, but their oncoming had a knock-on effect on others further west. They overcame the Alans (a people who had moved west from the Iranian steppe) about AD 372, then the Ostrogoths between the Don and Dneistr rivers, about AD 375. (The Ostrogoth king, Eormenric, took his own life.) The Visigoths were overthrown about AD 376, and were allowed by the Romans to settle south of the Danube. Some Ostrogoths bowed to Hunnic rule, others moved into the Visigothic lands. The Huns, now with Ostrogoths, Gepids, Rugians and others under their rule, came next through the Carpathians, into Pannonia (roughly the Hungary of today). This was about AD 400-410, and it seems that the Germanic Vandals and Suebi, together with the Alans now found themselves squeezed between the Huns and Rome's Rhine frontier. These crossed the frozen Rhine on the last day of December, 406, and poured into Gaul. The Salian Franks had been settled as federate troops of Rome, in Gallia Belgica (the Flanders and southern Netherlands of today), since the 350s. The Vandals and their friends therefore moved further south, plundering as they went. The Roman emperor Honorius enlisted the help of the Visigoths, and rewarded them with lands in Aquitaine. The Vandals crossed the Pyrennes into Spain (409) then, under Gaiseric (king, 428-77) they overleapt the Straits of Gibraltar, and went on to build a kingdom of sea-rovers, based in North Africa. (Gaiseric and his Vandals sailed to Italy in 455, and sacked Rome – and the ill-fame they won gave us the word 'vandalism'.)

The Roman general and statesman, Flavius Aëtius (c.396-454) strove for more than twenty years to hold the Western Empire together, his chief work being the defence of Gaul. He fought against the Visigoths thrusting up from Aquitaine and pushed them back. With the help of the Huns he overthrew the Burgundians, and settled the remnant of them in Savoy (436). After this the Huns were warring in the Balkans in the 440s, under Attila. And then about 450, Attila turned his mind to the West again. Valentinian III was now western emperor. He had given his troublesome sister, Honoria, as wife to one of his supporters in the senate. Honoria was seeking a way out, and she sent a ring and a plea for help to Attila the Hun. Attila chose to take the ring as an offer of marriage and he told Valentinian he must give up half his kingdom as wedding gift. This demand was denied and, early in 451, Attila led his war-host into Gaul. Besides his Huns he had with him an army of Ripuarian Franks under Gundebaud, Ostrogoths under the brothers Wallia (or Walamir), Theodemir (father of the later king Theodoric the Great) and Widimir, Gepids under Ardarich, and others. The host made their way slowly through northern Gaul (tied to the speed of the ox carts) burning, killing, and raping as they went. In June, 451 they reached Orleans and its key river crossing over the Loire. If Attila was to go any further he had to take the city and its bridges, to secure his rear. Sangibanus king of the Alans offered to hand over the town, but he was foiled by men faithful to the warrior bishop of Orleans, Anianus, an Alan himself. In those tense days Anianus again and again made the rounds of the walls, bearing holy relics. He saw that in holding out against Attila he was also shielding the peoples south of the Loire.

Meanwhile Aëtius sought help from Theodoric, king of the Visigoths of Aquitaine. The king's son, Thorismund, warned his father against believing the Romans, and Theodoric acknowledged that Aëtius was not to be trusted 'beyond the length of his sword'. Nevertheless he agreed to come in on the side of the Romans, the Salian Franks (under Merovech) and the Burgundians, against their common foe, Attila. (There were Saxons, too, who fought alongside the Romans. They came from the settlements around Bayeux, and those on islands at the mouth of the Loire.)

Theodoric and Aëtius came to Orleans on the 14th June. Rather than fall back Attila made up his mind to stand, after his seers told him that though he might be defeated in the battle, his foe would fall in the fighting. He took this to be Aëtius. But Attila put off the opening of the battle until the ninth hour, thinking that if things went badly he could get away under the shield of darkness.

Aëtius set Sangibanus (who was now mistrusted by both sides), in the middle of the Roman line, on a low hill, with his own two and a half Roman legions behind him. Thus there was no way that Sangibanus could slip off. (Over against Sangibanus was Attila himself.) On the left wing of the Roman host was Theodoric the Visigoth facing the Ostrogoths of Walamir. The Salian Franks and the Burgundians were on the right wing facing the Ripuarian Franks and the Gepids.

Attila began the onset in the middle of the line, and in the fighting Sangibanus was shot dead by an arrow through the throat. On the other side Gundebaud, leader of the Ripuarian Franks was slain. Meanwhile Theodoric, on Aëtius' left had his men give way before Walamir, drawing him and his Ostrogoths away from Attila. A word-bearer sent by Attila to call Walamir back was shot down by an arrow. With the light fading, Theodoric left a covering screen of warriors and took his Visigoths right round the Ostrogoths and so into the rear of the Huns. After a short and dreadful fight the Huns fled, but Theodoric himself was thrown from his horse and trampled to death. (Walamir the Ostrogoth also fell on the Catalaunian Fields.)

It has been suggested that Aëtius did some two-faced dealing that night. It is said that he did not want the Hunnic war-host wholly overwhelmed lest the Visigoths should afterward feel they no longer needed Rome. So (it is suggested) he went to see Attila in his earth-walled fortress, and agreed to let him get away, in return for his help later against the Eastern emperor, and against the Visigoths. Back in his own camp Aëtius was met by Thorismund, seeking his advice as to what he should do now that his father, Theodoric, was dead. Aëtius pointed out to him that he had five brothers back in Toulouse, and that if he did not move quickly one of them might forestall him and take his father's throne. Thorismund duly left for home, to take the kingship.

Attila waited until he was sure the Visigoth withdrawal was not a trick, then he went home. Two years later he was dead. The year after that (454) the Gepids and Ostrogoths threw off the Hunnish yoke. (Attila's son Ellak was killed in the battle on the Netad river in Pannonia.) After this the empire of the Huns fell apart. The other players in this drama also passed from the scene. In 454, Valentinian III, with no heir, and jealous of Aëtius for seeking a marriage alliance (he demanded the emperor's daughter for his son), had him murdered. The following year he, in turn, was assassinated by two of Aëtius' officers.

How was Britain, on the outskirts of this wider world, affected by the drama played out in Gaul? The answer offered here is that Hunnish thrustfulness kept the Roman mind focused on that great threat, and held them back from any thoughts of stepping into British affairs once more. It also kept the Franks busy, so that their eastern neighbours the Frisians were freer to face down (if they could) the rising power of the Danes. And it is against this background that Hengest the Jute (if there was such a war-leader) fought and plotted, and carved out for himself a kingdom.

Let us turn, then, to the tale of Late Roman Britain, and to the folkdoms of the southern and eastern North Sea rim.

# Late Roman Britain and the North Sea rim

## *The 'north-west frontier' province*

To defend its north-west frontier Rome used client tribes, scouts, the Wall, the Pennine forts and, of course, the army. The Roman diocese, or province, of Britain had a garrison amounting to about one tenth of the empire's standing army. This gave the high-ranking senator who governed the island a key role. Here was a temptation to someone who would bid for imperial power, and Britain became a springboard for military adventures.

This was the case in the civil war of AD 193-7. In the next century Carausius, and his supplanter Allectus, led a breakaway state for ten years. Marcus Aurelius Mausaeus Carausius (the first two of his names were adopted as part of his imperial claims) was a Menapian from the lower Rhine, who proved himself to be an able soldier. Diocletian's co-emperor, Maximian, gave him the task of combating the Saxon and Frankish pirates who were raiding the northern coasts of Gaul. From his base at Boulogne he caught pirate ships as they made their way back through the narrows (the Dover Straits). Carausius' success aroused the suspicion, or jealousy, of Maximian, who accused him of only intercepting pirates on their way home, relieving them of their booty and failing to restore it. Perhaps there were grounds for the second charge, but the first charge is hardly fair, for this was the way the system worked best. Raiders might slip through the narrows, but once they had begun raiding their presence would be known, and Roman navy ships could lie in wait to catch them on their way back. Carausius broke away from Rome in 286/7, and ruled until his assassination in 293. Allectus, his supplanter, was not overcome by Rome until 296.

It was in York in AD 306 that Constantine the Great began his rise to overlordship of the whole empire. In AD 350-53 one Magnentius rebelled against Rome. The so-called 'barbarian conspiracy' of AD 364-7 plunged the land into even greater upheaval, as Roman Britain was attacked from all sides (by Picts, Scots and Attacotti). The attack on Hadrian's Wall was helped by the treachery of the frontier scouts. Both Fullofaudes, Duke of the Britains, and Nectaridus, Count of the Saxon Shore (Germans, judging from their names) were killed. Troops deserted and joined in the plundering. The emperor Valentinian had to send Count Theodosius the Elder to retake the island.

Then Magnus Maximus set out from Britain in his bid for the imperial throne (383-88). It has been suggested that he may have made arrangements for defence in his absence, by giving responsibility to native chieftains.[1]

---

[1] L Alcock, *Arthur's Britain*, p.96.

In 398, there was a campaign against the Picts led, or initiated, by Stilicho. In 401, in the face of the Gothic threat to Italy he may have moved the 2nd legion to Rutupiae (Richborough) and withdrawn the 20th to the Continent.[2] At this time greater emphasis may have been placed on a mobile field army, led by a Count of the Britains. The force of infantry and cavalry was probably no more than about 6,000 strong.[3]

Constantine III made a bid for empire in AD 407-11. He was at length overthrown, but Rome was too heavily committed elsewhere to be able to retake Britain. It seems that the British leadership expelled the Roman administration.[4]

## *The administrative structure re-shaped*

We have seen that the very size of the garrison in Britain was a temptation to imperial pretenders. At some point Rome made up its mind to divide the diocese and the power that went with it. This most likely happened after the civil war of AD 193-7, but it may have been later, about AD 216.[5] From the one diocese were made the two provinces of Britannia Superior (nearer to Rome) and Britannia Inferior. Then, after the overthrow of the Carausius/Allectus breakaway government, another re-shaping was carried through. The date is not clear, but the new framework was in place by AD 312. Britannia Superior was now split into Britannia Prima (with its capital perhaps at Cirencester) and Maxima Caesariensis (its capital perhaps in London). Britannia Inferior became Britannia Secunda (with its capital at York) and Flavia Caesariensis (capital at Lincoln).[6] Another reorganization followed the overcoming of the 'barbarian conspiracy' of 364-7. (The name of Valentia province now appears. This may have been a new province, or a new name for one of the existing provinces.[7]) Each of these provinces had its provincial council, but there is no clear evidence for a diocese-wide 'Council of Britain'. (If anything the Romano-Britons should have been sending representatives to the council of the Gallic prefecture to which they belonged.[8]) Perhaps after the break with Rome such a council for Britain was formed, this being the one referred to in the writings of Gildas and in the *Historia Brittonum*.

[2] E Foord, *The Last Age of Roman Britain*, pp.122, 124, 128.
[3] L Alcock, *Arthur's Britain*, p.98.
[4] L Alcock, *Arthur's Britain*, p.99.
[5] B Jones and D Mattingly, *An Atlas of Roman Britain*, pp.143, 145.
[6] B Jones and D Mattingly, p.148.
[7] AS Esmonde Cleary, *The Ending of Roman Britain*, p.48.
[8] P Salway, *Roman Britain*, p.501n.

## *Late Roman defence measures: the Saxon Shore, foederati and laeti*

From the third century AD there was a growing threat to Britain and Gaul from seaborne raiders. A number of burnt sites, including the great palace at Fishbourne, near Chichester, may be evidence of Frankish or Saxon raids on the south coast of Britain. However, Roman Britain seems to have known reasonable prosperity in the early years of the fourth century, which suggests that the pirate raids were for the moment on a fairly small scale (at least compared with cross-border raiding by land on the continent).[9]

Yet the threat to Britain and Gaul was taken seriously, the clearest evidence being the great programme of building forts on the coasts of both lands. We get some information on the forts, and the late Roman military structure, from a document called the *Notitia Dignitatum* (the 'Record of Official Posts'). The part of this document relating to the eastern empire dates from about 395, and that relating to the western empire was most likely put together in the 420s. It lists court officials, vicars and provincial governors, and military commanders. It is the only source we have for the name *Litus Saxonicum* ('Saxon Shore'). See map page 16.

In Britain there were already forts at Reculver and Brancaster, built early in the third century.[10] The walls of these forts were thicker than those of earlier forts, but otherwise they were close in style to the typical 2nd century fort, having rounded corners, and watch towers flush with the outsides of the walls.[11] In the late third century a programme of building more specialist forts got under way. The strength of these new forts is seen in the semi-circular external bastion towers, even thicker walls, and more massive gatehouses. From bastion towers at each end of a stretch of wall the defenders could fire down at the attackers along the whole line of the wall. The towers may also have mounted heavy catapault weapons such as the ballista. The forts were clearly built to withstand a siege if need be, and it would seem that the threat was now more than of small-scale piracy. Haywood writes, 'we must conclude that the Romans had enough respect for Frankish and Saxon naval power to believe them capable of mounting a major seaborne invasion of Britain.'[12] As to the siting of these forts, the main factors were suitability as a naval base, and the guarding of the mouth of a river by which raiders might make their way inland. The sites were also well suited for use as strategic supply depots, and there is evidence of industrial activity at many of the forts.[13]

---

[9] J Haywood, *Dark Age Naval Power*, p.55.

[10] L Alcock, *Arthur's Britain*, p.95.

[11] S Johnson , 'Late Roman defences and the *Limes*', p.68.

[12] J Haywood, *Dark Age Naval Power*, p.57.

[13] J Haywood, *Dark Age Naval Power*, p.58.

Haywood thinks that most of the forts were built in a planned programme of works in the years following the collapse of the Gallic empire in 273, with completion by 285. Haywood goes on to note that some building may even have been carried out in the time of the Gallic emperor Postumus, namely, earthwork defences and a watch tower at Richborough, and the fort at Burgh Castle, guarding the mouth of the Yare. Then in the years following 273, wholly new fortifications were built at the old *Classis Britannica* (fleet) bases at Boulogne, Lympne and Dover. A new stone fort was built at Richborough. Forts were built at Walton and Bradwell, to guard the northern shore of the Thames estuary. Colchester would have had a harbour nearby (as would Rochester), and there was a defended port at Caister-by-Yarmouth. A Roman site at Skegness, on a stretch of eroded Lincolnshire coast, may have been a fort built at this time. There may also have been a fort near Dunwich, also eroded away. At Brough-on-Humber the earlier earthworks were replaced by stone walls shortly after 270. At the other end of the Saxon Shore 'Wihtgaræsbyrg' (named in the *Anglo-Saxon Chronicle* annal for 530) may have been a Saxon Shore fort, sited where Carisbrooke Castle now stands.[14] Haywood thinks the fort at Portchester was probably a late addition to the network, built in the period 285-93.[15] Pevensey was built some time after 335, to plug the gap between the Dover Straits and Portchester, while Lymnpe was abandoned about 340.[16] (We should note that Bidwell thinks that most of these forts were built by Carausius and Allectus, 286-96, as a defence against the emperor Maximian.[17])

On the other side of the Channel the fortifications at Oudenburg were rebuilt in a similar style to the British forts. The *Notitia Dignitatum* lists one fort as *Locus Quartensis sive Hornensis*, which may have been built in this period. (It is generally thought to have been near either Étaples on the Canche, or Cap Hornu on the Somme.) The two continental *Litus Saxonicum* forts of *Marcae* and *Grannona* may have been built at this time, or perhaps earlier in the century. *Marcae* was in Belgica Secunda, and so must have been on the coast between the mouth of the Scheldt, and Dieppe. (Marck has been suggested.) *Grannona* was in the territory of the *Dux Tractus Armoricani*, and so must have been west of Dieppe. It was most likely at the mouth of the Seine, perhaps at or near Le Havre.[18] Another suggestion is that it was at Port-en-Bessin. The main naval base on the Gallic side of the Saxon Shore was at the late Roman city of Boulogne.[19]

In Britain the chain of coastal forts was perhaps designed as much to protect Gaul as Britain, so that it was almost an extension to the Rhine frontier. And it is likely that

---

[14] L Alcock, *Arthur's Britain*, p.345.

[15] J Haywood, *Dark Age Naval Power*, pp.56, 58-9.

[16] J Haywood, *Dark Age Naval Power*, p.65.

[17] P Bidwell, Roman forts in Britain, p.43.

[18] S Johnson, 'Late Roman defences and the *Limes*', pp.65, 67.

[19] S Johnson, Later Roman Britain, p.131, Cleary, The Ending of Roman Britain, p.17.

the command of the *Comes Litoris Saxonici*, 'the Count of the Saxon Shore', once extended to the Gallic side of the Channel, as well as to the British side.[20] Why the name 'Saxon shore'? Does it mean 'the Shore where Saxons dwell', or 'the Shore attacked by Saxons'? The Romans did not normally guard a frontier with troops raised from among the enemy who threatened it, so the *Litus Saxonicum* was probably 'the shore attacked by Saxons'.[21]

For the Saxon reavers the richest pickings lay beyond the Channel Straits, in southern Britain and western Gaul, where there were large villas and landed estates. But to get there they had to pass through the Straits, which formed a natural bottleneck. If the Straits were held against them, there was no real need for complete cover further west. And it was only in the Straits that regular patrolling was possible. Even so a lone raider could slip through at night or in misty conditions. Pevensey, Portchester, and *Grannona* were well-placed to chase any pirates who slipped through, and they had their own small fleets. As soon as raiders landed their presence would be known. Probably all the forts had mounted troops, so that they could seek to head off Saxons who went raiding inland. And then there would be the further chance of catching them as they sailed back through the Straits. (We have seen that this was how Carausius operated.)

To complete the defensive picture we may note that on the west side of Britain there were forts at Lancaster and Cardiff (the only ones similar to the Saxon Shore forts), and perhaps at Caer Gybi (Holyhead). These may have been part of a defensive system against the Scotti and the Picts.[22] Carmarthen, Caerwent, Chester, Caernarfon and, to a lesser extent, Gloucester, assumed a new importance as points of defence. Carmarthen was linked to the sea along its river, by a series of signal stations. Loughor and Pembroke, and possibly Neath, seem to have been late Roman bases.[23]

How would naval warfare have been waged? Light Late Roman warships found at Mainz in 1981/2 seem to have had much in common with native 'Celtic' ships of the Rhine area. The best preserved type-A ship is Mainz ship 9. It was long and sleek (about 60 feet long, ten feet broad), with a shallow draught, drawing only about 18 inches of water. It would have been stable, seaworthy, manoeuvrable and, with a full crew of 30 oarsmen, capable of cruising at up to seven knots. It could have reached ten knots over short distances. It may also have carried a mast and a light, possibly lateen, sail. There was a fighting platform at the bow, and an unusual protruding forefoot, possibly a short ram. One of the type-A ships provided evidence of a shield rail around the sides, providing both storage, and protection to the oarsmen. The type-A ships may have been the *lusoria* referred to in Late Roman sources, or the

---

[20] S Johnson, 'Late Roman defences and the *Limes*', p.67.

[21] J Haywood, *Dark Age Naval Power*, p.78.

[22] J Haywood, *Dark Age Naval Power*, p.67.

[23] S Johnson, *Later Roman Britain*, pp.115-6, W Manning, *Roman Wales*, p.111.

scoutships described by Vegetius. The Mainz type-A would have been similar in size and performance potential to the Saxon or Anglian Nydam ship.[24]

Vegetius, a 4th/early 5th century military writer, refers to light, camouflaged craft (*scafa exploratoria*) used for scouting. They had twenty rowers a side, and were painted sea-green for camouflage – hulls, sails, men's clothes, faces and all.[25] Action at sea may have involved the use of bows and arrows and slings, like enough followed by boarding, and hand-to-hand fighting.

Note that it seems likely the Saxon Shore forts and the signal stations along the Yorkshire coast fell out of use early in the fifth century.[26]

## *Were there foederati and/or laeti in Late Roman Britain?*

Germanic troops had been stationed in Britain from the time of the conquest onwards. For example, we know of Frisian cavalry units at Burgh-by-Sands and Housesteads. In the late Roman period, at Housesteads, there was the *numerus Hnaudifridi* ('Nottfried's troop').

In the later Roman period the authorities made use of Germanic troops as 'poachers turned gamekeepers'. Roman written sources refer to *foederati*, who held their land under a *foedus* or treaty, and *laeti*, who were settled on empty lands within the borders of the empire, and who undertook hereditary obligations to military service. This was the cheapest solution to the problem of obtaining protection from enemies, but it has been argued that it would have brought with it the risk that the newcomers might seize power as Roman authority waned. (It has been suggested that Vortigern and his council brought in Hengest and his warband as *foederati*, and that in doing this they were following precedents set by the late Roman government in Britain, and afterwards followed by the 'post-colonial' authorities.)

It used to be held that the archaeological evidence pointed to an early Anglo-Saxon presence, of *foederati*, or *laeti*, or both. Anglo-Saxon cremation urns found at two burial grounds near Caistor-by-Norwich were held to date from the late third century (this on the basis of comparisons with those from the Danish island of Fyn). Other early burials were identified near the walled towns of Cambridge, Great Chesterford, Leicester, Great Casterton, Ancaster, Lincoln, York, and Dorchester-on-Thames. Then there were finds of pottery and metalwork. Two classes of pottery, and the art-style of certain belt-buckles and other fittings, were thought to be Germanic. These have been found in Germanic graves on the Continent, and in Anglo-Saxon graves in Britain. It seemed that they could have been issued to Germanic *foederati*. Such material has been found at four Roman cities: Canterbury, Colchester, London, and

---

[24] J Haywood, *Dark Age Naval Power*, pp.71-3.

[25] RG Collingwood, *Roman Britain*, p.279, Esmond Cleary *The Ending of Roman Britain*, p.61.

[26] AS Esmonde Cleary, *The Ending of Roman Britain*, p.144; J Haywood, *Dark Age Naval Power*, p.81.

Winchester (that at Winchester being dated to AD 390-410). It has also been found near strategic points, such as along Roman roads, and at some of the Saxon Shore forts. At Portchester archaeologists have found timber buildings arranged in no distinctively military plan, dated to the late 3rd/4th centuries.[27] A 'grubenhaus' has been found there, with a sherd of Anglo-Saxon pottery from 400-450, and a brooch of 450-500. Cunliffe concluded that the site was 'Germanised' in the first half of the 5th century.[28] Alcock suggested that Portchester may have had a 'numerus' from the Low Countries in the early 5th century.[29]

It was also noted that some early Anglo-Saxon settlements were sited on less fertile farming land, but close to much better land. This suggested that the more fertile land was still in the hands of Romano-Britons.[30]

These conclusions are now questioned. Esmonde Cleary argues the case in the 'Postscript' to his *The Ending of Roman Britain*.[31] He says that the dating of the Caistor-by-Norwich cremation urns rests on a chain of associations with datable Roman objects, and that scholars of the Anglo-Saxon period would not now wish to put so early a date on them. He adds that most scholars now believe that even the earliest Anglo-Saxon objects found in this country should not be dated before 400.

Of the two classes of pottery, the first is that made by hand and in typical Anglo-Saxon fabrics, but imitating Romano-British pottery. It is now said that none of the pottery vessels in question need be earlier than the general run of Anglo-Saxon pottery, that is, the fifth-century. The second class is pottery made in the Romano-British tradition, from well-prepared clay and on a fast wheel, but decorated in a style felt to be reminiscent of Anglo-Saxon pottery of the fifth and sixth centuries. There was a concentration of such pottery in East Anglia, where early Anglo-Saxon cemeteries have been found. It was thus felt to be of Romano-British manufacture, but designed to appeal to Anglo-Saxon tastes, implying that Anglo-Saxons were present in eastern Britain in the fourth century. It was called 'Romano-Saxon' ware. But re-assessment of this pottery has led to it being seen as standard late Roman provincial, with no ethnic overtones. The decorative styles are in fact those of the later fifth century onwards. Moreover, the bulk of fourth-century pottery from the Anglo-Saxon homelands is plain, or has little decoration. The decorative motifs on the 'Romano-Saxon' ware can be paralleled on other pottery, and on glassware and metalwork, of Roman manufacture and fourth-century date. Moreover, the kilns from which the East Anglian pottery finds came were in Hertfordshire and Cambridgeshire. The designation 'Romano-Saxon' pottery should probably be abandoned. Of the metalwork it is now said that it was the fourth-century Roman

---

[27] AS Esmonde Cleary, *The Ending of Roman Britain*, p.61.

[28] B Cunliffe, *Wessex to AD 1000*, p.285.

[29] L Alcock, *Arthur's Britain*, p.184.

[30] AS Esmonde Cleary, p.196.

[31] AS Esmonde Cleary, pp.189-93.

styles that influenced the fifth-century Germanic. Further, it is held that these belts were in fact standard insignia of office not only for military personnel, but for late Roman civilian officials as well.

As to early Anglo-Saxon material found at cities in Britain, the most substantial case for British/Saxon contact can be made for Canterbury. But none of the Anglo-Saxon pottery found was recovered from the latest Roman levels, and the *grubenhäuser* (sunken-floored huts) were dug into the 'dark earth' (which layer betokens the abandonment of the underlying town). It is now thought that there was a gap of at least a generation between the latest Roman and the earliest Anglo-Saxon occupation. Cleary also holds that there was probably a break in occupation at Portchester at some time between 400 and 450.[32] As to Germanic federate leaders betraying their employers and seizing the reins of power, it has been said that those who seized power on the Continent in the fifth century were not those already within the Empire, but those coming from outside.

In Cleary's assessment, the disappearance of Roman rule and culture in Britain, in the early fifth century, came about through the breakdown of the Roman social structure and systems of surplus extraction. (This refers to the economic activity which generates a surplus, thus supporting a centralised administration, and further economic development.) It seems that there was a return to a localised, agrarian, kin-based society with little capacity for surplus extraction. [33] Elsewhere Cleary writes, 'Such a situation helps explain the ability of the incoming Anglo-Saxon groups to establish themselves in Britain, and why their culture was not swamped by that of the indigenous population'.[34]

## *'A house asundered'*

The threats to late Roman Britain were not all from outside. Britain (and, indeed, the empire) was a house divided against itself. Among the faultlines of the late Empire the following have been noted: the army against the state, the people against the army, rich against poor, drop-outs against society, pagan against Christian.[35]

In Britain we may note, first, divisions between Pelagians (see below) and orthodox Christians. The strength of the Pelagians was such that outside help was needed in order to check them. Then we may note the difference in outlook between the upland folk of the North, Wales, and the South-west, and that of the lowlanders. For example, chieftains in the west were re-occupying old hill-forts[36]

---

[32] AS Esmonde Cleary, *The Ending of Roman Britain*, p.143.

[33] See AS Esmonde Cleary, *The Ending of Roman Britain*, chapters 4 and 5.

[34] AS Esmonde Cleary, 'Romano-British and Early Anglo-Saxon Archaeology', *ASSAH*, 6, p.61.

[35] See Michael Grant, The Fall of the Roman Empire.

[36] L Alcock, *Arthur's Britain*, p.93.

(such a move might have owed something to late Roman military ideas[37]). At the same time there were lowland families (such as that of Gildas) still having their sons educated for roles in the Roman administration. A third difference is seen in the response to the military threat. Some turned naturally to Rome for help (witness the appeal to Aëtius), but others perhaps thought to take matters into their own hands and buy in barbarian help. What we may have here is rivalry between a pro-Roman/ Catholic party upholding 'Romanitas', and a 'nationalist'/ Pelagian / pagan party asserting 'Britishness'.

The Christian Church was troubled by the heresy of Pelagius (*fl.* 390-418) who is said to have had British roots. He denied 'original sin', the belief that everyone born of human flesh partakes of the sin of Adam. Pelagius understood God's grace as being an enlightening of the believer after being cleansed from sin in baptism. This enlightening enabled the believer to see what was right, and then to do it by his own freewill and strength. The Pelagians preached the rejection of property and sex (the two things tying men to this world), and they denied the worth of infant baptism. The teaching of Pelagius was strongly opposed by Augustine, bishop of Hippo (AD 354-430), who taught that fallen men and women have inherited the sin of Adam and cannot turn to God, or do anything good and right, apart from the grace of God. The heresy of Pelagius drew followers in his native Britain. In his annal for 429 Prosper records that Agricola, son of the Pelagian bishop, Severianus, had infected the British church with his father's heresy. It has been suggested that Severianus was an Italian bishop, and that Agricola came to Britain to escape the anti-Pelagian legislation of 418-25. It would seem, then, that Britain was a safe haven for threatened Pelagians.[38]

The Catholic party sought help from the bishops of Gaul, who, with the blessing of pope Celestine, sent two of their number to confront the Pelagians. These were Germanus of Auxerre and Lupus of Troyes. A public debate was called. When the Pelagians arrived their showy clothing made plain their vanity ('free will is, after all, an arrogant doctrine'[39]). The Pelagians were routed in the theological debate. The two bishops then visited the shrine of Alban, and Germanus healed the blind daughter of a *vir tribuniciae potestatis* ('a man with the authority of a tribune'), placing a bag of relics against her eyes. Afterwards, in the face of a threat from Picts and Saxons, the bishops gathered an army of raw recruits, baptised them, then led them into battle. Their foes fled, overawed by a great shout of 'Alleluia'.[40] This was

---

[37] Ian Wood, 'The end of Roman Britain: continental evidence and parallels', in M Lapidge and D Dumville, *Gildas: New Approaches*, p.21.

[38] Ian Wood, in Lapidge and Dumville, *Gildas: New Approaches*, p.8.

[39] Ian Wood, p.10.

[40] AS Esmonde Cleary, The Ending of Roman Britain, p.162; C Thomas, Christianity in Roman Britain to AD 500, p.55.

in AD 429. (Germanus seems to have made another visit, perhaps about 435-44.[41]) These accounts show that, at this time, communications with Gaul were still open, that the churches in Britain and Gaul were still sufficiently in touch to be able to fight against Pelagianism together (the latest recorded contact is the council of Arles, 455), and that it was possible to cross the Channel without too great a threat from Saxon pirates. Clearly Britain was still under the Roman church, if not under the emperor.

As a footnote to this account we may note that Ian Wood sees it as allegory. The restored sight of the blind girl is taken as an allegory of the restoration of true doctrine to Britain. He acknowledges that the story of the 'Alleluia' victory may be based on an account of a campaign against Picts and Saxons, but he sees it as primarily an allegory about a bishop leading a people to true faith, and therefore to physical safety. Wood suggests that the episode of the healing of the withered son of Elafius (the head man of a district), during Germanus' second visit, may be taken as an allegory of the weakness of Britain.[42]

## *The folkdoms of the North Sea / West Baltic margins*

It is only in historical writings covering the last 100-200 years before the Christian era that the names of Germanic folkdoms start to appear. It was likely somewhere around this time that the Vandals, Burgundians, Goths and others moved to mainland Europe from Scandinavia. The fact that the Roman historian Cornelius Tacitus (c.AD 56/7 to c.AD 115) names them among the mainland Germans shows that they must have moved before the end of the first century BC. It is not known why they moved, though a worsening of the climate of northern Europe from about 800 BC may be one of the reasons.

It is Tacitus who first paints for us a picture of the early Germanic folkdoms. There is not space to look at all those he names, so we will look at those most nearly related to the world of the Finnsburg tale, in the fertile salt marshes and estuaries of the southern North Sea (or Wadden Sea). These have been exploited by man for fish, shellfish, fowl and wild plants since 5,000-4,000 years BC. Long-term settlement began 600-500 years BC, when the Groningen and Frisian coastal marshes were colonised, most likely by migrants from further east. The Schleswig-Holstein marshes were colonised in the first century AD. The settlers farmed the stiff clay soils, growing salt-resistant crops such as barley, broad beans, flax and kale. They kept cattle, drew fresh water from wells and ponds, and had dried cow-dung or peat for fuel. Timber had to be brought in from elsewhere.

Beginning in the west, we have the Batavi at the mouth of the Rhine. Beyond them (in Tacitus' account) were the Frisii (*Germania* 34). Tacitus refers to Lesser

---

[41] JM Wallace-Hadrill, 'Bede's Ecclesiastical History of the English People: A Historical Commentary, Oxford Medieval Texts, p.26.

[42] Ian Wood, in Lapidge and Dumville, *Gildas: New Approaches*, pp.10-12, 17.

Frisians, west of the lakes of the Low Countries (later the Zuyder Zee) and the Greater Frisians (later Finn's folk), who dwelt east of those lakes, beyond the reach of Rome. The head town of the Frisians was Dorostates Frisionum, that is, Dorestad, near Utrecht on the Lower Rhine. (In the sixth century AD it was known as far away as Italy.) Finds of Roman pottery and metalware at the sites of *terpen* (man-made mounds) show that the Frisians traded with the Roman provinces.

In the Rhineland, to the south of the Frisians, were the Franks. The Frankish confederation, most likely began to come together somewhere about AD 230. The main folkdoms among them were the Chamavi, Bructeri, Chattuari (the Hetware of the *Beowulf* saga), Salians, Amsivari, Twihantes, Usipi, and Tubantes. The name 'Frank' (perhaps meaning 'bold') must have been one they gave themselves. These tribes were settled between the Zuyder Zee and the river Lahn, and eastwards as far as the Weser. They were settled most thickly around the Ijssel, and between the Lippe and the Sieg.[43]

Eastwards of the Frisians, in Tacitus' portrayal, were the Chauci, and beyond them a group of seven tribes who shared together in the worship of the Earth Mother, Nerthus. The sanctuary of Nerthus was on an island in 'the Ocean', and since Tacitus calls the Baltic 'Mare Suebicum' the Ocean must be the North Sea (*Germania* 40). This group together were known as the Suebi or Suevi (later the 'Swæfe'). Tacitus says nothing of the Saxons, but Ptolemy in his *Geography* (written about AD 150) places the Saxons next to the Chauci, on the North Sea shore between the Elbe and the neck of the Cimbric peninsula (modern Holstein), and also in the North Frisian islands. It seems these Saxons were there by the first/second centuries AD, and that they were likely a confederation of Reudigni and Aviones (the first two named of Tacitus' seven tribes) and perhaps others. In the third century the Saxons spread south-westwards across the lower Elbe to the Ems, and either drove out the Chauci or made them part of their own folkdom. They may also have overrun some Frisian land.

The five other tribes of the Suebi were the Anglii, Varini, Eudoses, Suarines, and Nuitones. The land of the Anglii was called Angeln (that is, it was at the 'angle' in the coast). This was the southern third of the Cimbric (or Jutland) peninsula, as far north as the earthwork known as the 'Olgerdiget'. (This north-facing earthwork was perhaps first built about AD 50, and was then further developed in the third century.) Anglii territory also seems to have included most of the island of Fyn. To the south, the oldest fragment of Anglian tradition tells how Offa of Angeln set the boundary with the Myrgings at 'Fifeldor', which is thought to be a poetic name for the Eider.

The Varini of Tacitus (the Werns of the Old English poem *Widsith*) lived to the north of the Anglii. The first known homeland of the Jutes was likely beyond the Varini, in the north of the Cimbric peninsula. What we know of Jutish life and

---

[43] AS Esmonde Cleary, The Ending of Roman Britain, p.144; Haywood, Dark Age Naval Power, p.81.

culture (from archaeological work in Kent) suggests links between the Jutes and both the Frisians and the Franks.

Another folk-group known to have been in what is now Denmark was the Heruli, who were settled there in the late third century. As for the Danes, they had long lived in the southern part of Sweden and in Seeland, with the Geats to the north of them and the Swedes further north still, beyond the lakes. The Danes moved from Skåne to Sillende and other islands in the late fourth/ early fifth century.

## *Unsettled times*

The fifth century was a time of upheaval in the region. What caused this unsettledness? A number of factors seem to have been at play. First, there was pressure from rising sea-levels. Then it is said that depopulation in the Roman empire created a vacuum to draw in the barbarians, and that the empire's material wealth also acted as a magnet. Third, as we have seen already, there was likely pressure from the Huns, with ripple effects in the north. At the same time the spreading out of the Danes may have unsettled the smaller folkdoms – the Jutes, the Angles, and others – leading them to seek new homes to the south and west. Lastly, it has been suggested that blood-feuds drove war-leaders into exile seeking their fortunes.[44]

The Germanic folk dwelling by the salt marshes of the southern rim of the North Sea had to battle with periods of rising and falling sea levels. One way in which they responded to rising sea levels was by settling on man-made mounds of sods. Such a mound settlement has come to be known by the German word *terp* (plural *terpen*), a word akin to Old English 'thorp', Dutch 'dorp'. These *terpen* are found from the Elbe mouth in the east, as far as northern Holland in the west. The first phase of *terp* building is dated to 400-200 BC, during the Dunkirk Ib marine transgression.

After about AD 200 the coastal tribes began to feel the effects of the Dunkirk II marine transgression (AD 200-600), caused by a combination of eustatic and isostatic effects. At the peak of the transgression in the 4th century, the absolute rise in sea level was probably 3-8 feet above modern levels, but in the southern North Sea area subsidence of the land combined with this to produce an effective sea level rise of 12-14 feet around the Rhine mouths.[45] Coastal dwellers had to cope with flooded fields, drowned cattle, salted wells, and the spread of malaria (which became a main cause of death in the marshlands).

In the account of JNL Myres excavations at Feddersen Wierde, on the Weser estuary, give us a picture of these times. Several mounds were linked up in the first century AD, to make one large *terp* that could house more folk, and make more cropland available. In the second century a lord's house, and workshops were added, and later still a great hall, granaries and bronze- and iron-workings. The settlement

---

[44] L Alcock, *Arthur's Britain*, pp.351-2.
[45] J Haywood, *Dark Age Naval Power*, p.46.

then came to an end about the middle of the fifth century AD. Myres comments, 'it is tempting to connect this desertion with the possibility of movement overseas to Britain.' He adds that the pottery and other finds from Feddersen Wierde are much like finds from an early English settlement such as Mucking, Essex, on the Thames estuary, in a geographical area much like the Weser estuary.[46]

Dutch archaeological evidence also points to marked population movements at this time. The finds (from Friesland and Groningen) are modest during the Dunkirk II period, suggesting a fall in population. And in the western Netherlands from the fifth/sixth centuries there are no finds, so the population must have been very thin. In a paper on the excavations at Wijnaldum, Danny Gerrets notes[47] that at the Wijnaldum-Tjitsma *terp* there are almost no finds from between about AD 300/350 to about 425. There seems to have been more going on than simply a fall in population. Evidence from a number of *terp* excavations shows changes in settlement layout and in house construction (from buildings with a roof-bearing structure of wooden posts to sod-built structures). Changes in burial customs (to a mixed ritual of cremation and inhumation) have also been noted. Gerrets sums up, 'From the archaeological evidence we have to conclude that the Frisians mentioned in the Roman written sources were not the Frisians that we encounter in the written sources from the Early Middle Ages'.[48]

Boeles was struck by the finding of cruciform brooches and Anglo-Saxon pottery in the *terp* of Hoogebeintum, in Oostergo. Writing in 1906 he declared this to be evidence of an Anglo-Saxon invasion. He repeated this view in 1951, pointing to the presence of a burnt layer, together with the appearance of sunken huts, in the Ezinge *terp* excavation. He believed that most of the population were killed by the invaders.[49] (However, Gosses 1929, saw evidence of acculturation rather than slaughter.)

Since the 1950s opinions among Dutch archaeologists have changed, and they now think in terms of continuous occupation of the *terp* region. It has been urged that 'recent geophysical research at Wijnaldum and in northern Westergo has shown that the sea cannot have played a role of any importance in the abandonment of the region'.[50] Thus Gerrets suggests that there was not absolute discontinuity in the *terp* region in the fourth/ early fifth centuries, but that a much-reduced population continued to occupy some of the *terpen*. Likewise Heidinga says that the overall picture is of depopulation on a large scale from the third century onwards, then step by step filling up of the region again. Yet the reduced population was hardly enough to have been responsible for the rapid population

---

[46] JNL Myres, *The English Settlements* (Oxford: Oxford University Press, 1989), p.52.
[47] D Gerrets, 'Evidence of Political Centralization in Westergo' in *Anglo-Saxon Studies in Archaeology and History*, 10, pp.119-26.
[48] D Gerrets, *ASSAH*, 10, p.121.
[49] See D Gerrets, *ASSAH*, 10, p.121.
[50] D Gerrets, *ASSAH*, 10, p.121.

growth later in the fifth century. So Heidinga sees the population recovery as due mainly to immigration to the northern salt-marshes.[51]

Where might the immigrants have come from? Their material culture shows that they came from Schleswig-Holstein, from the 'Elbe-Weser triangle',[52] and perhaps from other areas of the eastern North Sea littoral. Like enough they were a mixture of peoples with a common Germanic background, who now settled down on the land which historically belonged to the Frisians. These settlers became the new 'Frisians', the people who lived on the land which once belonged to the Frisians.[53] Heidinga suggests that these Frisians filled the role of federates of their powerful neighbours the Merovingian Franks, in a way not unlike the relationship of the Roman Empire with their barbarian neighbours beyond the *limes*.[54]

HR Loyn thought that the 'mysterious Jutes' were among those who passed through the Frisian lands at this time.[55] (FM Stenton thought it more likely that Bede was misled by a chance resemblance between the names of two unrelated Germanic peoples, one people group in the Rhineland and the other in Jutland.[56]) It may be that the Germanic immigrants to Britain came from the whole stretch of coastland from Rhinemouth to Schleswig, and possibly from South Sweden as well, and that the Frisian lands played a key part, as a short-lived home before folk made the sea-crossing to Britain.

As we have seen, rising sea levels were part of the background to this time of restlessness in the fourth/fifth centuries. But Härke thinks that migration caused by this factor would have been small scale, and would have spanned quite a long period. He thinks that a more significant factor would have been the economic downturn resulting from the falling apart of the Western Empire. He goes on to argue that young men turned to piracy, and that this was often the first stage of migration, because they acted as the explorers.[57] Likewise, Louwe Kooijmans sees the fall in population as the outcome of economic collapse after the Roman withdrawal. He says that deposits once dated to Dunkirk II are now attributed to Dunkirk IIIa.[58])

---

[51] A Heidinga, 'The Frisian Achievement in the First Millennium AD' in *ASSAH*, 10, p.12

[52] C Hills 1996; Taakye, personal communication, cited in D Gerrets, *ASSAH*, 10, p.123.

[53] See D Gerrets, *ASSAH*, 10, p.123.

[54] A Heidinga, *ASSAH* 10, p.15.

[55] HR Loyn, *Anglo-Saxon England and the Norman Conquest* (Harlow: Longman, 1962), pp.27-8.

[56] FM Stenton, in DM Stenton, editor, *Preparatory to Anglo-Saxon England* (Oxford: Oxford University Press, 1970), p.267.

[57] Härke, responding to Ian Wood, 'Before and after the migration to Britain', in J Hines, editor, *The Anglo-Saxons from the migration period to the eighth century: An ethnographic perspective* (Woodbridge: The Boydell Press, 1997) p.58.

[58] LP Louwe Kooijmans, Archaeology and Coastal Change in the Netherlands, p.129.

Then there is the factor of leaders of warbands seeking out new fields. Reinhard Wenskus (1961) suggested that tribal groups were fluid, tending to form around successful military leaders, and then breaking up just as easily.[59] Wood thinks studies of the northern Germanic tribes point to the comparatively recent origins of most of those settled to the east of the lower Rhine in the fourth and fifth centuries'.[60] One key factor to weigh is the role of land as a social resource fundamental to status and power.[61] Charles-Edwards has argued[62] that in early Anglo-Saxon society status as a free man depended upon a minimum landholding. If land was not to be had then status by birth could not be kept up. So if there was population growth there would be an urgent need to gain more land. This would be so whether the land of the kindred was shared among all the sons of the house, or all went to the first-born (though the pressure would arise more quickly under the latter system). One result might then be out-migration. Another outcome might be a growth in the number of higher-status men entering into a client-lord relationship with a local chieftain or clan head. This would concentrate political power and, indirectly, control of land in fewer and fewer hands. Christopher Scull notes that, 'This model works best if it is accepted that there was some movement of population from the continent to Britain in the fifth century.' [63]

Scholars from a number of fields joined in a study project at Flögeln, near Cuxhaven (1992), looking at the archaeological and environmental evidence from one small defined region. The study seemed to show a clear gap in settlement from about the middle of the sixth century to the end of the seventh century, or even perhaps to 750.[64] The evidence of a break in settlement came more from pollen analysis than from excavation. This seemed to show a break in cereal cultivation, and the regrowth of forest. But some pollen diagrams suggested the presence of rye during the settlement gap. Maps of recorded cemeteries in North Germany and Denmark show a sharp contrast between dense distributions up to the fifth century, and very sparse distribution afterwards. According to Hills emigration should not perhaps be seen as the only explanation. She argues that famine and plague should also be considered.[65] Or there may have been concentration at fewer, larger cemeteries, or perhaps burials of a later period were sited near the cemeteries that ended in the fifth century.

Having outlined something of the background to the events of the fifth and sixth centuries, we turn now to look at the written sources for this period of history.

---

[59] Wenskus, cited by Ian Wood, 'Before and after the migration to Britain', p.42.

[60] Ian Wood, 'Before and after the migration to Britain', p.43.

[61] See C Scull, 'Social Archaeology and Anglo-Saxon Kingdom Origins', *ASSAH*, 10, p.22.

[62] 1972, cited in C Scull, *ASSAH*, 10.

[63] C Scull 1995, 77-79), cited in C Scull, *ASSAH*, 10, p.22.

[64] C Hills, *Origins of the English*, pp.78-79.

[65] C Hills, p.80.

# The written sources

In weighing the truth of a story we have to consider the trustworthiness, or otherwise, of the witnesses. There are two main British sources for the period, namely, Gildas's *De Excidio*, and the *Historia Brittonum*, and two main Anglo-Saxon sources, that is, Bede's *Historia Ecclesiastica*, and the *Anglo-Saxon Chronicle*. From outside Britain, we have the Gallic Chronicles.

## Gildas

Gildas wrote a book called *De Excidio Britanniae* (*DEB*), 'On the Ruin of Britain'. There is historical information in the book, but the work is not, first and foremost, a history book. Yet, as one writer has put it, scholars have 'picked over every word'.[66] Why? Because there is no other near-contemporary source of any length, for the history of these islands in the late fifth and early sixth centuries. Also, Bede drew on *De Excidio Britanniae* when he wrote his *Historia Ecclesiastica.*

In later centuries Gildas was named 'Sapiens' ('the Wise'), a title given to those who were learned in the scriptures and in Latin letters. There are two *Lives* of Gildas, written a long while after his time. The first of these was written by a monk of the monastery of Rhuys in Brittany. It has been dated to the eleventh century, but may be based on ninth century material. The other is the *Life* written by Caradog of Llancarfon about 1130-50. Today these works are seen as of little historical value. So the answer to the question, 'What do we know about Gildas?' is 'very little'. We have no sure knowledge of his roots, of his dates, of where he lived and worked. Even his name is a puzzle. It is not recognizably British, nor has anyone traced it in any other language.[67] It has even been suggested that it is a false name, hiding the identity of a wanted man. (He attacked the morals of the British political leaders of his day, and we may suppose that they might not have taken that lightly.)[68]

We can be almost certain that Gildas was a native Romano-Briton, and, like enough, he spoke a Brittonic dialect (though this cannot be proved from the *DEB*).[69] In later Welsh genealogies his father is named Caw of Britain. The eleventh-century Breton *Life* of Gildas names his father Caunus, and four brothers and a sister are also named. The Welsh genealogies give Gildas two sons.

---

66 François Kerlouégan, *Dictionary of National Biography* volume 22, p.224.

67 See P Sims-Williams, 'Gildas and the Anglo-Saxons', in *Cambridge Medieval Celtic Studies*, 6 (1983), p.3.

68 NJ Higham, *The English Conquest* (Manchester: Manchester University Press, 1994), p.97, François Kerlouégan on Gildas, in the *Dictionary of National Biography*, volume 22, p.223.

69 Sims-Williams, 'Gildas and vernacular poetry', in Lapidge and Dumville, editors, *Gildas: New Approaches*, p.169.

The time-scale of Gildas's life is very hard to work out, even though he tells us the year of his birth. This is in *DEB* 26.1 where he writes of the siege of Badon Hill, and says, 'That was the year of my birth; as I know, one month of the forty-fourth year since then has already passed.' If only we knew when Badon Hill was fought! But we do not. There are a range of dates offered:

The *Annales Cambriae*, which is probably a late eighth century work, says 516.

Bede took it that the battle was fought forty-four years after the coming of the Saxons to Britain (*HE* 1.16), so either about 490, or perhaps 493-99[70]

NJ Higham would date *De Excidio* between 479 and 484, so pushing Badon back to the 430s. In truth, Higham sees the reference to Gildas's birth year as 'a literary contrivance with some of the characteristics of a birth-related miracle, such as occur widely in the Bible and in much early hagiography'.[71]

Ian Wood suggests that Gildas meant that forty-three years passed between Ambrosius' victory over the Saxons (*DEB* 25.3) and the siege of Badon Hill, and that a month had passed since Badon. In other words Gildas was born in the year of Ambrosius' victory.[72]

Others suggest that Gildas wrote 'about 540', so giving a date for Mount Badon, and a birth date for Gildas, of 'about 500'. This dating depends on Maglocunus, or Maelgwyn, who was king of Gwynedd from about 534 to about 549. (He is one of the five kings attacked by Gildas.) Maelgwyn died in a great plague, dated 547 in the *Annales Cambriae*, 549 in the Annals of Ulster. This is thought to be the plague referred to by Byzantine and western writers, starting in the east in 541/2, spreading to southern Gaul by about 544, and probably reaching Britain a few years later.

Leslie Alcock notes that the *Historia Brittonum* 62, seems to make Maelgwyn the contemporary of Ida of Bernicia and of the early Welsh poets Aneirin and Taliesin. This would place him in the second half of the sixth century,[73] and the date of Badon would then be perhaps 'about 520'.

The *Annales Cambriae* gives 570 as the year of Gildas's death, but we have no means of cross-checking this date.

Where was Gildas's home area? Some argue for a northern, others for a southern, context. David Dumville strongly backs the northern theory. In a two-step argument, he holds, first, that if we place Gildas in the first half of the sixth century, and we also believe that there was extensive Anglo-Saxon settlement in the east Midlands and the South before the last quarter of the fifth century, then we have little choice but to place

---

[70] JM Wallace-Hadrill, 1988, p.214.

[71] NJ Higham, *The English Conquest*, p.49.

[72] Ian Wood, 'The end of Roman Britain: continental evidence and parallels', in Lapidge and Dumville, *Gildas: New Approaches*, p.23.

[73] L Alcock. *Arthur's Britain*, p.23.

Gildas in the west of Britain, far away from the 'front-line'. He then argues that Gildas cannot have been in the arc from north Wales to South-west England, where ran the writ of the five kings he attacked. Other pointers to a northern home are said to be the role of the Picts and Scots as *the* enemies of Britain (they were a threat mainly to the north), and the references to mountains and mountain pastures. Thus Dumville places Gildas in the north-west, and he takes 'the East' (where the Saxon federates were planted), to be the Newcastle area or Lothian. He thinks that this was the 'home' to which the Saxons went back after they had done raiding.[74]

There are, however, some weighty arguments against the northern theory. First, there is the matter of Gildas's ignorance of the north. He believed that the Walls (Hadrian's, and the Antonine) were built after the Romans had formally left Britain. In Gildas's account the Romans came back twice in answer to British pleas for help against the Picts and Scots. During the first expedition they advised the building of a wall (which the Britons made of turf), and during the second the Romans themselves built a stone wall. And Gildas took the wall forts to be towns (*DEB* 18.2). Dumville explains Gildas's ignorance about the Walls as the outcome of distance in time, rather than space. He remarks that Gildas must be dated to the 460s at the very earliest.[75]

Those who hold the southern theory say that Britain's northern enemies (the Picts and Scots) did not confine their raiding to the north. As for the mountains and mountain-pastures these need be no higher than the uplands of South-west England. And anyway, the 'mountains' might be part of Gildas's 'rhetorical topography', whose function (according to Higham) was rarely geographical.[76]

Other geographical evidence may throw light on the north/south question. Gildas repeats Orosius' mistaken figure of 200 miles for the width of Britain. (Gildas seems to have drawn information from Paulus Orosius, perhaps gained indirectly, through some geographical compilation.[77]) Gildas does go some way towards putting things right by adding that the 200-mile figure left out 'various large headlands' (*DEB* 3.1). Higham thinks that the Kentish and Cornish peninsulas best fit this description. He goes on to argue that Gildas was aware of the key importance of the Kent-Gaul channel crossings, that his reference to the 'noble' Thames perhaps suggests some familiarity with it, and that he had a town-based viewpoint, suggesting that he was based 'south of the Mersey and east of Long Mynd'. Higham goes further, to suggest that he was no more than 1-2 days' ride from the south coast. In *DEB* 18.3 Gildas refers to 'towers overlooking the sea at intervals on the south coast', by which he may have meant the Saxon Shore forts. Higham concludes that Gildas was a thoroughly southern lowlander.

---

[74] D Dumville, 'The Chronology of *De Excidio Britanniae*, Book I', in Lapidge and Dumville, *Gildas: New Approaches*, pp.72-80.

[75] Dumville, 'The Chronology of *De Excidio Britanniae*, Book I', p.78.

[76] NJ Higham, *The English Conquest*, p.103.

[77] P Sims-Williams, 'Gildas and the Anglo-Saxons', in *Cambridge Medieval Celtic Studies*, 6 (1983), p.5.

There is also the evidence of Gildas's political knowledge. He noted that British pilgrims could not now go to the shrines of the martyrs, that is, Alban of Verulam and Aaron and Julius of Caerleon (*DEB*, 10.2). This hardly fits in with Gildas being based in the north. But if he was in the south, it may be that the middle Thames Saxons barred the way for the pilgrims. The lands of the five rulers Gildas condemned stretched from Dumnonia in the south-west to Gwynedd in North Wales. Unless Gildas (for reasons of personal safety) kept out of the lordships of these rulers (perhaps moving from place to place), it would seem that he was writing from the province of Britannia Prima. Higham thinks we can narrow this down. He says that Gildas has more specific information about Constantine of Dumnonia than of the other kings, and he says this suggests he was writing from 'next door', in the *civitas* of the Durotriges – roughly modern Dorset. (A *civitas* was a Roman administrative unit based on an existing tribal territory. There were a number of *civitates* making up each of the four – or five – provinces of Roman Britain. Towns such as Winchester, Cirencester, and Lincoln were *civitas* capitals. Each *civitas* was divided again into *pagi*, based on the smaller towns.)

And one final point about Gildas's geographical outlook: what did he mean by 'Britannia'? Neil Wright[78] believes the answer is 'the whole island', the '*Britannia insula*' of *DEB* 3. What, then, did Gildas mean when he referred to the Scots and the Picts as 'overseas nations' (*DEB* 14)? Did he modify his understanding of 'Britannia' to mean 'Britain south of the Forth-Clyde line'? Certainly this was Bede's understanding of the geography. For him 'Britannia' was the area of the Roman diocese of Britain, 'overseas' referred to the lands beyond the Firths of Forth and Clyde, and the 'Irish' were the Scots of Dál Riata. But Wright thinks that when Gildas said 'overseas' he meant just what he said – that these nations were based outside mainland Britain, the Scots in the north-west (that is, Ireland), and the Picts in some unnamed area to the north. Thus when they fled from the Romans they fled across the sea (*DEB* 17.3). And when Gildas wrote (in *DEB* 21.1) that 'for the first time the Picts in the far end of the island kept quiet from now on', Wright takes this to mean that, having been until now based overseas from the British Isles, the Picts now settled in the far north. (And perhaps the Scots from here on were coming from settlements in Dál Riata, rather than from Ireland.)

There are different traditions about where Gildas received his education. The earlier *Life* of Gildas, written in Brittany, says that his parents entrusted him to the monk Illtud, to learn the scriptures and the liberal arts, at the monastery of St Illtud at Llanilltud Fawr. Among his fellow pupils there were said to have been the future saints, Samson and Paul Aurelian. Gildas is then said to have studied in Ireland, Rome, Ravenna, and finally Brittany. This is hard to believe. Yet it may be that Gildas did spend part of his life in a monastic environment, for he shows some sympathy for asceticism and the monastic movement.

---

[78] N Wright, 'Gildas's geographical perspective: some problems', in Lapidge and Dumville, editors, *Gildas: New Approaches*, pp.85-105.

If Gildas did not study in a monastery, where might he have gained his learning? In the traditional system of classical education a youth spent five years (from the age of eleven to sixteen) under a *grammaticus*. From him he would learn right Latin, that is, the Latin of highly-thought of authors such as Vergil. Then at about the age of 16 the young man moved on to study public speaking with a *rhetor*. It was the rhetorical schools who turned out the trained men needed to make the huge Roman bureaucracy work, and to plead as advocates in the courts.

Many Christian leaders rejected traditional classical education. Sulpicius Severus, for example, reminded people (in his *Vita S. Martini*) that salvation was not preached by orators, but by fishermen. Cassian equated rhetorical skill with the sin of vainglory. Thus the Church set up its own 'episcopal' or 'presbyteral' schools to provide itself with enough literate bishops and priests. (Yet many of those Church leaders who rejected classical letters had in fact first received a thorough training in the traditional Roman schools.)

What can be learned of Gildas's education from a study of his Latin? (Lapidge notes that 'the marks of the traditional Roman education were indelible'.[79]) Gildas's writing shows no evidence of spoken, or vulgar, Latin, such as a native speaker might use.[80] But his Latin is utterly correct by Late Latin standards, and there are no signs that he drew upon glossaries and word-lists. (Those who did sometimes show unawareness of all the connotations of a given word.) Gildas consistently used technical words precisely and accurately, words such as *foederati, annona, hospites,* and *epimenia.* He is thoroughly familiar with Vergil. So it seems likely that Gildas did receive a traditional education from a *grammaticus*.

Is there any evidence that he had been further trained by a *rhetor*? In his essay on Gildas's education Michael Lapidge[81] notes that *De Excidio* is a well planned piece of literature. In *DEB* 1-2 Lapidge sees a standard *exordium*, setting out the reasons for speaking – Gildas wrote out of sorrow for his country. This is followed by a historical account of the matter in hand (*DEB* 3-26). Then there is the *propositio*, setting forth the speaker's case, and the *argumentatio*, the detailed argument of the case. Gildas had two targets for his *propositio*: first, the holders of secular office *DEB* 27-36 (and this is followed by the *argumentatio* in *DEB* 37-63), then the holders of ecclesiastical office, *DEB* 64-75 (followed by the *argumentatio* in *DEB* 76-105). In the manner of the *rhetor* Gildas then calls his 'witnesses', in this case the Scripture writers. Like a *rhetor* he closes with the *epilogus*, the aim of which was to stir his hearers either to wrath or mercy. In *DEB* 106-110 Gildas reminds the wrong-doers of the punishments for their evil deeds, but he ends with a prayer for mercy for his 'clients', the few good shepherds to be found in Britain.

---

79 M Lapidge, 'Gildas's education and the Late Latin culture of sub-Roman Britain', in Lapidge and Dumville, editors, *Gildas: New Approaches*, p.33.

80 M Lapidge, 'Gildas's education', p.34.

81 M Lapidge, 'Gildas's education', pp.41-2.

It seems safe to say that Gildas had been trained by a *rhetor*. Yet Roman government and rhetorical education went hand in hand, and by the late fifth century the fabric of Roman government was falling apart. It seems, then, that Gildas, and others like him, must have had private tutors. (Such a system continued in Gaul into the early sixth century.) This surely means that he came from a well-to-do home, probably from a land-owning family, able to afford the luxury of a good Latin education.[82] And if the traditional dating of Gildas (about AD 500 to about 570) is correct it would mean that in the early sixth century some form of Roman government was still in place, offering career openings to a man like Gildas. It also implies that there was an audience of cultured, Christian, aristocratic, Romanised Britons for whom Gildas wrote.[83]

Lapidge sums up with the following hypothesis: that Gildas trained for a government administrative career, that he was afterwards ordained, that he was perhaps converted to the monastic way and renounced his earlier secular training, and that he then took up a career in the British Church as an outspoken critic of corruption in Church and State.[84] It would seem that through his preaching against ecclesiastical corruption Gildas became the leading reformer of the sixth century Church in these islands.[85]

In his *De Excidio* Gildas shows knowledge of Juvenal, Jerome, John Cassian, the *Vita S. Martini* of Sulpicius Severus, and, above all the *Aeneid* of Vergil, and especially Book II, with its the vivid picture of the sack of Troy. Gildas also used Eusebius's *Historia Ecclesiastica*, in the translation of Rufinus, and the *Historia adversum Paganos* of Orosius. But Gildas relied more on oral tradition than on written records, and he gives 'an impressionistic version of events'. Yet his sketch of British society in the west in the sixth century is broadly in keeping with what can be learned from later charters, saints' *Lives* and annals from Wales.[86]

The text Gildas draws on most often is the Bible, and as he writes for a 'besieged Britannia'[87] he presents a view of history that sees it as providential. He is interested in the past only as it reveals the pattern of history and explains the present, thus enabling him to point out what happens when God's laws are ignored. Gildas believed that the present was the continuation of biblical history. He saw the Britons as a chosen people, their life being a continuation of the history of Israel. As God had made his covenant with Israel, so was there a 'contract' or treaty between God and his people, the Britons. By their sins the Britons had broken the treaty. For this

---

[82] NJ Higham, *The English Conquest*, pp.97-8.
[83] NJ Higham, *The English Conquest*, p.98.
[84] M Lapidge, 'Gildas's education', in *Gildas: New Approaches*, p.48.
[85] Richard Sharpe, 'Gildas as a Father of the Church', in *Gildas: New Approaches*, p.199.
[86] Yorke, *Kings and Kingdoms*, (London: Seaby, 1990), p.2.
[87] AH Merrills, *History and Geography in Late Antiquity* (Cambridge: Cambridge University Press, 2005), p.277.

the inevitable outcome was the withdrawal of God's protection. They had also broken faith with the Romans, so that Roman protection of Britain had failed, too. This meant defeat and suffering. But such chastening could (indeed, should) lead to repentance and restoration. So Gildas set out to list the afflictions of Britain, to explain their causes, and to identify those responsible. Contrition would then lead to the renewal of divine protection. So the victories of the Saxons were less a political and military matter, much more a matter of breach of faith on the part of the Britons. Gildas wrote graphically of Saxon ferocity and duplicity. He saw these folk as 'wolves', 'dogs', 'barbarians', 'easterners', 'devils'. He likened them to the Philistines of old, and cited the words of the Old Testament God against the unrighteous land of Israel, 'If I cause wild beasts to pass through the land ... ' (Ezekiel 14:15). These Saxons were destroyers of 'Romanity'. But they were also the instruments of God's wrath.

Gildas drew parallels with the days of Zedekiah, the last king of Judah. That king had broken his treaty with Nebuchadnezzar of Babylon, and the result was the dreadful siege of Jerusalem (589-587 BC). Gildas identified with the contemporary prophet, Jeremiah. As that prophet had denounced the sins of Judah, so Gildas denounced the sins of his own people. He condemned heresy (such as Arianism), apostasy (there was a resurgence of paganism – perhaps the gods of the conquerors seemed more powerful), and even the church (which was generally characterised by greed, and neglect of duty). Gildas wrote of churchmen as plunderers, as wolves, in effect equating the priesthood with the heathen Saxons. Thr thrust of his work has been summed up as follows: 'Kings Britain has, but usurpers; judges has she, but ungodly; priests Britain has, but foolish ones'.[88]

Gildas shows a distrust of the untamed wild, and he makes a lot of use of beast imagery. We have seen that he speaks of the Saxons as 'wolves' (*DEB* 23.1). He also calls them 'a pack of cubs burst forth from the lair of the barbarian lioness' (*DEB* 23.3). The Picts and the Scots are 'wild, barbarian beasts' (*DEB* 18.3), while the Arian heresy is a 'savage snake' (*DEB* 12.3). Beast images are also applied to the five 'tyrants', the five rulers in Wales and the south-west condemned by Gildas. (Perhaps he meant to recall the four beasts of Daniel 7, and also the beast from the sea in Revelation 13:2.) Gildas also uses plant pictures. He speaks of 'tyrant thickets', and of the usurper Magnus Maximus as 'a sprig of its [the island's] own bitter planting'(*DEB* 13.1). The Saxons are 'the sprig of iniquity, the root of bitterness' (*DEB* 23.4). Gildas laments that 'the vineyard that had once been good ... degenerated into sourness' (*DEB* 24.4).

Patrick Sims-Williams suggests that Gildas may have made use of imagery from two streams of panegyric tradition (the Celtic, and the classical/biblical), and exploited the differences between them.[89] For example, Gildas referred to

---

[88] See L Alcock, *Arthur's Britain*, p.29.

[89] P Sims-Williams, 'Gildas and vernacular poetry', in *Gildas: New Approaches*, pp.169-192.

Maglocunus as the 'dragon of the island'. In biblical tradition the dragon is an image of Satan. But in Welsh lore of the twelfth century and later, dragon images always occur in a favourable sense. Did Gildas use the image of the dragon (and other images) from the Celtic stream, and then undercut them by placing them in a context in which the biblical or classical significance would be to the fore? Perhaps 'dragon' was an epithet used by the court bards (the 'parasites' of *DEB* 35.3?) which Gildas echoed with back-handed praise of Maglocunus.[90]

There are a few further points to be made about Gildas. He was very sparing of names, and chronology was not a high priority for him. He collected anecdotes not for historical purposes, but as illustrations to support his understanding of historical cause and effect. His description of the geography of the land presented an idealised, Eden-like Britain.[91] And he presented an idealised Christian past with Christianity reaching Britain in the time of Tiberius (*DEB* 8), that is, within four years (at most) of the crucifixion.

We must acknowledge that Gildas never meant to give us formal history. Yet 'picking over' his work is not a wholly foolish enterprise. When he was dealing with events of only one or two generations back he would have needed to be more sure of his facts, otherwise he would have lost credibility. The letter to Aëtius, the siege of Mount Badon, and the long period of peace which followed, would have been public knowledge, and Gildas's credit as a preacher would surely have been lost if he was wildly out. Alcock acknowledges this, then goes on to ask, 'But how far back is this argument valid?'[92]

## Bede

The writings of the English monk, Bede (who lived from about AD 673 to 735) included many Bible commentaries, the lives of Christian saints, and two important and influential works on chronology and computation, *De temporibus* and *De temporum ratione*. Bede had a longstanding interest in chronological scholarship and its implications for historical writing. He made use of regnal and consular years, but he also set everything into the *annus Domini* frame. This form of dating seems to have been first used by Dionysius Exiguus (died about 527). There is evidence that AD dating was finding its way into legal instruments from 670 onwards,[93] but it was Bede's use of it in the *Historia Ecclesiastica* which led to its coming into general use.

Today it is Bede's *Historia Ecclesiastica gentis Anglorum* ('History of the English Church and People') for which he is best remembered. This *Historia* is the only work, other than parts of the Bible, which has been read by every English generation from

---

[90] P Sims-Williams, 'Gildas and vernacular poetry', in *Gildas: New Approaches*, pp.175-6.
[91] NJ Higham, *The Englsih Conquest*, p. 14.
[92] L Alcock, *Arthur's Britain*, p.26.
[93] K Harrison, *The Framework of Anglo-Saxon history to A.D. 900* (Cambridge: Cambridge University Press, 1976), p.134.

his own day to the present.[94] There are two early manuscripts of this work, the Moore MS dated to about 737, and the St Petersburg MS which is not later than 747. Both were written in Northumbria, the St Petersburg manuscript most likely at Bede's monastery of Jarrow. Thus the text is of 'an exceptionally uncontroversial standard'.

Where did Bede get his material from? In the Preface that he wrote to the *Historia Ecclesiastica* he addresses king Ceolwulf (king of Northumbria 729-737). To allay any doubts that the king, or others, might have, he names his sources. We learn that his principal authority and adviser was Abbot Albinus of St Peter's and St Paul's (later St Augustine's), Canterbury. This was the most important centre of intellectual life in England at this time, having been established by Archbishop Theodore. Bede tells us that Albinus had carefully passed him material, either verbally or in writing, through Nothhelm, a priest of the church of London (and later archbishop of Canterbury, 735-739). Albinus took his facts 'from written records or from the old traditions' (annals and regnal lists may have been kept at Canterbury). Nothhelm himself visited Rome, where he was allowed to examine the archives, and to copy papal letters. Some version of the Kentish origin story is likely to have been known in Kent in Bede's day. Certainly it is hard to think of any who, apart from Bede's Kentish informants, would have been concerned about Hengest and Oisc and the line of descent of the Kentish kings, or about Horsa's monument in East Kent.

Albinus and Nothhelm also provided Bede with information on the East and West Saxons, the East Angles and the Northumbrians. Another informant was Daniel, bishop of the West Saxons, who sent Bede, 'in writing', something of the history of the church among the West and South Saxons, and on the Isle of Wight. The monks of Lastingham monastery gave Bede a careful account of the conversion of Mercia. Bede gained information on the church of the East Angles 'partly from the writings or the traditions of men of the past, and partly from the account of the esteemed Abbot Esi'. He got information on Lindsey either from the letters of Bishop Cynebert, 'or from the lips of other trustworthy men'. For the history of the church in Northumbria Bede drew material from 'the faithful testimony of innumerable witnesses' who knew the facts, apart from what he knew himself.

For most of his knowledge of the history of the English churches in the seventh century Bede had to turn to oral witness by men of his own day. He did, however, weigh the reliability of witnesses. One example quoted is an account given by the priest Deda, abbot of Parteney ('a most truthful man', *HE* II.16). He told how he had heard from an old man who, with others, had been baptized by the missionary bishop Paulinus in the days of king Edwin of Northumbria. From this record we get a picture of Paulinus as 'tall, with a slight stoop, black hair, a thin face, a slender aquiline nose,' a man both 'venerable and awe-inspiring.'

What else can be learned about Bede's sources? Some eighty years ago Max Laistner reckoned that Bede had access to roughly 150 works by seventy-five authors, and J

[94] J Campbell, *Dictionary of National Biography*, volume 4, p.764.

Campbell has noted that this list could certainly be corrected and added to today.[95] Many, perhaps most, of these 150 works were available in the Wearmouth-Jarrow monastery library. Benedict Biscop had brought back books from Italy and elsewhere, and Bede says that the library had been doubled in size by king Ceolfrith.

Bede's account of Roman Britain came largely from Orosius (*fl.* 414–17) and Eutropius (*fl.* 363–4). He also drew on Josephus, Jerome's translation of Eusebius' *Chronicle*, Rufinus' version of Eusebius' *Ecclesiastical History*, Grosius, Gildas's *De Excidio Britanniae*, and a good selection of chronicles, including that by Marcellinus Comes.[96] He had access to an account of the martyrdom of St Alban, and drew on the *Life of St. Germanus* written by Constantius (*fl.* 480) for his record of the fifth-century visits to Britain by Germanus. For the period after 597 he had a handful of biographies of saints that he could refer to.

His account of the physical geography of Britain, in *HE* I.1, draws on the work of Pliny, Orosius, and Gildas, while Solinus' *Collectanea rerum memorabilium* and Isidore clearly influenced his account of Hibernia (Ireland).[97] For local geography his use of the Anglo-Saxon land measurement of the 'hide' might suggest that he went to tax or tribute records, or he may have drawn on common knowledge.

It may sometimes be possible to see where a passage in the *Historia Ecclesiastica* has been taken from a written source. For example, Bede almost always uses *Australes* to refer to the South Saxons, while he uses the word *Occidentales* of the West Saxons. But in the well-known passage in *HE* I.15, giving the origins of the German invaders, they are called the *Meridiani* and the *Occidui* respectively. This would seem to suggest that the wording here is not his own.[98]

Bede's letters, and his account of his sources, show that he was in communication with ecclesiastics over much of England and beyond. He has preserved material which would otherwise have been lost to us, such as the extracts from early English synods and from the *Life of St Æthelburh* of Barking.[99] Some of the most important centres of learning in Europe were Irish, and Bede emphasizes the importance of Irish learning for Englishmen. Archibald Duncan has suggested that Bede's information on the Scotti came from an Ionan source, almost certainly written and not oral.[100] (The question whether Bede had access to an early version of the *Anglo-Saxon Chronicle* will be looked at when we consider that source.) Clearly Bede belonged to a quite extensive world of information.

---

[95] J Campbell, *DNB*, volume 4, p.763.

[96] MLW Laistner, 'Bede as a Classical and Patristic Scholar' *Transactions of the Royal Historical Society*, 16 (1933), p.77.

[97] AH Merrills, History and Geography in Late Antiquity, p.250.

[98] J Campbell, *DNB*, volume 4, p.761.

[99] B Yorke, *Kings and Kingdoms*, pp.22-3.

[100] A Duncan, cited in Merrills, p.287.

What did Bede set out to do in his *Historia Ecclesiastica*? We may note that this work is both parochial and universal.[101] Bede still felt himself to be an Anglo-Saxon, a Northumbrian, but he was also linked to the sacramental redemptive community of the church.[102] It has been said that 'Bede succeeded in giving the Anglo-Saxons a new history by incorporating them into the history of the island of Brittania and the history of the church of Rome'.[103] He wrote an ecclesiastical history in the tradition of Eusebius, and a 'national' history in the tradition of such as Jordanes and Gregory of Tours.

This parochial-universal outlook is seen in another of Bede's thrusts. Through wide reading in the Old and New Testaments, and most likely learning much of this by heart, Bede gained an unrivalled knowledge of the Bible text. And he wished to set before his readers Christian moral object lessons and universal truths. With this in mind he quotes 1 Corinthians 10:11 time and again. In this passage the apostle Paul writes of the exodus of Israel from Egypt and their time in the wilderness, with all their grumbles and complaints, and the judgments of God upon them. Paul goes on, 'these things happened to them as a warning, but they were written down for our instruction'. So Bede peopled his history with Christian champions (and a few villains to shun). The kings, bishops, missionaries and others of his story are compared to biblical archetypes, so that the players of Bede's drama become embodiments of 'the familiar characters on the great Christian stage', and are seen to be relevant to believers throughout the world.[104] Here we touch on one of two aspects of Bede's sense of history noted by Jan Davidse, the relation between time and eternity (the other is the relation between Christianity and history).[105] For Bede, time is always moving on, creating a growing gap between 'then' and 'now'. But when one discovers a meaning in the past, something that we may learn from, then it is found that the past is not wholly past and gone, and the gap is bridged. So Gregory the Great, the Fathers, Queen Aethelthryth (in fact an older contemporary of Bede's) are not only figures of the past, they also become contemporaries.

As to the relation between Christianity and history, we may note that when Bede set his *Historia* in the *annus Domini* framework, this was not simply a way of organising historical facts in relation to a fixed point. It brought the history of the world into relationship with redemption. Bede saw the incarnation of the Word as the decisive turning-point in world history. And in the history of the world since the redemption it was the position of the church, and not the rise and fall of empires, that was central.

---

[101] AH Merrills, History and Geography in Late Antiquity, p.235.

[102] J Davidse, 'The Sense of History in the Works of the Venerable Bede', *Studi Medievali* 3rd series, xxiii (1983), p.691.

[103] JN Stephens, p.13, cited in Davidse, p.674.

[104] AH Merrills, History and Geography in Late Antiquity, p.239.

[105] See J Davidse, pp.651, 657.

The story of the growth of the church begins in the book of Acts, and now Bede sees himself writing the latest, perhaps even the last, chapter in that ongoing story.

For Bede Britain was set almost at the outermost edge of the world, and this was even more true of the island retreats of Iona and Lindisfarne and Farne, with the unknown and unknowable width of the Ocean beyond. These lands seemed to border the otherworldly, having a role like that played by the desert in the literature about saints' lives in Europe and North Africa.[106] As for Hibernia (Ireland), it is pictured as a land of milk, honey and vines, another Canaan. The two islands (Britain and Ireland) are seen in 'spiritual interdependence', coming to their fullest potential only through contact with each other.[107]

Furthermore, had not the Lord said that the gospel must be preached to all nations and then the end would come (Matthew 24:14)? Several factors were holding off that end: the non-conversion of the Jews, the way that the heathen clung to their idolatry, false faith within the church. Nevertheless, the conversion of the English located the story of Britain near the end of time.

It is sometimes said that Bede had no interest in the pagan past of his people. This is not wholly true. Bede would have known from the Old Testament that God intervenes in the affairs of non-Christian peoples, and he could see God fulfilling his purposes in the life of the heathen Æthelfrith of Bernicia, and working in the life of Edwin of Northumbria while he was yet a pagan. Yet it is true that Bede had little to say about the secular origin stories of the Germanic inhabitants of Britain, or of their migration traditions. He did not, in truth, find the origins of the English nation in a shared military past.

Nor did he see the English as a 'new Israel'. In this he differed from the *Exodus* poet who, in his tenth century/early eleventh century work pictured the Israelites at the Red Sea as Germanic warriors – the implication being that the Anglo-Saxons had also crossed the sea, going to their own promised land.[108] (However, it does seem that Bede saw the Anglo-Saxon migration as a necessary step towards Pope Gregory sending missionaries to convert them.)

It seems that Bede had a rather different 'origin myth' in mind. This is found in the account of Gregory and the English boys (*HE* II.1). Like the stories of the origins of the Goths, this tale is set in a far-off place (Rome in this case). Gregory is the founding hero, who sets the great journey in train, and he plays a key role in the later succession of power within the group. As Patrick Wormald quaintly noted, 'Symbolically at least, Napoleon's nation of shopkeepers began in Gregory's

---

[106] AH Merrills, History and Geography in Late Antiquity, pp.251-2.
[107] AH Merrills, p.264.
[108] Scott M Langston, *Exodus Through the Centuries* (Oxford: Blackwell Publishing, 2006), pp.132-4.

market-place in Rome'.[109] The first book of the *Historia* had told how 'they' – the Angles, Saxons and Jutes – had settled in Britain. With the coming of the gospel (*HE* I.23ff) we move on to the real history, that of 'our' united people.[110] Merrills concludes that for Bede the English were a people whose very being as a nation was dependent upon their conversion.[111] Likewise Davidse has noted that Bede saw the Christianization of the Anglo-Saxon people as the turning-point in their history.[112]

In making an assessment of Bede's historical writing it is important to stress that he was not writing for 'a concourse of antiquaries' (to use Harrison's words).[113] Harrison goes on, 'No estimate of Bede's work should neglect the limits he imposed upon himself.' Bede was interested in the foundation of Kent, as the kingdom where the only archbishopric of the seventh century was situated. Perhaps he could have found out more about the *adventus Saxonum* if he had been so minded. But that was not his purpose.

How shall we assess Bede as a witness? It has been noted that he was hard on the Britons because, in his view, they failed to reach out to their English neighbours (and conquerors) with the gospel, and because they stubbornly held to the Celtic dating for Easter against that of Rome. He has also been accused of bias in not including any Mercian kings in his list of those who held the 'Bretwaldaship', or overlordship of all Britain (*HE* II.5).[114] (Note that the concept of the 'Bretenanwealda' – usually shortened to Bretwalda, 'Britain-ruler' – perhaps continued a British understanding that Britain had had, and should have, one high overlord.) In answer it must be said that Bede lived before the time of Mercia's greatness in the later eighth century. The only early Mercian candidate for the Bretwaldaship would be Penda. Perhaps Bede could not bring himself to acknowledge the might of that militant pagan. Yet it could be that Penda, for all his deeds in war against Northumbria, never gained general acceptance as overlord of the English.

These may be flaws in Bede's writing, but where does he stand, overall, when his truthfulness is weighed? K Harrison singles out ('without trying to be exhaustive'), four factors which might affect Bede's accuracy. First, he might have lacked a key date which would have helped him to sort out a sequence of events. Second, while Bede preferred primary sources to derived ones[115] there

---

109 Patrick Wormald, 'Bede, the *Bretwaldas* and the Origins of the *Gens Anglorum*', in Patrick Wormald (ed.), *Ideal and Reality in Frankish and Anglo-Saxon Society: Studies Presented to J.M. Wallace-Hadrill* (Oxford, 1983), p.129 of 99-129, quoted in AH Merrills, p.306.

110 AH Merrills, History and Geography in Late Antiquity, p.304.

111 AH Merrills, p.307.

112 J Davidse, 'The Sense of History in the Works of the Venerable Bede', pp.694-5.

113 K Harrison, *Framework*, p.18.

114 See P Sims-Williams 'The Settlement of England in Bede and the Chronicle' in *Anglo-Saxon England*, 12 (1983) pp.25-26.

115 K Harrison, *Framework*, p.54n.

might yet be mistakes in the material he drew upon. Third, there are his own mistakes, such as errors in transcription or arithmetic, or faulty deductions. And fourth, there are mistakes that are not of his making, but which arise 'when it is assumed that considerations which apply to modern history should be applicable to pre-Conquest England'.[116]

And what of Bede's dependence on oral witness for much of his information? For many scholars today it seems that oral witness is taken as a negative. In noting that most of Bede's material came to him by this means Barbara Yorke comments that some of it was certainly influenced by the conventions of both Germanic and Christian story-telling, so that we have set-piece scenes of heroic action, on the one hand, and miracle-working, on the other'.[117] John McNamara sees Bede as a man who 'inevitably entered the world of legends, and these legends shaped his work as much as his work shaped them'. He sees Bede as not only a listener and recorder, but as one who 'authorized' and circulated stories. [118] (Note that the stories from Bede discussed by McNamara in his paper are not accounts of the migrations, but later accounts of miraculous healings.)

Yet Harrison, in discussing oral witness notes that the dates of truly notable events might well be faithfully handed down by word of mouth until Bede's day. One example might be king Edwin's baptism on Easter Day in the eleventh year of his reign (*HE*, II.14). Another example could be Oswiu's victory at the river *Winwaed*, at a time of heavy rains and flooding, in the king's thirteenth year (*HE*, III.24). Harrison concludes that 'the main sequence of dates from 596 to 729 appears to be reliable and free from systematic error'.[119]

FM Stenton remarked that Ceolwulf, king of Northumbria, to whom Bede addressed his *Historia*, was well known for his interest in the history of the English people. He was acquainted with much heroic verse which has since disappeared. The fact that he should have read and approved a first copy of the *Historia* must be given due weight.[120] And Bede himself declares (in the Preface to his *Historia*), 'I have laboured honestly to examine whatever I could ascertain from common report for the instruction of posterity.' And we may also note that when Bede was less than sure about the truth of his information he would write *perhibentur* ('it is said'). Hengest and Horsa are a case in point. Speaking of the English peoples Bede says, 'Their first chieftains are said to have been Hengist and Horsa' (*HE* I.15).

---

[116] K Harrison, *Framework*, p.78.

[117] Yorke, Kings and Kingdoms, p.23.

[118] J McNamara, 'Bede's Role in Circulating Legene in the *Historia Ecclesiastica*', *ASSAH*, 7, p.67.

[119] K Harrison, *Framework*, p.96.

[120] Stenton, *Preparatory*, p.268.

On the whole, Bede's careful work is acknowledged even by critical scholars. It is agreed that he 'used language with great precision'.[121] Barbara Yorke acknowledges that 'Bede believed that the course of events would reveal God's will towards man and so he set out to reconstruct as accurately as he could the history of the Anglo-Saxons since their arrival in Britain and adoption of Christianity'.[122] As an example of Bede's concern for truth we may note his second commentary on the Acts of the Apostles (called the *Retractatio* by reference to an earlier work to which it adds, and which it puts right in places). He tells us that he has been able to refine the meaning of *scapha*, 'small boat'. He has referred to Vegetius' pamphlet on military tactics and now takes the word to mean 'a kind of canoe hollowed out of a single log.'[123] P Meyvaert made a detailed study of Bede's lengthy transcript of Pope Gregory's reply to some questions from Augustine (*HE*, I.27), comparing it with other copies. He found many errors, but concluded that Bede had transmitted the text 'warts and all'.[124] In transcribing a number of Pope Gregory's letters 'Bede chose fidelity rather than consistency'. [125]

Certainly Bede had his own standpoint. *But if he was to convince and persuade he had to record events as accurately as possible.* Bede's achievments are very great. Compared with some of his modern critics he stands as a 'giant among grasshoppers'.

## The Anglo-Saxon Chronicle

The first 'edition' of the *Anglo-Saxon Chronicle* known to us was completed in 892. After that date the *Chronicle* was kept up at a number of different monasteries, and the versions differ slightly. The *Chronicle* archetype, sometimes referred to as the 'common stock', has not survived.

If the whole work was put together in the late ninth century then it is a very late source indeed for the period of the coming of the English to Britain. Might there have been earlier editions of the *Chronicle*? Ealdorman Æthelweard, who died about 998, and who claimed descent from Æthelred I, Alfred the Great's elder brother, wrote a Latin version of the *Anglo-Saxon Chronicle*, down to 975. He seems to have had before him an older, fuller version of the *Chronicle*, different from any which has come down to us.

We might ask whether the historical work of Bede was a spur to the writing of annals in Wessex as well as in Northumbria. HM Chadwick suggested that the annals from 755, at least to 840, and perhaps to 855, were the work of a writer of the

---

[121] For example, Fanning 1991, cited in Yorke, *ASSAH*, 10, p.27.

[122] Yorke, Kings and Kingdoms, p.22

[123] See MLW Laistner, 'Bede as a Classical and Patristic Scholar', p.85.

[124] P Meyvaert 1971, p.32, quoted in K Harrison, *The Framework of Anglo-Saxon History*, p.79.

[125] P Meyvaert 1970, p.166, quoted in K Harrison, p.79n.

time of king Æthelwulf (839-58). And FM Stenton argued,[126] that soon after King Alfred's accession in 871 the *Chronicle* which we have today was updated as far as 858 (and later carried as far as 891). He thought that the chronicler of 858 probably had before him an older set of annals, running from about 750.

Could the roots of the *Chronicle* go even further back than that? Might Bede, writing his *Historia Ecclesiastica* in 731 have had access to an early version? In another paper[127] Stenton argued that traces of archaic grammatical construction in the pre-750 annals, the employment of methods of computation so ancient that their meaning cannot now be recovered, and the frequent reference to obscure place-names, led to 'an almost overwhelming presumption' that part at least of these annals go back to the seventh century. He noted the 'remarkable precision' of the annal for 661 (recording that Cenwalh fought at 'Posentes byrig' *at Easter*), and the recording of 'the great mortality of birds' in 671 (Æthelweard's version refers to the foul stench). It is recorded of Cuthred that he was the godson of Birinus (*Chronicle* 639) – a detail which few would remember for long.[128] Another annal which perhaps has the stamp of a contemporary record is 664, when there was an eclipse of the sun, and a great pestilence. And GH Wheeler argued that it was hard to see why the annal of 674, with its genealogy for the short-lived king Æscwine, should have been composed in 892, more than 200 years after his death. Wheeler further argued, from a study of the genealogies embedded in the annals, that the section from 648-750 incorporated a contemporary record of events.[129] (Kenneth Sisam, writing about 'Anglo-Saxon Royal Genealogies' in 1953, did not agree that pedigrees like those of Æscwine, and of Oswald the Atheling (728), must have come from contemporary sources. But he did suggest that they came from an eighth century written source, which might be presumed to give Ine's pedigree as well.[130])

If there was an eighth century source whose annals went back to 648, there might be implications for annal-keeping before that date. Stenton saw the entry for 648 as the first annal which contains within itself an indication of contemporary writing, but he thought that it would hardly do as the beginning of a West Saxon Chronicle. He thought it likely that the writer would have carried the record back at least to the start of the mission of Birinus in 634 and the baptism of the West Saxon king Cynegils in

---

[126] In a paper entitled 'The South-western Element in the Old English Chronicle' (*Essays in Medieval History presented to Thomas Frederick Tout*, Manchester, 1925, reprinted in *Preparatory to Anglo-Saxon England*, 1970, pp.106-115.

[127] FM Stenton, 'The Foundations of English History', in *Transactions of the Royal Historical Society*, 4th series, ix (1926), reprinted in *Preparatory to Anglo-Saxon England*, 1970, pp.116-126.

[128] K Harrison, *Framework*, pp.133-4.

[129] GH Wheeler, *English Historical Review*, xxxvi, 1921, pp.161-2.

[130] Kenneth Sisam, 'Anglo-Saxon Royal Genealogies' 1953, in EG Stanley, editor, *British Academy Papers on Anglo-Saxon England*, 1990, p.195.

635.[131] The Easter Tables of the Dorchester-on-Thames *scriptorium* could have provided a framework for the setting down of contemporary annals.[132] (However, Damian Tyler cautions that Christianity, and therefore the organizational background needed to produce documentation, was weak in Wessex until at least the 680s.[133])

What of the sixth century annals? Stenton thought that a mid-seventh century chronicler might have written down oral traditions about Cerdic, Cynric, and Ceawlin. He notes, as marks of antiquity, the integrity seen in the refraining from smoothing away inconsistencies, the triviality of some entries, the enigmatical character of others, and 'laconic allusions', in the manner of heroic poetry. [134] The *Chronicle's* reference, under 584, to Ceawlin's victory and anger might be an example of such allusion. Elsewhere Stenton notes that 'there are indications that, in part at least, it [the tale of Hengest and Horsa] had been handed down in alliterative verse'. [135] Leslie Alcock is another who sees poetry as one strand in the oral tradition behind the earlier annals of the *Chronicle*. He thought that the names of battles and warriors could have been drawn from battle poems about the heroic deeds of the dynasties of Hengest of Kent, Ælle of Sussex, and Cerdic of Wessex. He further suggests that the 'fire and slaughter' imagery of the English settlement comes from Anglo-Saxon heroic poetry.[136]

Kenneth Harrison also suggests that the materials for the *Chronicle* annals for 450-660 may have been collected together soon after the latter date. Malmesbury (founded about 640) or Sherborne might have been the place of compilation. He says of the early *Chronicle* entries 'there is no padding or embroidery, no attempt to link the earliest entries together or breathe life into a fossil record'.[137]

Harrison further suggests that there may have been early written annals from Kent to draw on. He begins his line of argument by suggesting that the marriage of Æthelberht of Kent to Bertha, daughter of Charibert, King of Paris, took place before his accession to the throne in 560, though likely enough not by more than a year or two. We know from a letter to Bertha, written by Gregory the Great in 601, that she was 'instructed in letters'. She came, indeed, of a literate family (her father was praised for his Latin by Venantius Fortunatus), and we may take it that her bishop-chaplain, Liudhard, would also have been literate. This would mean that there were literate folk in Kent from the time of Æthelberht's marriage, and perhaps a few records began to be

---

[131] FM Stenton, 'The Foundations of English History', in DM Stenton, editor, *Preparatory to Anglo-Saxon England*, p.119.

[132] L Alcock, *Arthur's Britain*, p.42.

[133] DJ Tyler, 'Bede, the *Anglo-Saxon Chronicle*, and Early West Saxon Kingship', *Southern History*, 19, 1977, p.4.

[134] Stenton, 'The Foundations of English History', in *Preparatory*, p.119-21.

[135] FM Stenton, *Anglo-Saxon England*, p.16.

[136] L Alcock, *Arthur's Britain*, pp.42, 44.

[137] K Harrison, *Framework*, pp.134-5.

noted down. The Merovingians were very aware of heredity, and Æthelberht may have learned from them. 'Thus the record of his pedigree, as given by Bede (*HE*, II.5) might belong to the sixth century rather than the seventh'.[138] Bishop Liudhard may have had a copy of the Easter tables drawn up in 457 by Victorius of Aquitaine. With these the user would be able to work out which calendar year he was in, and which regnal year, and then employ an elementary knowledge of Roman history gained from such chronicles as those of Prosper. The approximate date of the coming of the Saxons could be arrived at. However, Harrison acknowledges in the end that record-keeping in sixth century Kent is possible rather than probable.[139] (Many scholars today doubt that Æthelberht can have enjoyed quite so long a life and reign. They suggest that the fifty-six years of his reign were in fact the years of his life. In this case his marriage, and the bringing in of literacy which may have followed, would not have happened until around 580.)

It almost goes without saying that others dissent from such theories of early record-keeping. Barbara Yorke, for example, allows the possibility of near contemporary mid-seventh century annals, but doubts that the hypothetical compiler(s) also wrote up the fifth and sixth centuries. She thinks, rather, that the early annals 'read as a seamless whole in the form in which they were cast in the ninth century and it is impossible to detect now any earlier stages in their compilation'.[140]

Can a study of the wording and turns of phrase of an Old English prose text tell us about authorship and dating? In theory it can. FM Stenton argues that an occasional archaic case-ending, or pre-Alfredian form of a proper name, show that truly old material has been brought in.[141] In her study of the vocabulary of the *Chronicle* Janet Bately says that we should be able to see words and turns of phrase that are typical of an author, and other words that are rarely or never used by him. We should also be able to determine whether a text is the work of one author or several. But in practice things are not so simple.[142] She does, however, note that for the most part the *Chronicle* is marked by a plain style, and generally unemotional language. She says that the annals for 449-584 are marked off from the rest of the *Chronicle* by their regular use of the formula 'the place called'. (This could have been present in a Latin or vernacular source used by the compiler.) She also notes that the eighth-century annals, stretching from at least 716 to 741, and the entry for 755, show some distinctiveness.[143]

---

[138] K Harrison, *Framework*, p.123.

[139] K Harrison, *Framework*, p.140.

[140] Yorke, *ASSAH*, 6, p.47.

[141] FM Stenton, *Anglo-Saxon England*, p.15.

[142] J Bately, 'The compilation of the Anglo-Saxon Chronicle, 60 BC to AD 890: vocabulary as evidence', *British Academy Papers on Anglo-Saxon England*, p.262.

[143] J Bately, pp.271-3, 282.

## *The Historia Brittonum*

The *Historia Brittonum* was long thought of as the work of Nennius, who lived around 770-810. Mommsen believed that Nennius took a late seventh century work and added bits of his own here and there. Liebermann thought he put the whole work together using written authorities (now unknown to us) and oral tradition. However, the authorship of Nennius is now largely discounted.[144] The work may be dated to about 829-30.[145]

The writer, whoever he was, had no trained or disciplined mind. In his Preface he engagingly acknowledges that he has gathered up all he could find and 'made a heap' of it, and he asks his readers to forgive him as he goes on like a chattering bird. Leslie Alcock takes up the metaphor of the heap and says that the book is 'like a cairn of stones, uneven and ill-fitting, not worked into a smooth whole by the craftsman's tools'. But, he says, it has the virtue of its defects, and the individual 'stones' can be traced.[146]

The 'heap' includes accounts of British and Irish origins, a sketch of the Roman period, chapters about St Germanus and St Patrick, the tale of Ambrosius or Emyrs, an account of the campaigns of Arthur, the Northern British History (thought to be a hybrid Anglian-British document, focused on the Ida dynasty), and a list of the Wonders of the British Isles. (Among these wonders we have the burial mound of Amr son of Arthur, which is never measured the same twice running. It might be six, nine, twelve or even fifteen feet long – and 'Nennius' has tried it himself and found it to be so!) From our point of view the most significant parts of the 'heap' are the 'Kentish Chronicles' (*HB* 31, 36-8, 43-6). It is thought that the writer drew this Kentish material from an English rather than a Welsh source. This conclusion is based on the fact that he gives the English form of some place-names before their Welsh form.[147] Thus he says that Vortigern 'handed over to them [Hengest, Horsa and their followers] the island that in their language is called Thanet, in British Ruoihm' (*HB* 31). And the second of the four battles in Kent was 'at the ford called Episford in their language, Rhyd yr afael in ours' (*HB* 44). Also, Old English is used in the story of the murder of the 300 British elders – *Eu, nimet saxas*, that is, 'English, draw your knives!' (*HB* 46).

A key question is, what sort of historical writing is this *Historia Brittonum*? Dumville sees it as 'synthetic' history, meaning that it is 'an expression of a sense of national unity projected back into a legendary past'. In the view of Charles-Edwards it is this

---

[144] See, for example, David Thornton's article in the *Dictionary of National Biography*, volume 40, pp.423-4.

[145] Yorke, Kings and Kingdoms, p.3.

[146] L Alcock, *Arthur's Britain*, p.32.

[147] See Sowerby, 'Hengest and Horsa' in *Nottingham Medieval Studies*, 2007, p.6, citing N Brooks in S Bassett, editor, *The Origins of Anglo-Saxon Kingdoms*.

categorization, rather than any rule of historical method, which enables Dumville to take up such a sceptical position with so much confidence. [148] Elsewhere Dumville lays down the rule that we may accept as true witness only contemporary evidence, or evidence that can be shown to come from contemporary sources by a clear line of transmission.[149] Charles-Edwards finds this rule to be too limited. He notes that later evidence may help us understand contemporary evidence which is otherwise unclear, and there may be good reason to accept the later evidence, even though we do not now know where it has come from. We may also note the point that a contemporary source might be constrained by political or other pressures, so that it cannot tell the truth, whereas a later text, free from these pressures, may give a truer picture (though, again, we may not know where its information has come from). There are examples of this from the Carolingian period.

Charles-Edwards acknowledges that there is synthetic history in the *Historia Brittonum* (for example, the accounts of the origins of the Irish, and the British). But if an interest in origin legends is to be enough to brand a whole text as synthetic (and therefore worthless as evidence), then we would have to write off Paul the Deacon's *Historia Langobardorum*, and Bede's *Historia Ecclesiastica*. Charles-Edwards notes Paul the Deacon's tale of the dealings of Woden and Frea with the Lombards. This may be recognised as 'synthetic', but this does not mean that the whole *Historia Langobardum* is synthetic history.

Rather than take the *Historia Brittonum* as wholly synthetic, Charles-Edwards puts forward the case for viewing it as synchronistic history. And it had to be synchronistic as the writer wove the histories of the Romans, the Irish and the English into his account of the Britons. A further point is that in the early middle ages we find two genres of history which interact: the history of a people (for example, Jordanes' *Historia Gothorum*), and ecclesiastical history. In Bede there was a conscious weaving together of the two. Likewise, the *Historia Brittonum* begins with the Six Ages of the World, a theme fitting for an ecclesiastical history, then we have an account of the origins of the British, followed by the record (in the tale of Germanus, Gwrtheyrn or Vortigern, and Hengest) of the fates of two peoples, the Britons and the English. We also hear something of the progress of Christianity. Charles-Edwards ends, 'If such history is unhistorical, so also are all the major histories of the early Middle Ages'.

---

[148] See T Charles-Edwards, in Bromwich, Jarman, Roberts, editors, *The Arthur of the Welsh*, 1991, pp.17-21.

[149] Dumville, 'Historical archaeology and Northumbrian History', 1987, cited by T Charles-Edwards in *The Arthur of the Welsh*, 1991, p.19.

### *Continental sources*

An entry in the Gallic Chronicle of 452 tells us that, 'The Britains at this time have been handed over across a wide area through various catastrophes and events to the rule of the Saxons'. The annal has been taken as referring either to 445/6 or to 441/2. The second Gallic Chronicle (511) has a like entry, dated 440: 'The Britains, lost by the Romans, fell under the control of the Saxons'. The two annals may have a common source. It is not at all clear how these annals might be reconciled with Gildas's record of an appeal to Aëtius in 446.[150]

## What story do these sources tell us?

### *Gildas's De Excidio Britanniae*

Gildas tells how, beset by her foes, Britain appealed to Rome for help. Although Rome twice sent punitive expeditions, the foes of the Britons still came back, and so a third appeal was sent, addressed 'To Agitius, thrice consul: the groans of the British'. They complained that 'The barbarians push us back to the sea, the sea pushes us back to the barbarians; between these two kinds of death, we are either drowned or slaughtered' (*DEB* 20.1). (It may be that here Gildas had in mind the plight of the Israelites at the Red Sea and their cry for help.)

We have noted that Gildas gives few names and dates, and one wonders where this material could have come from. Was there still a government archive in Britain where Gildas might have got a copy of the letter?[151] And who was 'Agitius'? The name seems closest in form to 'Aegidius', a Roman general in Gaul who died in 464. This is rather late to fit in with the British time scheme, and, anyway, Aegidius was never consul. Bede quietly amended the name to Aëtius, and most scholars since have reached the same conclusion. JM Wallace-Hadrill notes that the spelling 'Agitius' is not a serious problem if we allow for the influence of Vulgar Latin.[152] The Aëtius in question was Flavius Aëtius, *magister militum* in the west, and four times consul. The date of this letter was thus likely 446 or soon after (Aëtius was consul for the third time, 446-54).

The cry from the Britons fell on deaf ears. (Higham suggests that Gildas may have had in mind Judah's vain hopes of outside help, in the days of Jeremiah.[153]) What was to be done next? The Romano-British aristocracy would very likely have resisted demands on their own estate manpower (and anyway such recruits would have been very raw). The attacks on Britain were, apparently, seaborne, so why not

---

[150] See Ian Wood, 'The end of Roman Britain: continental evidence and parallels', in Lapidge and Dumville, *Gildas: New Approaches*, pp.18-20.

[151] Higham, The English Conquest, p.131.

[152] JM Wallace-Hadrill, 'Bede's Ecclesiastical History of the English People: A Historical Commentary, 1988, p.211, citing KH Jackson, Language and History, p.603.

[153] Higham, *The English Conquest*, p.145, note 75.

employ Saxons, who were used to the sea, to fight them off? (In truth, if a Roman general in Gaul *had* sent a force to Britain at this time, it would almost certainly have been made up mostly of barbarian troops. So why not go straight to the source?) This is what the council, with the *superbus tyrannus* or 'proud tyrant', decided to do. But Gildas says that in following this course the council members were like 'foolish princes of Zoan' and the proud tyrant was as a latter-day Pharaoh. The Saxons would prove to be wolves in the sheepfold (see *DEB* 23.1-2).

The Saxons came to Britain in three ships, and Gildas tells us that the Saxon word for ships was *cyule* or 'keels'. (As a curious aside we may note that this is almost certainly the earliest extant example of written Old English.) He also says that the Saxons came after gaining favourable omens and auguries (*DEB* 23.3). Higham thinks that Gildas's knowledge of the auguries, and his use of the Germanic term for ships, implies some familiarity with things Saxon. Yet Higham also thinks that the augury text 'depends more on the *Aeneid* than on the actual wording of whatever augury had actually been taken in distant Saxony'.[154] He agrees with Sims-Williams that the three ships suggest a folklore element, but he says the number need not be far out.[155]

The treaty arrangements made were modelled on recent Roman practice. That the Saxons were to be treated as Roman soldiers is implicit in the statement that they were to be 'invited under one roof' (a phrase reminiscent of the Roman practice of *hospitalitas* – billeting on provincials). The Saxons were to be given *annona* ('grain tax') and *epimenia* ('monthly doles of provisions'). In addition they were subject to a *foedus* ('treaty'). Higham comments, 'Concerning those matters which could have been reported to him by well-informed Britons – such as pertain to the decision-making process and the conditions of Saxon employment – Gildas's account is devoid of the miraculous, and of elements which are obviously derived from folklore. On the contrary, his information betrays considerable comprehension of late Roman practice, both in the generation which invited in the Saxons and that for which he himself wrote. Gildas's contextualisation of the employment of Saxons is, therefore, generally plausible, and lends a significant degree of historicity to the entirety of this episode'.[156] Later, Higham sums up, 'Gildas's account of the employment of Saxon mercenaries is internally consistent, logically presented and sufficiently empowered by the technical vocabulary of late Antiquity to be accepted as factual, if the rhetorical – even at times hysterical – content be set aside.'[157]

The Saxons were settled *in orientali parte insulae* 'on the east side of the island' (Gildas does not specify Kent). They drove back the Picts and Scots, but it was not long before they were in arms against the Britons. Gildas offered three explanations for the Saxon rebellion: 1) Saxon duplicity, 2) 'incidents' between Briton and Saxon,

---

[154] Higham, *The English Conquest*, pp.41, 135.
[155] See Higham, *The English Conquest*, p.60, note 32.
[156] Higham, *The English Conquest*, pp.41-2.
[157] Higham, The English Conquest, p.205.

3) Saxon complaints of insufficient supplies. Higham thinks that the first explanation 'is really no more than a literary device of his own fashioning' (to underline the folly of asking in the Saxons). But he sees the second and third explanations as realistic enough. The government might well have found it hard to lay their hands on the precious metal needed for making payments. It seems that most of such metal then in Britain was in the form of obsolete coinage, of religious accessories, and of tableware and similar vessels in wealthy households. It would not have been easy for a government to twist the arms of the wealthy, when they were so heavily dependent on their support.

Now, according to Gildas, the Saxons went on the rampage, burning, raping and plundering. Their onset was like 'that of the Assyrians of old on Judaea' (*DEB* 24.2). Sims-Williams suggests that Gildas saw a parallel between the Fall of Troy and the Ruin of Britain, and that much of his account of barbarian devastation (like many Continental accounts), was influenced by the Fall of Troy in *Aeneid*, Book II, the book of Vergil he quotes most often.[158] Whether this is so or not, Gildas tells next of the rise of a *vir modestus* (in contrast to the *superbus tyrannus*), as leader of the Britons, one Ambrosius Aurelianus. Gildas adds two things about his parents: that they 'had worn the purple' and that they had been slain in the wars (*DEB* 25.3). 'Wearing the purple' most often meant the holding of imperial power. But there was no lawful emperor of this name, and we do not know of any usurper who bore the name. (And Gildas would hardly have spoken well of such. He had a keen sense of rightfulness, and saw usurpers as 'sprigs' from a 'thicket of tyrants', *DEB* 13.1.) Thus it seems more likely that 'wearing the purple' here means someone from the highest ranks of the Romano-British nobility. In Roman terms this would have been a man of senatorial or magisterial rank. The kindred name also suggests a link of some kind with Ambrose bishop of Milan (373-97) and the orthodox Catholic Christianity that he stood for. (The father of Saint Ambrose was Aurelius Ambrosius.) Altogether Gildas seems to be saying that this was someone whose true 'Roman-ness' marked him out as a rightful leader in the eyes of God.

Under Ambrosius the Britons found new strength. Sometimes they had the upper hand, sometimes their foes, until the siege of Badon Hill, 'pretty well the last defeat of the villains [the Saxons], and certainly not the least' (*DEB* 26.1). It is not clear who besieged whom, or who led the British force (Ambrosius, or another). And the location of Badon is unknown. Many (perhaps most) scholars take it that it was a hill-fort (though Higham thinks it may have been a walled settlement). Old English 'Baddabyrig' or 'Baddanbury' means 'the fort of Badda', who was perhaps an Anglo-Saxon hero or lesser god. On the other hand the name may be Celtic.[159] Was a British 'Din Badon' assimilated to the name of an Anglo-Saxon hill-fort hero? In

---

158 P Sims-Williams, 'Gildas and the Anglo-Saxons', in *Cambridge Medieval Celtic Studies*, 6 (1983), p.12.

159 M Winterbottom, editor, *Gildas*, p.151.

fact, in the Latin 'Badonis', the 'd' is a 'th' sound, and this would become 'Baðon' in Old English. If 'Badonis' was the native British name for Bath, this may have evolved into the name we have today. Alcock thinks Mount Badon was probably a hill outside Bath, [160] while Higham thinks the siege may have been of Bath itself.[161] Copley says that Badon may have been near Severn mouth, and he adds that this is in fact stated in an interpolation into one manuscript of Gildas.[162] Grinsell suggests that the site was Badbury Hill camp, west of Faringdon, or Liddington.[163] Much depends on which direction one supposes the English came from.

Anglo-Saxon sources do not mention the battle, and it is sometimes suggested that this is because they were only interested in English victories. Yet the Anglo-Saxons weighed highly the 'worth of defeated valour', as in the poem 'The Battle of Maldon'. Barbara Yorke acknowledges, 'The battles which were most memorable to the early Anglo-Saxons might include great disasters as well as great victories'.[164])

What of the outcome of this battle? Peter Salway judges that this victory 'set back further Saxon aggression in Britain for fifty years or more'.[165] Leslie Alcock notes that the sequence of pottery styles in the upper Thames settlements seems to have been dislocated in the early sixth century (that is, after Badon[166]).

In Gildas's scheme of things a great British victory must have stemmed from a return to righteousness. But by his own day Britain was once again in the hands of tyrants, and he goes on to 'name and shame' five of them. (We should note that in the fifth and sixth centuries the word 'tyrannus' did not mean quite what we mean by it today. The power of a tyrant was not necessarily oppressive, but it was illegitimate. Thus the tyrant was what we would call a 'usurper'.[167]) The first of the five was Constantine, 'tyrant whelp of the filthy lioness of Dumnonia', that is, the south-west (*DEB* 28.1). He was guilty, first, of the murder of two royal youths, also of adultery and sodomy. Then there was Aurelius Caninus 'lion whelp' (*DEB* 30.1) who may have ruled the Silurian lands of Glamorgan, perhaps with the Gloucestershire area. He is accused of parricides, fornications, adulteries, civil wars and plundering. There was Vortipor, 'tyrant of the Demetae' (roughly modern Dyfed). He is vaguely accused of murders, adulteries and rape (*DEB* 31.1). Cuneglasus (*DEB* 32.1), who may have been king in Ceredigion or Powys, is condemned for divorce, and re-marriage to a sister-in-law. The fifth ruler was Maglocunus (Maelgwyn) of Gwynedd. Gildas's tone is more deferential here. Condemnation of wrong-doing is mingled with acknowledgement of

---

160 L Alcock, *Arthur's Britain*, pp.70, 359.

161 NJ Higham, *The English Conquest*, p.166.

162 GJ Copley The conquest of Wessex in the sixth century, p.171.

163 LV Grinsell, *The Archaeology of Wessex* (London: Methuen, 1958).

164 B Yorke, Kings and kingdoms of early Anglo-Saxon England, p.135.

165 P Salway, *Roman Britain*, p.498.

166 L Alcock, *Arthur's Britain*, p.115.

167 See CA Snyder, *An Age of Tyrants'*, p.xvii.

this ruler's greatness. He was 'first' (in evil), 'mightier' (in power, and in malice), 'more generous' (in giving gifts), *DEB* 33.1. He had a 'royal neck', and his predecessor (his uncle, who he had supplanted and killed) had been *rex*. Perhaps in Gildas's view Maglocunus could have been a saviour under God. Gildas was looking for a British leader who would be another 'David' against the Saxon 'Goliath'.[168] (There are allusions in Gildas to a leader more powerful than Maglocunus. Some speculate that this was Arthur.)

## *Bede's additions*

Only two episodes in Gildas gave Bede any chronological clues: the usurpation of Magnus Maximus (383-8), and the letter to Aëtius (dated by Bede to 446). Bede explains that the Romans could not come in answer to the British appeal of 446, because of the Hunnish threat. (Attila was then away in the Balkans, but he might soon return.) So it was that the Britons looked elsewhere for help. Bede sets the *adventus Saxonum* in the time of the eastern emperor Marcian (AD 450-57) and the western emperor Valentinian III (425-55), in other words between the years 450-55. (According to Harrison he writes this 'as if it were a matter of common knowledge, which with great probability it was'[169]). Rough datings elsewhere are very slightly different. In *HE* I.23 the sending of Augustine by Gregory the Great in 596 is said to have been 'about 150 years after the coming of the Angles to Britain'. In *HE* II.14, Edwin of Northumbria's baptism in 627 takes place 'about 180 years after the coming of the English to Britain'. In *HE* V.23, the year 731 is 'about 285 years after the coming of the English to Britain'. If Bede had a date within the period 450-55 in mind, he might have been expected to write 'about 280 years'. (In *Chronica Maiora* Bede places the British recovery under Ambrosius in the reign of Zeno (474-91), 'presumably by intelligent guesswork'.[170])

The unnamed *superbus tyrannus* of *De Excidio Britanniae* now has a name, 'Vurtigernus'. In Bede's *Chronica Maiora* the form is 'Vertigernus', In the *Anglo-Saxon Chronicle* it is 'Wyrtgeorn', in the *Historia Brittonum* 'Guorthigirnus', and in Welsh 'Gwrtheyrn'. Wallace-Hadrill thinks that for this name Bede must have drawn on a written tradition, and not eighth-century oral informants, either British or English. This is because the forms of the name given by Bede preserve the *i* in -*tigernus*. In Old English this *i* had been 'syncopated' (that is, shortened in the middle of the word) by AD 700. Bede also has the *t* which developed into *th* in Welsh about 600. This does not have to mean that Bede's sources were earlier than 600, but they must have had the form of the name from earlier texts.[171] It may be that Bede found this name in an annotated manuscript of *De Excidio*. But Hindley thinks

---

[168] NJ Higham, *The English Conquest*, p.148.
[169] K Harrison, *Framework*, p.125.
[170] P Sims-Williams, 'The settlement of England in Bede and the Chronicle', 1983, p.18.
[171] JM Wallace-Hadrill, 1988, pp.211-12.

that it may be Bede's loose translation of *superbus tyrannus*.[172] The title *superbus tyrannus* implies lordship over minor *tyranni*. This Vortigern seems to have ruled with a group of 'consiliarii', like a Roman provincial governor.[173]

Vortigern invited in barbarian mercenaries. In a well-known passage Bede says that the Germanic newcomers were from 'three very powerful Germanic tribes', the Saxons, Angles, and Jutes (*HE* I.15). A longer list of ethnic groups is found in V.9: Frisians, Rugians, Danes, Huns, Old Saxons and Boruhtware ('Boructuarii' or 'Bructeri'). This second passage has been taken to be an expansion, even a correction, of the earlier passage. It has been noted that it is closer to the evidence of the archaeology of the early Anglo-Saxon inhumation cemeteries than the three groups of I.15.[174] Eric John believes Bede's own view is that found in V.9. He thinks the information in I.15 came to Bede late, and it was then 'cobbled clumsily' into the text.[175] However, the context of V.9 is not the migrations. It is actually a list of the nations in Germany that Bishop Egbert hoped to evangelize. It is likely that 'the passage was intended to accentuate the ambition of the planned mission, rather than to reflect accurately the historic origins of the insular Anglo-Saxons'.[176] W Pohl, however, has noted that the purpose of such lists was often to suggest 'the multitude of barbarians that threatened the Roman state or the Christian faith'. So it might be said that the aim of such a list was 'not ethnographic but atmospheric'. These lists usually included names that were more emotionally charged, such as 'Huns' or 'Scythians', and this might be the function of the *Boructuarii* in Bede's list.[177] Place-name evidence may point to other folk-groups who took part in the migration. FM Stenton drew attention to names (with Swaffham being the best known) which suggest that the Swaefas, the pre-migration neighbours of the Angles (*Widsith* lines 43-4) were among the invading tribes.[178]

Today it is commonly held that Bede's account reflects the political geography of his own day, rather than of the fifth/sixth centuries. Yet it is also acknowledged that 'he does seem to have been broadly correct in identifying the main North Sea provinces from which the bulk of the Germanic settlers in Britain came and their main areas of settlement within Britain.[179] The terms 'Angle', 'Saxon' and 'Jute' existed before the Germanic settlement, and 'Bede's use of them in the context of

---

[172] G Hindley, A Brief History of the Anglo-Saxons, pp.13-14.

[173] L Alcock, *Arthur's Britain*, p.357.

[174] Ian Wood, 'Before and after the migration to Britain', in John Hines, editor, *The Anglo-Saxons from the migration period to the eighth century*, 1997, p.41.

[175] Eric John, *Reassessing Anglo-Saxon England*, pp.4-5.

[176] AH Merrills, History and Geography in Late Antiquity, p.299.

[177] W Pohl, 'Ethnic names and identities in the British Isles: A comparative perspective', in John Hines, editor, *The Anglo-Saxons from the migration period to the eighth century*, p.15.

[178] FM Stenton, in DM Stenton, editor, *Preparatory to Anglo-Saxon England*, p.268.

[179] B Yorke, Kings and Kingdoms, p.6.

the *adventus* is certainly not anachronistic'.[180] Angles and Jutes appear in Tacitus' *Germania* (dating from the end of the first century AD). The Saxons appear around the beginning of the third century, probably as a newly-federated group. Bede's information, then, can be regarded as authentic, if incomplete.

Several important details of Bede's outline of the *adventus Saxonum* have been generally endorsed by modern archaeology. John Hines writes, 'We can identify culture-groups in the areas Bede points out on the Continent and follow the transference of these to Britain in the immediately post-Roman period. Assuming that the association of these culture-groups with the ethnic groups Saxon, Angle and Jute is generally valid – and that is not a significantly problematic thing to do – we can note that these fit with Bede's plan of the settlement of England in some substantial ways but certainly not perfectly'.[181] Bede's statement that Continental Angeln was deserted in his time may mean that he knew of no surviving group called the Angles on the continent.[182]

The Germanic mercenaries brought in by Vortigern were to receive land and *stipendia* ('pay'). It may well be that failure to come up with the promised money led to the Saxon revolt. As to the leaders of the newcomers Bede notes that the first chieftains 'are said to have been Hengist and Horsa'. In Bede's tale these two leaders are little more than names, associated only by implication with Vortigern's disastrous rule.[183] Wallace-Hadrill suggests that in making Hengest and Horsa leaders of a mixed Anglo-Saxon force Bede perhaps meant to claim for Hengest the kind of overlordship he talks of in II.5.[184] (Yet in the passage cited Bede clearly says that Ælle of the South Saxons was the first to hold this position.) Horsa was slain in the fighting, and was buried in east Kent where a monument bearing his name 'still stands'. Bede later adds that Hengest's son, Oeric, bore the surname Oisc (*HE* II.5).

## *Additions from the Anglo-Saxon Chronicle*

The *Anglo-Saxon Chronicle* sets the landing of Hengest and Horsa at 'Ypwinesfleot' or 'Heopwinesfleot' (Ebbsfleet in Kent?), in the time of Marcian and Valentinian, emperors in east and west. They overthrew the Picts, but then called in more of their own folk from the old homeland, and turned on the Britons. Four battles were fought between 455 and 473. In the first Horsa was slain, and in the other battles Hengest's son Æsc shared the leadership with his father. In 488 Æsc took the kingdom (presumably on the death of Hengest, though this is not said).

---

[180] J Hines, 'The Becoming of the English', *ASSAH*, 7, p.50.
[181] J Hines, 'Becoming', *ASSAH*, 7, p.50.
[182] J Hines, 'Becoming', *ASSAH*, 7, p.58.
[183] AH Merrills, History and Geography in Late Antiquity, p.296.
[184] JM Wallace-Hadrill, 1988, p.214.

Bede does not name the landing place, and according to Sowerby 'this has been judged likely to be a post-Bedan embellishment of the myth, as it is of a kind which Bede might have been expected to have included in his work had he known it'.[185] To go further, perhaps some scribe had Hengest land at Ebbsfleet because Augustine had landed there. But it might simply be that Ebbsfleet was the landfall for folk coming into Kent from Gaul, or from Frisia further east. And when we look closely, we find that we cannot be wholly sure that Ebbsfleet was said to be Hengest's landing place, for it is not certain that 'Ypwinesfleot'/ 'Heopwinesfleot', is rightly understood to be that place. And neither can we be sure that it was Augustine's landing place, because we are nowhere told this. Bede says that he landed in Thanet, but he does not say where (*HE* I.25).

## Additions from the Historia Brittonum

At the end of the *Historia Brittonum* (*HB* 66) we are told that Vortigern 'held empire in Britain in the consulship of Theodosius and Valentinian, and in the fourth year of his reign the English came to Britain in the consulship of Felix and Taurus, in the 400th year from the incarnation of Our Lord Jesus Christ.' (Here, 'incarnation' seems to be a mistake for 'passion', and the date intended is 428.[186]). Rachel Bromwich says that Vortigern's family connections seem to have been mainly with east-central Wales, though there was also a tradition that the family came originally from Gloucester.[187] Vortigern may have been the leading figure in the 'nationalist' party, and he may also have favoured Pelagianism as a native version of Christianity.[188] In 437 there took place 'the dissension' of Vitalinus (perhaps Vortigern's kindred name) and Ambrosius, who may have been the leader of the Roman party. This took place at Guoloph (which might be Wallop in Hampshire[189]). The *Historia* tells us that in calling in the Saxons Vortigern was moved by fear of the Picts and the Irish, and of a Roman invasion, but also and 'not least, from dread of Ambrosius' (*HB* 31).

In its account of the arrival of Hengest and Horsa and their followers the *Historia* adds something not found in Gildas or Bede, namely, that the three ships of the newcomers were 'driven into exile' (and this is only too likely). The island of Thanet was given to the newcomers. Perhaps Vortigern set them in eastern Kent to guard against any move by Ambrosius to link up with Roman forces in Gaul.

Vortigern seems to have been weak and shifty, and he could not hold the loyalty of a man like Hengest, who the *Historia* saw as 'shrewd and skilful'. Hengest sized up

---

185 R Sowerby, 'Hengest and Horsa', 2007, p.17.

186 L Alcock, *Arthur's Britain*, pp.104-5.

187 Ifor Williams, editor, *Pedeir Keinc y Mabinogi*, cited in Bromwich, editor, *Trioedd Ynys Prydein*, p.389.

188 JNL Myres, The English Settlements, p.15.

189 J Morris, *The Age of Arthur*, volume 1, p.73.

the weakness of Vortigern's position and, with the latter's ready agreement, brought over another sixteen longships of warriors. Hengest's fair daughter also came over. (Geoffrey of Monmouth names the girl 'Rowena'. This seems to be the Anglo-Saxon name, 'Hrothwyn', a name not known from elsewhere, but one that preserves alliteration with Hengest.[190]) The story goes that Vortigern became drunk at a feast given by Hengest, and Satan entered into his heart, so that he looked on the maiden and wanted her. Speaking through Hengest's interpreter, Ceretic, he asked for her hand, offering as bride-wealth up to half his kingdom. After taking counsel of his elders Hengest asked for the kingdom of the Cantiaci (Kent). Vortigern agreed, without any reference to the king, Gwyrangon. The *Historia* adds that Vortigern also gave Gwyrangon secretly into the hand of the Saxons (*HB* 37). But the Britons fought back, led by Vortigern's son, Vortimer. There were four battles in Kent, and the Saxon barbarians fled to their ships 'like women'. But Vortimer soon after died, and the barbarians came back again.

Even now, with their greater wealth and numbers, the Britons ought to have been able to withstand the small Jutish war-band, and the other bands of Anglo-Saxon adventurers who chanced their arm elsewhere in Britain. But they were never able to fight as one. They had not come together when the Romans invaded four centuries earlier, nor did they do so after they left. (And it went on in this way. As late as about 590 an alliance of four British kings headed by the famous Urien of Rheged hemmed in the Bernician Angles on Lindisfarne Island. A great victory was within their grasp, but during a three-day blockade Urien was murdered by a man sent by a rival king, and the British alliance broke up, *HB* 63.)

Hengest now turned to untroth. He spoke of peace and a long-term treaty, and it was agreed that the leading men of the two sides should meet, with everyone leaving his weapons behind him. Vortigern came to the meeting with three hundred of his elders, all unarmed. But Hengest told his men to hide knives in their shoes. When Hengest gave the word the Saxons fell on the Britons and slaughtered them. Vortigern alone was saved alive, and he agreed to ransom his life by giving up Essex, Sussex and Middlesex (*HB* 44-46).

In the view of the *Historia* the Saxon settlement led by Hengest succeeded not because of their strength, but because it was the will of God (*HB* 45). The message may be: a Gwrthefyr (Vortimer) or an Arthur may win glory for a while, but someone like Patrick may bring a whole people to salvation.[191]

These written accounts could fit into a picture of a Britain cut off from central government help, a Britain of strong local loyalties and rivalries, a Britain see-sawing between a pro-Roman party on the one hand, and a 'nationalist' party on the

---

[190] HM Chadwick, The Origin of the English Nation, p.46n.

[191] See T Charles-Edwards, in Bromwich, Jarman, Roberts, editors, *The Arthur of the Welsh*, 1991, p.20.

other. The Roman party must have had the upper hand when the letter was written to Aëtius. But when the pro-Roman policy fell to the ground, it was the turn of the British party, led by Vortigern. It would seem that this Vortigern got the backing of the British leadership for seeking help elsewhere, and with the North Sea rim also in upheaval at this time, there were foot-loose war-leaders around, with their war-bands, looking for work. Hengest the Jute was such a man. He was likely an exile from his homeland living by his sword, and he was shrewd and thrustful.

# The written sources: how trustworthy are they?

How trustworthy are our witnesses? We have seen that Gildas saw his task as calling his people back to a right relationship with God. He used history as a source of lessons and examples, but he was certainly not a writer of formal history. He never set out to be such. We look here at one specific question raised about his work.

The worth of Bede's work has been questioned because he wrote from a particular perspective, that is, he saw the hand of Providence in history.

And the standing of the *Anglo-Saxon Chronicle* has been challenged on the grounds that it is Wessex dynastic propaganda, that its record of the war in Kent is confused, that its account of Wessex origins is in conflict with archaeology, that it includes fictional characters and events, and that its early chronology is untrustworthy.

## *An interpolation in Gildas's De Excidio Britanniae?*

We are told that before the Saxons sailed for Britain they were encouraged by favourable omens and auguries, to the effect that they would live for three hundred years in the land to which their prows were directed, and for half that time would lay it waste (*DEB* 23.3) Did Gildas write this, or was it (as Alex Woolf argues[192]) added after his time? Woolf suggests that, first, a later hand wrote the material in the margin, or between the lines, then, at some stage in the copying of the manuscript this material was brought into the text. Here is the passage, with Woolf's 'suspect material' in italics:

> Then a pack of cubs burst forth from the lair of the barbarian lioness, *coming in three keels as they call warships in their language. The winds were favourable; favourable too the omens and auguries, which prophesied, according to a sure portent among them, that they would live for three hundred years in the land towards which their prows were directed, and that for half the time, a hundred and fifty years, they would repeatedly lay it waste.* On the orders of the ill-fated tyrant, they first of all fixed their dreadful claws on the east side of the island , ostensibly to fight for our country, in fact to fight against it.

Woolf argues that the passage makes good sense without the italicised material. When the supposed addition is taken out the picture of the cubs of the 'barbarian lionness' is at once carried forward with the reference to their 'dreadful claws'. Woolf is also suspicious of the three ships, and of some of the wording. He draws attention to the writer's use of the word 'keels'. It is the only Old English word in

---

[192] A Woolf, 'An Interpolation in the Text of Gildas's *De Excidio Britanniae*', *Peritia*, Volume 16, 2002, pp.161-167.

the book, and Woolf thinks it must be an allusion to an Anglo-Saxon origin legend. He notes that the writer of this passage makes use of Latin terms (*exprimitur, longa navis, uaticina, praesagio, euectus*) which are found nowhere else in *De Excidio*.

But it is the prophecy itself (that the barbarians would live in Britain for three hundred years, and lay it waste for half that period) which lies at the heart of Woolf's case. (It has been suggested elsewhere that the episode of the omens is to be compared with the twelve vultures seen by Romulus, which were supposed to presage twelve centuries of Roman rule.[193]) Woolf finds it hard to believe that Gildas, with his 'fundamentalist' Christian ideology, would cite a prophecy which presumably came from a pagan soothsayer. A further point he makes is that nowhere else does Gildas show 'any sympathy or understanding of the Saxon perspective'.[194] He goes on, 'It is the nature of prophetic literature that it legitimises itself by providing proofs. It does this by projecting the prophet back into the past and having him or her prophesying both things that have demonstrably come to pass and things that are yet to transpire. The fact of the former creates confidence in the expectation of the latter. If we assume this to be the case in the present case then we ought, perhaps, to look to the 150-year interval for clarification.' Woolf then turns to the reference to the Britons' appeal to 'Aëtius, thrice consul' in *DEB* 20.1. The third consulate of Aëtius was from 446-454, and Woolf suggests that the 150 years might run from 447 to the coming of the Augustinian mission to the English, in 597 (the time when the English might be said to have stopped behaving badly!)

In answering Woolf we may note, first, that he himself acknowledges that the passage he questions is found in all the complete manuscripts of *De Excidio* which have come down from the Middle Ages.[195] This is a very real problem for his theory.

Woolf questions whether Gildas really would have used the Old English word 'keels', even though it was (for him) an outlandish word, in truth a word from 'the enemy'. Yet it is something that people do. In our own era words such as 'gestapo' and 'blitzkreig' have gained a place of sorts in English writing. And it is not at all clear how Woolf makes the leap from the one word 'keel' to an Anglo-Saxon origin legend. As to the use of Latin terms which are found nowhere else in *De Excidio*, is not Gildas here writing of things recorded nowhere else?

Why should it be hard to believe that Gildas would use a prophecy taken from a pagan English source? Far from showing an unlooked-for sympathy for the Anglo-Saxon perspective, the passage surely portrays them in a rather bad light, as insatiable ravagers. And Gildas would likely be aware of the prophecies of the pagan soothsayer, Balaam, recorded in Numbers 23-24 (prophecies about the future history

---

[193] P Sims-Williams, 'Gildas and the Anglo-Saxons', in *Cambridge Medieval Celtic Studies*, 6 (1983), pp.22-23.

[194] Woolf, 'An Interpolation in the Text of Gildas's *De Excidio Britanniae*', 2002, p.163.

[195] Woolf, 2002, p.166.

of Israel). He may also have known Ezekiel's account of how the king of Babylon came to a crossroads, and had to decide whether to lead his army against the Ammonite city of Rabbah, or against Jerusalem. (He cast lots, and the lot came up for Jerusalem, see Ezekiel 21:18-23.)

Woolf assumes too much (he uses the word himself). He assumes that there cannot be true prophecy. He takes it as read that the three keels are 'folkloric', and could hardly be applied to real fifth-century events by a writer living only two or three generations later. He guesses that the first 150 years are the period 447-597, then guesses further that the prophecy (which he holds is no prophecy) has something to do with the completion of the conversion of the English to Christianity. He suggests that 672, the date of the council of Hertford, might be used as the key date in this process. That then becomes for him the earliest possible date for the questioned passage, while its full date range Woolf places between 672 and 900. But none of this 'works' if the assumptions along the way are in fact ill-founded. The mathematical factors in a hypothesis should be borne in mind. Each stage of a hypothesis may have a high probability, while the whole may have almost none. Thus Step A may have a 90% probability, and Step B the same, but AB has only an 81% probability – and so on.[196]

Is it not more likely that the prophecy is quoted by Gildas, first, because it portrayed the Anglo-Saxons as inveterate murderers and plunderers, and then also because it gave the Britons hope of deliverance, albeit three hundred years hence? In the outcome, the prophecy proved to be wide of the mark. The Anglo-Saxons did *not* spend 150 years in endless raiding – they had homes to build, fields to sow, and harvests to gather in. And they certainly did not stop all warring in 597, to live in Christian love with their British neighbours. Nor were they driven out three hundred years after the *adventus*. The fact that this pagan prophecy turned out to be so empty, should perhaps encourage us to believe that it was a genuine episode of the mid-fifth century.

## Bede and providential history

Bede has been judged guilty of interpreting history in the light of his own outlook. He had a thorough knowledge of the Bible and its teaching penetrated his work as a historian.[197] To him what mattered was the meaning of past events for the present and the future.[198] He wrote the tale of how God oversaw the bringing of the gospel to the English, and of the growth and upbuilding of the church in this land. (Nine tenths

---

196 See CS Lewis, *Fern-seed and Elephants*, p.120.

197 Jan Davidse, 'The Sense of History in the Works of the Venerable Bede', *Studi Medievali* 3rd series, xxiii (1983), p.647.

198 R Sowerby, 'Hengest and Horsa' in *Nottingham Medieval Studies*, 51, 2007, p.18, and see J Davidse, 'The sense of history in the works of the Venerable Bede', *Studi Medievali*, 3rd ser., xxiii (1983), 647-95 at 656.

of his *Ecclesiastical History* is about the time after the coming of Augustine in AD 597. That was what he really wanted to write about.) He believed that God spoke to men in his own day, as in Old Testament times, through the pattern of events.[199] In other words he wrote providential history.

For some scholars, an outlook so thoroughly shaped by the Bible places limits on the writer as historian. These limits are said to be seen in the need to educate and edify, and in the interest shown in miracles.[200] Richard Sowerby has written, 'Thus for an *Ecclesiastical History*, the interpreted meaning of events is of primary importance, though this necessarily precludes the accurate recounting of historical truth.'[201] Charles W Jones has gone so far as to assert that the *Historia Ecclesiastica* 'is not the work of a historian but of a teacher pursuing ethical and moral goals'.[202]

There is, surely, a misapprehension here. *Every* historian comes to his or her work with a perspective. It is not possible to do otherwise. No one can write dispassionate history. Depending on this perspective the historian will select what, for him or her, is important, and what is peripheral, what is trustworthy and what is unreliable, what is plausible and what is implausible. He or she will weigh the data, reach conclusions, draw lessons.

There is another issue here which may be related: the danger that a 'club' of historians may be writing for themselves, writing for each other's approval, but unaware how the outside world regards them. CS Lewis (tutor at Oxford University, then Professor of Medieval and Renaissance Literature at Cambridge) took certain theologians of his day to task, for the unreality of their scholarship. He noted that someone too long immersed in minute study in his own field might lack standards of comparison for his results.[203] Lewis also touched on the questions of the miraculous (a feature of the New Testament, as of Bede's writing) and the prediction of the future, and he noted the way in which such were ruled out by these scholars. He commented that this is very sensible if we start by knowing that inspired prediction, and the miraculous, never occur. But 'this is a purely philosophical question. Scholars, as scholars, speak on it with no more authority than anyone else.' Hence the ruling 'If miraculous, unhistorical' is one they bring to their study of the texts, not one they have learned from them.[204] In speaking thus the critics were obviously influenced by, and perhaps insufficiently critical of, the spirit of the age.

---

[199] Ray 1976; McClure 1983, cited in Yorke, 'The Origins of Anglo-Saxon Kingdoms', *ASSAH*, 10, p.27.

[200] See Wilhelm Levison's essay on 'Bede as Historian' in *Bede, His Life, Times and Writings*, 1935, cited in Davidse, pp.648-9.

[201] Richard Sowerby, 'Hengest and Horsa', 2007, pp.18-19.

[202] CW Jones, Saints' Lives and Chronicles in Early England, 1947, cited in Davidse, p.649.

[203] CS Lewis, *Fern-seed and Elephants*, 1975, p.107.

[204] CS Lewis, p.113.

## *The Anglo-Saxon Chronicle challenged*

The worth of the *Anglo-Saxon Chronicle* has been challenged on the grounds that it is Wessex dynastic propaganda, that its record of the war in Kent is contradicted by the *Historia Brittonum*, that its West Saxon leaders have British names, that archaeological evidence goes against the *Chronicle* record of West Saxon roots, that some characters and events are fictional, that its early chronology is suspect.

### The Chronicle as dynastic propaganda

At the time when the 'first edition' of the *Anglo-Saxon Chronicle* was completed (that is, in the late ninth century), the royal house of Wessex had gained the leadership of all England outside the Danelaw. Did they have the *Chronicle* record adapted to uphold that position? Barbara Yorke sees in the early sections of the *Chronicle* not simple accounts lovingly preserved, 'but complex versions of a mythical West Saxon past which had been overhauled between the sixth and ninth centuries as part of a constantly evolving tradition'.[205] In this view, as the house of Wessex absorbed its smaller neighbours (Kent, Sussex, and the Jutish lands of Wight and Hampshire), so were their foundation myths brought into the *Chronicle*. So we have Hengist and Horsa in Kent (and/or Hengest and Oisc), Ælle and his three sons in Sussex, Port and his sons in southern Hampshire, and Stuf and Wihtgar in the Isle of Wight all added to the story of Cerdic and Cynric in Wessex (*Chronicle* 449-514[206]).

It is also said that the *Chronicle* shows bias, tending to pass over anything good done by the foes of Wessex, that is, the Britons and the Mercians. There may be some truth in this – though it would be hard to prove, and it would not of itself make anything in the *Chronicle*, as we have it, untrue, other than by omission.

Sarah Foot makes the specific suggestion that the *Chronicle* material was brought together in the context of the Danish wars, when the break-up of the northern monastic houses threatened the loss of the means for the preserving of corporate memory. She argues that king Alfred then shaped an account of a past in which all the English might share. He did this by means of historical texts translated (and in the case of the *Chronicle* constructed), setting forth a past made in the image of the present, offering a teleological explanation of what had gone before. 'The historical writings of the Alfredian court fit the English past into the divine plan; they demonstrate the part played by the English within God's larger, linear scheme for humanity's progression to salvation.'[207] Thus did the compilers of the

---

[205] B Yorke, 'Fact or Fiction? The written evidence for the fifth and sixth centuries AD', *ASSAH* 6, p.48.

[206] Goody 1968, Scharer 1996, 178-85, cited in Yorke, 'The Origins of Anglo-Saxon Kingdoms', *ASSAH*, 10, p.25.

[207] Sarah Foot, 'Remembering, Forgetting and Inventing: Attitudes to the Past in England at the End of the First Viking Age', *Transactions of the Royal Historical Society* Sixth Series, IX (Cambridge: Cambridge University Press, 1999), p.198.

*Chronicle* make a version of a World Chronicle in which West Saxon affairs could be related to events of Roman and biblical history.[208]

If, as has been suggested above, the putting together of the *Chronicle* began about 648, then we might argue that material from the other southern English kingdoms was brought in because of its historical interest. We may also note that there is Mercian and Northumbrian material in the *Chronicle*, and the Wessex rulers were not masters there.

## The warring in Kent

It is said that in the *Anglo-Saxon Chronicle* the tide of war in Kent is from east to west, and it ends with the Welsh fleeing like fire. But in the *Historia Brittonum* it is from west to east, and it ends with the Saxons taking to their ships. We can only weigh this matter if we can rightly identify the places named. This is very far from being a straightforward task.

The landing by Hengest and Horsa takes place at 'Ypwinesfleot'which, Brooks comments, seems to be significantly close to, but not the same as, 'Yppelesfleot', that is, Ebbsfleet on Thanet.[209] The first battle (in which Horsa was slain) was at 'Ægelesþrep', that is, Ægel's 'thorp' (farm). Most take this to be another name for Aylesford ('Ægel's ford') near Maidstone. This identification turns on the assumption that the familiar word 'ford' was substituted for the word 'threp' before the tenth century.[210] Next there is a battle at 'Crecganford' which 'is close to, but not an acceptable form of, *Cræganford*, Crayford'.[211] The identification 'depends on the bare possibility that all extant manuscripts of the *Chronicle* go back to the original in which the name was misrepresented'.[212]

The *Chronicle* says the Britons now forsook Kent and fled to London. But they must have been back, for there was then a battle at 'Wippedesfleot'. Twelve leaders among the Britons were slain there, together with an Anglo-Saxon thane named Wipped. The site of this battle cannot now be found out. A 'fleot' is a creek, but which creek was fought over we do not know. Morris thinks it likely that it was the Wantsum Channel between Thanet and the mainland, a long way east of Aylesford.[213] (The creek name looks very much as if it has been made up on the basis of the personal name 'Wipped'.)

A fourth battle, in 473, brought Hengest and Æsc/Oisc great spoil, and the Britons fled 'like fire'. But the *Chronicle* does not say where the battle was fought. Thus we have: a) two uncertain sites, b) another battle at a sea inlet, 'somewhere', and c) a fourth battle whose site is not named at all.

---

[208] See B Yorke, 'Fact or Fiction?' *ASSAH*, 6, p.46.
[209] N Brooks, Anglo-Saxon Myths: State and Church 400-1066, p.41.
[210] See FM Stenton, *Anglo-Saxon England*, pp.16-17.
[211] N Brooks, Anglo-Saxon Myths: State and Church 400-1066, p.41.
[212] FM Stenton, *Anglo-Saxon England*, p.17.
[213] J Morris, *The Age of Arthur,* Vol.1 (Chichester: Phillimore, 1977), p.81.

And nor is it clear that the *Historia Brittonum* draws a picture of warring from west to east. Chapter 43 has Hengest's folk penned up in Thanet, besieged there three times, before sending for more fighting men from Germany. Then Chapter 44 speaks of four keen battles. The first was fought on the river 'Derguentid', which is taken to be the Derventio or Darent. This river is not far from the Cray, so we might suppose that this is the same battle as the *Chronicle*'s 'Crecganford'. The next was fought at 'Episford' (Rithergabail, or Rhyd yr afael in Welsh) or Horseford. The *Historia* tells us that Horsa (as well as Catigernos son of Vortigern) fell here, so we may take this to be the *Chronicle*'s 'Ægelesþrep'. The third battle was 'by the Inscribed Stone on the shore of the Gallic Sea', which just might be the great marble arch at Richborough. (Fragments of the arch's dedicatory inscription have lasted until our own day.[214]) The barbarians were overthrown, and fled to their ships 'like women'. The *Historia* then passes over the fourth battle, and ends by telling of the death of Vortimer. So we have three battles which might be placed on the map (though with nothing like full certainty), but with the fourth battle we are wholly in the dark.

The different understandings of these puzzling place-names illustrate a point about what might be called changing fashions in interpretation in the last half-century or so. (Barbara Yorke does acknowledge that while the written sources have remained the same, historians have changed in their approach to them.[215]) For Frank Stenton (1967), 'These names must have been taken over by the original West Saxon annalist as an integral part of an ancient tradition, and it is greatly to his credit that he did not translate them into forms intelligible to himself or his readers.'[216] But Esmonde Cleary (1989) sees the recorded names as 'conscious and inaccurate archaisms by the compilers of the *Chronicle*'.[217] (One cannot but wonder how a historian of the twentieth century can thus enter the mind of a chronicler of the ninth century or earlier, and *know* that the man was making up half-realistic old names.)

Brooks follows Wallenberg[218] in seeing the first three names as mangled forms of the names of known places. 'Such consistent error suggests that the compilers of the Anglo-Saxon Chronicle were not following a Kentish written account of the origins of the dynasty, but rather drawing on oral tradition, which after the demise of the independent Kentish kingdom would have been kept alive through the ninth century only in a West Saxon context'. Brooks goes on, 'The West Saxon dynasty of Egbert (802-39) may have had ancestors in the Kentish royal family, and a West Saxon *scop* [court poet], ignorant of Kentish geography, could have garbled the place-name forms in a way that would not have been acceptable to a Kentish audience'.[219]

---

214 J Morris, *The Age of Arthur* Volume 1, p.81.
215 B Yorke, 'Fact or Fiction?' *ASSAH*, 6, p.45.
216 FM Stenton, *Anglo-Saxon England*, p.17.
217 AS Esmonde Cleary, *The Ending of Roman Britain*, p.171.
218 JK Wallenberg, *Kentish Place-Names*, Uppsala, 1931, pp.83-4, 286-8, 320-3.
219 N Brooks, Anglo-Saxon Myths: State and Church 400-1066, 2000, pp.41-2.

There is nothing unlikely in the tide of warfare flowing first one way, then another, and British and Saxon writers might choose to emphasise one thing or the other. Take a battle that is much closer to us in time: Waterloo. An English writer might stress the high deeds of the 'thin red line' of English infantry, and have the Prussians coming up only when the battle was more or less won. But a Prussian writer might picture the British infantry brought almost to their knees, saved in the nick of time by the Prussians. And a French writer might say that it was only through the failure of Marshal Grouchy to bring his corps into battle that victory was denied to Napoleon.

## The leadership of Cerdic and Cynric

The leadership of Cerdic and Cynric in founding the kingdom of Wessex has been questioned because the name 'Cerdic' (and perhaps 'Cynric', too) is British.[220] Cerdic is an Anglicised version of 'Caraticos', or 'Coroticus'.[221] There is no independent authority for Cerdic's pedigree (it seems to have been put together from that of the Bernician kings). Thus it looks as if he could not claim descent from any important Germanic family.

The *Chronicle* is a source not over-friendly to the Britons, and it would hardly give the forebears of the kings of Wessex British names if they were not the true ones. We find, in fact, a surprising number of British personal names in the Wessex royal house, suggesting either inter-marriage, or perhaps a gesture to subject Britons. We should perhaps recall that the fifth century was a time of great upheaval, of peoples moving and mingling. Is it so hard to believe that Cerdic's father took a wife from some high-born Romano-British kindred, and that their son should become an adventurer, the leader of a warband seeking a place for themselves? In the *Chronicle* entry for 495 Cerdic and Cynric are referred to as 'ealdormen', and Myres suggests this may imply that Cerdic once had some administrative role, under the Romano-British authority, for a stretch of the Saxon Shore.[222]

## Where was the cradle of the West Saxon kingdom?

The evidence of fifth century Anglo-Saxon cemeteries in the middle and upper Thames valley points to this region as the first home of the West Saxons, or 'Gewisse' (a name mentioned by Bede, thought to come from an Old English adjective meaning 'sure' or 'reliable'[223]). Cemeteries have been found along the Kennet and Thames valleys, underlining the importance of rivers for penetration.[224] The settlements (parallel to the line of the Icknield Way) connect by a chain of early

---

[220] AS Esmonde Cleary, *The Ending of Roman Britain*, p.170.

[221] B Yorke, Wessex in the Early Middle Ages, p.49.

[222] JNL Myres, The English Settlements, pp.147.

[223] B Yorke, Wessex in the Early Middle Ages, 1995, p.34.

[224] B Yorke, Wessex in the Early Middle Ages, 1995, p.32.

settlements in Berkshire with the region of the middle Ouse and Cam,[225] suggesting that the incomers made their way up from the Wash, rather than by way of the river Thames. Later, 'princely' burials, and other prestige goods, found through archaeological work, and dated to the late sixth century, fit with the middle Thames region being the powerbase of an emerging kingdom. After the conversion to Christianity the first West Saxon see was at Dorchester-on-Thames.[226]

Furthermore, Stenton notes the number of 'heroic' names that occur in place-names in the country round Oxford, and says that this cannot be wholly fortuitous. Hinksey contains the personal name Hengest. Witney and Wittenham contain the name Witta (a king of the Suevi, named in *Widsith*). Beckley and Begbroke come from the name Becca (ruler of the Baningas, in *Widsith*), and Handborough is from Hagena (ruler of the Holmryge, in *Widsith*). The name Elsa, which is prominent in the saga of Theodric of Verona, occurs in Elsfield. Seacourt, the name of a lost village west of Oxford, contains the name Seofeca, a sinister counsellor of king Eormenric in one of the most famous of ancient stories. Frithela is the name of a man associated with Seofeca in the story, and it occurs in the compound *Friþelabyrig* in the tenth century boundaries of Seacourt, and in the name of Frilford, a few miles away. Clearly the people who chose thus to name these places knew that these were folk famous in the old tales that were handed down.[227]

When we turn to the *Anglo-Saxon Chronicle*, however, we get another picture of how it was. Cerdic and Cynric land on the Solent and gradually extend their conquests northwards. It is worth noting that the Salisbury area seems to have been a centre of Saxon 'princely' power long before the *Chronicle's* battle there in 552. (It has been suggested that this battle was not the first step in a Saxon advance, but 'the defence of a generation-old settlement against a British counter-attack'.[228]) But we do not know if these settlers were West Saxons or Jutes. Bede says the lands on both sides of the Solent were 'Jutish' provinces, and they were not conquered by the West Saxons until the 680s. So it would seem that the *Chronicle* narrative may have been written to give historical justification for the late seventh century takeover.[229] One might perhaps have expected the Jutish leaders to be cut out of the record, but in fact Alfred claimed descent from them through his mother.[230] Thus, in the *Anglo-Saxon Chronicle* the creation of Wessex is seen as a Saxon/Jutish venture, and Alfred could be taken as the embodiment of his people.

---

[225] DM Stenton, editor, *Preparatory*, pp.117-8.
[226] Yorke, Kings and Kingdoms, p.132.
[227] DM Stenton, editor, *Preparatory*, p.104.
[228] L Alcock, *Arthur's Britain*, p.363.
[229] See B Yorke, 'Fact or Fiction?' *ASSAH*, 6, p.48.
[230] Asser, *Life of King Alfred*, chapter 2.

There might be a way to fit the two Wessex pictures together. For example, it may be that the settlements in the south were small and marginal in the early days of the migrations, but from them sprang the leaders (Cerdic and his kin) who later rose to the over-kingship of Wessex. However, in Sims-Williams' view 'any attempt to reconcile the *Chronicle* with archaeological evidence is premature until it has been shown that the quality of the traditions the *Chronicle* preserves justifies the exercise.'[231]

## Fictional characters

Many early English place-names feature personal names: 'Frithela's ford' (Frilford), 'Æbbe's down' (Abingdon), 'Beornmund's island' (Bermondsey), and so on. We have no stories about these people, and no reason to think that they were not real people. There are characters in the *Chronicle*, however, who seem to have been created to explain the origin of historic places. From the Kentish annals we have, for 465, 'Wipped' and the battle at 'Wippedesfleot'. The annal for 477 names Cymen, Wlencing, and Cissa as the sons of Ælle of Sussex. These names are thought to be linked with a lost 'Cymenes ora' (once south of Selsey Bill, but now under the sea[232]), Lancing, and Chichester. Then there is Port (said to have given his name to Portsmouth), Wihtgar (whose name seems to be based on that of the Isle of Wight), and a British king, Natanleod (said to have left his name to the district of Netley Marsh, where he was killed in battle). Others who are linked with these figures may or may not be fictions as well. Stuf is named as the brother of Wihtgar, and Bieda and Mægla are named as the sons of Port. Acknowledging that these could be real people might be held to be 'selective', but there are no overt reasons for rejecting them.

## Fictional events

It has also been suggested that historic places (what Sims-Williams calls 'conspicuous antiquities') have inspired fictional events in the wars, those events being unsupported by the discovery of war cemeteries. Examples quoted are the Saxon Shore fort at Pevensey, Old Sarum, Barbury, Dyrham, Gloucester, Cirencester and Bath. Sims-Williams also finds it 'odd' that towns captured from the Britons in 571 have English names. He accepts that the names of the three British leaders at Dyrham in 577 are recognisably Welsh. 'Coinmael' is Welsh 'Cynfael' (Conmail in Old Welsh). 'Condidan' is probably Welsh 'Cynddylan' (OW *Condilan). 'Farinmail' is presumably southern Welsh 'Ffernfael/Ffyrnfael' (OW Fernmail).[233] He goes on to find a 'curious coincidence' in there being a Welsh leader named Cynddylan, slain by the English in the Wroxeter area in the mid-

---

231 P Sims-Williams 'The Settlement of England in Bede and the Chronicle', 1983, p.29.

232 FM Stenton, *Anglo-Saxon England*, pp.17-18.

233 P Sims-Williams, 'The settlement of England in Bede and the *Chronicle*', 1983, p.33.

seventh century. Sims-Williams suggests the 577 entry in the *Chronicle* may be a composite, drawing on a Welsh triad of defeated kings.[234]

Are the 'conspicuous antiquities' named above really so conspicuous? Archaeologists now accept that Old Sarum was more than a posting inn (*mansio*) with a few other houses, set at a cross-roads. But it was not one of the great cities of Roman Britain. And Barbury? Surely there are many other hill-forts more striking than this site. This is all a far cry from the work of the twelfth century writer, Geoffrey of Monmouth, who set his tale of British history in truly 'conspicuous' places, such as London, York, Oxford and Winchester. And the lack of warrior graves and battle gear need not worry us. War-bands were mostly small, perhaps two hundred to a thousand warriors, and would surely leave little mark of their passing. The gear found on the field after a battle would have been taken away as plunder, not left there for the archaeologist.

And why should it be 'odd' to find captured towns now with English names? Some names with British roots survived ('Gloucester' and 'Cirencester' for example), but most names would have changed when ownership changed. Why use names that were many years out of date at the time the *Chronicle* was written down?

As for Condidan at Dyrham in 577, and Cynddylan of Powys killed about 655, where is the 'curious coincidence'? Death, and the same name, seem to be the only likenesses. The 577 entry just might be based on a Welsh triad of defeated kings, but then, where is the evidence?

## The chronology

Even if we were to grant the historical worth of the early annals of the *Chronicle* (and many would not), it is unlikely that a true time-scale was handed down orally from the pre-Christian era. Barbara Yorke sees the *Chronicle's* dates as among 'the most unreliable and unstable elements' in the narrative.[235] (Yet she does concede that 'the sources cannot be seen as completely fictional works; she suggests that 'factional' might be a better way to describe them'.[236]) Sims-Williams finds the chronology most suspicious and beyond putting right.[237] After discussing a number of matters he turns away 'in despair'. Brooks sees the work of a chronicler striving to fit a dynastic origin story into some sort of chronological order.[238] Leslie Alcock, looking for a space in the chronology where Gildas's forty-four years of peace after Badon might be fitted, noted that the chronology of the *Chronicle* for the period 449-550 is likely to be guesswork.[239] Like enough it is, though this does not mean that the folk named, and the events of which these annals tell, are necessarily fictitious.

---

234 P Sims-Williams, 1983, p.34.
235 B Yorke, 'Fact or Fiction?' *ASSAH*, 6, p.49.
236 B Yorke, 'Fact or Fiction?' *ASSAH*, 6, p.49.
237 P Sims-Williams 'The Settlement of England in Bede and the Chronicle', 1983, p.34.
238 N Brooks, Anglo-Saxon Myths: State and Church 400-1066, pp.41.
239 L Alcock, *Arthur's Britain*, p.43.

In considering the issue of chronology we may note, first, the way in which annals were drawn up. It became the practice to make notes, historical in nature, in the margins of an Easter Table. These Easter or Paschal annals could then be extracted to form a set of annals pure and simple. Such notes are usually short and to the point, and they can help to 'characterise' (in Plummer's words) years.[240] Material derived in this way has been detected among the early entries of both the *Chronicle* and Bede's *Historia Ecclesiastica*.[241] It is said that this makes the early dating seem artificial, governed by the conventions of writing annals which required that everything be entered under a specific AD year.[242] Some see a plan of eight or four year periods. GH Wheeler (1921) thought he could see resemblances in the general ideas and wording of the accounts of the beginnings of Kent, Sussex and Wessex (449-560). He suggested that the chronicler had sought to distribute his materials as evenly as possible.[243]

Sims-Williams sees artificial time-spans in the six-years between Hengest's landing in 449 and his succeeding to the kingdom in 455. He compares this with the tradition recorded in the regnal list that Cerdic and Cynric conquered Wessex about six years after their landing. He notes further that Æsc succeeds to the kingdom of Kent in 488, in the fortieth year after the Kentish landing, and Cerdic dies in the fortieth year after the landing on Southampton Water. He adds that this is 'a good biblical figure'.[244] It would seem that Sims-Williams is thinking of a monk-chronicler, well-versed in the Bible, who did not know the length of the founders' lives, and made use of the forty years often assigned to a biblical generation. As regards the first point, the invaders may have gained footholds within six years of their landings, but both in Kent and Wessex fighting went on for years. As to the fortieth years, this really is only a suggestion, with no means of proof. It is not evidence.

Another aspect of the chronological question concerns a seeming duplication of events (though the later series of annals is certainly not a word for word repeat of the earlier). The duplication (if that is what it is) was noted by FM Stenton, [245] and it has been discussed more recently by David N Dumville in a paper on the West Saxon Genealogical Regnal List.[246] Dumville lists the duplicate entries thus:

---

240 See K Harrison, *Framework*, pp.44, 47.

241 L Alcock, *Arthur's Britain*, p.9.

242 Yorke, 'Fact or Fiction?' *ASSAH*, 6, p.46.

243 GH Wheeler, 'The genealogy of the Early West Saxon Kings', *The English Historical Review*, April 1921, p.171.

244 P Sims-Williams, 1983, p.35.

245 FM Stenton, *Anglo-Saxon England*, pp.22-3.

246 DN Dumville, 'The West Saxon Genealogical Regnal List and the chronology of Wessex', *Peritia*, Volume 4, 1985, pp.21-66.

| | | |
|---|---|---|
| 494/5 | | Arrival of West Saxons |
| | 514 | |
| 500/1 | | Taking of land and kingdom |
| | 519 | |
| 508 | | Battle with Britons |
| | 527 | |
| 516 | | End of Cerdic's reign; Cynric king |
| | 534 | |

Thus when the dates of this parallel series of events are compared, the difference varies between eighteen and twenty years. This chimes in with a key fact of early time reckoning. The Greek astronomer Meton (about 430 BC) discerned a cycle of nineteen years, having noted that 235 lunar months were almost exactly equal to 19 solar years. Put another way, new moons recur on the same solar days or nights as 19 years before, with only a small margin of error. The Metonic cycle was adopted in the Easter calculations of the Church.[247] Might the same series of events have been entered twice, in two successive nineteen-year cycles?

From a careful comparison of the reign-lengths of later Wessex kings Dumville believes that the boundary of an undisputed AD chronology can probably be put at 641/2, the date of the end of the reign of Cynegils, the first Christian king of Wessex. [248] (This, by the way, suggests that from the first setting up of Christian institutions a good system for handing on chronological information, seemingly without intentional manipulation of reign-lengths, was set up.) Dumville then added up those reign-lengths which he thought were the most likely original readings, and suggested that the beginning of Cerdic's reign should be placed 104 years before 641/2, that is, in 537 or 538 (instead of the 494/5 of the *Chronicle*). This led Dumville to conclude that the record had been moved back by *two* 19-year periods. He suggests that Cerdic's arrival date should become 532, and the years of his reign run from 538-554. (Note that 532 is the first year of the first AD-dated Easter-cycle of Dionysius Exiguus.[249])

Why should the beginnings of West Saxon dynastic history in the *Chronicle* have been set 38 years earlier (if this has indeed been done) than the Genealogical List had it? Perhaps the most likely reason was a wish to narrow the gap between the first coming of the West Saxons and the beginnings of the Kentish kingdom (the earliest recorded Anglo-Saxon kingdom). Also it might have been felt that the sequence of *Bretwaldas* (overlords) of the southern English needed to be more evenly spaced

[247] K Harrison, *Framework*, p.2.
[248] DN Dumvile, 'The West Saxon Genealogical Regnal List', 1985, p.63.
[249] DN Dumville, 1985, p.51, note 79.

out. Dumville's suggested dates for Ceawlin, the second of the *Bretwaldas*, are 581-88,[250] The first *Bretwalda* was Ælle of Sussex, who, in the *Chronicle's* dating, was active in the 470s to 490s. This gap could be narrowed by lengthening Ceawlin's reign, making it begin in 560. And it would have given Ceawlin a reign-length of about thirty years, which may have seemed more fitting for so formidable a warrior-king. (In Dumville's view, seven years – short, glorious, and violent – would fit the *Chronicle*'s Ceawlin very well.[251])

It is interesting to note that bringing the obscure Creoda back into the picture does not seem to have been considered. There is enough evidence to show that Creoda was Cerdic's son and Cynric's father, but for some reason, now unknown, the compiler of the *Chronicle*-archetype disapproved of him, and his name was cut from the record (though not completely).[252] To have restored a whole reign-length would certainly have helped with the gap-filling, but it was not done.

Other studies have focused on the chronology of the life and kingship of Æthelberht of Kent. According to Bede (*HE* II.5) and the *Chronicle* annal for 616, Æthelberht died in that year, after a reign of fifty-six years. This would be a truly long reign for that time, and it has been suggested that a fifty-six year life-span has been confused with the reign length. Now this Æthelberht married a Frankish princess named Bertha, and because of this link we can turn for help to the *Historia Francorum* of Gregory of Tours (539-94). Bertha was the daughter of Charibert I, who lived from about 517 until 567. In 561 he became king in Neustria, Aquitaine and Novempopulana, with his capital at Paris. In Book IV, 26 (written between 575 and 581), Gregory notes, 'Moreover king Charibert married Ingoberga, by whom he had a daughter who afterwards married a husband in Kent and was taken there.' It is usually assumed that the daughter was Bertha. And some writers read these words as meaning that she was only born after Charibert had become king. They also take it that Æthelberht was not yet king at the time of his marriage, and that the marriage took place during the time that Book IV was being written, say about 578.[253] (Bede's statement that Æthelberht received Bertha *a parentibus* is not a problem, for the word means kindred, not parents.) Bertha's mother, Ingoberga, is thought to have lived from 520-89. In *HF* IX.26, Gregory reports Ingoberga's deathbed will (of 588-9), which states that she had a daughter who married the son of a king in Kent. Again, some take this to mean that even then Æthelberht had not begun his kingship. (But Ingoberga might simply be referring to Æthelberht's status at the time of the marriage.)

---

[250] DN Dumville, 1985, p.51.

[251] DN Dumville, 1985, pp.58, 59.

[252] See Dumville, 1985, pp.59-60.

[253] See, for example, N Brooks, in S Bassett, editor, *The Origins of Anglo-Saxon Kingdoms*, 1989, pp.66-7, and D Kirby, *The Earliest English Kings*, 1991.

This matter of possible confusion in the chronology of Æthelberht's life and kingship is serious. If there was muddle in Canterbury, the oldest centre of Anglo-Saxon Christianity, it would weaken confidence in all early Kentish dates, and indeed early dates from the other Anglo-Saxon kingdoms too.[254]

Might Bede have misunderstood a statement that Æthelberht had lived for 56 years? Yet surely so careful a historian would have cross-checked the truth of a fifty-six-year reign. It is not impossible that his Kentish informants could have talked with folk about what they had heard from their grandparents, and maybe about what those grandparents heard from their elders in turn. So the oral tradition could take one back to about 600, though not much further than that.

One possibility might be that Æthelberht served as under-king to his father, perhaps in west Kent, for many years. The fifty-six years could then be the whole of his years in government, first as under-king and then as sole king. If he was born about 545, he would have been about thirty-three at the time of his marriage, perhaps being then a widower. And perhaps Bertha was herself a widow, for other sources suggest that Charibert and Ingoberga were married about 540, and that Bertha was born about 541.

To sum up, we might guess that Æthelberht lived from 545-616, his father, Irminric, from about 520-590, and Octa from 480-550, with Oeric/Oisc living from about 440-512. If this series of seventy-year life-spans is deemed not believable, we would then have to acknowledge that we seem to have lost a generation.

---

[254] B Yorke, 'The Origins of Anglo-Saxon Kingdoms', *ASSAH*, 10, pp.25-6.

# We set out with the question, How trustworthy are our witnesses? What are we to conclude?

Gildas was a rhetorician rather than a historian. From the recent history of the Britons he took examples which he could use to forward his goal of calling his people back to righteousness. He never set out to write history for its own sake. We may bemoan the things he might have told us, but did not. We should not take him to task, however, for he did not have us in mind when he wrote. His work should be used with care, bearing in mind the restricted purpose of *De Excidio Britanniae*, but there is no need to write off the whole. References to events within the knowledge of Gildas's audience deserve to be taken seriously.

Bede's *Historia Ecclesiastica* certainly presents providential history, and much of what he wrote draws on oral witness. But these facts do not mean that his work is of no lasting academic worth. If his thrust was to convince and persuade it had to be based on careful work. Bede himself declared that he had laboured honestly. He deserves to be accepted as a witness who set out to be truthful, though he was not infallible.

The *Anglo-Saxon Chronicle* as we have it is a late ninth century work. Even if the early material was first put together in the mid-seventh century, that is still 150-200 years or so after the age of Hengest and Cerdic. And we may acknowledge that the early chronology of the *Chronicle* has to be guesswork, and that some names have been made up. Nevertheless, the *Chronicle* reads as a plain, matter-of-fact, record, and it is not lightly to be put aside.

We have seen that the writer who put together the *Historia Brittonum* freely acknowledged that he had gathered up everything he could find and 'made a heap' of it. So in answer to the question, 'Is it trustworthy?' the overall answer must be 'No'. But this does not mean that it should be thrown out altogether. Mingled with the tall stories (such as that of the burial mound which is never measured the same twice running, *HB* 73) there is other matter which might be true. This can help us if it is 'handled with care'.

## *'Hengest': history or legend?*

The early settlers were a mixed Germanic group, and it has been suggested that they would have needed a story of common roots to hold them together. Some scholars have claimed that there are features of the tale of Hengest and Horsa that are more the stuff of legend than of history. Among these features are: the three cries for help, the small number of ships, the leadership of two brothers with unusual names (which alliterate), Horsa's monument, the treacherous massacre of the British elders, the puzzle of the Kentish dynastic name (Oiscingas).

## *The three cries for help*

Gildas's account of the three appeals of the Britons for Roman help (*DEB* 15, 17, 20) has provoked comment. To Sims-Williams this is a 'suspiciously folktale-like threefold repetition'.[255] RG Collingwood held that, in literary form, the story is a 'triad' in the Welsh tradition. It might be called the 'Three Groans of Britain'.[256] (Rachel Bromwich acknowledges 'a tendency towards triple groupings'[257] in the work of Gildas.) Sims-Williams comments, 'Celtic triads are rarely marked by the sequential and climactic features of the folktale threefold repetitions'. [258]

There is really nothing here either to strengthen or weaken the picture as given by Gildas. Perhaps there were only two appeals (or four, or five), and perhaps Gildas made it three because that seemed a fitting number. But perhaps he says three because there were three. If you have asked twice, it may seem worthwhile to try one more time. But 'no' three times can seem like the end of the matter.

## *Three ships*

Bede, following Gildas, writes of 'three longships' (see *HE* I.15, *DEB* 23.3). One writer remarks facetiously that 'The three boats seem about as historical as the Three Bears'.[259] It has even been suggested that when Bede wrote of the invaders coming in three groups – Saxons, Angles, and Jutes (*HE* I.15) – he was perhaps influenced by the three keels referred to by Gildas![260] More seriously, it is held that the coming of the first representatives of a nation in a small number of ships is a standard legendary theme. Thus the *Anglo-Saxon Chronicle* records that Ælle and his sons came in three ships (477), and likewise Stuf and Wihtgar in 514. Jordanes (in *De origine actibusque Getarum*, 'The origin and deeds of the Getae/Goths', AD 551) tells us that in the 1st century AD 'the Goths went forth from the bosom of the island of Scandza with Berig, their king, sailing in only three ships toward the hither shore of Ocean, namely to Gothiscandza.'[261]

Yet, was the number three truly so very common? Cerdic and Cynric came with five ships (495), Port and his two sons (501) had only two ships. The Picts (Bede tells us) sailed from Scythia out into the ocean with 'a few ships'. We might argue that 'three' could be rough short-hand for a small force. Even if it is not a tally that an accountant would accept, it does not mean that the seafaring never happened. Anyway the figure of three ships may not be far off the mark. Each ship might have

---

[255] P Sims-Williams, 'The settlement of England in Bede and the Chronicle', 1983, p.7.

[256] RG Collingwood, *Roman Britain*, pp.293-4.

[257] R Bromwich, editor, *Trioedd Ynys Prydein*, 2006, p.liii.

[258] P Sims-Williams, 'The settlement of England in Bede and the *Chronicle'*, 1983, p.7n.

[259] Eric John, Reassessing Anglo-Saxon England, p.5.

[260] AH Merrills, History and Geography in Late Antiquity, p.297.

[261] See P Sims-Williams, 'Gildas and the Anglo-Saxons' 1983, pp.22-23.

carried as many as fifty warriors, a total of one hundred and fifty men. In an age when local wars were probably waged with armies of no more than a thousand men each, a hard core of 150 experienced warriors might make all the difference in battle. It has been noted that the 'invasion' of Britain was based mainly on the coming of small contingents or family groups.[262] (Note how, in 786, Cyneheard came near to snatching the kingship of Wessex with a warband of only eighty-four followers. See the *Chronicle* entry for that year, and the full story inserted, out of place, under 755.)

## *The leadership of two brothers*

The theme (if that is what it is) of the leadership of two brothers, Hengest and Horsa, has been linked with other tales of brothers: the Castor and Pollux of classical legend (the 'Dioscuri' or 'sons of Zeus'), and Romulus and Remus the founders of the Roman folkdom. The tales of the Lombards begin in the island of Scadanan (Scandinavia), where, by the help of the gods, the brothers Ybor and Agio defeat the aggression of the Vandal brothers, Ambri and Assi. [263] Then in the legends of the Vandals there are the brothers Raus and Raptus, second century AD leaders of the Hasdingi, one of the two tribal groups of the Vandals (the other being the Silingi). Merrills notes other brotherly pairs in Anglo-Saxon genealogical tradition.[264] In sum, Turville-Petre says that it 'seems likely' the Germanic historians drew on the same matter that the Romans used.[265]

We may note that in the lawless world of fifth/ sixth century northern Europe, it was the custom for the leader of a warband to have his own close kin with him. Even so, is the the leadership of two brothers so very widespread? The biblical Israelites traced their line back to the *twelve* sons of Jacob. The legendary forebear of the Britons was one man, Brutus. He had no brother at his right-hand, but a fellow 'Trojan', Corineus.

## *Animal names*

'Hengest' means 'stallion' or 'gelding', and 'Horsa' means 'horse'. The names are unusual and, for some, improbable. (Yet animal names were not unknown in early Germanic times. We read, for example, of 'Eofor' (boar) and 'Wulf' in *Beowulf* lines 2964-5.) Some have taken 'Hengest' and 'Horsa' for nicknames or, in the case

---

[262] See G Ausenda, in J Hines, editor, The Anglo-Saxons from the migration period to the eighth century, 1997, p.419.

[263] G Hindley, 2006, p.14. The source for the Lombard story is the anonymous seventh century work *Origo Gentis Langobardorum* ('Origin of the Lombard Nation'). Paul the Deacon also wrote a *History of the Lombards*.

[264] AH Merrills, History and Geography in Late Antiquity, pp.294-5.

[265] JE Turville-Petre, 'Hengest and Horsa' in *Saga Book of the Viking Society*, 14 (1953-7), p.282.

of Hengest, a kind of title and a mark of fame. Another suggestion is that one out of Hengest and Horsa was a historical figure, and the other added to make up a standard pair.[266] Sims-Williams comments that, on his own, Hengest is more acceptable – we might see him as a figure from the world of *Beowulf* and the *Finnsburh Fragment*.[267] (We may note that Sims-Williams does not believe in Hengest's historicity, but he does acknowledge that there is no way in which it can be proved or disproved.[268] We may compare Gwyn Jones's comment that the one thing harder to prove than the existence of Hrothulf in sixth century Denmark, or Finn in fifth-century Frisia, is their non-existence.[269]) Another theory is that Horsa was added to the tale through misreading a gloss in a manuscript, written to define the name Hengest as meaning 'horse'. Then there is the suggestion that what we have here is 'thinly disguised equine deities', comparable with continental Germanic horse-cults.[270] For Sowerby the horse-cult explanation is compelling. He does, however, acknowledge that the evidence for it is thin and sometimes unconvincing. It is based on continental examples, on Kentish horse-brooches, and on the Church prohibition of the maiming, or eating, of horses in the England of 786.

The names 'Hengest' and 'Horsa' may be unusual, but are they so improbable? Why would a maker of false history undermine his own work by using names that no one would believe in? Harald Kleinschmidt says, 'claims for Hengest's fictitiousness should not be based on his name, for stallion names are well attested on the Continent'.[271]

Allen Mawer made a study of animal and personal names in place-names.[272] He noted that in some Old English place-names the first element might be the name of an animal, or a personal name derived from such. He found good evidence from place-names that the following could be used as personal names: *bucc* ('buck'), *bulla* ('bull'), *cocc* ('cock'), *crawe* ('crow', a woman's name in a charter classified as BCS 1288[273]), *hana* ('cock'), *heafoc* ('hawk'), *hroc* ('rook'), *mūl* (mule), *seolh* ('seal'), *wifel* ('beetle', 'weevil'). He noted that *Wulf* and *Wulfa* ('wolf') may be shortened names for men whose full name was one or other of the many compound names in *Wulf*.

266 R Sowerby, 'Hengest and Horsa' in *Nottingham Medieval Studies*, 51, 2007, p. 11.

267 P Sims-Williams, 'The settlement of England in Bede and the Chronicle', 1983, p.23.

268 P Sims-Williams, 'The settlement of England in Bede and the Chronicle', 1983, p.4.

269 Gwyn Jones, *Kings, Beasts and Heroes*, 1973, p.33.

270 R Sowerby, 'Hengest and Horsa', 2007, p.10, citing JRR Tolkien, *Finn and Hengest*, p.174; also B Yorke, 'Fact or Fiction?' *ASSAH*, 6, p.47.

271 H Kleinschmidt, 'Bede and the Jutes: A critique of historiography', *NOWELE*, p.38, note 25.

272 A Mawer, 'Animal and Personal Names in OE Place-names', *The Modern Language Review* Volume XIV, Number 3, July 1919, pp.233-44.

273 Birch classified Anglo-Saxon charters in his *Cartularium Saxonicum*, 1885-93. 'BCS' refers to this classification.

*Hengest* occurs in place-names such as Hinksey, Berkshire (BCS 1002), and Henstridge, Somerset (in a late copy of BCS 923). Mawer concludes that, 'There is no evidence that this name was in general use in the O.E. period except possibly as naming someone after Hengest the Kentish king (whether mythical or not), or after Hengest the Danish leader in *Beowulf.* That these heroes were so named shows that at one time the animal name must have been considered a suitable man's name'. *Hors* occurs in Horsington, Somerset, and Horsington, Lincolnshire. 'The evidence leads to much the same conclusion as for *hengest*.'[274]

Mawer concluded that it 'seems clear that these names, for the most part at least, form a very old stratum in English personal nomenclature and were not in living use at the end of the Old English period. They most of them probably go back definitely to heathen times and there is no evidence that they were given as nicknames, i.e. as additional names, supplemental to the names given at birth. They are real personal names, traditional with the race, given at birth with little or no thought of any application of the name to the appearance or disposition of the child'.[275]

As for the sound-likeness, this was part of the tradition of early English kindred groups. Among the early Wessex kings we have (after Cerdic and Cynric) Ceawlin, Cutha, Ceol, Ceolwulf, Cynegils, Cwichhelm, Cenwealh, Cuthred, Caedwalla. There are a number of Os- names among the early Northumbrian kingly houses – Osric, Oswine, and Osfrith of the Deiran house, and the brothers Oswald and Oswiu of Bernicia. In the Kentish genealogy given in *Historia Brittonum* 58 (Octha – Ossa – Eormenric – Æthelbert – Eadbald – Erconbert – Egbert) there is vowel alliteration. FM Stenton notes that, in name-giving, gaining alliteration seems to have been more important than meaning. Hence there are contradictory names such as *Friþuwulf* ('peace-wolf'), and *Wīgfriþ* ('war-peace').[276] Alliteration is sometimes treated as a test of authenticity.

## Horsa's monument

Sims-Williams suggests that the story of Horsa's death may be based on the monument in east Kent, while Hines finds in the death 'the scent of an heroic legend'.[277] The suggestion has been made that Horsa owes his 'existence' to a damaged Roman monument on which HORS appeared as part of the word COHORS.[278] The suggestion is certainly ingenious, yet it would make our forebears who were thus misled seem very foolish indeed.

---

[274] A Mawer, p.240.

[275] A Mawer, p.244.

[276] FM Stenton, 'Personal names in place-names', in *Preparatory*, pp.86-7.

[277] J Hines, 'The Becoming of the English', *ASSAH*, 7, p.50.

[278] See JNL Myres, *The English Settlements*, p.358n.

It is true that legends have been made to explain other wonders. Thus, Geoffrey of Monmouth tells how the seer Merlin, by his wonder-working, brought the stone circle of Stonehenge from its place in Ireland.[279] The Neolithic and Bronze Age monuments known as the Rollright Stones (on the Oxfordshire/ Warwickshire border) are said to be a king and his men turned into stone by a witch. The city of Bath was said to have been built by a legendary prince who was healed of his leprosy there, as he smeared his body with the muddy ooze of the warm springs. But is Horsa's monument such a tale? A monument to a fallen war-leader (a great barrow on a hill-top, perhaps), is not hard to believe in. Why should so heedful a writer as Bede say the monument still stands (*HE* I.15) if someone of his day could go and look, and prove him wrong?

## *The massacre of the British elders*

To Sowerby the material which the *Historia Brittonum* adds to our story is reminiscent of tales in the Icelandic sagas, peopled with 'vibrant characters and circumstantial details, presented to fulfil other goals than the purely historical'.[280] The account of the massacre of the 300 British elders in *HB* 46 might be taken as one example. It is pointed out that a like story is found in the origin tale of the continental Saxons, as recorded in part by Widukind of Corvey in the 10th century, and more fully in the *Annales Stadenses*. Other treacherous episodes have been noted, for example in Xenophon (*Anabasis*), and in the saga of Harald Hardrada of Norway (13th century). For Sowerby 'the proposition that the massacre episode is a later addition to an otherwise Jutish myth of the first ancestors of the present-day *Oiscingas* is plausible ... The episode could have originated in a Saxon kingdom and become accommodated into the Kentish version of the *adventus* at this time of Æthelberht's overlordship [over neighbouring Saxon kingdoms]'.[281] And in the view of Nicholas Brooks, 'This is clearly a Germanic folktale or formulaic myth which, suitably adapted, is likely to have been part of the stock repertoire of many an Anglo-Saxon court *scop* or praise singer'.[282]

Yet it is hard to believe that the Anglo-Saxons would adopt this story. Why would any folk choose to place on record, for all time, such a tale of treachery and breach of hospitality on the part of their forefathers? Sowerby acknowledges that it is odd, but suggests that 'the distinction between cunning and treachery may be largely one of perspective'.[283] In other words, some folk might see it as a tale of admirable cunning, paying back the earlier wrongs of the enemy. Yet it seems more the sort of

---

[279] Geoffrey of Monmouth, *Historia Regum Britanniae*, VIII, 10-12.

[280] R Sowerby, 'Hengest and Horsa', in *Nottingham Medieval Studies*, 51, 2007, p.1, citing B Yorke, *ASSAH* 6.

[281] R Sowerby, 'Hengest and Horsa' in *Nottingham Medieval Studies*, 51, 2007, p.15.

[282] N Brooks, Anglo-Saxon Myths: State and Church 400-1066, pp.44-5.

[283] R Sowerby, 'Hengest and Horsa' in *Nottingham Medieval Studies*, 51, 2007, p.14.

tale that one believes about enemies. Note that this (tall) story is not found in Bede or the *Chronicle*. We might set it aside as one of those 'stones' in the *Historia Brittonum* 'heap' which is not really worth keeping.

## The Oiscingas

Bede gives us two short kindred 'trees' for Kent. In *HE* 1.15 he traces the line of Hengest and Horsa back through Wihtgisl, Witta, and Wecta to Woden. In *HE* II.5 he says that 'Æthelberht was the son of Eormenric (or Irminric), the son of Octa, the son of Oeric whose surname was Oisc, whence the kings of Kent were known as *oiscingas*. Oisc's father was Hengest'. A variant on these traditions is found in the *Historia Brittonum* 58, and in the genealogy of Æthelberht II of Kent in the so-called Anglian collection. (This is the fullest gathering of genealogies that has come down to us. The oldest manuscript we have was written in Mercia between 805 and 814, but it is thought that the material was put together in Northumbria between 765 and 774.[284]) In *HB* 58 Hengest's son is Octha or Ocga (presumably Octa), who is the father of Ossa or Oese, and he of Eormenric the father of Æthelberht.

The key figure is Oisc. He (and not Hengest) gave his name to the dynasty, so presumably a claimant to the kingship of Kent had to show descent from him. Was he truly the son (or grandson) of Hengest, or have two lines been artifically merged? Was Oisc perhaps a lesser pagan god?

The name 'Oisc' seems to be an early spelling of 'Oesc'. This might have been expected to become 'Ēsc', but the *Anglo-Saxon Chronicle* has 'Æsc'. (Sisam thinks this has come about through a misreading of the unfamiliar 'Oesc' in a written source and unthinking copying thereafter.[285]) 'Oisc' goes back to an earlier *Oski, *Anski. It is related to the Norse word for a god *áss* (compare Old Norse *ǽsir*) and to the Old English personal name element 'Os-'. (Chadwick says that the sound-change from 'ans-' to 'os-' must have taken place well before the end of the sixth century.[286]) Jordanes tells us of the Gothic demi-gods, *Ansis*, who stood at the head of the royal genealogies of the Goths.[287] The name is said to mean 'divine'. This name seems to have reached the Ravenna Cosmographer (writing about AD 700) as 'Ansehis', which is commonly emended to 'Anschis'. This leader is said to have been the 'princeps' of the Saxons who came into Britain from Old Saxony.[288] Ian Wood suggests that the name 'Ansehis' might be seen as a corruption of either 'Hengest' or 'Oisc'.[289] Kleinschmidt says that the correspondence between 'Oisc' and 'Anschis' indicates

[284] DN Dumville, 'Kingship, Genealogies and Regnal Lists', 1977, p.76.

[285] K Sisam, 'Anglo-Saxon Royal Genealogies' 1953, in EG Stanlty, editor, 1990, p.196.

[286] HM Chadwick, The Origin of the English Nation, p.47.

[287] N Brooks, *Anglo-Saxon Myths: State and Church 400-1066*, pp.39, R Sowerby, 'Hengest and Horsa' in *Nottingham Medieval Studies*, 51, 2007, p. 12, n.55.

[288] See ALF Rivet and C Smith, p.205.

[289] Ian Wood, 'Before and after the migration to Britain', in John Hines, editor, The Anglo-Saxons from the migration period to the eighth century: An ethnographic perspective, p.50.

that Oisc followed the sound change from West Germanic to Old English and must therefore have been introduced to the British Isles during the Migration Age.[290]

Note that the Cosmographer was a cleric (his name is lost to us), that the surviving manuscript copies of his work date from three or four generations after AD 700, and that there are many mistakes of spelling, word division, omission and mishearing (it seems that some of the text was dictated). On matters English the Cosmographer can hardly be seen as a better authority than Bede, who was in touch with Kentish and West Saxon sources.

How far back can we trust this kinlore? Barbara Yorke is reasonably confident that Irminric was the name of the father of Æthelberht. (Note that the element 'Eormen' or 'Irmin' is rare in Anglo-Saxon names, but relatively common among the Frankish royal house and aristocracy.[291]) She also thinks that Oeric/Oise was probably a historical figure. But by this stage (in her view) we are in 'the problematic world of divine ancestors'. Hengest she sees as belonging to the world of Germanic heroic poetry, and the link with him 'crudely made and lacking in credibility.[292]

So are we faced with two traditions of the founding of the kingdom of Kent? Has the Hengest-Oisc link been made in order to shape a father-son dynastic legend, as against a brother-brother invasion myth featuring Hengest and Horsa? Sowerby thinks that the battles of Oisc and Hengest seem to be independent of the stories of Hengest and Horsa, and he suggests that what we have is a composite of two origin-myths, most likely put together during the kingship of Æthelberht when perhaps Hengest was first added to the ancestry of the Oiscingas.[293] Perhaps, then, Hengest was one of those heroes of war and adventure that kingly houses liked to add to their lineage.

Nicholas Brooks's assessment is that, 'We need not assume these heroic tales and origin myths to be total fictions, but we certainly cannot establish what element of historical truth they may contain. We can therefore learn something of the stories which kings and courts liked to hear, but have no means of knowing how far an Anglo-Saxon *scop* or court-poet may have both possessed and exercised a freedom to invent (or to adapt) his stories to suit the gullibility (or the ambitions) of his audience'.[294]

In defence of the record as it stands it might be suggested that it was only in the time of Oisc that the kingdom was set on a sure footing. Also, there are other cases from the early English period where a kingly house took its name not from the known founder, but from his son or from another. The *Historia Brittonum* says that Wehha

---

[290] H Kleinschmidt, 'Bede and the Jutes: A critique of historiography', *NOWELE*, p.38, note 30.

[291] B Yorke, *Kings and Kingdoms*, p.27.

[292] B Yorke, 'Fact or Fiction?' *ASSAH* 6, p.47, 'Joint kingship in Kent', *Archaeologia Cantiana*, 1983, pp.3-4.

[293] R Sowerby, 'Hengest and Horsa' in *Nottingham Medieval Studies*, 51, 2007, p.12-13.

[294] N Brooks, Anglo-Saxon Myths: State and Church 400-1066, p.79.

was the first king of the East Angles (*HB* 59), but the later kingly house called themselves the Wuffingas, after Wehha's son Wuffa. The kings of Mercia were known as the Iclingas, taking their name from Icel, who probably lived about the 460s. Yet there were war-leaders in Mercian tale much better-known than Icel, both before his time (Offa of Angeln) and after (Penda).

## A case study

Having seen the story of Hengest and Horsa compared with the tale of Lombard origins. let us have a look at that record, as found in the *Origo Gentium Langobardum* ('The Origin of the Lombard Nation'), written about 650. Here is the opening chapter:

'There is an island that is called Scadanan, which is interpreted "destruction," in the regions of the north, where many people dwell. Among these there was a small people that was called the Winniles. And with them was a woman, Gambara by name, and she had two sons. Ybor was the name of one and Agio the name of the other. They, with their mother, Gambara by name, held the sovereignty over the Winniles. Then the leaders of the Wandals, that is, Ambri and Assi, moved with their army, and said to the Winniles: 'Either pay us tribute or prepare yourselves for battle and fight with us.' Then answered Ybor and Agio, with their mother Gambara: 'It is better for us to make ready the battle than to pay tributes to the Wandals.' Then Ambri and Assi, that is, the leaders of the Wandals, asked Godan [Woden] that he should give them the victory over the Winniles. Godan answered, saying: 'Whom I shall first see when at sunrise, to them will I give the victory.' At that time Gambara with her two sons, that is, Ybor and Agio, who were chiefs over the Winniles, besought Frea, the wife of Godan, to be propitious to the Winniles. Then Frea gave counsel that at sunrise the Winniles should come, and that their women, with their hair let down around the face in the likeness of a beard, should also come with their husbands. Then when it became bright, while the sun was rising, Frea, the wife of Godan, turned around the bed where her husband was lying and put his face towards the east and awakened him. And he, looking at them, saw the Winniles and their women having their hair let down around the face. And he says, 'Who are these Long-beards?' And Frea said to Godan, 'As you have given them a name, give them also the victory.' And he gave them the victory, so that they should defend themselves according to his counsel and obtain the victory. From that time the Winniles were called Langobards.'

How very plain and matter-of-fact is the record of Hengest and Horsa, in Bede and the *Chronicle*, when seen side by side with this! (Kenneth Sisam has noted that, 'The Anglo-Saxons were often content to state bare facts where we expect them to be coloured or explained.'[295]) And one is reminded of the response of CS Lewis when he heard it said of John's Gospel that it was 'a spiritual romance, a poem not

[295] K Sisam, 'Anglo-Saxon Royal Genealogies' 1953, in EG Stanlty, editor, 1990, p.194.

a history'. He answered: 'I have been reading poems, romances, vision-literature, legends, myths all my life. I know what they are like. I know that not one of them is like this.'[296]

CS Lewis's friend, Professor JRR Tolkien, was another scholar in the field of English, and he was someone who surely knew far more about myths and legends than do most historians. In his essay 'On Fairy-stories'[297] he noted that a common single thread does not explain the origins of a whole story. (And may this not apply to two threads, such as ships and brothers?) He notes that in the fields of archaeology, or comparative philology, scholars may study an artefact or a word that has parallels in other lands. But what they have before them may not be a case of straightforward borrowing. So with a story: it may have come from a common ancestor, or it may have spread, at various times, from one or more centres. Or, again, each story may have come into being independently. Tolkien concluded that it was now 'beyond all skill but that of the elves' to unravel the intricate web of a story.[298]

As a last thought at the end of this discussion of history and legend, we may note that there are sometimes surprises outside the ivory tower. The *Navigatio*, a work of the late ninth or early tenth century, tells of a voyage across the North Atlantic by the Irish monk, Saint Brendan (486-575), and his companions. In one episode (see *Navigatio* 10) the monks spend a night on a small island, and next morning light a cooking fire. Then the island begins to heave like a wave, and it turns out that it is no island, but a great creature of the deep (presumably a whale). We may smile at this tall story, but we now know that it is not to be written off as utterly fanciful. In 1976-77, Tim Severin and friends sailed an Irish-type curragh of wood and leather from the west of Ireland to Newfoundland. They found that whales were drawn to their strange boat, and would swim close to it, seemingly out of curiosity.[299]

## *Footnote: 'a layman among the historians'?*

So much seems to depend on how a writer approaches our written sources, that is, whether he or she comes to these with respect, or with unshakeable confidence in the modern age as the era when we can read between the lines and expose the foolishness of our forebears. From the latter stance there seems to grow a determination that we shall not believe unless driven to do so. In the writings of some of these scholars we are told that some things seem 'likely' and others 'unlikely', some statements 'plausible' and others 'clearly fictitious'. Yet such words are opinions, not evidence. One's confidence in such writing is not helped by the use, at times, of rather melodramatic language, when we are told, for example,

---

[296] CS Lewis, Fern-seed and Elephants, p.108.

[297] Published in JRR Tolkien, Tree and Leaf, Smith of Wootton Major, The Homecoming of Beorhtnoth Beorhthelm's Son, pp.11-79.

[298] JRR Tolkien, *Tree and Leaf*, pp.26-7.

[299] T Severin, *The Brendan Voyage*, p.142.

that the problems in the way of believing Gildas are 'appalling', or that the early chronology leaves one 'in despair'.[300]

Back in 1973 Norman Anderson, Professor of Oriental Laws in the University of London, wrote a book with the title 'A Lawyer among the Theologians'. He took to task those theologians of his day who, as he saw it, were unrealistic in their demands for evidence in such matters as the authorship and dating of biblical writings. Evidence that would be accepted as reasonable in other academic fields was said to be not enough.

He set out some of the principles which guide lawyers as they weigh up statements. By their training they are minded to allow written evidence to speak for itself, to sift oral witness carefully, and to allow that circumstantial evidence can, at times, be very persuasive. When writing of oral witness Anderson quotes from Dorothy Sayers, who spoke of 'that storehouse of trained memory which, among people not made forgetful by too much pen and ink, replaces the filed records and the stenographer's notebook.[301] In the case of written evidence, the lawyer should seek for meaning within the document itself, and that document must be construed as a whole. When a lawyer believes that a witness is truthful and sincere he must accord his or her testimony the respect which it deserves. He should not reject the basic assumption that the witness is intrinsically unlikely to have contradicted himself. Words and intentions must prevail, not subjective conjectures. The need for 'proof beyond a reasonable doubt', must not be allowed to become a demand for proof beyond a shadow of doubt. And while no one can ever wholly shed his own stance, it should be noted that there is a great difference between the man who truly does his best to be objective, who tries to give full weight to any evidence which seems to go against his own point of view, and the man who holds certain preconceived ideas so strongly that he is ready to impose them on the available evidence.[302]

Turning to New Testament criticism Anderson notes the staggering assurance with which some critics make categorical statements on points which are, on any showing, open to question. Some will state opinions as though they were incontrovertible fact. Others will go from the assertion that not every detail in a work is necessarily historical to the conclusion that almost no detail is historical. There is also perhaps a lack of awareness that fashions and trends of thought (in one's own discipline, or in the world around us) have a strong influence, conscious or unconscious, upon us.[303]

---

[300] See DN Dumville, in *Gildas: New Approaches*, p.79, and P Sims-Williams 'The Settlement of England in Bede and the Chronicle' in *Anglo-Saxon England*, 12 (1983) p.21.

[301] Dorothy Sayers, quoted in JND Anderson, *A Lawyer among the Theologians*, p.62.

[302] See JND Anderson, *A Lawyer among the Theologians*, 1973, pp.15-26.

[303] JND Anderson, A Lawyer among the Theologians, p.14.

Coming as 'a layman among the historians' one cannot but be struck at times by examples of the 'staggering assurance' referred to by Anderson. Here are a few cases:

> 'I am convinced that the received accounts of our [Anglo-Saxon] migrations, our subsequent fortunes, and ultimate settlement, are devoid of historical truth in every detail.'[304]
>
> '(T)he interpreted meaning of events is of primary importance [for Bede], though this necessarily precludes the accurate recounting of historical truth'.[305]
>
> 'My conclusion is simple. Where Bede's sources are extant we should read and judge them for ourselves; where they are not extant, we should treat the traditions Bede reports with at least the reserve that he himself displays, probably with more.'[306]
>
> '(S)o many events [in the *Chronicle*] are clearly fictitious'.[307]

And there is other familiar ground, striking likenesses between critical biblical studies and the work of some modern historians of the early Middle Ages. Here are some common features:

1) In stage one of an argument a suggestion may be made. It is unprovable, but by stage two the assumption can become a 'fact'. So although the critical historian may condemn, in others, theories accompanied by 'perhaps', 'possibly', 'probably',[308] they may yet use such themselves.

2) Awkward material may be cut out on the grounds that it is an interpolation (it may, for example, be seen as a marginal gloss mistakenly brought into the text).

3) One passage may be seen as the duplicate of another, or two passages may be said to be fused into one.

4) Oral witness is unregarded. It is claimed that, 'The unreliability of oral tradition needs no emphasis.'[309]

5) Interpretative history is deemed incompatible with integrity as a historian. (But interpretation is inescapable.)

6) Rearrangements of the text are put forward, as when it is suggested that Bede *HE* V.9 may be earlier than *HE* I.15.

---

[304] JM Kemble, quoted in P Sims-Williams, 'The settlement of England in Bede and the *Chronicle*', 1983, p.1.
[305] R Sowerby, 'Hengest and Horsa', in *Nottingham Medieval Studies*, 2007, p.19.
[306] P Sims-Williams 'The Settlement of England in Bede and the Chronicle',1983, p.26.
[307] P Sims-Williams, 'The settlement of England', p.34.
[308] P Sims-Williams, 'The settlement of England', p.40.
[309] PH Sawyer, *From Roman Britain to Norman England* (London: Methuan, 1978), p.13.

7) There seems to be a resistance to the early dating of sources. Is it such a threat to scepticism?

8) Sims-Williams, following Kemble, would reject the plausible. But given that the implausible is bound to be rejected, what is left to believe? (JM Kemble wrote *The Saxons in England*, 1849. He was a significant Anglo-Saxon scholar. Yet it was said of him that, at times, his work lacked 'acuteness and precision', and that he could put forward strange views with vehemence, and in language that might be bombastic, even nonsensical.[310])

9) Tolkien comments on a scholarly 'anxiety to be original'.[311] It does seem at times that some feel a need to see something others have missed, or to demolish something others have upheld.

And another thing, too readily overlooked by some scholarship today: early medieval writers certainly knew fewer things than we do (we have the benefit of building on the scholarship of former generations). But they had no less brain power than folk today. Furthermore, do we have the right to say that their integrity was less than ours? If Bede, for example, was arguing a case, what would be the worth of false or carelessly handled information? Truth would be vital in such a situation. And surely truth must be the goal for every historian. Over-readiness to believe will undermine the standing of our work, but so will determined scepticism.

Two final points in this section: first, it is possible to take unbelief too far. In 1819, Richard Whately, a Fellow of Oriel College, Oxford, had a little dig at the freethinking philosopher, David Hume, who questioned everything not backed up by 'evidence'. Whately asked, can it be shown that Napoleon Bonaparte ever really lived? There had long been reports about him in the British press, but the only sources the writers could cite were other journalists or unknown correspondents. Certainly it was in the interest of newspaper owners to spread these reports abroad, for they encouraged sales. And there were disagreements about episodes in this Napoleon's career. Had he won the battle of Borodino, or had he lost? And while there might be folk who said they saw Napoleon on shipboard in Plymouth (on his way to exile in St Helena), in truth all they saw was someone who they were *told* was Napoleon. Whether he was or not was quite another matter. This little book was an exercise in satire, but Whately had a sound point. If we have made up our mind to doubt, then almost everything is, or should be, doubtful. [312]

And the other point: CS Lewis (who we have cited before), spoke and wrote tellingly of theologians of his own day, who did not share the language and culture of the early Christian centuries, yet who seemed to think they were the first ones to

---

[310] See Bruce Dickins, 'John Mitchell Kemble and Old English scholarship'in *British Academy Papers on Anglo-Saxon England*, 1990, pp.57-90.

[311] JRR Tolkien, *Tree and leaf*, p.58.

[312] D Bebbington, *Patterns in history*, 1979, pp.9-10.

read the New Testament documents aright, and to unearth their sources. Lewis was the more sceptical when he saw the way critics 'saw into' his own writings. He could not be wholly sure (because he did not keep records of the matter), but he had the impression the guesses made by the critics were always wrong. He adds that you would think mere chance would ensure they hit as often as they missed. But, no, they seemed to miss every time.[313] When we read the works of those early historians of the Anglo-Saxon age – even a muddler like the compiler of the *Historia Brittonum* – we should not be over-quick in assuming that we can 'see through' them. There may be times when we can unravel mistakes and emend miscopyings. Nonetheless those old writers had one advantage that can never be ours: they lived within the language and culture of the Old English period, and we do not.

---

[313] See the essay 'Fernseed and elephants' in the book of that title (Glasgow: Fontana/Collins, 1975), pp.114-5.

# Kinlore (genealogy)

Tacitus implies that kinlore was important among noble Germanic families. And later, in the Heroic Age (in the *Beowulf* poem, for example), we see men taking pride in their memory for relationships (though the purpose was, like enough, the practical one of identifying a man). Kinlore was needed for right succession, though it was not the only factor in the choosing of new leaders, and there is no evidence of long pedigrees in the poetry. Nor is there evidence that genealogies were recited on formal occasions, or used to fix the order of long-ago events.[314]

Kinlore was a much more serious matter in the Celtic world. Indeed knowledge of one's forebears became a legal necessity, essential in such matters as the inheritance of land, the settlement of disputes, the evidence (on oath) of witnesses, and the seeking and paying of compensation. By the Laws of Hywel Dda (died 949 or 950) all families had to know their relatives to the ninth remove. Giraldus Cambrensis, who travelled through Wales in 1188, confimed that even the lowliest could tell their family tree through at least six or seven generations.[315] And Dumville cites the occasion of the inauguration of Alexander III (king of Scotland, 1249-86) when a Gaelic-speaking Scot read the king's genealogy back through the ninth century Cinaed mac Alpine, back to the fifth century Fergus mac Erca, and on right back to 'Scota, daughter of Pharaoh'.[316] Alone in western Europe the Celtic countries seem to have had a class of professional learned men. In Ireland, for example, we hear of the *filidh* (usually translated 'poets') who were responsible for kinlore, king-lists, origin tales, and so forth. After the conversion some of the *filidh* became clerics, and it may be that Irish missionaries, besides bringing the gospel, and their orthography and art, also brought the business of pedigree-writing.

There were a number of reasons why genealogies became ever more important among the Anglo-Saxons. There was the need for someone claiming the throne to prove that he truly belonged to the kingly line (and the church wished to ensure that no one of illegitimate birth was included). There was the wish to hold on to cultural links. The Anglo-Saxons remained aware of their ties with continental kindred, and they were interested in the tales of the migrations. C Scull suggests that for an Anglo-Saxon kingly house continental forebears could strengthen the claim to legitimacy.[317] Then there was the powerful motive of social prestige. The names of gods and heroes could enhance the glory of the house. And a pedigree might also undergird political alliances and overlordship. In sum, kinlore could be an expression of learning, a legal title, and a political weapon.

---

314 K Sisam, 'Anglo-Saxon Royal Genealogies' 1953, in EG Stanley, editor, *British Academy Papers*, pp.180-81.

315 Hafina Clwyd, in J Rowlands, *Welsh Family History*, p.1.

316 DN Dumville, 1977, p.73.

317 C Scull, 'Social Archaeology and Anglo-Saxon Kingdom Origins', *ASSAH*, 10, p.22.

Dumville focuses on the political aspect. He says social anthropologists today hold that 'pre-literate peoples only preserve versions of their history which explain current social groupings and institutions, and that these versions may bear little relation to an historical sequence of events.'[318] Through genealogy the ruling dynasty could present the past (and, by implication, the future) in the light of its own history. It must follow from this that changes in the social and political situation would mean that the genealogy had to be changed. Against this some argue that kinlore was such an important factor in holding society together, that it would have been recited on public occasions, and corrected by the common memory. On the other hand, it might be held that in a heroic society, with its violence and its frequent changes of ruler, there would always be bards ready to re-write the kinlore on behalf of *de facto* rulers. The record might then bear little relation to biological and historical facts. Dumville cites Gilla in Chomded Hua Cormaic, a poet of early twelfth century Ireland, who noted two factors in the falsification of kinlore: 'invincible ignorance' (a category which could include the work of other scholars with whom one disagreed!), and bribery and corruption of the learned.[319]

Dumville considers the case of two figures in West Saxon kinlore, Freawine and Wig. Their presence in the kingly line helps the alliteration. Perhaps even more importantly they were known from heroic legend as subordinates of Offa of Angeln, who is portrayed as the forebear of the eighth-century Offa of Mercia. This might be a way of underlining Offa II's overlordship of Wessex.[320] Dumville goes on to suggest that the eighth-century Offa was named after Offa of Angeln, and that he then arranged to have his famous namesake placed in his pedigree. Dumville thinks that figures such as Icel (the forebear of Offa of Mercia), and Wuffa of East Anglia, made themselves kings not by virtue of ancient royal descent, but by their own force of hand.[321]

Kenneth Sisam has gone into the matter of 'old names of kings and shadows' in West Saxon royal genealogy.[322] He notes that RW Chambers brings out the perfect alliterative structure of the Cynric to Woden genealogy in the *Chronicle* (under the years 552, 597 and 855). Thus we have:

(Cynric Cerdicing), Cerdic Elesing,
Elesa Esling, Esla Giwising,
Giwis Wiging, Wig Freawining,
Freawine Friðogaring, Friðogar Bronding,
Brond Bældæging Bældæg Wodening.

[318] DN Dumville, 'Kingship, Genealogies and Regnal Lists', 1977, p.85.
[319] DN Dumville, 1977, p.83.
[320] DN Dumville, 1977, p.81.
[321] DN Dumville, 1977, pp.92-3.
[322] K Sisam, 'Anglo-Saxon Royal Genealogies' 1953, in EG Stanley, editor, *British Academy Papers on Anglo-Saxon England*, 1990, p.146.

Chambers thought that these lines were likely to be truly old, going back to a time when the names of forebears, both real and imaginary, were recorded by memory, and 'were doubtless chanted by retainers of the West-Saxon kings in heathen days'.[323] Sisam clearly sees the perfect alliteration as too good to be true. He notes that with continuous hereditary succession it is not too difficult to maintain alliteration. 'But', he asks, 'by what foresight could it be arranged, in the troubled days of migration and conquest, that the names of successive kings would make such perfect verse?'[324] He believes that from Ecgberht back to Ingild, Ine's brother, the Wessex genealogy may reasonably be trusted, and that from Ingild to Cerdic the genealogy is 'defensible'. He says that there is conflicting evidence of Cerdic's immediate successors, while, 'Beyond Cerdic all is fiction or error'.[325] Sisam suggests that Cerdic's pedigree was copied from part of that of Ida of Bernicia, with 'Giwis' instead of 'Bernic' (whose name is clearly linked with 'Bernicia'). If so then we must acknowledge that Cerdic's true roots are unknown. This does not mean that Cerdic himself is a fiction. His British name, and the *Chronicle's* description of him as merely *ealdorman* ('leader') are matters unlikely to have been made up, and suggest that he was a historical figure.

As time went on gods, heroes, and biblical figures were brought into genealogies. One of the most striking additions is that of the god Woden. He is named in all the kingly lines other than that of Essex, where we have the god Seaxnet instead. Clearly the Church did not see Woden as a god, but it seems that a hero of old bearing the same name could be accepted. Dumville thinks that for Bede this was no more than a means of defining royalty.[326] Some might go further and say that this was a way of claiming that all these kingly lines (and the folkdoms they 'summed up') were boughs of the one tree.[327]

As well as Freawine, Wig and Woden, the shadowy figures of Sceaf and Beaw were added to the Wessex kinship 'tree', linking the royal house with the old heartlands of northern Europe. The last gap to bridge was that between the northern world and the Great Flood and the early patriarchs of Genesis.[328] That book told nothing of the origins of the Germanic peoples. But in the works of the Fathers Japheth son of Noah was taken to be the ancestor of the Europeans. So now Sceaf was said to be a son of Noah born in the ark.

Names could also be taken out of a genealogy, through the practice of *damnatio memoriae*, known in classical culture as the creation of an 'unperson'. We have

---

[323] RW Chambers, quoted in Sisam, 1953, p.158.

[324] K Sisam, 1953, p.159.

[325] K Sisam, 1953, pp.179-80.

[326] DN Dumville, 1977, pp.78-9.

[327] Leslie Webster and Janet Backhouse, editors, *The Making of England*, 1991, pp.45-7.

[328] On this subject see D Anlezark, 'Sceaf, Japheth and the origins of the Anglo-Saxons', *Anglo-Saxon England*, Volume 31, December 2002, pp.13-46.

already noted the case of Creoda. In Northumbria the kings who followed Edwin, Osric of Deira and Eanfrith of Bernicia, were soon 'justly punished' (in Bede's words) for apostasy, each falling in battle within a twelve-month. Bede goes on to tell how it was settled that the memory of them should be wiped away, and their year added to the time of the king who came after them, the godly Oswald (*HE*, III.1).

How far back might we trust the Anglo-Saxon genealogies? The second half of the sixth century has been suggested as the limit of oral tradition at the time when it came to writing these things down.[329] Dumville says that this fits in with potentially reliable records in Welsh and Irish accounts, and with the great plague of the 540s, when some lines of descent would have been cut off. However, for a slightly different perspective, see the next section, on oral tradition.

# On oral tradition

Early Anglo-Saxon England was a 'pre-literate' society, and Barbara Yorke asks whether such a society would have had the same concepts of historical truth as are found in the classical and Christian traditions of record-keeping.[330] She says it has been too readily assumed that humans have an inherent desire to record the past accurately, and she argues, further, that anthropological studies have taught us much more about other societies analogous to that of the Anglo-Saxons. These studies are said to show, first, that pre-literate societies assume that present conditions must have existed in the past as well. Next, accounts of the past might mingle real and mythological figures, while the folk passing on the traditions, having no written records to refer to, might be unaware of this. Third, there might be 'set-piece scenes' (such as the slaughter of the 300 elders) which could be told of any hero, but whose details might be anachronistic. Lastly, forebears might be created from place-names, for example, 'Wihtgar' from the Isle of Wight.

Sarah Foot discusses the question of individual and collective memory.[331] She takes the act of memory to be a personal one, and she says that what is remembered may change under the influence of time, age and experience, and through the intrusion of subsequent events, or conflicting recollections. Commemoration (that is, collaborative remembrance) may alter separate memories by embodying them in a constructed account of a shared past. She holds that this is more likely to be 'fictive construction' than long-acknowledged and collectively remembered 'truth'.

We certainly live in an age which finds it hard to value oral witness. (We have already encountered the bald claim that 'the unreliability of oral tradition needs no

---

[329] B Yorke, Kings and Kingdoms, p.4.
[330] See B Yorke, 'Fact or Fiction?', *ASSAH*, 6, pp.45-50.
[331] S Foot, 'Remembering, Forgetting and Inventing', 1999, pp.185-200.

emphasis.'[332]) This is surely a twentieth century perspective on a past with a very different culture from ours. For us, paper and ink (and now the CD and the USB flashdrive) are everything. But for earlier ages the oral witness of knowledgeable and trustworthy men counted for more, and the written record might be seen as only a help to memory. Here are some points from the other side of the argument.

Kenneth Harrison comments that it is perhaps too easy to suppose that because men cannot read or write they fall short in other ways. That the Anglo-Saxons were far from primitive is shown by, for example, the sophistication of their calendar.[333] Harrison notes that the ninety clauses of Æthelberht of Kent's law code must be largely founded on the memory of ancient customs and penalties. For this both facts and figures had to be remembered.[334] Guthlac (died 714) knew stories of the ancient kings of past ages. Bede knew that the battle of *Degsastan* took place in Aethelfrith's eleventh year which, with the help of a Northumbrian king-list, enabled him to fix the date to AD 603. Harrison stresses that Bede is usually careful and clear-headed in the handling of chronology, and that he would not have invented a date.[335]

In his essay on Welsh pedigrees Michael Siddons notes that, 'The possibility of accurate oral transmission of rulers' pedigrees over long periods was confirmed in the Pacific islands where there were populations which had migrated centuries ago from a common source to widely scattered islands and which had had no further contact. In many cases the royal lines from different islands converge backwards to common ancestors referred to independently by the same names and at the same periods.'[336]

Stenton notes that, 'It is easy to underestimate the length of time covered by two good memories'.[337] Thus, if, about 650, a seventy-year-old was telling what he had heard as a boy from a grandfather, also living to seventy, this would be enough to span the period from 520-650. (One might add that if written record-keeping began in Kent with Bertha and bishop Liudhard, say about 580, the time span for two good memories would be pushed back to about 450.) Kenneth Sisam acknowledges that, 'One may still find villagers who, without a written record, can trace back their descent through a century and a half to an undistinguished great-grandfather. In Anglo-Saxon times when the conception of kindred was vital, the descendants of kings might reach back still farther in memory'.[338]

---

[332] PH Sawyer, From Roman Britain to Norman England, 1978, p.13.
[333] K Harrison, *Framework*, p.137.
[334] K Harrison, *Framework*, p.131.
[335] K Harrison, *Framework*, p.139, citing Jones 1947:43.
[336] M Siddons, 'Printed and Manuscript Pedigrees' in John Rowlands and others, editors, *Welsh Family History*, p.209, citing Thor Heyerdahl, *American Indians in the Pacific* (London: Allen & Unwin), 1952, p.35.
[337] FM Stenton, 'The Foundations of English History', in *Preparatory*, p.121.
[338] K Sisam, 1953, p.195.

Patrick Geary writes of the relationship between land, and oral and written witness. He notes that, 'Land not only formed the basis of a family's wealth and power: land was the means by which a family knew itself in historical perspective.'[339] This meant that assured property bounds were important. Geary discusses the boundaries of donated properties in the East Frankish world where (unlike in England) the practice was simply to record the names of the places on the donated property. If there was a boundary dispute, it was through oral witness that the written evidence was filled out. There had to be a beating of the bounds, led by a group of knowledgeable and trustworthy men, who would show where the boundaries were, and speak forth their witness. Their sworn statement had to be heard and recorded first in the memory of witnesses who would then confirm it in writing, and the written document could later be used as a help to memory of the events.[340]

Adam Fox[341] cites Thomas Bewick who recalled how, on winter evenings, in his Tyneside village of Mickley in the 1750s, tales were told of men who had been leading figures in the border wars, of others who had been good landlords or kind neighbours, and also others who had simply been bold, independent and honest. These tales were set in the local landscape. Many of them served to explain local place-names and landmarks. 'Indeed, the landscape all around was a vast repository of memory ... from which people derived a sense of identity and pride based upon place'.[342] (In such reminiscences of the elders there was often a nostalgia for the old days when 'there were fewer lawyers and all things were cheap'![343])

Old people were revered as the keepers of ancient wisdom and communal memory. 'We old men are old chronicles', says the 'countryman' in a dialogue of 1608, 'and when our tongues go they are not only clocks to tell only the time present, but large books unclasped; and our speeches, like leaves turned over and over, discover wonders long since passed'.[344] Aubrey talked to Goodwife Dew of Broad Chalke who died in 1649, at the age of 103. She remembered Edward VI visiting Wiltshire. When more than one generation was involved, inherited memory could reach back a good way, and with some reliability. John Smyth of Nibley (1567-1640), estate steward to the earls of Berkeley, heard old men and women, born in the reign of Henry VII, talk about the battle of Nibley Green in 1469. As children they had heard the tale from fathers, mothers, kinsfolk and neighbours. Smyth heard in lively detail how Thomas Talbot, Viscount Lisle, was

---

339 Patrick J Geary, 'Land, Language, and Memory in Europe 700-1100', *Transactions of the Royal Historical Society* Sixth Series, IX, Cambridge: Cambridge University Press, 1999, p.171.

340 PJ Geary, 1999, p.178.

341 Adam Fox, 'Remembering the Past in Early Modern England: Oral and Written Tradition', *Transactions of the Royal Historical Society* Sixth Series, IX, Cambridge: Cambridge University Press, 1999, pp.233-56.

342 Adam Fox, pp.234-5.

343 Adam Fox, p.238.

344 Adam Fox, p.236.

slain by the arrow of 'Black Will'. Old Charles Hiet was able to tell the same story in 1603, having heard it from his father and grandfather 'as if the same had been but yesterday'.[345]

There was duty laid on the old to treasure the communal memory, and to pass it on to the young, and thereby maintain the common voice. If this was true in the 1600s, a thousand years after the wonders of written records were introduced to the English, how much more true must it have been in, say, the sixth to eighth centuries!

Having weighed the witness given by our written sources, and briefly looked at the matters of kinlore and oral tradition, we go on to consider 'models' of the Anglo-Saxon settlement. But first we take a short look at Anglo-Saxon seacraft.

---

[345] Adam Fox, p.237.

# Anglo-Saxon seacraft, and the crossing

What is known of Anglo-Saxon ships? The one buried at Sutton Hoo in Suffolk was 89 feet long, 14 feet in the beam, and 4½ feet deep, though it would have drawn only about two feet of water unladen. It was clinker-built, probably in oak. The ship's stems were raked at angles similar to those of the Nydam ship, and rose at least 12½ feet above the keel. There was a side-rudder, on the starboard side at the stern. The flat bottom, with the keel formed by a flat, heavy plank which thrust only about two inches below the hull, made the boat fit for the shoaly waters of the southern North Sea. It would have been able to go close inshore, and far up rivers. Assuming a rowing speed of about three knots an hour for twelve hours, a Sutton Hoo-type ship would have made only about 36 nautical miles a day if rowed. But the Germanic folk were probably using the sail by the mid-first century.[346] Haywood cites Edwin and Joyce Gifford, who point out that the leaf-shaped plan of the Sutton Hoo ship is more like a sailing ship. (Rowing galleys had nearly straight sides, to lower hull resistance and get the most from the output of the rowers.) When a half-size copy of the Sutton Hoo ship, fitted out with mast and sail, was tested, it was found that it could be readily handled, and could sail at up to 10-12 knots.[347] For short-range warfare the advantages of sail would have been less clearcut. For example, the sail would have made the ship more visible to coast-guards.

The numbers involved in early sea crossings would have been small. An early English ship probably carried 40-60 warriors, so that the 'three keels' of Hengest and Horsa, for example, would imply a warband of somewhere between 120 and 180 men.

By what way did the Anglo-Saxon reavers (and later settlers) come? While a few hardy sailors may have come straight across the North Sea from the Cimbric peninsula to the east and south of Britain, most would probably have hugged the coast, resting in lonely coves and inlets on the way. By this means they would have reached the *fretum gallicum*, the present-day Pas de Calais, and would then have had 22 miles of sea to cross.

However, some Anglo-Saxons may have first settled for a while in the western coastal marshes of Frisia and at the Rhine mouths. (These parts seem to have been resettled after sea encroachments, some time after AD 425.) They could then have made the sea-crossing from there.[348] The direct passage from Frisia to the Yarmouth area is about 125 miles, which would have taken thirty hours or more, rowing (during which time the weather might change a lot). It would seem that many Frisians also came into

[346] J Haywood, *Dark Age Naval Power*, p.38.

[347] J Haywood, pp.101-3.

[348] Otto S Knottnerus, 'The Wadden Sea Region: A Unique Cultural landscape' in *Wadden Sea Ecosystem* no.12, 2001, p.32.

south-east England.[349] (It has also been suggested that Anglo-Saxon reaving and folk movement was launched from settlements in north Gaul.)

Winter travel must have been rare (see Bede, IV.1, on Hadrian's delayed journey to Britain). The Danish and German North Sea coast is too dangerous in winter. Folk would not set out before March. But spring is the worst time to travel, according to a poem in *Maxims* II, line 5. The best time for a crossing was between late spring (perhaps at the beginning of May) and early leaf-fall. Reconnaissance and preparation would have to be done a year before. Fowler suggests that raiders would have set out in April/May, because then they would have had little left in the way of food supplies at home, and they would have been looking for profit from raiding. June/July might also have been a possible time for seafaring from areas where the seasonal movement of livestock between winter and summer pastures was part of the yearly cycle. The women and children would be away with the livestock, leaving the menfolk with less on their hands. The latter might have gone out raiding and prospecting.[350] Another view is that migration in considerable numbers would have been possible only after the harvest had been brought in. In two successive years, 488 and 489, Theodoric and the Goths set out in August, after harvest time.[351]

---

349 JNL Myres, The English Settlements, p.48.

350 See Fowler, in John Hines, editor, The Anglo-Saxons from the migration period to the eighth century, 1997, p.63.

351 See Pohl, in John Hines, editor, *The Anglo-Saxons from the migration period to the eighth century*, 1997, p.62, and G Ausenda, p.418.

# 'Models' of the Anglo-Saxon settlement

A number of models have been proposed.

## *The 'going concern' model*

It is the contention of KR Dark[352] that the sub-Roman kingdoms were identical in territory to the Romano-British *civitates* and that these in turn had been shaped from the pre-Roman Iron Age polities. He believes that this resurrection of Iron Age states happened before the incoming Angles and Saxons gained control. He bases this conclusion on his belief that the territories of seventh century Anglo-Saxon kingdoms match closely the pattern of the Roman *civitates* in lowland Britain.[353] (Alan Vince takes a similar line, arguing that there is a close correlation in the boundary between Saxon and Anglian areas and the borders of two late Roman provinces, those of Flavia and Maxima Caesariensis.)[354]

Further evidence comes from names. The name of Kent continues the name of the Roman *civitas*, and the name of Lindsey seems to come from the *civitas* capital, Lincoln. Wight is a Germanization of the Latin name of the island, and Bernicia and Deira (later welded into one kingdom, Northumbria) are thought to be originally British district names. If this line of thought is correct, then it would seem the Anglo-Saxons took over the *civitates*/ kingdoms as 'going concerns', and there was no call to begin the process of state-formation all over again.

Dark sees the new Romano-British rulers of the *civitates* rising to power in two different contexts, that is, in the lowland and the highland zones. He believes that in the lowlands of Britain they took power in a civilian, urban context, perhaps at the *civitas* capitals – places such as Canterbury (for the Cantiaci tribe), Wroxeter (for the Cornovii), Dorchester (for the Durotriges). This may have happened while Constantine III was in Gaul in AD 409, in his bid for the throne. Dark suggests these lowland dynasties took on Anglo-Saxon and Irish *foederati* to defend their kingdoms in the fifth century. Then towards the end of that century they moved their political centres from the towns to neighbouring hill-forts. South Cadbury was probably one example.

In the highland zone of Britain it seems that native dynasties were restored following the end of Roman rule, perhaps in the early fifth century.[355] Dark further suggests that in warfare the tactics, and perhaps the organization, used by the new

---

352 KR Dark, Civitas to Kingdom: British Political Continuity 300-800, 1994.

353 KR Dark, pp.133, 135.

354 Alan Vince at the 47th Sachsensymposium, see B Yorke, 'The Origins of Anglo-Saxon Kingdoms', *ASSAH*, 10, p.28.

355 KR Dark, pp.94-5.

rulers were based on Roman methods, but built around the warriors of the king's court instead of the legions.[356]

Dark believes that the Romano-British political framework lasted so long partly because it was so local. Power was in the hands of a string of tribal kingdoms, and there was no 'core' which incomers could strike at to bring the system down at a blow. There was, furthermore, local economic independence. Dark further suggests that the Christian Church played a key role, putting down roots unusually early in rural Britain, and helping to hold British society together.[357] He believes that the towns were still the seats of British bishops through the fifth and sixth centuries, perhaps even in areas where the Anglo-Saxons gained political control after the middle of the fifth century.

The takeover of 'going concerns' is also seen at the local level. Barbara Yorke draws attention to landscape studies which have highlighted examples of continuity of territorial boundaries. There are cases where the boundaries of medieval estates, as marked out in early charters, seem to be identical with those of Roman villa estates.[358] What we see is probably the continuity of a unit of administration rather than one of economic exploitation. Barbara Yorke explains: 'The basis of both the internal organization of both the Anglo-Saxon kingdoms and those of their Celtic neighbours was a large rural territory which contained a number of subsidiary settlements dependent upon a central residence which the Anglo-Saxons called a *villa* in Latin and a *tun* in Old English. These 'vills' (as they were later known) were centres of royal administration and were visited by the kings and their entourages on regular circuits of their kingdoms when food rents which had to be rendered at the royal vill would be consumed. In Anglo-Saxon England of the seventh and eighth centuries groups of royal vills and their dependent territories formed *regiones*, discrete territories within kingdoms for administrative purposes.'[359]

The takeover of going concerns need not mean change without upheaval. Christopher Scull paints a picture of economic trauma and political fragmentation in post-Roman Britain. He writes, 'The subsistence economy need not have suffered major disruption, but the Romanized superstructure which it supported, and which served the needs of élites and the state, collapsed'.[360] Post-Roman Britain may thus have more closely resembled (in political structures and economic level) the continental societies from which the Anglo-Saxons came. 'A politically-fragmented indigenous society offers a plausible context both for the permanent settlement of incoming groups, and for their subsequent establishment

[356] KR Dark, p.197-8.

[357] KR Dark, p.253-5

[358] B Yorke, Kings and Kingdoms, p.8.

[359] B Yorke, Kings and Kingdoms, p.8.

[360] C Scull, 'Archaeology, Early Anglo-Saxon Society and the Origins of Anglo-Saxon Kingdoms', *ASSAH*, 6, p.70.

of a political ascendancy'.[361] If post-Roman Britain did indeed fragment, the main beneficiaries were likely the incoming Germanic groups. It may be suggested that these came with the agreement of British political entities needing fresh support, or that they simply took advantage of British political weakness.

This would seem to fit in with the accounts given by Gildas and Bede of federate troops, quarrels over pay, treachery and apocalyptic disaster. HR Loyn thinks that for Kent, at least, there is no reason to doubt that this was the way it was.[362] He writes, 'The story of federates rebelling against their paymasters is plausible, and the possibility that more of the structure of the 'Roman-Britain of the tyrants' survived in Kent than elsewhere is not unlikely'.[363]

## *The pirate base model*

Another model is that of the pirate base, perhaps under the leadership of an exiled Anglo-Saxon prince. Haywood notes that among those who raided Britain and Gaul were Franks and Saxons, Heruli (then settled in Denmark), the *Chaibones* (probably the Saxon tribe of the Aviones) and, most likely, Frisians.[364] (Alcock notes that the rising power of the Franks, especially after 486, diverted the Saxons across the Channel.[365]) Barbara Yorke notes that the continental historians Gregory of Tours and Sidonius Apollinaris depict the 'Saxons' (their all-embracing name for non-Frankish Germans from the North Sea area) behaving throughout the fifth and sixth centuries like the Vikings of later centuries. They were raiding the Channel coasts, establishing colonies and bases in Francia, and on occasion lending their armies to help Frankish leaders and factions. The identification, in Frankish sources, of 'Saxon' bases in Normandy, just across the Channel from the two Jutish provinces of Kent and the Solent region, may suggest the likelihood that they also established bases there.[366]

## *The folk migration model*

In weighing the folk migration model the question of the numbers involved must be considered. Alcock says that the estimate of the Anglo-Saxon element in the population in the sixth century has been put at 50,000-100,000. What of the Romano-British population? By one estimate the rural population of the lowland zone of Roman Britain is said to have been 'at least one million' at the end of the second century. It is then held that numbers had fallen markedly by the fifth century,

---

[361] C Scull, p.70.

[362] HR Loyn, Anglo-Saxon England and the Norman Conquest, p.28.

[363] HR Loyn, p.41.

[364] J Haywood, *Dark Age Naval Power*, pp.59, 60.

[365] L Alcock, *Arthur's Britain*, p.112.

[366] B Yorke, 'The Origins of Anglo-Saxon Kingdoms', *ASSAH*, 10, p.26.

though hardly to the level of the Anglo-Saxon population.[367] Another estimate has suggested that, 'The density of settlement in Roman Britain was comparable to, or greater than, it was at the time of the Norman conquest, which implies a population of at least the two million estimated from Domesday Book, probably more.'[368]

Now when two ethnic groups are thrust together, and (as happened in lowland Britain) the language, customs and traditions of one group prevail after a while, then one of two possible social mechanisms must have been at work: a) gradual acculturation through assimilation of one group by the other, or b) the disappearance of one group (by genocide, or by them leaving the area). It does seem strange that it was the Anglo-Saxon language and customs that should prevail, when they must have been far fewer in number. And the acculturation (if that is what happened) would have to have taken place within about 150 years, generally a short time for such a wholesale change. Again, acculturation generally goes from the higher socio-cultural level (the Romano-British in this case) to the lower (the Anglo-Saxon).

The archaeological evidence seems to go against any theory of genocide. There are hardly any signs of battle cemeteries (like those connected with native British sites dating from the time of the Roman invasion), though early Saxon cemeteries of warriors, seemingly not associated with settlements, may be such.[369] Some villas were burned down, but most simply fell into ruin by neglect. The absence of layers of burning from the stratification of Roman towns is against conquest by 'fire and slaughter'.[370]

Margaret Gelling approaches the question of folk migration from the place-name perspective.[371] It has long been noted that many Celtic river and stream names have survived, as well as forest names (Lyme, Arden, and the lesser woodlands of Cannock in Staffordshire, Morfe and Kinver in the Severn valley, Kemble in Gloucestershire, Melchet and Pamber in Hampshire, Braydon, Savernake, Chute, and Panchet in Wiltshire, Mendip in Somerset).[372] Gelling focuses on settlement names. She begins by noting, 'The change of language which took place after the Roman period has never been fully explained, and this is probably the obscurest question in the whole of English history.'[373] She goes on to state very clearly that the place-name evidence makes theories about the invading Anglo-Saxons carrying out wholesale massacre, or completely displacing Celtic-speakers, untenable. 'There is an identifiable corpus of pre-English place-names which could only have been

---

[367] L Alcock, *Arthur's Britain*, p.310-11.
[368] C Hills, *Origins of the English*, 2003, pp.91-2.
[369] J Wacher, *The Towns of Roman Britain*, 1974, pp.413-4.
[370] L Alcock, *Arthur's Britain*, pp.355.
[371] See M Gelling, 'Why Aren't We Speaking Welsh?' *ASSAH*, 6, pp.51-56.
[372] FM Stenton, 'The Historical Bearing of Place-Name Studies', 1939, in DM Stenton, *Preparatory*, 1970, p.258.
[373] M Gelling, p.51.

adopted and preserved by English speakers in conditions of peaceful coexistence.' The same place-name evidence also rules out any thoughts that the numbers of Germanic settlers were very small. There was 'a massive replacement of the general stock of British names by Old English toponymns ... the renaming of the vast majority of settlements is inconceivable without the influx of a mass of peasant settlers. (The arrival of a Latin-speaking ruling class in the first century AD did not cause a wholesale renaming of settlements ... The same is true of the Norman conquerors at a later date; we have only a handful of French place-names in any area of England'.[374])

The archaeological record confirms the fact of large-scale Anglo-Saxon settlement in Kent, the East Midlands and East Anglia. In parts of the West Midlands and of south west England there is no archaeological evidence for Anglo-Saxon peasant immigration, yet the replacement of British place-names by English ones happened on an equally massive scale, and this is the crux of the problem. In Shropshire and Devon in particular Celtic names are very scarce. On the other hand in the Penge/Croydon/Leatherhead part of Surrey the frequency of Celtic names, and names referring to Celts, is remarkably high.

Gelling says that Frank Stenton and Dorothy Whitelock are among those who have minimised the evidence for a Celtic strain in the population of Anglo-Saxon England.[375] Both comment on the lack of any habitation names with clear British roots. According to Gelling these scholars were misled through their overlooking the corpus of names which are recorded from Roman Britain. The people of Roman Britain did not use names of the -ton, -ham, and so on, type. 'In all the recorded names from Roman Britain there is no explicit reference to farms or hamlets, and only one to a villa. Where habitation terms are used the reference is to something out of the ordinary, such as a fort (-dunum) or town walls (Duro). Romano-British Celts defined their settlements by giving them the names of adjacent topographical features, such as hills and rivers.

The Old English language was 'remarkably immune to Welsh influence',[376] and borrowings were very, very few. This has naturally been used as an argument against there being much contact between the speakers of the two languages. But, 'It is a historical anachronism to attribute the modern Englishman's poor linguistic skills to his Dark Age forebears. In the Dark Ages everybody, irrespective of ethnic affiliation, would be able to hear and pronounce names correctly. Philologists have shown that Old English forms of Primitive Welsh and Latin names are remarkably accurate and systematic, sometimes involving substitution of the closest Old English sound for one for which they had no exact equivalent'.[377] Gelling goes on to suggest that the fact of

---

[374] M Gelling, p.51.
[375] M Gelling, p.53.
[376] M Gelling, 'Why Aren't We Speaking Welsh?' *ASSAH*, 6, p.56.
[377] M Gelling, p.55.

few borrowings 'is not proof of lack of contact, but rather of community of interests [as farmers] ... Words are borrowed when people encounter objects or concepts not catered for in their own vocabulary'. Her clear conclusion is that there was a period of coexistence between speakers of Primitive Welsh and Old English.

Alcock notes that Welsh folk appear in the Laws of Ine. Doubtless many were serfs, but some were substantial landowners. It is likely that in some parts of Wessex the English communities were small, and engaged in farming alongside larger British communities. (Perhaps they fitted into gaps left through Roman decline, or in some cases the expulsion or killing off of Britons.) In other areas the English would have been in the majority.[378]

## *Place-name evidence*

Place-name evidence can throw light not only on Romano-British/Anglo-Saxon relations, but on early settlement.

The old Germanic suffix *-ing* has several functions and forms in place-names. It seems to have had the root meaning of 'that which pertains, or belongs to, something or someone'. Some *-ing* names may be old, but we cannot safely regard names of this type as evidence of early settlement.[379]

AH Smith says that in Old English the *-ingas* formation is limited to certain place-names, to the earlier heroic poetry, and to the oldest historical traditions. The general meaning of folk-names in *-ingas* is 'an association of people dependent in some way upon the leader whose name forms the first theme'. (Such names can refer to a single family, to a household, or to a whole tribe.) Smith notes that the lack of evidence for the creation of folk-names from personal names in later times led scholars to think that such names belonged to the age of migration and early settlement. (But *-ingas* names formed from old local names, for example, 'Avening', 'the folk living near a river *Avon*', were not thought to be necessarily old.[380]) A further point was that words with a Christian association (bishop, monk, priest) are never known with *-ingas* or *-ingahām* names (and they are rare with *hām* names).[381] Folk-names in *-ingas* were noted in east and north Kent, in the coastal districts of Sussex, and in eastern Hampshire. They are also frequent in Essex and East Anglia. And it was thought that some groups, such as the Hæstingas, had early on crossed in a body from the Continent to Britain. This understanding is now challenged, and it is said to be over-simple. Alcock notes that the distribution of *-ingas* names has not always coincided in detail with the early cemeteries. Thus, pottery and ornaments which suggest fifth-century settlement have been found outside the *-ingas* areas, in

---

378 L Alcock, *Arthur's Britain*, pp.312-3.
379 AH Smith, 'Place-names and the Anglo-Saxon settlement' 1956, in EG Stanley, editor, *British Academy Papers on Anglo-Saxon England*, 1990, p.213.
380 AH Smith, p.215.
381 AH Smith, p.221.

Nottinghamshire, Lincolnshire, east and central Yorkshire, and up the rivers flowing into the Wash. According to Alcock, 'It is now thought that the *-ingas* names really belong to a mature rather than a primitive phase of settlement.'[382]

The old element *gē* ('a district') is found only in certain south-eastern names, such as Surrey, and Eastry, Wester and Sturry in Kent. In such names the first element is also ancient, and is found in older place-names, for example, the 'wester' in Westerham.

Heathen names are clearly earlier than the conversion. Among these are: *alh* (as in Alkham, Kent) and *hearg* (Harrow, Harrowden) denoting a temple, and *wīg* (Wye in Kent, Patchway, Willey) meaning a grove. Some names denote groves or hills devoted to the gods, for example, Woodnesborough in Kent, and Thundersley, Thundridge, and Tuesley. Some place-names where an animal name is compounded with 'head' are also likely heathen. When such a place-name cannot, on topographical grounds, refer to a headland, to the head of a river, or to the upper end of a valley, then we may have a reference to the head of an animal sacrificed to the god. An example is Farcet ('bull's head'), Huntingdonshire.[383] Other names with *bēl* 'funeral pyre' (as in Beald, Belstead), recall the heathen practice of cremation.[384] Names of heathen origin are of very uneven distribution. The majority are in certain localities, such as the Canterbury district, the Wey valley in Surrey, and Essex. (On place-name evidence, Essex might be called the most strongly heathen of English kingdoms.) There is also a scattering of heathen names along the rest of the Thames valley. When heathen names are compared with heathen burials some anomalies can be seen. Thus, burial grounds found in Essex do not give the same picture of intensive and widespread settlement suggested by the county's archaic place-names. (The accidents of discovery of archaeological sites may be a factor here.) In the Trent valley heathen burials far outnumber archaic place-names (this might be a problem of not being able to recognise other types of archaic place-names).[385]

From its combination with archaic words like *wester* (Westerham), or words with heathen associations (Alkham), the word *hām* also belongs to the earlier phases of the settlement. It is common in the south-east, in East Anglia, and in the more easterly parts of the northern counties.

The lack of very old names in certain districts has an obvious explanation in the character of the landscape, for example, Romney Marsh, the Weald of Kent and Sussex, the Fenlands around the Wash. In other areas the longer survival of a British population may be the reason, as in the Hertfordshire Chilterns (here the heavily wooded terrain was probably another factor), and the south-west of the West Riding.[386]

---

382 Alcock, *Arthur's Britain*, p.306.
383 AH Smith, p.209.
384 AH Smith, p.220.
385 AH Smith, p.222.
386 AH Smith, p.223.

## *'Case studies'*

### Essex

While the Romano-British *civitates* were taking over political power, it seems that the Angles and Saxons were beginning to settle in a number of places in eastern Britain. Barbara Yorke writes, 'Sites like that of the Roman villa at Rivenhall and Roman town at Great Chesterford seem to show the peaceful interaction of Romano-British and Germanic peoples and throw light on the circumstances through which the late Roman cities of the Trinovantes became an Anglo-Saxon kingdom. Recent studies of the Essex landscape and the relationship between Roman and Saxon sites suggest that the structure of the Roman countryside largely survived and that any changes in rural settlement were a gradual response to changing economic and political circumstances. Saxon settlers would have been in the minority and their cemeteries are centred on the coast and eastern waterways ... Sites like Mucking show that the territory of the East Saxon kingdom was among the first areas of Britain to receive Anglo-Saxon settlers in the early years of the fifth century.'[387] To begin with, this may have been through *foederati* arrangements. For example, excavations at Mucking between 1965 and 1978 brought to light scores of sunken huts and two burial grounds in use from the early 400s to the early 700s.[388] The site gives fine views down the Thames estuary, and the settlers may have been placed there by a sub-Roman British state (or states) of the Catuvellauni and Trinovantes tribes, to guard the sea approaches. This state may at first have centred on St Alban's or London, or both. Note that 'The original bounds of the diocese of London, that is the East Saxon see, seem to have included not only Essex, but also Middlesex, south-eastern Hertfordshire and Surrey'.[389] It has been suggested that a ring of Anglo-Saxon burial grounds a little south of London (at Mitcham, Beddington, Croydon, Orpington and Darenth), mark the presence of federate troops here, too. The sites seem to be closely related to the Romano-British settlement and road pattern.[390] As the Saxons took over it may be that a rump Romano-British state lived on into the 6th century, steadily shrinking to an enclave in the woodlands of the north Chilterns,[391] before it was finally overrun.

---

[387] B Yorke, *Kings and Kingdoms*, p.456.

[388] G Hindley, A Brief History of the Anglo-Saxons, p.3.

[389] B Yorke, *Kings and Kingdoms*, p.46.

[390] KR Dark, pp.89, 127, and J Hines, The Anglo-Saxonsfrom the migration period to the eighth century, pp.63-4.

[391] D Hooke, The Landscape of Anglo-Saxon England, 1998, p.142; AC Thomas, Christianity in Roman Britain to AD 500, 1981, p.260.

## East Anglia

We are short of detailed written sources here. It is likely that the archives of the kingdom (held by the two episcopal sees and the major religious houses) were lost, or severely impoversished, during the ninth century Viking raids and conquest. Bede received some information from Albinus and Nothhelm, some from the writings or traditions of men of the past, some from Abbot Esi, also a *Life of St Fursa* and probably oral traditions about St Æthelthryth.

Angles may have first settled in East Anglia in the early to mid-fifth century. Norfolk and Suffolk seem to represent the original territory of the Iceni. (The north-south division may have had its origins in the sub-Roman period.[392]) In his study of the origins of the Anglo-Saxon kingdoms Christopher Scull focuses on East Anglia. He says that here the archaeological evidence points to free settlement spread over a longish period of time. (It has been suggested that East Anglia was perhaps the first region to receive independent – that is uninvited – Anglo-Saxon settlers.[393]) Scull says that Myres' early dating of cremation pottery is not supported by associated metalwork. Thus the earliest Anglo-Saxon material from East Anglia would fit with settlement in the period 425-50, or a little later.[394] The great majority of migration period sites in the region were in use by about AD 520, but only a few can be shown to have been established by AD 475. The great expansion in the number of new cemeteries from 475 onwards need not mean a new episode of migration, or population growth among the Germanic incomers. It could be the outcome of a process of acculturation, that is, the adoption by indigenous groups of new cultural practices, expressing new affinities and identities. Scull suggests that, 'The initial invisibility of the indigenous population in the 5th century may be attributed to material poverty and/or servility, or to cultural practices which left no distinctive visible trace in the archaeological record'.[395]

The Spong Hill, Norfolk cemetery shows many similarities with North German material. The brooches are like those from Schleswig-Holstein, and the stamped decoration on pottery is like that on the pottery of Lower Saxony. Issendorf (close to the Elbe, on the boundary of these two regions) shows a similar range of material to that at Spong Hill. A detailed statistical analysis of the pottery from the two sites showed that they were closer to each other than either was to sites in their own regions. It does look as if we have here an example of direct connection through migration.[396]

---

[392] B Yorke, *Kings and Kingdoms*, p.61.

[393] See B Yorke, *Kings and Kingdoms*, p.61.

[394] C Scull, 'Archaeology, Early Anglo-Saxon Society and the Origins of Anglo-Saxon Kingdoms', *ASSAH*, 6, p.71.

[395] C Scull, p.71, and see Esmonde Cleary, *The Ending of Roman Britain*, pp.178-187.

[396] C Hills, *Origins of the English*, 2003, p.82.

The fact that early centres of power such as Ipswich and Sutton Hoo, were close to rivers suggests that it was not a central site that was important, but access to the cultural arena of the North Sea. There seems to have been continuing close contact with Denmark, south-west Norway and the Swedish Uppland.[397] Finds from Mound 1 at Sutton Hoo show some 'striking iconographic parallels' with the Vendel period in Sweden. Links with the poem *Beowulf* have also been noted. It has even been suggested that the Wuffingas were descended from an eastern Swedish dynasty, or that they were members of the royal house of the Geats. However, the parallels may be more a matter of cultural contacts and influence, perhaps (in the words of Barbara Yorke) an example of what might be called the 'out of Scandinavia myth'. This would mean that royal houses sought to show links, for themselves and their peoples, with the most powerful peoples of the Scandinavian world, both past and present.[398]

## Lindsey

The kingdom of Lindsey occupied only the north of Corieltauvi territory. (Perhaps the Corieltauvi *civitas* broke up after the Romans left.) Lindsey was surrounded by the sea, the Humber estuary, and the marshes of the Trent and Witham, making it in a very real sense an island – *Lindesege* or Lindes island.[399] At Kirmington and Hibaldstow there is some evidence of the presence of Germanic women about AD 400. It has been suggested that these may have been the wives of *laeti*, settled here to help defend the *civitas*. The Hibaldstow site is on Ermine Street, and that at Kirmington is at a strategic cross-roads.[400] Stafford says there was a dramatic increase in the size of Anglo-Saxon cemeteries, such as at Kirton-in-Lindsey, in the late 5th/early 6th centuries.[401] The name Cædbæd (an anglicisation of Romano-British 'Catuboduos') in the genealogy of the Lindsey rulers suggests British/Anglo-Saxon intermarriage.[402] (The names of members of other royal families could point to intermarriage: 'Cerdic' of Wessex has already been noted, and there is also 'Æthelwalh' king of Sussex.[403])

---

[397] Martin Carver 'Kingship and material culture in early Anglo-Saxon East Anglia', in Steven Bassett, editor, *The Origins of Anglo-Saxon Kingdoms*, p.147-52.

[398] B Yorke, 'Political and Ethnic Identity', in WO Frazer and A Tyrrell, editors, *Social Identity in Early Medieval Britain*, 2000, pp.81-2.

[399] P Stafford, The East Midlands in the Early Middle Ages, p.135.

[400] B Eagles, 'Lindsey', in Steven Bassett, editor, *The Origins of Anglo-Saxon Kingdoms*, p.208.

[401] P Stafford, The East Midlands in the Early Middle Ages, p.81.

[402] B Eagles, 'Lindsey', in Steven Bassett, editor, *The Origins of Anglo-Saxon Kingdoms*, p.206.

[403] P Drewett, David Rudling and Mark Gardiner, *The South-east to AD 1000* (London: Longman, 1988), p.265.

## Northumbria

The early Anglian kingdom of Deira probably occupied the former territory of the Parisi, the present East Riding of Yorkshire.[404] The *Historia Brittonum* refers to one Soemil who 'first separated Deira from Bernicia' (*HB* 61), which most likely means that he took it from the hands of the British. He may have been a leader of *laeti*, living about the middle of the 5th century.[405] The original nucleus of Bernicia was probably in the Tyne area (the Tees valley seems to have formed the boundary of Bernicia and Deira in the seventh century). 'Both kingdoms have British names and were surrounded by Celtic kingdoms; it is possible that both were in origin British kingdoms or tribal territories which were taken over by Anglo-Saxon warbands'.[406] A fragment of a Northumbrian chronicle based on the annals with which Bede closed his *Historia Ecclesiastica* records that Oessa, the grandfather of Ida of Bernicia was the first of the dynasty to come to Britain, though Ida seems to have been the first of the line to rule (reputedly from 547-59).[407] (Note that Deira has far more Anglo-Saxon cemeteries than the rest of Northumbria.[408])

## Early Wessex

We have already noted that the middle and upper Thames valley (from Cookham up river to the Gloucestershire border) was a centre of Saxon settlement from the early 5th century. It is not easy to understand why *laeti* (if that is what these were) should have been planted in the heart of the land. But given that the Romano-British kingdoms were rarely able to work together against the common foe, we might guess that one *civitas* planted Saxons here as border troops, while perhaps their rivals did the same. The *civitates* of the Catuvellauni and the Atrebates had common borders here, and the Dobunni might have been involved as well.

---

[404] KR Dark, p.128.

[405] JNL Myres, The English Settlements, p.188.

[406] B Yorke, *Kings and Kingdoms*, p.74.

[407] B Yorke, *Kings and Kingdoms*, pp.74-5.

[408] B Yorke, Kings and Kingdoms, p.5.

# The Jutish lands

## *Kent before the Jutes*

Kent was a kingdom before the coming of the Romans. To the Greek geographer-historians, Strabo and Diodorus, it was Κάντιον, a name which they presumably knew from the writings of Pytheas (the fourth century BC Greek geographer and explorer). The most likely meaning of the name is 'corner land, land on the edge', and Pytheas and the others perhaps understood it as referring to a headland. (Κάντιον or 'Cantion' was one 'corner' of Britain, then believed to be a three-cornered island – the other 'corners' being Land's End and Orkney,) To Caesar the land was 'Cantium', this name being extended by him to the hinterland.[409] Brooks says that these names probably all represent a monosyllable **C(h)ant* or *Cænt*.[410]

To Bede the land was 'Cantia'. There are two main ways in which the name Cantia, or Kent, might have been passed to the Anglo-Saxons. The first way is through Saxon seafarers learning the name in the fourth century.[411] The other way is through the incomers seizing control of the power structures of the *civitas*/kingdom from post-Roman 'tyrants' or kings, or having that power handed over to them. (The story in *Historia Brittonum* is of the transfer of control by means that were legal – if underhand – and not by warfare.) That the latter is the stronger possibility is suggested by the concentration of early Anglo-Saxon settlements in areas where the major Romano-British sites had been.

## *Archaeology: the Scandinavian link*

Early grave goods in Kent have been read as indicating close links with Jutland.[412] Some very worn cruciform and square-headed brooches, with relief designs similar to Scandinavian brooches, have been found in east Kent graves. This has been taken as evidence that they were brought from Scandinavia and kept for a long time before burial. However, linking grave objects with ethnic origin may be misleading. Few urns and pots of the fifth century have been found in Kentish graves, and they have lacked distinguishing features to mark their origin. And as well as the Scandinavian-type brooches, Kentish graves have yielded objects of Kentish manufacture. There are also Frisian finds in fifth century Kent.[413] Again, many of the brooches, headbands, glasses and weapons found have been Frankish, and those necklaces with bracteates which could be reconstructed seemed to follow Frankish fashion as

---

[409] ALF Rivet and C Smith, *The place-names of Roman Britain*, p.300.

[410] N Brooks, 'The creation and early structure of the kingdom of Kent', in S Bassett, editor, *The Origins of Anglo-Saxon Kingdoms*, p.57.

[411] N Brooks, p.37.

[412] P Drewett, David Rudling and Mark Gardiner, *The South-east to AD 1000*, 1988, p.256.

[413] GJ Copley, The conquest of Wessex in the sixth century, p.133.

well. It is thought that the Frankish goods came in through wedlock ties and trade links, rather than settlement.[414] The concentration of Frankish imports in Kentish cemeteries of the late fifth and the sixth centuries contrasts with the lack of such imports in other parts of Anglo-Saxon England. This suggests that long-distance trade was controlled by a central authority in eastern Kent, most likely the king.[415]

Recent archaeological research in Scandinavia has focused on the identification, characteristics and importance of central places which can be identified as *villae regales*. In this rcsearch the finds of numerous bracteate hoards have been important. (Bracteates were dress fasteners, and they were produced, and used, only for a fairly short time, probably between the mid-fifth century and the mid-sixth century AD. The bracteate iconography seems to show that the main god represented on these amulets was Odin/Woden.[416]) Forty-six bracteates have been found in Anglo-Saxon England, twenty-eight of them in eastern Kent. All the Kent bracteates save one (a B-bracteate from a grave at Bifrons) belong to type D. The largest find concentration of type D bracteates outside eastern Kent is in Jutland, But no die links have been found, and these bracteates were likely made in Kent using Jutish or northern German D-bracteates as models.[417]

Another point to be noted is that twenty-six of the Kentish bracteates were found in graves, while two were from unknown find-spots. None have been found in hoards. In southern Scandinavia, however, bracteates have been found in hoards (most often associated with female dress objects) or as single finds, but they have not been found in graves. The comparative analysis of Kentish and Jutish cemeteries of the fifth and sixth centuries carried out by Sorensen shows that graves in Jutland differed significantly from contemporary Kentish graves, not only in their grave goods, but also in terms of burial rites.[418]

However, there do seem to be parallels between Kent and Scandinavia in terms of the relationship between jewellery finds and places of significance in the king's administration. In a female grave, D3, at the Finglesham cemetery there was found a very worn, silver gilt, great square-headed brooch which, according to Haseloff, belongs to his Jutlandic brooch group. It has been dated to AD 480-500.[419] The Old English form of the name Finglesham is **þengels-ham* 'home or manor of a prince'. It is only a mile from Eastry, which, with Lyminge, Sturry and Wester, was probably part of the early administrative structure of the Kentish kingdom established before the integration of West Kent. (Wester, the western **ge* or district, was east of the

---

[414] P Drewett and others, 1988, pp.258, 279.

[415] C Behr, 'The origins of kingship in early medieval Kent', in *Early Medieval Europe*, 9, 2000, pp.46-8.

[416] C Behr, pp.35, 36.

[417] C Behr, 'The origins of kingship in early medieval Kent', pp.49-50.

[418] C Behr, p.30.

[419] C Behr, p.41.

Medway.[420]) The rich graves at Finglesham, the evidence for a royal villa in Eastry, and the place-name indicating an administrative centre, point to the presence of members of the Kentish royal family.[421] Behr suggests that beliefs about the roots of the Germanic people of eastern Kent were preserved and expressed not only in oral tradition, but also in well-chosen dress accessories. In other words, the latter were not simply dress fasteners but were symbols of origin and status. 'It is most likely that the people in Kent who wore the bracteates understood the meaning of their images which were clearly linked to the cult of Woden and to Scandinavia'.[422] Since the jewellery was worn by women Behr further suggests that women of the highest rank in early Anglo-Saxon society in Kent played 'an ostentatious role in the religious and ideological legitimization of early Kentish kingship'.[423]

## *West Kent and East Kent*

It seems that the early Jutish kingdom of Kent was made up of the eastern half of the shire alone. (There had long been an east/west divide. Caesar noted differences between the West Kent folk and East Kent's Belgae.[424]) The extent of west Kent is not clear. The second century AD geographer-astronomer, Ptolemy, attributed three towns to the Cantii: London, Canterbury and Richborough. Scholars have all rejected the idea that London was in Cantium, but this leaves us without any firm evidence of the western boundary of the Celtic kingdom of Kent, or of the Romano-British Cantium, the land of the Cantiaci. Some have held that British Cantium included not only all of Kent, but also the eastern marches of what we know as Surrey,[425] and perhaps, too, the Weald to the north and east of Pevensey.[426] Some have guessed that there were two *pagi*, centred on Rochester and Canterbury, but this is based only on the existence of the two towns, and the later division of the county.[427]

Economically West Kent belonged with East Surrey (they had common links with the wood-pastures of the Weald), and the Anglo-Saxon grave goods found there are more akin to those of the Saxons of Surrey and Essex, than to those of East Kent. There was perhaps a tug-of-war between the Essex and East Kent kingdoms over the West Kent lands. Near Rochester, where Watling Street from London crosses the Medway, the burial ground of a well-armed community has been found. There is

---

[420] C Behr, p.42, citing Yorke.

[421] C Behr, p.43.

[422] C Behr, p.50.

[423] C behr, p.52.

[424] M Lyle, *Canterbury*, 1994, pp.14, 26.

[425] ALF Rivet and C Smith, *The place-names of Roman Britain*, p.299.

[426] M Welch, 'The kingdom of the South Saxons: the origins', in S Bassett, editor, *The Origins of Anglo-Saxon kingdoms*, pp.78,83, and Drewitt, p.275.

[427] Nicholas Brooks, *Anglo-Saxon Myths: State and Church 400-1066* (London: Hambledon Press, 2000), p.37.

another at Aylesford, on the Pilgrims' Way track along the North Downs. It would seem these were marcher settlements of the East Kent kingdom.[428] (West Kent was most likely taken over by the East Kent leadership some time in the sixth century.[429])

## *The settlement*

Early Germanic settlement sites in Kent were coastal and along rivers and creeks. Fifth century Kent was heavily wooded, and it was the rivers that gave a way in (and a way out, if things went wrong). Moreover boats could get further upstream in the fifth century, than they can today. The earliest Germanic settlements were on the light, fertile soils of the Canterbury/ north-east Kent region. There were early settlements up the Stour valley as far as Wye or Ashford, and up the Medway to Teston or Yalding. The Germanic settlement of the Darent valley, as far as Otford, goes back to the earliest days, though this would seem to have been an incoming of Saxons.

The Jutish/Saxon settlers next took over what Alan Everitt calls the 'Foothills', and the springheads of Holmesdale (see his study, *Continuity and Colonization: the evolution of Kentish settlement*). By 'Foothills' Everitt means the low-lying, coastal plain, between the North Downs and the marshlands of the Thames and the north Kent coast over against Sheppey. This land was fertile, and near the sea. Here the great Roman road, Watling Street, ran from east to west, while the key river valleys of the Stour, Medway, and Darent cut northwards through it. Holmesdale is the name of the wide upland vale between the North Downs and the Chart. Strictly speaking the name belongs to the valley to the west of the Medway, but Everitt uses it of the valley as a whole.

Everitt argues that the areas of early Germanic settlement were also the areas of Romano-British settlement. He points, first, to the evidence of archaeology. Roman remains are to be found in the neighbourhood of almost every major Jutish settlement. At Richborough and Reculver there were Roman forts, at Sturry there was a Roman settlement and a quay by the river, at Eastry there was a Roman ritual site, at Worth a temple and a burial ground. In the neighbourhood of Milton Regis, which was a seat of the Kentish kings, there were at least twenty-five major archaeological sites, mostly dating from the Roman period. Faversham was a centre of metal-working in the Roman period, and this may have been continued in the Anglo-Saxon period. It early became a royal villa. Everitt identifies forty or so Jutish 'estate centres', from which wider settlement, and local government, grew. Four fifths of these, he says, are close to Romano-British remains.[430] At almost every major Roman site in the shire there are early Saxon or Jutish burials. Finds at the

---

[428] P Drewett and others, *The South-east to AD 1000*, pp.257, 275.

[429] B Yorke, *Kings and Kingdoms*, p.27.

[430] A Everitt, *Continuity and Colonization: the evolution of Kentish settlement* (London: Leicester University Press, 1986), pp.101-2.

Roman burial ground at Martyrs' Field, outside Canterbury, show that the Anglo-Saxons made use of that burial ground in the fifth/sixth centuries. At Deal, too, graves of Romano-Britons and Anglo-Saxons have been found close together.[431] The goal seems to have been to stand in rightful heirship. Or perhaps the early English sought thus to harness or, if need be, to undermine, the spiritual 'force' of the place.[432] (For the same reason, like enough, the early English also buried their dead in prehistoric barrows, or at sacred sites.)

At places like Eastry, Woodnesborough, Sturry, Rainham, Maidstone, Rochester and Dartford it is noteworthy that the main street of the Roman settlement is still the main street today. Maidstone is a good example of ongoingness from Romano-Britons to Jutish settlers. There was a Romano-British settlement here, at a key river-crossing. It was also a religious site, and nearby Penenden Heath was later a meeting-place for the whole Kentish folk. (It may indeed have been a folk meeting-place right from prehistoric times.) It would seem that the early English took over land that had been farmed from Roman villas, without any significant opposition.[433] Almost every church between Dartford and Otford, in the Darent valley, is close to a Roman villa. The church at Lyminge stands on the site of a Roman temple. Many of the churches of Holmesdale are sited by sacred springs that may once have been heathen places of worship. (Otford and Kemsing are examples.) However, at the springline settlements in Holmesdale, the marks of Roman/Jutish ongoingness are not so clear.

There is evidence from administrative and economic development. Everitt says that the administrative framework of Kent was not laid down from above, but was of local growth. He suggests this points to the takeover of a settlement pattern that was already in place. Then there is the pattern of 'transhumance' stock rearing, the seasonal movement of sheep and pigs to the Weald, to be fattened on the pannage of oak, chestnut, hornbeam and beech. The system goes right back to the early days of Jutish settlement, and perhaps to Romano-British times and beyond.

There is further evidence from place-names. There are more Celtic place-names in Kent than in the 'highland zone' county of Devon (though they are still only a small percentage of the whole).[434] The Germanic folk who settled in Kent held to the Celtic name 'Cantium', and they called themselves the 'Cantware' or 'Kentings'. (The incoming Saxons, on the other hand, put their own names on the lands they took over. The Saxons who settled to the east named the land Essex. Those to the south named Sussex, and those to the west, Wessex.) In Kent the name of Thanet is Celtic, and the names of rivers such as the Medway, the Darent, and the Cray. The British word *ceto* ('wood', 'forest') is found in five place-names: Chatham, Chattenden, Chetney, and the

---

[431] P Drewett and others, *The South-east to AD 1000*, p.272.

[432] S Pollington, *The English Warrior* (Hockwold-cum-Wilton: Anglo-Saxon Books, 1996), p.61, 61n.

[433] P Drewett and others, pp.254, 271-2.

[434] A Everitt, Continuity and Colonization, p.5.

lost Chathurst and Chetham, all lying within the former Blean Forest that stretched for some forty miles between the Thames estuary and the Stour Levels. (Until well into the Jutish period Kent was largely a forested land. The dense woodland of the Kent/Sussex Weald was long a forbidding 'wild', like the fells and moorlands of the north.)

Altogether, there are about thirty-five place-names that certainly have Celtic roots, a further dozen or so that may be Celtic, and between twelve and twenty for which a Celtic root has been suggested by reputable scholars (though challenged by others). All are in areas of early Jutish settlement. Among settlement names (as distinct from topographical names) there are twelve or thirteen names of early 'head' settlements with clearly Celtic roots – Dover, Reculver, Lympne, Lyminge and others. There are nine or ten lesser places, closely linked with Jutish estate centres, having Celtic names ('Pennycrych' and 'Billerica' are examples). There are also some names with 'wealh' (the Old English for 'foreigner', 'Briton'), suggesting the presence of Celtic-speaking settlements. It may be that some 'combe' names – near to early estate centres and to early Jutish archaeological sites – are Celtic (though Dr Gelling now questions whether 'combe' truly comes from a British word[435]). Everitt notes that there are some forty or forty-five place-names of British 'ambience' in the Foothills and Holmesdale.[436] He further notes a substantial number of very difficult names in Kent, and suggests these may have 'a very primitive Germanic lineage, perhaps going back to the Teutonic peoples brought into Kent in the Romano-British period.'[437] He names Aylesford, Davington, Faversham, Otford, Wrotham and other examples.

FM Stenton, addressing the place-name evidence in Kent, argued that, 'Words which are rarely, if ever, found elsewhere in England, occasional peculiarities of sound-development which must have arisen far back in the history of the Old English language, and a considerable number of personal names, which are both archaic and unique, give a distinctive character to the place-names of Kent.' He goes on, 'Among the characteristic features of Kentish local nomenclature is a large number of place-names consisting of a first element – a common noun, an adjective, or a personal name – followed by a particle *-ing*. Some of them are names of settlements, others, of natural features, but in either case they are wholly distinct in structure and meaning from the more familiar plural names in *-ingas*, which were originally names of tribes, families, or other groups of human beings.' In some, 'a locative case-ending has caused palatalization of the final *g*, and produced such forms as Arpinge, Geddinge, and Ruckinge.' (Among examples of *-ing* names from the other Jutish areas (that is, the Isle of Wight and Hampshire), are Brading, Swaythling, and Nursling.[438])

---

[435] M Gelling, Place-Names in the Landscape, pp.88-9.

[436] A Everitt, Continuity and Colonization, p.105.

[437] A Everitt, Continuity and Colonization, p.107-13.

[438] See FM Stenton, 'The Historical Bearing of Place-Name Studies: The English Occupation of Southern Britain', 1940, in DM Stenton, *Preparatory*, 1970, pp.271-2.

Stenton also noted heathen names (which must go back to the period before 597) in the south-east. Augustine and his fellow-missionaries worked in a land where the sanctuaries of a living heathenism were so many that some of their names survive even after thirteen hundred years. There are five places of heathen worship which can still be identified within twelve miles of Augustine's church of Canterbury. Stenton adds that it is not surprising that the conversion advanced by generations rather than by decades.[439])

In sum, while acknowledging that there was probably a break in the story of human settlement in some parts of Kent (Canterbury is cited), Everitt holds that overall the picture is of continuity. He thinks there is good evidence that the Jutish takeover was largely peaceful, rather than an overcoming in war and a sharing out of the kingdom. This would not be at odds with the tale of war found in the *Chronicle* and in the *Historia Brittonum*. Fifth-century war-bands were small, and for the common folk the tide of war would, like enough, mean little more than new landlords and new men gathering taxes.

## Canterbury *(see maps)*

The first (pre-Roman) settlement was at a ford where a North Downs trackway came down through the alder swamps of the Stour valley bottom, and crossed the river. The settlement was named 'Durovernum Cantiacorum', that is, 'the stronghold of the Cantiaci by the alder grove (or swamp)'.

Roman Canterbury was the *civitas* capital of the Cantiaci, and an industrial centre and market. An industrial suburb (metal-working, pottery, and tile-making), with a network of lanes west of the river, was left outside the town when the walls were built about AD 270. These industries withered in the 4th century AD.[440] The theatre was too large for anything but occasional use in Roman times. The temple area opposite was cleared in the 4th century, perhaps to make a market place.[441] There was no great clustering of villas round Canterbury. Perhaps the east Kent landowners preferred to live within the security of the town, and run their estates from there. Perhaps town properties functioned as working farms.[442]

Archaeology gives us some picture of the withering of city life in late Roman Canterbury. The baths had fallen out of use by the 350s. Cobblers and bone-workers set up business in the old baths *palaestra* (exercise yard), and wooden lean-to shops were set up against the *palaestra* wall. Another bath-house, with gaming house, was damaged by fire, and by 360 was left a ruin. The public sewer

---

[439] FM Stenton, 'The Historical Bearing of Place-Name Studies: Anglo-Saxon Heathenism', 1941, in DM Stenton, *Preparatory*, 1970, p.297.

[440] M Lyle, *Canterbury*, pp.19, 33, P Drewett and others, *The South-east to AD 1000*, p.203.

[441] M Lyle, *Canterbury*, p.29.

[442] P Drewett and others, *The South-east to AD 1000*, p.214, M Lyle, *Canterbury*, p.36.

system broke down, so that blockages led to the backing-up of foul water.[443] The south gateway of the Riding Gate was closed up, and the carriageway became a smith's workshop. New buildings of timber encroached on to the streets. The latest small coins are dated 380-90 (but were current for much longer).[444] Sometime in the first part of the fifth century a family was buried within the temple precincts. (This was against Roman law, which banned burials within cities, so clearly official control had broken down.) These were a man, a woman, girls of about 11 years and 8 years, and the old family dog. The woman was laid with one girl in her arms, and the other at her feet, and the man was laid with the old dog on his lap. The females had Roman keys, chains and bangles, and imported glass beads. It has been suggested that these deaths are evidence of disease amid decay.[445] A silver hoard buried outside the London gate, about 410, is a mark of how unsafe the times were. As the fifth century wore on the north and south fourths of the city were left empty of folk, and the land may have been farmed. Much of the west part of the town was flooded by the Stour. 'Dark-earth' layers of varying depths seal nearly all excavated Roman buildings. ('Dark earth' is the waste ground of late Roman Britain. It may be the rotted remains of late Roman wooden, or wattle and daub, buildings.[446]) Anglo-Frisian pottery (handmade and not fired in a kiln) and some forty sunken-floored huts, dated about 450, have been found in one 'insula', on top of leveled Roman buildings. Was the insula given to them by a 'skeleton' late Roman council, or was this simply a good enough place for newcomers to settle?[447] And then, among a scattered goldsmith's hoard a South Gaulish Visigothic *tremiss* of about 480 has been found. It was not used as currency, but was clipped for melting. One wonders who the goldsmith would have been working for.[448]

Esmonde Cleary sees Canterbury as a place where there was a gap in human settlement of at least a generation between the latest Roman and the earliest Anglo-Saxon finds.[449] However, we do see one thread of continuity in the influence of the Roman theatre in Canterbury on the layout of the city in the early Middle Ages.[450] It was probably used by the king for assemblies, and this suggests a desire to connect with the Roman past.[451]

---

[443] AS Esmonde Cleary, *The Ending of Roman Britain*, p.132.
[444] M Lyle, *Canterbury*, p.35.
[445] M Lyle, *Canterbury*, p.36; AS Esmonde Cleary, *The Ending of Roman Britain*, p.151.
[446] AS Esmonde Cleary, pp.147-8.
[447] S Johnson, *Later Roman Britain*, pp.178-9.
[448] M Lyle, *Canterbury*, p.38.
[449] AS Esmonde Cleary, *The Ending of Roman Britain*, p.193.
[450] N Brooks, Anglo-Saxon Myths: State and Church 400-1066, p.36.
[451] B Yorke, *Kings and Kingdoms*, p.19.

## Early development of the Kentish kingdom

John Hines acknowledges that the story of fifth-century Jutish settlement in Kent is 'apparently true', but he goes on to say that perhaps the story was preserved not so much for its truth as because it gave the Men of Kent an identity. It made them different from the Angles and Saxons.[452] And it may have helped bind together a multi-racial community consisting of Romano-Britons, Jutes, Saxons, Frisians, and some Franks.

The early kingdom of (east) Kent was small, in area and in population. So were the other early Anglo-Saxon states. In such a context power tended to be impermanent. It would die with the individual leader, and his successor would then have to begin again. One outcome was that the leader had to consume much of the product of holding power, in gift- or ring-giving, feasting and the like. This would make it hard for him to accumulate the land and wealth which could be transferred to others and used to uphold a more stable power structure.[453] How could small and short-lived lordships grow to become larger and more permanent kingdoms?

Two mechanisms for growth have been suggested: 'competitive exclusion', [454] and core-periphery interaction, making use of prestige-goods. Both could apply to Kent. The first is a model put forward by Bassett (1989). This proposes competition between local political groupings with the winners becoming progressively more powerful. Bassett likened the process to the FA Cup competition, where teams are knocked out in the successive rounds.[455] This is, in truth, a back-projection from the era chronicled by Bede, when dynasties were striving for power. Such developments might be furthered through population growth, alliance, marriage, or warfare, until one group gained enough land and resources to give it a competitive edge over neighbours. Then it might either absorb them or place them in a relation of dependency. The development of higher- and lower-rank kings, kingdoms, and sub-kingdoms, can still be seen in the Tribal Hidage.[456] This may be what happened as Jutish east Kent took over Saxon west Kent. (The Tribal Hidage was most likely drawn up in Mercia in the mid-seventh century. It lists thirty-five peoples, and it seems to be an assessment for tribute, based on hides of land held.[457])

As to core-periphery interaction and the prestige-goods model, Cleary notes that this is seen in late British prehistory (from 55 BC to AD 43), a time of new kinds of settlement, more differentiation in burial practices, more goods coming in from the continent, the bringing in of coinage, and the emergence of greater and lesser rulers.

---

452 J Hines, 'The Becoming of the English', *ASSAH*, 7, p.51.

453 AS Esmonde Cleary, 'Approaches to the Differences between Late Romano-British and Early Anglo-Saxon Archaeology', *ASSAH*, 6, p.60.

454 Carneiro 1978, see C Scull, 'Social Archaeology and Anglo-Saxon Kingdom Origins', *ASSAH*, 10, p.20.

455 See C Scull, *ASSAH*, 5, p.68.

456 AS Esmonde Cleary, *ASSAH*, 6, p.62, and see Yorke, *Kings and Kingdoms*, pp.10-13.

457 B Yorke, *Kings and Kingdoms*, p.10.

These developments are seen, in particular, in Kent, and along the Thames estuary and the south coast. Key to the processes in both late British prehistory and early Anglo-Saxon history was the influence of the neighbouring parts of the continent (Belgic Gaul in the first case, Merovingian Francia in the second). From these continental neighbours came new objects, new ideas, new politics. Access to the continent and its prestige goods would have been a vital tool in building status and strengthening control over territory and people. 'Archaeologists have long recognized amongst the grave-goods from sixth-century Kentish burials a significant Frankish element, particularly of luxury items such as belt fittings, garnet jewellery, glassware and bronze bowls'.[458] This need not imply any large numbers of Frankish settlers. Such goods may have come in as trade goods, as marriage gifts, or as gifts between rulers. HR Loyn notes that, 'There is a growing body of evidence for such intercourse in the fifth and sixth centuries between north Gaul and Kent'.[459]

## *Was there joint kingship in Kent?*

In Kent there seems to have been regularly a senior king based in Jutish east Kent and a junior partner (generally a close relative) in the Saxon west.[460] The west may have been, for some time, land for which the east Kent kingdom strove with the East Saxons. The need to keep a firm eye on this important marcher land may provide an explanation of the origins of a junior kingship based in western Kent. The system of dual kingship persisted up to the third quarter of the eighth century.[461] (Kent was not alone in having a joint kingship. Among both the East and West Saxons the number of kings varied. The Hwicce seem to have had a number of instances of brothers ruling jointly, but with no sign of a division of power between them.[462])

How far back might this system go? Barbara Yorke thinks that it would be unwise to argue for the existence of joint kingship in the fifth century on the basis of references to Hengest and Horsa, and Hengest and Oisc. She suggests that joint kingship having become the norm (from the sixth/seventh centuries) this was explained, and justified, by projecting that arrangement back into an earlier period'.[463] Yet we have seen that the east/west division in Kent goes back to pre-Roman times. In the early Anglo-Saxon period the fact of there being two Kentish bishoprics (Canterbury and Rochester) suggests that the east/west division 'was a significant administrative division within the kingdom before the arrival of Christianity'.[464]

---

[458] N Brooks, Anglo-Saxon Myths: State and Church 400-1066, p.46.
[459] HR Loyn, Anglo-Saxon England and the Norman Conquest, p.41.
[460] B Yorke 'Joint Kingship in Kent', 1983, p.19; N Brooks, 'The creation and early structure of the kingdom of Kent', in S Bassett, editor, *The Origins of Anglo-Saxon Kingdoms*, 1989, pp.67-74.
[461] B Yorke, 'Joint Kingship in Kent', 1983, p.15.
[462] B Yorke, 'The Origins of Anglo-Saxon Kingdoms', *ASSAH*, 10, p.27.
[463] B Yorke, 'Joint Kingship in Kent', 1983, p.4.
[464] B Yorke, 'Joint Kingship in Kent', 1983, p.5.

## *The Isle of Wight and the Hampshire coast*

With East and Middle Saxons to the north and west of Kent, and expansion to the south-west blocked by the Weald, the only opening for growth was by sea. It seems likely that the sixth-century rulers of Kent did have an interest in the only other two areas which Bede says were settled by Jutes, the Isle of Wight and the Hampshire shore roughly from Lymington to Hayling Island. Ashton and Lewis suggest that the Isle of Wight, along with the Hampshire coast, may once have been a separate 'pagus' of the Belgae, perhaps centred round Portchester, and that it was ceded by treaty to the Jutes, or conquered by them.[465]

Common features in grave goods (especially female dress accessories) from Kent, the Isle of Wight, southern Hampshire, and West Sussex, suggest some relationship among the élite families in these areas in the later fifth and sixth centuries. Their shared tastes were in part derived from Francia and in part from Scandinavia. [466] (Note that only one object has come to light which might have been imported from Jutland. This was found at the Apple Down cemetery on the South Downs in West Sussex.[467])

The richest grave so far known from the Isle of Wight is that of a young woman buried at the Chessell Down cemetery. She was buried with three great Kentish square-headed brooches on her breast, as well as the more usual brooches on either shoulder (one of which was a rare Frankish import). The rest of her jewellery consisted of a silver and a gold ring, an elaborate necklace of beads, and a headband of gold braid in Frankish fashion. Between her legs were a crystal ball and a perforated spoon, and at her sides were an iron weaving batten and another large iron artefact (possibly a key). At her feet there was a bronze pail from Byzantium, and two silver-rimmed wooden cups.[468] These objects are characteristic of the rich female graves at Sarre in Kent. They may be evidence for wedlock ties between the two royal houses (of Kent and Wight) in the second half of the sixth century.

Further evidence of these ties is found in the kinship rolls for Kent. These suggest that at the time the rolls were put together there was an awareness of common Kentish/Wight origins. Hengest is said to be the son of Wihtgils, the son of Witta/Wihta, son of Wehta of the line of Woden. (The folk of the Isle of Wight were the 'Wihtware'.)[469]

---

[465] M Ashton and C Lewis, *The Medieval Landscape of Wessex*, p.25. See also JNL Myres, *The English Settlements*, p.114.

[466] B Yorke, in S Bassett, editor, *The Origins of Anglo-Saxon Kingdoms*, pp.88-9.

[467] C Behr, 'The origins of kingship in early medieval Kent', in *Early Medieval Europe* 9, 2000, p.28.

[468] B Yorke, Wessex in the Early Middle Ages, p.37.

[469] B Yorke, Wessex in the Early Middle Ages, pp.36-7.

The name of the Jutes is found in a number of old place-names. Florence of Worcester records that the New Forest was known as *Ytene*, 'of the Jutes'. The name *Ytingstoc* (modern Bishopstoke) seems to indicate that the lower Itchen was in Jutish territory. There was also *Ytedene* (valley of the Jutes), near East Meon. These places may have marked the western and northern bounds of the Jutish lands. The Meonware were a group of Jutes settled on the river Meon. The bounds of the two minster parishes of Titchfield and East Meon may delineate the territory of the Meonware.[470] The Jutish coastal plain would have been separated from the chalklands to the north by the woodland which was known as the Forest of Bere. The hillfort of Winchester Hill was Jutish. The Netley Marsh area could have been a no-man's land.

Might the incomers have penetrated to the Salisbury area? DJ James says the coin loss indicates that the site of *Sorviodunum* (Old Salisbury) was occupied into the 5th century. There may have been a sub-Roman population and authority in the Salisbury area as late as the mid-sixth century.[471] Ten graves at the Winterbourne Gunner cemetery (four miles north-east of Salisbury) were excavated in 1960. A throwing axe ('francisca') of Frankish type was found in Grave VI. According to Böhner's classification the date should be AD 450-525. Also in Grave VI there was a late Roman strap end, with an engraved beast of 4th/5th century workmanship. A figure-of-eight buckle, inlaid with bronze wires, from Grave VI, is thought to date from the last half of the 5th century. The design of brooches found in Graves VII and IX is adapted from Kentish disc brooches of perhaps the second quarter of the 6th century. Thus the Winterbourne brooches must be dated to the second half of the century, and they seem to have been worn out before they were put into the graves. A provisional view would be that the associated settlement began not later than about 520, and that the settlers came up from Southampton Water.[472]

There are two groups of graves at the Petersfinger cemetery, south-east of Salisbury, a group orientated west-east, and another orientated north-south. The first group appears to be earlier, as in two instances north-south graves cut into the west-east graves. It is possible that the west-east graves are of the same period and settlement group as those at Winterbourne Gunner, where the graves are also west-east. According to Ashton and Lewis among the west-east burials there was a warrior with a fine Frankish sword.[473] (Both Winterbourne Gunner and Petersfinger are at strategic points where roads leading to Old Sarum ford the river Bourne.) The cemeteries at Charlton and Harnham also show Frankish links, possibly spread from Kent.[474]

---

[470] B Yorke, in S Bassett, editor, *The Origins of Anglo-Saxon Kingdoms*, pp.90.

[471] DJ James, '*Sorviodunum* – A Review of the Archaeological Evidence', *WANHM*, 95, 2002, p.16.

[472] J Musty and JED Stratton, 'A Saxon cemetery at Winterbourne Gunner, near Salisbury', *WANHM*, 59, 1964, pp.86-104.

[473] M Ashton and C Lewis, *The Medieval Landscape of Wessex*, pp.14-15.

[474] Bruce Eagles, 'Anglo-Saxon presence and culture in Wiltshire c. AD 450 - c.675', in Peter Ellis, editor, *Roman Wiltshire and after*, WANHS, 2001, pp.218-9.

Some of the earliest pottery and metalwork found in Hampshire are of types found on the Isle of Wight. However, most of the sixth century burials at Droxford, Hampshire do not closely parallel those of the Island, and have just as much in common with the neighbouring Saxon areas of North Hampshire, South Wiltshire and Sussex.[475] Indeed, the material culture of the Hampshire Jutes was never so very different from that of their Saxon neighbours. The distinction was probably more political than cultural, that is, it was a feeling of being different and having different rulers.

The Isle of Wight was assessed as an independent province in the Tribal Hidage. It is followed in that list by the *Noxgaga* and *Ochtgata*, who may perhaps be the peoples of the Jutish mainland provinces.[476] (Surrey and east Berkshire have also been suggested.[477])

In Bede's thinking a people could not flourish as Christians unless they had their own king and bishop.[478] In the *Historia Ecclesiastica* thirteen political entities meet Bede's definition of a *gens* as having their own kingly house and their own bishopric (or the potential for that): Kent, the East Saxons, the East Angles, the West Saxons, Mercia, Hwicce, the South Saxons, Deira, Bernicia, the Isle of Wight, Lindsey, the Middle Angles, the Magonsæte.[479] Bede evidently believed that the Jutes of the Isle of Wight, who dwelt in a distinct *provincia* with their own kings, should have had their own bishopric. Yet it was not to be. Bede tells of the conquest of Wight by Cædwalla of Wessex in 686, and Wight was added to Winchester diocese.

The *Chronicle* tells of the coming of Stuf and Wihtgar in the year 514, and it names them West Saxons. But king Alfred's biographer, Asser, makes it clear that in ninth-century Wessex they were believed to be Jutish and to be the founders of the royal house of Wight. Osburh, the wife of Æthelwulf of Wessex, and mother of Alfred the Great, was of Jutish descent (Asser, *Life of King Alfred*, 2). There is nothing in Bede's narrative to make one think that the West Saxons had any prior claim to the Isle of Wight. It has been suggested that when the *Chronicle* narrative says that Cerdic and Cynric overran the island in 530, it was in fact attributing to them the deeds of the Jutish leaders, or using them as a model.[480] (For Wessex the gaining of the Jutish lands was to be of great economic and trading importance.)

---

[475] B Yorke, Wessex in the Early Middle Ages, p.39.

[476] see B Yorke, in S Bassett, editor, *The Origins of Anglo-Saxon Kingdoms*, p.92.

[477] P Drewett and others, *The South-east to AD 1000*, p.275.

[478] B Yorke, 'Political and Ethnic Identity', in Frazer and Tyrrell, editors, *Social Identity in Early Medieval Britain*, pp.74, 76.

[479] Bede does not give any information on a royal house for the Magonsæte, but see Kate Pretty, 'Defining the Magonsæte' in Bassett, editor, *The Origins of Anglo-Saxon Kingdoms*, pp.171-83.

[480] B Yorke, in S Bassett, editor, *The Origins of Anglo-Saxon Kingdoms* p.95.

# Constructed ethnicities?

John Moreland contends[481] that generations of archaeologists, historians, politicians, and churchmen have been 'beguiled' (a rather loaded word) by Bede's statement that the English were sprung from 'the three most formidable races of Germany, the Saxons, Angles, and Jutes' (*HE* I.15). He believes that a national story has more to do with culture and history than with blood ties, and he says that the 'English' are not, in fact, biologically descended from the Germanic stock of Bede's account. He argues against seeking to create a national myth through what he calls the 'culture-history' approach. The features of this approach are (in the case of the English), first, a linking of ethnicity with material culture, second, the claim that the Angles, Saxons, and Jutes were distinct groupings in their Continental homelands, and remained so in the early period of their settlement in England, and, third, the belief that these groupings then coalesced to form the nation that we know as the English. As an example of this approach Moreland cites the work of JNL Myres. Myres matched pottery and jewellery from English cemeteries with that from northern Germany and southern Scandinavia, and then applied ethnic names drawn from the historical sources.

Against this approach Moreland baldly states that 'there is no immediate and direct relationship between ethnicity and material culture'.[482] He does, however, acknowledge that to move from the rejection of a direct link between ethnic identity and material culture, to argue that there is *no* relationship, would be 'a debilitating step'.[483] Moreland argues, further, that seeking to identify distinct Anglian, Saxon, and Jutish groups in England is fruitless, because on the Continent these groups were really 'loose confederations drawn from a variety of people'.[484]

Moreland then cites Chris Arnold, who holds that cemetery evidence from the Isle of Wight shows 'nothing more than the movement of people or objects between families maintaining a traditional link between Kent and the island'.[485] But if there were no ties of kindred, what were these 'traditional links'? Moreland sees them as simply one element in a series of traditions, memories, or aspirations used when new regional identities (or ethnicities) were 'constructed' in the sixth century. He says these constructions were matters of *power*, and were of concern to the élite within the larger entity (what might be called a 'restricted ethnicity'). He cites Patrick Geary who concludes that 'the peoples of the migration period acquired their

[481] See J Moreland, 'Ethnicity, Power and the English', in Frazer and Tyrrell, editors, *Social Identity in Early Medieval Britain*, pp.23-51.

[482] J Moreland, 'Ethnicity, Power and the English', pp.29-30.

[483] J Moreland, 'Ethnicity, Power and the English', p.40.

[484] C Hills, 'Archaeology in the pagan period', 317, also Scull, 'Early Anglo-Saxon society', 71, cited in Moreland, p.33.

[485] Arnold, 'Anglo-Saxon cemeteries of the Isle of Wight', 170, quoted in Moreland, p.43.

identity through their adherence to particular royal or ducal families'.[486] As well as deciding who belonged, the construction of these identities involved the creation of 'outsiders' by 'social closure'. Moreland adds that the lack of evidence for upheaval in the countryside of late Roman Britain means that we must assume that the great majority of the population of the early middle ages was *not* of Germanic origin. He even doubts that the élites were mainly Germanic.[487]

However, the evidence of language (English replacing Romano-British) and place-names, are surely the rocks on which such theories must founder.

# An aside on the genetic story

In the last few years genetic anthropology has been coming into its own, and some interesting studies have been published. ME Weale and others at the Centre for Genetic Anthropology, University College, London, brought out a report in 2002. This concerned a study of a sample of 313 males from seven towns in an east-west line from East Anglia to North Wales. These were small market towns (with less than 20,000 people), and only men whose paternal grandfathers were born within 18-19 miles (30 kilometres) of the towns were sampled. Likewise data was gathered from 177 samples from Friesland and Norway. It was found that statistically the Central English and Frisian samples could not be told apart. But the two North Welsh towns differed both with each other and with the English towns. The researchers concluded that the best explanation was a substantial incoming of Anglo-Saxon Y-chromosomes into Central England (contributing 50-100 per cent to the gene pool at that time), but not into North Wales. (Note that the five English sample groups all came from the Danelaw.[488])

A study like this assumes that migration was not on such a scale that the continental homelands were left deserted, and thus open to being repopulated by new people groups. It has been stressed that we ought to ask, who was living in Friesland in the fifth century, and is it their descendants that we are now comparing with the samples from Central England? The population of the Friesland area seems to have fallen drastically in the late Roman period. It afterwards picked up, and then grew rapidly in the later fifth century. Yet the reduced population was hardly enough to have been responsible alone for the rapid growth, suggesting there had been immigration from elsewhere. The material culture of the immigrants seems to show that they came from Schleswig-Holstein, from the 'Elbe-Weser triangle', and perhaps from other areas of the eastern North Sea littoral. Like enough they were a mixture of peoples with a common Germanic background. Catherine Hills thinks that the similarities

---

[486] P Geary, 'Ethnic identity as a situational construct in the early middle ages', *Mitteilungen der Anthropologischen Gesellschaft in Wien*, 113 (1983), cited in Moreland, p.45.

[487] J Moreland, 'Ethnicity, Power and the English', p.50.

[488] C Hills, Origins of the English, p.70.

between England and Friesland could then be explained as being the result of migration into both areas from the same parent population.[489]

Capelli and others (2003) looked at the spread of Y-chromosomes throughout the British Isles, and in southern Denmark, northern Germany and Norway. The Danish and German samples were taken to be the afterkin (descendants) of the same source population from whence the Anglo-Saxons came. The researchers arrived at a mean figure of a 54.1 per cent contribution to the English gene pool. Accounting for such a high genetic input by immigration alone would apparently have required the movement of 500,000 people or more. This is way beyond any documented people movements of the early Middle Ages. For example, the number of the Ostrogoths moving from the Balkans into Italy in the late fifth century has been put at 100,000.[490] But the figures could be explained by what has been called an 'apartheid-like' shaping of society, that is, keeping apart an élite immigrant minority and a disadvantaged homeborn population. Such separation is found in periods following conquest. In post-Roman times the Visigothic king Euric (AD 466-484) banned marriage between his followers and the homeborn of southern France and Spain. After the Norman conquest in 1066 the English were made of lower legal standing, and such marriages as did take place between Normans and English were nearly all one way, that is, Norman men marrying English women. Such legal barriers to mingling would be a matter of self-preservation, for the incoming group would be greatly outnumbered by homeborn folk. There are no written records of population figures for Britain before 1086, and estimates are extrapolations from very fragmentary evidence. We have seen that it has been suggested the population of Britain at the end of the Roman period was two million or more, whereas the Anglo-Saxon element in the population in the sixth century has been put at 50,000-100,000.

The Law Code of king Ine of Wessex (dated 688-694) gives us clear evidence of a legally sundered society (and, like enough, the story would have been the same in the other Anglo-Saxon kingdoms). It is most unlikely that this was a new development. Rather it was probably the upholding of a separation put in place in the immediate post-conquest period. Under Ine's laws the 'wergild' (the money payable in compensation for death or wounding) was between two and five times more for a Saxon than for a 'Welshman' (Briton). There are perhaps other signs of the Saxons in society having both higher standing and higher wealth. Thus if it is granted that the presence of weapons in a grave is a pointer to a Saxon rather than a British burial then, altogether, the Saxon graves have on average four artefacts, and British graves only 2.3 artefacts. (The Britons had been, on the whole, unarmed and untrained in Roman times.)

---

[489] C Hills, 2003, p.71.

[490] Heather, 1991, cited by Mark G Thomas, Michael PH Stumpf and Heinrich Härke: 'Evidence for an apartheid-like social structure in early Anglo-Saxon England', 2006.

The higher standing and wealth of the incoming group would spell higher reproductive success. In their 2006 study, 'Evidence for an apartheid-like social structure in early Anglo-Saxon England',[491] Mark G Thomas and others report how they used computer simulations to test out a number of plausible patterns of Anglo-Saxon advantage. They found that the proportion of 'incomer' Y-chromosomes rose from 20 per cent or less straight after the settlement period to 50 per cent or more within fifteen generations. (They see 50 per cent as a conservative estimate of the proportion of Y-chromosomes in today's English gene pool that originate among Anglo-Saxon incomers of the fifth century.) If a generation is taken to be about 25-30 years, then fifteen generations would fit the time span between the incomings in the mid-fifth century and the Laws of king Alfred (about AD 890) where there are no signs of an ongoing Saxon/British legal sundering. The researchers go on to say that, with some plausible computer simulations, the genetic contribution of the incoming population could rise from less than 10 per cent to more than 50 per cent in as little as five generations.

In 2006 Stephen Oppenheimer (a career paediatrician who later took up an interest in genetics) brought out his book *The Origins of the British*. In it he holds that most dwellers in the British Isles have forebears who were here in Neolithic times. He outlines his case in an article in 'Prospect' magazine[492] saying: 'The genetic evidence shows that three quarters of our ancestors came to this corner of Europe as hunter-gatherers, between 15,000 and 7,500 years ago, after the melting of the ice caps but before the land broke away from the mainland and divided into islands. Our subsequent separation from Europe has preserved a genetic time capsule of southwestern Europe during the ice age, which we share most closely with the former ice-age refuge in the Basque country. The first settlers were unlikely to have spoken a Celtic language but possibly a tongue related to the unique Basque language.' He holds, further, that the genetic division between a 'Celtic' west and north, and an 'English' south and east, itself dates right back to Neolithic times. He then argues that there is no evidence (linguistic, archaeological or genetic) that confirms the long-held identification of the Hallstatt or La Tène cultures of central Europe as Celtic. He says this belief stems from a mistake made by the historian Herodotus (who lived from about 490 BC to about 425/420 BC). In a 'passing remark' about the 'Keltoi' Herodotus placed them at the headwaters of the Danube, which he thought to be near the Pyrenees. Oppenheimer goes on: 'Given the distribution of Celtic languages in southwest Europe, it is most likely that they were spread by a wave of agriculturalists who dispersed 7,000 years ago from Anatolia, travelling along the north coast of the Mediterranean to Italy, France, and Spain, and then up the Atlantic coast to the British Isles. There is a dated archaeological trail for this. My genetic analysis shows exact counterparts for this trail both in the male Y chromosome and the maternally transmitted mitochondrial DNA right up to

---

[491] See the 'Proceedings of the Royal Society' website.

[492] S Oppenheimer, 'Myths of British Ancestry', *Prospect* magazine, 21/10/06, issue 127.

Cornwall, Wales, Ireland and the English south coast.'[493] Next, we are told that when the Celts came to the British Isles, they settled only the traditionally Celtic western and northern areas. The south and east were never inhabited by Celtic-speakers, but were colonised by folk from northern Europe speaking the Germanic language which, over time, evolved into English. This happened not after, but long before, Roman times. The later Anglo-Saxons were smallish élite groups whose cultural impact may have been large, but whose impact on the bloodlines was very small. 'When I looked' (writes Oppenheimer[494]) 'at exact gene type matches between the British Isles and the continent, there were indeed specific matches between the continental Anglo-Saxon homelands and England, but these amounted to only 5 per cent of modern English male lines, rising to 15 per cent in parts of Norfolk where the Angles first settled.'

Oppenheimer's case, though put forward with much confidence, seems to be at odds with well-founded linguistic evidence, if nothing else. If we look at place-names, for example, it is clear that in the south and east names from Anglo-Saxon roots far outnumber those from Celtic roots (though if Oppenheimer is right in saying that the Celts never lived in this area, then there should not be any Celtic place-names here at all). According to Sims-Williams one of the main concentrations of Celtic-rooted names, in Roman times, was the area between London and the Wash, in the English heartland while, oddly, the proportion in Wales was lower than in almost any part of England.[495]

The belief in a large Germanic presence in Britain before the Roman conquest is very ill-supported. The only evidence for the Germanic descent of the Belgae is the report by Julius Caesar, who himself contradicted the claim elsewhere by making a clear distinction between Belgae and Germani. The ambiguous evidence for their migration to southern England has been debated for several decades. The only safe conclusion is that if the Belgic migration happened it would have added continental ancestry to southern England, but not specifically Germanic ancestry. Concerning Germanic soldiers in Roman Britain, their numbers have been overstated in the literature.[496]

As regards links with the Basque country, it should be pointed out that Basque is a 'language isolate', that is, it has no proven link with any other language. It has been compared with every living and extinct Eurasian language family known, and even with the Afro-Asiatic Berber group of North Africa. But there have been no conclusive results.

---

[493] S Oppenheimer, *Prospect* magazine, 127.

[494] S Oppenheimer, *Prospect* magazine, 127.

[495] P Sims-Williams, Ancient Celtic Place-Names in Europe and Asia Minor, 2006.

[496] H Elton, *Warfare in Roman Europe, A.D. 350–425* Oxford Classical Monographs, Oxford: Clarendon Press, 1997)

As to English developing into a separate branch of Germanic in England, well before Roman times, this is wholly at odds with two centuries of careful language research in Europe. According to this research Proto-Germanic split into Proto-West Germanic, Proto-North Germanic, and Gothic, early in the Christian era. A little later Proto-West Germanic split into the forebears of the West Germanic languages we know today, among them English, Frisian, Dutch and German. The split which led to English developing separately from the others began when West Germanic speakers emigrated across the North Sea to eastern Britain from the mid-fifth century. They were then physically separated from the West Germanic peoples on the Continent, and although there would have been ongoing social contacts, these would not have been enough to keep speech habits on either side of the North Sea in line with one another. So West Germanic in Britain inevitably began to diverge from its Continental sister languages.

If the Iberian/Neolithic theory is right, then we would have to say that a long line of able and upright scholars (historians, archaeologists, philologists and others) have all been wrong, or mostly wrong. Surely those who claim to have found truth hidden from so many before them, need to weigh their theories against the findings of scholars in other fields, and to do this in great humility. We are in something of a cleft stick here. There is, clearly, a great need to draw together a range of specialist studies, in genetic anthropology, history, archaeology, linguistics and place-name studies. But who is to do this? The danger is that someone taken up with his or her own field of study may miss their way when they venture into another area. So a geneticist straying, say, into linguistics, or an archaeologist of the Bronze Age straying into biblical studies, may go badly wrong. Those working in these fields need to remind themselves, all the time, how little, really, they know.

# Hengest: taking stock

Before going on to think about the Hengest saga in Part 2, we will take stock, noting things which we can say that may not be provable, but which are at least defensible.

First, we hold that to see Hengest as a real historical figure, a foot-loose outlaw-adventurer of the mid-fifth century, is a perfectly tenable position. Bliss argues that in a long-lived tradition the following matters are likely to be handed down truly: the names of the leading figures, their links with one another, and something of the outfalling of events. The weakness will be in the dating, though events may be remembered in the right order. He holds that the fixed points in the tradition, on which we may rely are: the Jutish origin of the Kentish kingdom (whether or not Hengest himself was a Jute – Bliss himself thinks he may have been an Angle[497]), the names of the leaders Hengest and Horsa, their landing in Thanet about the middle of the fifth century, Horsa's early death in battle, and the foundation of the Kentish kingdom by Oisc.[498] Certainly the evidence against Horsa is not overwhelming, so we may accept him, though his place in the story is not key. We might accept that the Oisc who gave his name to the dynasty was a real person, yet not perhaps blood kin to Hengest. (Hengest was the sort of hero that a dynasty might like to add to its family tree.)

Next, it is certainly believable that Hengest and his war-band (like enough a mixed group of Jutes, Frisians, Franks and others) were employed by the Romano-British authorities as *foederati*, in accordance with Late Roman practice. After the failure of the appeal to Aëtius (perhaps because of the threat posed by the Huns) the authorities may have been searching for Germanic mercenaries at the very time (about 450-55) when Hengest was looking for new openings, perhaps having made Frisia too hot to hold him. If the Picts had been the only threat the obvious place to set the newcomers would have been in the north, or at least, as far north as East Anglia (at the northern end of the Saxon Shore defences). However, if we may accept that Vortigern was the British leader at this time (and that is a defensible line to take), we can see that he may have been playing more than one game. There was a Roman party led by Ambrosius. Vortigern may have managed to sideline them for the moment, but they might yet try to bring back Roman power, and Vortigern needed to guard himself against such a move.[499] It is perfectly credible that Vortigern would set Hengest's war-band on Thanet, a key base from which to intercept shipping in the Straits. It is possible that the Jutish settlements in Hampshire were also the result of a treaty settlement, whereby the Portchester end of the Saxon Shore network could be held.[500] But it would seem that in

---

497 A Bliss, *Finn and Hengest*, pp.168-80.
498 A Bliss, *Finn and Hengest*, pp.68-69.
499 JNL Myres, *The English Settlements*, pp.14, 18.
500 JNL Myres, p.114.

seeking to prevent a Roman takeover of his affairs Vortigern became too deeply involved with his Saxon mercenaries.[501]

Third, the reason given for the Saxon revolt (inadequate *annonae*) might be well-founded, given the increasing numbers of the newcomers. There are parallels on the Continent. For example, about 476, *foederati* quartered in Italy asked the *magister militum*, Orestes, for homes and lands of their own. When Orestes refused their petition they asked Odoacer (who was likely of Germanic stock, and an officer in what remained of the Roman army) to lead their revolt. Orestes was killed, and the Germanic *foederati*, with a large part of the Italic Roman army, then proclaimed Odoacer 'king of Italy'. That Hengest soon changed his plans from warrior service to carving out a kingdom, is highly likely.

## *Towards a chronology of Hengest's career*

Bede's dating of the first coming of Germanic groups to Britain gives us one fairly fixed point, within the years 450-455. Tolkien suggests a date of about 450/51 for the 'Freswæl' (the Frisian slaughter), and about 453 for Hengest's coming into Britain.[502] We may have one clue about Hengest's years in that he is called a 'hyse' in the *Finnsburg Fragment*. The word means 'youth, son' (but also 'man, warrior'). Another clue is the coming to the kingship (of Kent) of Æsc/Oisc in 488, presumably on the death of Hengest (though the *Chronicle* does not say that in so many words). Tolkien suggested a date around 420/25 for the birth of Hengest, making him 25-30 years old at the time of the 'Freswæl', and 63-68 years old when he died. Hnæf was perhaps about 30 years old, and his sister-son about 15 years old.

Tolkien suggests a birth date for Oisc of about 450. But if 455 is a reasonable date for the death of Horsa, it would mean that Oisc was only about five years old when he took Horsa's place at Hengest's side. We would then have to say that the chronicler, or his source, had made the shared leadership happen too early. But the *Chronicle* seems fairly sure about its facts here, naming Æsc/Oisc alongside Hengest in 456, 465, and 473. Perhaps, then, Oisc was born about 440, so that he came to warrior years in 455. He would then have been about 72 years old at the time of his death (the *Chronicle* says that he was king for twenty-four years from 488). We could also put back Hengest's birth year a little, say to 415. This would make it easier to fit Hrothwyn into the time scheme. If Hengest had fathered her say, about 438, he being then about 23 years old, Hrothwyn would have been 16 or 17 years old at the time Vortigern saw her.

---

[501] Stephen Johnson, 'Late Roman defences and the *Limes*' p.67.

[502] See A Bliss, *Finn and Hengest*, pp.72-6.

# Part 2: The Hengest saga and its setting

The tale of Finnsburg and of Hengest and the fighting in Kent, fit well with the life and outlook of the Germanic 'Heroic Age' (about AD 325-575), and to this we now turn.

## *Heroic society in the fifth century AD*

Germanic heroic society was a society geared for war. To its members war was the business of life, their 'meat and drink', the spring of their gladness. The Roman historian Tacitus bears witness that the German warrior thought it tame and spineless to gather wealth slowly by the sweat of his brow when it might be got quickly by the loss of a little blood. All else that this world might hold – ease, profit, women and wooing – came well down his list for weal and worth. To a warrior a land at peace was a land stagnating and, like enough, he would be off, seeking out a folkdom that had a war in hand, and a warband that would take him (*Germania* 14).

The men of a warband looked to their lord to seek out openings for war-making. Among the things that led to warring in the Heroic Age were the settling of grievances, answering the smearing of one's name, and holding the defeated to their tribute payments. When it came to warring the lord must take his share in the fighting, do deeds of daring, heap up spoil and share it open-handedly with his followers. The bond between lord and man was no mercenary one, however. Or, rather (as we shall see), it went far deeper than that. How was this warfare carried on?

## *The warcraft of the Heroic Age*

A full war-host was made up of the 'building blocks' of a number of war-bands, each given its own mission, and each band fighting together. The holding of river-crossings, the storming of strongholds, the dawn onset, the use of woodland cover, the war-chant and, in battle, the shieldwall, were key features of the warfare of the age.

A river-crossing could be a key battleground, with one war-host seeking to force a passage, and the other set on withstanding them. A river might also serve to guard the flank of a war-host. And with boats to hand, a river could also be used for bringing in war-supplies, as well as offering a way of escape if a battle was lost. (That the Cray, the Darent and the Medway, with their crossing-places, should have been much fought over – as pictured by the *Chronicle* and the *Historia Brittonum* – is thus very credible.)

Strongholds were held, though they were not perhaps so key as in other wars, before and since. Among the besettings (sieges) of which we have record is the South Saxon storming of Anderida (Pevensey), with the slaying of all the Britons within (*Chronicle* 491). Gildas writes of the battle of Mount Badon as a besetting (*DEB* 26.1). On a smaller scale there was the onset against a hall, such as Finnsburg. A hall of this kind would likely have an enclosing earthwork and palisade wall. The gates would be key in the first onset, then the doors of the hall itself. If the hall was strongly held one shift might be to fire the thatch, and so drive the withstanders out into the open. Bede tells how, in 651, the heathen Penda of Mercia beset the Northumbrian fortress of Bamburgh. Penda had the nearby settlements torn down for their beams, rafters, and thatch. He then had these stacked against the walls, and set alight. However, the saintly Aidan prayed, and a shift of the wind drove back the fire against the onsetters, causing them to give up the attack (*HE* III.16).

The dawn onset, taking the other war-host unawares, was also a well-known part of warcraft in the Heroic Age. And there was another gain here. With war being carried on mostly in the summer, a dawn onset made use of the cool of the morning. Making use of nearby woodland for cover was, like enough, another shift of the warcrafty. (The Vikings are known to have done this, in their war-making, AD 800-1000.) It would have been hard to tell the numbers of men screened among the trees, and hard to see their goings to and fro. And if an onset from woodland was withstood, the war-host might withdraw to its shelter.

The Anglo-Saxons do not seem to have cared for fighting on horseback. The horse might be ridden to battle, but it did not play a great part thereafter (though a few warriors, working on their own, might ride out and seek to harass the foe). In truth the horses of Britain (and throughout northern Europe at this time) were only 8-10 hands – about the size of a Shetland pony – and too small for cavalry work.[503] If the British war leader, Arthur, did indeed turn the tide of war about AD 500, and if his 'knights' were horse-warriors, then their horses must have been bought in. For it would have been no light matter to bring on home-bred horses that were great enough and strong enough for cavalry warfare. The mares would have had to be fed a good diet when carrying their foals, and this would be in the winter months when food was hard to find.[504] The business would have taken several generations.

So the Anglo-Saxons did their fighting on foot, and were by no means easy prey for horse-warriors. War-hardened men could well throw back an onset by cavalry. Indeed, in a battle of the Heroic Age (as in any age) the overcoming was not merely a matter of force or weaponry, but of strength of heart and of the ties that bound one to friends in the shieldwall. A man might also call up thoughts of his forebears, as did Ælfwine at Maldon (*The Battle of Maldon* lines 216-9).

Tacitus tells us that before a battle the host sent forth their war-chant. This was a harsh roar, rising and falling as the warriors set their shields before their faces, so that the sound might swell out through being 'thrown back'. And the chant was not only for stirring up the heart-strength of the warriors. By listening to the sound men might foretell the outcome of the battle about to begin. So would they put fear into their foes – or themselves! (*Germania* 3)

---

503 RHC Davies, quoted in SS Evans, *Lords of battle*, p.38n.

504 S Pollington, *The English Warrior*, p.189.

The heart of the battle array was the shieldwall, with the warriors in line, each man bracing his shield on the left shoulder and knee, and overlapping his neighbour's shield a little. Thus each man helped to guard his neighbour, and was guarded in turn, while the foe came up against a thicket of spears. The battle would open with light spearmen, bowmen, and slingers in small groups, sending their missiles against each other, seeking to thin and break up the other's line. (And there may have been something more. Later Viking sources show that the casting of a spear over, or at, the foe, was believed to bring down their doom.) This first stage of the battle would end as the two shieldwalls drew close, and the light spearmen and bowmen withdrew to the flanks or rear.

The onset against a shieldwall might be by means of a wedge-shaped battle line that would seek to breach the wall. This tactic was known to the Romans, and the military writer Vegetius says that soldiers called it the 'boar's head'.[505] If a breach was made then the withstanders would be broken up into smaller groups, but if the wedge crumbled and was driven back it would be the onsetters who would be left splintered. The standard answer to the wedge was to draw men back in a 'V'-shape, over against the wedge, and crush it between the two arms of the 'V'. (The Romans called this the pincer or 'forceps'.)[506] Another approach was to seek to turn the flanks of the other's line. It is likely that part of the war-host would be kept back behind the line, to be sent to strengthen a threatened flank.

The breaking point of a battle might come through the death of a leader, or of a leading warrior, or perhaps through the taking of a standard. Men who turned and ran were like to be cut down, and it was at this stage that the worst of the slaughter happened. The closing act of the drama would be the last stand of the 'hearth' warriors over their fallen lord.

## *Weapons*

It was the right of every free Anglo-Saxon to hold weapons and, indeed, he was bound to bear them. They were a mark of his standing, both in this life and in the grave and the life beyond. The giving of weapons played a key part in social ritual. The sword and the axe were the 'higher' weapons (though the axe less so, after the fifth century). Perhaps some ten to thirty warriors in every hundred would have had a sword. The thrusting spear was the weapon of the common warrior, though a sword might be given him as a reward for some outstanding warplay.

---

[505] Vegetius III.19, quoted in R Underwood *Anglo-Saxon Weapons and Warfare*, p.131.

[506] See R Underwood *Anglo-Saxon Weapons and Warfare* pp.131-4, and S Pollington *The English Warrior* pp.182-3.

## Swords

These might be shorter or longer. The early English warrior might wield a weapon with a narrow blade 3-12 inches long (more a war knife than a sword). Or he might wield the 'seax' (21-30 inches long), or the longsword (about 34-37 inches).

The kind of furnace in use in Anglo-Saxon times did not work that well, and the iron ore was not of high worth.[507] Yet Anglo-Saxon smiths were skilled at their task, and they made better steel than either the Romans or the Normans.[508] There were simple laminated and forge-welded weapons, but the best swords were made by pattern-welding, in which the iron was beaten into strips, then twisted together and forge-welded. These swords were 'lithe' and springy, and thus hard to break. Cutting edges were sharpened with a grindstone. The hilt was made from wood, horn or bone, and was often decorated with metal fittings. The balance of the early English sword meant that it was better for the slash stroke, rather than for hacking or thrusting. Sometimes mere strength might be a man's undoing, as in the case of a warrior whose downward stroke left his sword stuck fast in the other's shield. A deft twisting of the shield might then wrench the sword from his hand.

A study of the skeletons at an Anglo-Saxon graveyard (such as those at Eccles, Kent) may show the marks of sword, arrow or throwing spear.[509] And there must have been many cases of men dying from blood-poisoning, after being wounded by weapons that were not surgically clean. This may have led to the belief in the venomous blade.[510]

The sheath for a sword was made of wood, covered with leather. The inside was often lined with fleece or fur, and the grease would help to hold off damp, thus keeping the blade from rusting.

Sometimes a bead of glass or amber was attached to the neck of a sheath, by a strap or thong. This may have been a charm, or it might have been a kind of 'healing stone', for healing the wounds given by the sword. (Two Icelandic sagas speak of such stones, though they were kept in a bag, and either tied to the sheath or hung around the neck.)[511]

Warriors were sometimes called upon to swear great oaths on their swords, the meaning being that if the warrior afterwards broke his troth the sword would forsake him in time of need, or even turn against him. The warrior might also swear troth to his lord with his hand on the hilt of his lord's sword.

---

[507] R Underwood, p.48.
[508] S Pollington, p.108n.
[509] R Underwood, p.65.
[510] S Pollington, p.152n.
[511] R Underwood, p.61.

A sword was not merely a blade with a market price, it was a 'maððum', a treasure above price. The stored up 'life' of the sword – the battles in which it played a part, the warriors who had wielded it, the oaths sworn upon its naked edge, the feuds it had stirred or settled – these together were the sum of its 'force'.[512] Such a sword might bear a name. One of the best known was 'Mimming', the great sword wrought by the smith, Welund. Another was 'Hrunting' the sword that Hrothgar loaned to Beowulf (*Beowulf* lines 1455-64). Beowulf's own sword was 'Nægling', that is, 'Nailing' (*Beowulf*, line 2680). And there was 'Screp', the sword wielded by Offa of Angeln. A sword might also be marked with a short runic text (nearly always on the hilt). The 'maððum' sword was closely bound up with the ongoing life and well-being of the kindred. It was part of the kindred's 'luck'. The sword was perhaps handed on by father to daughter, to be passed on to her children. (So would the weapon 'rest' between generations.)[513]

The keen edge of a sword might be undone by witchcraft, through 'blunting' spells (perhaps wrought by someone looking at the sword[514]). So a warrior who would outwit rather than be outwitted – one who was bent on fame and booty, a true follower of Woden – might keep another sword, perhaps the shorter 'seax', and hold it out of sight, beyond the reach of spells. This was a more chancy weapon, perhaps a bringer of ill-luck. It might be stained with death already, through having been picked up after a battle, or plundered from a grave-mound. It was a weapon for stabbing, for dealing deep-thrust wounds.

## Spears

Spear shafts were traditionally made from ash, though hazel, apple, oak and maple were also used. Spear length ranged from about five feet to nine feet. The common warrior had two spears, the first a throwing spear, and the other for thrusting, or for use as a pike. The thrusting spear had 'wings' lest it sink in too deeply, so making it hard to pull out quickly in the press of battle. At the point of balance of the spear, about one third down the shaft from the blade, a cord or thong was wound tightly, to serve as a grip. A spear might be wielded underarm, giving more force to the thrust, or overarm striking at the foe's face and shoulders over the top of his shield. The thrusting spear was also a hunting weapon, and a weapon for swineherds (to hold off bears, wolves or boars).

The 'angon' spear was based on the Roman 'pilum', and was likely a status weapon. It had a short head (which might be barbed), an iron shank about two feet long, and a wooden shaft six feet long. When it pierced a shield the barbs would stop it being withdrawn, and with the long iron shank it could not be cut free. Its weight would then bear the shield down.

---

512 S Pollington, p.35.

513 S Pollington, p.46

514 S Pollington, p.112.

## Bows

Finds of bows and arrows are rare in England, so that it is sometimes said that the Anglo-Saxons did not use bows in war. It does seem that the high-born warrior looked on the bow as more a hunting weapon than a weapon for battle. Yet it is hard to believe that so forceful a weapon was put aside. Perhaps it was left to the common fighting man. It was cheap, and something that he would have anyway. As to so few being found in England, this may be because they have not often survived in English soils.

Germanic bows were 'longbows', some five to six feet long, traditionally made from yew, though ash or elm was also used. The bow stave was so chosen that the back of the stave was sapwood, and the 'belly' heartwood. The elastic sapwood worked under tension, the resilient heartwood under compression.[515] The 'horn-bow' must have been made of wood and horn – unless the term is simply a poetic word referring to the curve of the weapon. Bowstrings were made from animal sinew. Arrow-shafts were made of ash, poplar or hazelwood. Arrowheads were made from bone or iron, and they were of three kinds: the barbed head, the triangular or square-sectioned 'bodkin' (which had a long tapering point that could even pass through the links of a mail shirt), and the leaf-shaped head. An Anglo-Saxon bow likely had an accurate range of 160-200 feet, and a far range of 500-650 feet. But the speed and force of an arrow fall quickly, because of air friction, so that at 160 feet penetration is only three-fourths of that gained at 30 feet.[516]

## Other weapons

The 'fransisca' was a throwing axe, with a range of about 40 feet. It was a weapon of the Franks, but it is found quite often in Kent, and also in Essex, Sussex and Wiltshire. The axe-hammer was used in Europe, and one has been found at Howletts, in Kent, probably gained through trade with Merovingian Gaul. The so-called 'staff-sword' may have been a pole-axe.

## Shields

The shield ('hildeboard', or battle-board), was the warrior's main defence in battle, and with its long, spiked metal 'boss' it could also be a formidable thrusting weapon. A hole was cut behind the boss, and a grip fitted in place. This would have been a handle made of wood or iron, with cloth or leather bound round it. There may also have been padding inside the boss. An early English shield was 18-27 inches across, about one fifth to one third of an inch thick, and likely weighed 6-11 pounds. A small shield was good in that it was light and easy to handle in a one-to-one fight. But the greater shield was needed in the 'shieldwall' of the pitched battle. There the warrior must first ward off thrown weapons (spears, axes), then face the foe right in

---

[515] R Underwood, p.28.

[516] R Underwood, p.32, 34.

front of him, and also those either side of him, threatening to get past his guard. A warrior with a shield was still at risk about the head and neck, and also the sword arm and the lower leg.

Alder, willow and poplar were the woods most often used. (The lime or linden so often spoken of in song, was in truth fairly rare.[517]) These are all light woods, fibrous and tough. The boards would often be covered with cow-hide on the outer side, and perhaps on the inner side too. The hide would be put on wet, and allowed to shrink on to the board. The hide would help to slow down the splintering of the wood in battle, and (if treated with dubbing) to weather-proof it. Plaques of wild beast figures were sometimes set into the shield. These would have strengthened it, and they may have had some heraldic or religious meaning, too. Sometimes a shield may have been fitted with leather straps so that a warrior could carry it slung over his shoulder. A high-born warrior might have a 'shield-bearer' with him, carrying a spare shield.

## Mail shirts

Such chain-mail as was to be had in the fifth century was likely Roman, though some of it may have been home-wrought. A mail shirt from Vimose, Denmark, dated to the fourth or fifth century, was made from 20,000 riveted iron rings.[518] Such a shirt would blunt the force of cutting strokes, but a strong thrust could burst the links asunder, not only wounding the wearer, but driving some of the links into the flesh. And such a shirt was heavy, so that in a fast-moving battle the wearer would be somewhat hampered. Only the highest leaders in an early English war-host would have had mail. Others may have had stout leather jerkins, and perhaps strips of toughened leather forming a kind of kilt guarding the thighs.

## War-helms

Helmets, like mail, were only for the highest-born in the war-host. Some of those around were plundered Roman helmets, but Germanic smiths also made them, having Roman helmets for their model. Sometimes a helmet had a boar crest, probably meant to keep watch over the warrior. (The boar symbolised strength.) The 'grimhelm' was a helmet with a face-plate that was meant to over-awe and to stir dread. A helmet might have a mail 'curtain', shielding the neck. (Leslie Alcock says there is no evidence that either the Britons or the Anglo-Saxons wore such helmets on the field of battle.[519]) Simpler helmets could be made from leather, boiled and shaped.

---

[517] S Pollington, p.136.

[518] R Underwood, pp.91-2.

[519] L Alcock, *Arthur's Britain*, p.334.

# The warband and the hall

The high point of life in the Heroic Age is summed up in the lord and his warband, seated in hall, feasting and glorying after warlike deeds wrought.

## *The lord and his warband ...*

The warriors of a warband (who were single men), were known as the 'gesiþas', that is, 'those who fare forth together'. It was a fitting name for a band whose ties were strengthened in a shared life of hardship. Another name was 'heorðgeneatas', that is, 'hearth-retainers' (in Latin the 'comitatus'). As well as heart-strength and hardihood the warrior was to be marked by 'maegen' (modern English 'main'), that is, 'force' and inborn skill. In the warband there would be both young warriors and 'doughty' men, hardened in battle. These latter were also wisemen or 'redesmen'. While the lord of a warband would have his own close kin in leadership within the band, a war-tried leader would draw men from elsewhere and further strengthen his hand.

Warlike training may have begun as early as eight years with wrestling, running, leaping, and other drills and games. Going out with the hunt would have helped the youth learn to handle spear and bow, and also to face up to the threat of boars, or even bears. Fosterage of boys from seven to eight years old, up to fourteen years, was well-known among those lords who were bound in friendship. A youth became a warrior at about fourteen years, and he would then stay in the warband, perhaps, until he was about forty years old.

The early English set great store by ties of kinship and lordship, and they fostered those ties through two-way giving. A lord had to be open-handed with gifts of gold and weapons, and he must needs keep open house, setting meat and mead before the warband gathered in hall. For his part the warrior must 'earn his mead' by keeping troth with his lord. Even if his lord were driven from the land, the warrior must go with him, though there was no outcome more dreaded than to be a 'wrecca' (exile). In battle he must be 'hot-handed', hardy, fearless. He must be steadfast even when all was lost and death near at hand – yet always without 'show'. His heart's longing must be for good fame, his heart's dread the shame of outliving a fallen lord. If their lord fell in battle, all true warriors would have but one goal, to fight on and shed blood for blood, 'to lay down their lives, or to avenge their lord' (*Battle of Maldon* line 207). For both lord and man such giving and gaining was their 'law' (and that word is not too strong). Keeping troth with one's lord came before even troth towards one's own kindred. Often the two troths went together, though not always. In the Cynewulf/Cyneheard fight in the *Chronicle* annal for 755 there were a number of warriors who had kinsmen on the other side.

## ... Seated in hall

The Anglo-Saxon timbered hall could be as much as eighty feet long, and some thirty feet wide, often with simple length:width ratios, such as 2:1 or 4:1. One way of building the hall was by setting upright planks in trenches (which might be dug as much as eight feet down). This is called a 'stave' building. Another way of building was to set the uprights further apart, and then either lay planks, one atop the other, between them ('bulwark' construction), or fill the spaces with wattle and daub. Sometimes the infill might be dry-stone or turf. The evidence for buttresses shows that many hall-buildings were lofty.

The inside of the hall was open, though there might be aisles (as evidenced by post-holes). Sometimes there may have been partitions at one or both ends of the hall, making sleeping rooms for women and children. (On the other hand these may have slept in outlying huts.) The floor of the hall might be packed earth, or it might be cobbled or planked. Wooden planking was sometimes several feet above ground-level. (In *Beowulf* lines 1316-17, the 'hall-wood' boomed as Beowulf and his men crossed the hall, and in the *Finnsburg Fragment* line 30, the burg-floor 'spoke' as the fighting ebbed and flowed.) The floor was often strewn with straw and/or sweet-smelling herbs. The roof (which could be gabled or hipped) was usually thatched, though turf or wooden shingles may also have been used.

The way into the hall was through doors on the long sides. The doors would have had hinges made of iron or wood, and they were closed with a latch. The hall was also a stronghold, so windows were, like enough, few and small. (They must keep out winter draughts, too.) These may have had vellum (calf-skin) stretched over them, as this would help keep out draughts, but would also let in some light. More often the windows were likely shuttered. The inside of the hall would have been dim, even in day-time, lit mostly from the fire in the middle of the hall, and from candles and lamps burning animal fat. Braziers burning charcoal may have been used to give more heat in corners away from the great hearth. There would have been draughts, smoke, hounds (stretched out, or snarling over bones), mice or rats scuttling in and out of dark corners, and in winter a sparrow flying in one door, out of the snow and rain, then out again by the other door (Bede, *HE* II.13).

The walls and beams of the hall may have had carvings wrought in them, and some of these may have been painted. There may also have been tapestries and woven standards hanging up, together with swords, spears, axes and shields won from fallen foes. These would call past battles to mind and foster the war-like feel of the place.

There would have been little in the way of furniture: chests (some iron-bound and lockable), shelving, tables (often of the trestle type), benches, stools, with some cured skins and fleeces giving a little in the way of comfort. The hall was also the sleeping place of the warband. At the end of the evening the mead benches would be moved aside, and bedding and pillows laid on the floor.

Around the hall there would often be an enclosing earthwork and ditch. (The hall 'Heorot' in *Beowulf* had a manned palisade wall.) Ranged about within the earthwork there would be thatched huts, hearths for metal-working, pits (refuse pits, quarry pits, latrines), byres, pens for livestock, drainage ditches, pathways, perhaps a well. Sunken-floored huts (such as those found at Sutton Courteney) were common in early English settlements. These were about 10-13 feet long, 8-10 feet wide, and sunk some eighteen inches to two feet into the ground. It is thought that there would have been a floor built over the sunken part, making a place for storing goods, or perhaps to be filled with straw in winter, to help keep the building warmer. Some of these buildings may have been sleeping rooms, but others were workshops for weaving, dairying and other tasks. Cooking was carried on either in huts such as these, or outside in the yard.

## *… Feasting and glorying after warlike deeds wrought*

The hall was the setting for feasting and gift-giving, most often in the evening. (Welsh songcraft, too, speaks of logs blazing and lighted candles. In other words, the main goings-on in the hall happened in the evening.) The 'symbel' was a high and solemn feast, an almost 'religious' gathering when, on a set day in the year, the lord sat upon the high settle, with his warriors about him on the mead benches. There was strong drink and ritual speech, and then, as the lord sat with drawn sword across his lap, each warrior would lay head and hands on the lord's knee, most likely as a sign that he was his man up to, and beyond, death. This ritual was thought of as taking place outside time and outside earthly geography, in a sacred landscape.[520]

The 'symbel' happened in the evening, with the gift-giving the following morning. Then, seated on the gift stool, the lord would hand out weapons, mail-shirts, horses, rings and other treasure. (A good lord would keep only a third of the hoard won in war, and give away two-thirds to his men.) From this gift ritual the hall was sometimes called the 'ring-hall', and the lord was 'ring-giver', 'ring-lord', or 'treasurer-giver'.

It was only after the 'symbel' was over that the feasting took place. Here, everything was bound within strict rules, the warriors being seated by rank, and served with mead or ale from the foremost among them down to the least. (It was the lord's wife and daughters who bore the drinking horns among the seated warriors.) The feast was also the setting for listening to the poets, to their songs of the old heroes of the Germanic world, to tales of the forefathers and tales of the deeds of their own warband. It was part of a warrior's reward to have his deeds of high fame sung in hall. Then there might be riddles to be 'unrimed', kinship lists to be told, and boasts and vows about deeds to be wrought in the next warring. And older warriors might 'render rede' (give advice). Thus did Wulfgar speak to Hrothgar, without being asked and sure that he would be heeded (*Beowulf* lines 366-70). The gladness of the

---

[520] S Pollington, *The English Warrior*, pp.33-4.

hall bound the group together, and bound hall and warband together under the same doom. So, in the tale of Finn and Finnsburg, the overthrow of Finn's warband, and the burning down of his hall, are one and the same grief.

There was also another kind of hall, where there was no hall bliss, where treasure was not shared out, but rather hoarded so that it brought no good to the holder. The under-mere hall of the monster Grendel in the poem *Beowulf* (lines 1513-18, 1612-13) was one such hall. Another was the dragon's 'barrow hall' in the same poem (lines 2270-80, 2288-2302, 2756-81).

The life of the true hall was the best this earth held out to the heathen English. When Christianity was brought to the early English it struck a rich chord, for it, too, was about a lord – the Lord – eating and drinking with his followers. Our word 'lord' is from 'loaf' and 'ward', referring to the guardian of the loaf, the provider. As an Anglo-Saxon lord undertook to give his followers food and drink, and they in turn bound themselves to be true to him and to each other, so at the heart of the life of the church there was the Lord's Supper. The Lord Christ gave his followers bread and wine, a picture of spiritual food and drink, and those who took part in the Supper bound themselves to be true to him and to each other. And as the feasting in an Anglo-Saxon hall was an earthly foreshadowing of that 'Waelheall', where warrior-heroes were borne after death, so the Lord's Supper foreshadowed the wedding feast of the Lamb in the High Hall of heaven. What was new in Christianity was not the feast itself, but this being a feast for everyone, and not only for the high-born fighting men. Now all could be glad in the young hero, the Christ, who had opened the way for them.[521] Indeed, at the feasting of the Christ-folk, the last were first, and it was the greatness of the lowly that was held in high worth.

---

[521] K Herbert, Looking for the Lost Gods of England, p.32.

# Anglo-Saxon heathenism

No attempt is made here to give a full account of Anglo-Saxon heathenism. But something needs to be said about the god Woden, and about the lady Frija/ Freya, because they form part of the background of our Finnsburg tale. Some account is also given of the runes, and of lesser otherworld beings, such as elves.

## The Germanic gods

Woden was first among the Germanic gods. He was the god of 'onblowing' (inspiration). Another of his names was 'Grim' or 'Grimr'. He sometimes went about shrouded in a hood. Woden was the god of the lordly and the high-born fighting men.[522] (Thunor was the god of the common warriors.) The fraught figure of Woden could be the making of a warrior-hero, but also, in the end, his undoing. He would give out weapons to chosen followers, but those who took them were thereafter bound to serve him to death and beyond. And at the time set by Woden he would withdraw his help. In one later Norse tale Woden gives a wondrous sword to the hero Sigmund, but at the time that Sigmund is to die Woden appears on the battlefield and himself shatters the sword with his spear.

Woden would also give rede ('advice') of high worth, as when he showed Hadding how to form the battlefield 'wedge' of warriors for breaking a shieldwall. Again he met with Harald Wartooth of the Danes, and gave him word that he would not suffer any wounds. Later, Woden withdrew his favour, stirred up strife between Harald and his great friend King Ring, and showed Ring the high secret of the 'wedge'. As Harald was going to the battle against Ring he became aware that the driver of his war-wain was none other than the god Woden. Harald pleaded that he might overcome in battle one more time, and he swore that he would give Woden all the slain. But Woden was unmoved. He flung Harald from the wain, and slew him with his sword as he fell. In some of the poems there are bold words spoken against the trothlessness of the god Woden. In the tenth century poem *Hákonarmál* the slain Hakon is welcomed at the hall of Odin (Woden), but he answers coldly, 'Surely we have deserved victory of the gods ... We will keep our war-gear ready to hand.' In *Lokasenna* Odin is told to his face that often he gave victory to cowards who did not deserve it.[523] In Bede's record of Paulinus preaching the Christian faith before king Edwin of Northumbria, the priest of the old heathen faith, Coifi, says openly. 'For a long time now I have realised that our religion is worthless; for the more diligently I sought the truth in our cult, the less I found it' (*HE* II.13).

'Frija' is a truly old name, from an Indo-European root, akin to Sanskrit 'priya' (beloved one), and to Old English 'freo' (high-born lady), and 'freond' (friend). The

[522] P Stafford, The East Midlands in the Early Middle Ages, p.173.

[523] HR Ellis Davidson, Gods and Myths of Northern Europe, pp.49-50.

name can thus bear a number of meanings, from rank lust through to queenliness.[524] Later Northern mythology made two goddesses, Frigg the wife of Odin, and Freya the stirrer of lust, the sorceress. Kathleen Herbert has written, 'It is either ironic, or very subtle, that the queen should be called Frigg (the desired) and the witch-whore should be called Freya (the lady)'.[525] The English, however, did not split the goddess in two. Frija or Freya was a goddess of love, of war, of foretelling, of comeliness and alluring. When she rode to battle she went on the great boar 'Hildisvin' (battle-swine). In one Norse tale it is told of her that she longed to have the wondrous necklace, 'Brisingamen'. The four dwarfs who held it, named as their price a night each with her, and Freya in the end agreed.

## *The runes*

One of the most telling poems in Northern lore speaks of Woden and how he wrested knowledge of the runes. He hung on the World Tree for nine nights, starving and pierced by a spear, until at last he grasped the runes. Afterwards he did not tell the full twenty-four letters of the 'futhark' (the runic alphabet), but only eighteen (two nines), and these were spells for chanting, speaking or whispering.

The name 'futhark' is made from the first six letters of the runic alphabet ('th' being one letter). In Anglo-Saxon and Frisian areas new letters were wrought to fill new linguistic needs, and the 'futhark' was built up to twenty-eight or more runes. Some of the letters are clearly akin to the Roman alphabet, but others are nothing like. Early finds of rune-inscribed objects in eastern Europe (Roumania, Russia, central Germany) suggest possible origins in that general area, perhaps among the Goths, on the Danube frontier or on the Vistula.[526] Another suggestion is that they were forged by Romanised Germani in the Alpine valleys of southern Switzerland and northern Italy. R I Page leans towards the theory of the Danish scholar, Erik Moltke, that they originated in southern Jutland. The earliest inscriptions date from the second century AD, but they are so mature that it is fair to say that runic history probably goes back not less than a century or so before that. This would bring the invention of the runic alphabet back to near the beginning of the Christian era'.[527]

Runes were cut on wood, metal, bone, horn or stone, hence their straight-sidedness (curved letters being much harder to cut). Sometimes runes were used for very straightforward things, like carving the owner's name on a sword. But the word 'rune' is thought to be rooted in Old English 'run' meaning 'secret, mystery'. This has led to the conclusion that the script is related to magic and the occult, and that rune-masters were thought to have supernatural powers which enabled them to control or release magical power. Thus, for example, R I Page suggests that the

---

[524] K Herbert, Looking for the Lost Gods of England, p.25.

[525] K Herbert, *Lost Gods*, p.25.

[526] RI Page, *Runes*, p.9.

[527] RI Page, *Runes*, p.9.

runes on a stone slab that formed part of a grave chamber at Kylver on Gotland were meant to stop the dead body in the grave getting out.[528] Francis Owen notes that another word used of the runes means 'to paint', which would suggest that the letters were sometimes painted, or that paint was introduced into the inscribed lines. He suggests that the colour most often used was likely red, that is, blood-hue – perhaps thought to strengthen the magic.[529] Catherine Hills notes that 'some early inscriptions do seem so enigmatic that religious or magical interpretation is plausible. To illiterate people the concept of writing, the transmission of ideas without face-to-face contact or speech, might in itself seem supernatural'.[530] Yet the runes were also widely used as a practical everyday script.

'Each rune had a name that was also a meaningful word.'[531] Thus the name of the letter 'f' was *'fehu' meaning, first, 'cattle', then 'money, wealth'. The letter 'u' was *'uruz', perhaps referring to the aurochs, the great wild ox, and having the symbolic further meaning 'male strength, virility'. The letter 'ï' was *'i(h)waz' or *'eihwaz', that is, 'yew-tree', the letter 'e' was *'ehwaz' or 'horse'. It may be that cult or magical significance had become attached to certain words. Thus the spear-shaped 't' letter is named *'tiwaz/*tiewaz', that is, the god Tiw, and it points to a warlike concept. When marked twice on a sword, it would have laid a charm on it.[532] Owen suggests that the 'h' rune *'hagalaz' ('hail') signified destruction, and when cut on a gravestone was meant to call down destruction on the desecrator of the grave.[533] Runes were likely used to still the waves of a stormy sea, to ward off sickness or other evil, to ensure victory in the fight, to undo a hate-spell. In *Beowulf* line 501 Unferth 'unbound a battle-rune'. Runes were also used to tell of things to come. In *Germania* 10, Tacitus tells how the ancient Germans would cut a bough from a nut-bearing tree, slice it into strips, mark the strips with signs, and then cast them onto a white cloth. Then the priest (or the father of the family, in the case of a small private matter) would 'read' what had randomly fallen on the cloth – and yet not randomly, for the outfalling was surely guided from the Otherworld.

The earliest runic inscription known in England comes from the cremation cemetery at Caistor-by-Norwich, and dates from about 400. It is on a roe-deer's ankle bone, and it is likely that it was once a gaming piece. It reads 'raïhan', that is, 'roe-deer'. Page notes that the 'h' rune has the north European, not the Anglo-Frisian, shape, and he suggests that the folk cremated here may have come from southern Denmark. He adds that other, more recent, finds of early runic monuments seem to have Scandinavian affinities.[534]

---

528 RI Page, *Runes*, p.18.
529 F Owen, The Germanic People, p.213.
530 C Hills, Origins of the English, p.50.
531 RI Page, *Runes*, p.14.
532 S Pollington, *The English Warrior*, p.51.
533 F Owen, The Germanic People, p.219.
534 RI Page, *Runes*, p.32.

The most famed of English runic objects is probably the whale-bone ivory Franks casket, found in a French farmhouse in the nineteenth century and acquired by Sir Augustus Wollaston Franks who gave it to the British Museum. (One panel was missing. It turned up later, and was bought by a collector who gave it to an Italian museum.) The inscriptions are 'in Old English and Latin, using both conventional and encoded runes as well as Insular script', and the carver used a Northumbrian or north Mercian dialect of the early eighth century. The scenes mingle biblical, Germanic and classical story.[535]

There was certainly some rivalry between scripts in later Anglo-Saxon England, but it was not a religious rivalry. There is no reason to think that the Church disapproved of the runic script. (It is used on the coffin lid of St Cuthbert, and on the very Christian Ruthwell cross.) In the end the runic script lost out to the more prestigious Roman script.[536]

## *Otherworld beings*

To the early English (heathen and Christianised) there was a host of otherworld beings about them. The English were aware of 'wælcyrian', and of 'helrune' (women who sought knowledge from the dead), of the 'nihtgenga' and the 'nightmare' (a female monster who harassed folk while they slept). There were also the elves – dun or hill elves, water-elves (living in springs, pools and water-courses), wood-elves (in groves and wealdlands), sea-elves, and wild elves (dwelling on the moors). In *Beowulf*, elves, like the monster Grendel, are kindred of the murderer and outcast, Cain (see lines 107-112). Illness and other troubles might be traced to an elfish arrow, loosed in spite. But the early English also saw elves as passing fair. One of their words for womanly loveliness was 'ælfscine' (elf-sheen, lovely as an elf). Yet a lovely elf-woman was still harmfraught and like to be a man's undoing.

---

[535] L Webster and J Backhouse, The Making of England:Anglo-Saxon Art and Culture AD 600-900, pp.101, 103.

[536] RI Page, *Runes*, p.42.

# Some notes on the outlook of the early English

## *Of wisdom and wyrd*

The world of the heroic age was shot through with deeply held beliefs – in the worth of wisdom, in the ties of kinship and lordship, in the 'laws' of wrath-wreaking (vengeance) and of 'guest-right' (hospitality), in the weaving of 'wyrd' (doom).

The early English set a high worth on 'wisdom', and saw it as a manifold thing. It meant a right understanding of the things that happen, insight into the hearts of men and women, an awareness of rights and duties (one's own and those of the kindred). The poet of *The Wanderer* pictured the wise man as one who holds out, who is not too hot-hearted, not hasty in speech, who was not a weak warrior, who showed forethought, was not over-greedy for wealth, not over-glad nor over-mild, not given to high words without having a good understanding of a matter (lines 63-9). Such wisdom was gained partly through the teaching of the young by the old, partly through living life and finding its ins and outs, its ups and downs.

Then there were 'oughts' – laws almost – that threaded through daily life. In the midst of many 'oughts' lord and man might find themselves pulled two ways and well-nigh torn asunder. A lord was bound to welcome guests to his hall, but what if those guests turned out to be of the same folk as his father's slayers? He was bound to keep troth with his wife, but what if the wedlock had been forged as a deed of 'peace-weaving', to seal the ending of a feud – a feud that was not, in truth, dead? In after-time the husband might be put in mind that his wife's kin boasted of weapons taken from his own slain forebears. Thus it was that in one famous tale the love of the Heathobard, Ingeld, for his Danish wife Freawaru waned, and the doomed peace was unwoven. In the Waldere story Hagena is torn between troth to his friend, Waldere, and troth to his lord, Guthhere. And so, in the Frisian tale, did Hengest brood long over his two 'oughts' – to wreak wrath for Hnæf, to keep troth with Finn.

The belief that wrong could not be left to rest, but must be 'righted' by shedding the blood of the wrong-doer, was held so strongly that the Christian church made hardly a dent in it (though the righting might now be seen as wrought by God, through the avenger). So the monk Bede tells how Augustine called the leaders of the British church to a meeting, and would have them work with him in bringing the gospel to the English. But they thought him high-hearted and answered 'no'. Augustine is then said to have warned that if they would not take the gospel to the English then they would one day meet death at their hands. Some while after this, 'as though by divine judgment', some twelve hundred British monks who had gone with the British war-host, to pray for them in the battle at Chester (about AD 613-6), were slaughtered by the heathen king Æthelfrith of Bernicia (*HE* II.2).

The early English were deeply aware of 'wyrd', which is the root of modern English 'weird' (though the meaning of today's word is far other). A one-word rendering of 'wyrd' would be 'doom', or 'fate'. A fuller, truer rendering might be 'the way things happen', and the way things happen was shaped both by deeds wrought of old, and by things yet to come. Wyrd was seen as hard, unbending, unsparing. 'Wyrd is cruellest' quoth the poet.[537] Yet 'wyrd' might also help a man, if he was, in truth, undoomed: 'Weird saves oft the man undoomed if he undaunted be!' (*Beowulf* lines 572-3, Alexander's translation, see also lines 2291-3). But then, again, the Anglo-Saxon saw well that though a man were not doomed to fall in battle yet life is beset with sorrows, for man is earth-born, death-bound, a mere breath.

Willing or unwilling, men and women found themselves caught up in the unfolding of the great world-strife. For in the Northern world view the gods and heroes were arrayed against dread forces bent on evil, and at the last those gods and heroes would be overwhelmed. At the beginning of the end there would be the great winter, unbroken through three wearisome years. There would be an outbreak of untold wickedness, of bitter warfare among men, of grievous sorrows. After this there would be mighty earthquakes, the darkening of the sun, the great serpent rising from the sea, a last battle between gods and giants in which both hosts would fall. There would be flames climbing up to the heavens, and the sea covering the earth. Then, after the overwhelming (which the sons of the gods, alone, would live through) a new earth, green and rich, would come into being.

Meantime the hero fought on, alongside the gods. Though he did not have hope, yet a man need not be bowed by 'wyrd'. If he took upon him that which was fated then he overcame at the last. The true warrior felt deeply 'the worth of defeated valour'.[538]

Christianity, when it came, did change the picture, though not all at once. The Christian fought the same old foes, and those foes would be overcome in the end, though not while this world lasts. In *Beowulf* a sense of foreboding, of darkness drawing in, of man's life and how fleeting it is, are still very much the stuff of the poet's outlook. It is in the eighth century *Life of Guthlac*, that we see another picture. The young Guthlac had led a warband on the Welsh-Mercian border, waging war with earthly weapons. After nine years he threw it up, became first a monk, then a hermit on Crowland in the Fens, cut off from the world of men. And there, in the manner of the great Egyptian hermit, Anthony (AD 251-356), he fought with spiritual weapons against the devils who came to plague him. They came night after night, but they found that in this warrior of Christ they had met their match, and at the last they fled from him.[539]

---

537 'Maxims' II, line 5, in LJ Rodrigues, Anglo-Saxon Verse Charms, Maxims & Heroic Legends, p.125.

538 JRR Tolkien, quoted in H Mayr-Harting, *The Coming of Christianity*, p.236.

539 H Mayr-Harting, pp.236-9.

# Old English songcraft

## The early English poet

The Old English word for a bard was 'scop', a word that seems to be close kin to 'scieppan' (to shape, make, destine), and to 'scieppend' (maker, shaper). The Old Germanic world held skill with words in high regard, as high a skill as the right wielding of weapons. A poetic word might, in truth, be taken as no mere skill of man, but as a word from the god. And indeed, in later Old English, 'scieppend' could be used even of God himself.

Among the things asked of the early English poet there may have been the uttering of right words – for welcoming guests, for making much of friends, for saying the last words of farewell over a grave. It was his business to sing of the high deeds of a lord and his warband. It was also his business to uphold the things the warband (any warband) stood for – the bonds of their shared life, hardihood in war, troth to their lord in life, death and beyond. So would the poet uphold the bonds, and the shared life, of the folkdom itself.

To these ends the poet would go with the band when they went forth a-warring, and he would be there to watch the battle. Indeed, it must be so. How otherwise could he know what had happened and unfold its meaning for the men of his own time, as well as for those who came after? How otherwise would his song ring true, and be believed? The warrior would welcome the poet, for it was in his songs that he, the warrior, would find lasting fame. Yet he might also be on edge before the poet, for he knew that if he let himself down in the fight, then the mockery of the poet, or his simple overlooking, could unmake that warrior's name.

A poet might bide with an open-handed lord, or he might fare from hall to hall, and from land to land. Through such faring he would spread his tales further afield, and he would learn new songs in turn.

## The songcraft

There are only about 30,000 lines of Old English songcraft that have come down to us. (Over 3,000 of these are found in one poem, *Beowulf*.)[540]

No writer of Old English times has set out for us the why and wherefore of the patterns of Old English songcraft. Our understanding of those patterns has been gained by careful study of the poems themselves, and by setting them side by side with poems that have come down to us from other early Germanic tongues.

In manuscripts of Old English verse, there are no headings, and no capital letters to mark a new sentence. The poems are not gathered into 'stands' (or stanzas), nor even into lines, but are written out like prose. Yet the lines are there, the strong flesh

---

[540] See M Alexander's introduction to his translation of *Beowulf*, 1995), p.vii.

and bones of Old English songcraft. Each line of poetry is in truth two half-lines. (Perhaps the pause between them was marked by a stroke on the harp.) Sentences usually begin with the second half-line. And each half-line 'lives' of itself, whilst also being bound to its fellow by 'sound-likeness' (alliteration). The sound-likeness is important, but the stresses are key. There are two stresses in each half-line, which fall on the chief words for the sense (most often nouns, adjectives, and adverbs). The 'fore-sound' of the first stress in the second half-line (called the 'off-verse' or b-verse) sets the pattern of sound-likeness in the line. This stress is called the 'head-stave'. The most common pattern is for the two stresses in the first half-line (the 'on-verse' or a-verse) to share this sound-likeness. Sometimes only the first stress does so, and even more rarely it may be only the second stress that shares it. The second stress of the second half-line must not share in the sound-likeness. (In later Old English songcraft this last stress did sometimes share the sound-likeness, and rhyme also began to be used.)

Here is an example from *The Finnsburg Fragment*:

|  |  |
|---|---|
|  | The raven wheeled, |
| swart and sallow-brown. | Sword's flame gleamed |
| as if all Finnsburg | were afired |

(lines 34-36)

In seeking for words, the early English poet had a great 'wealth-hoard' to draw on, not simply of single words, but of phrases that could be used for key thoughts, the choice depending on the needs of sound-likeness. A breaking-down of the first fifty half-lines of *Beowulf* has shown that only thirteen are not matched, wholly or in part, elsewhere in Old English verse.[541] There was a wealth of 'likewords' (synonyms), words of 'given' meaning (metaphors), and kennings (double-barreled metaphors, such as those for the sea – 'gannet-bath', 'whale-mere', 'swan's riding' and the like). There was a host of likewords for the following: man, ship, sword, king, God, lord, joy, battle, death, exile, grief. Through the use of this rich word-store, something could be said again in a new way, thus strengthening and re-embodying the meaning, slowing down the movement, and giving depth and worth to the verse.[542]

There are other noteworthy features of Old English verse. There are 'bygoings' (digressions) and 'episodes'. The *Beowulf* poet was much given to such. (Episodes make up almost a fourth of his poem.) A good example of a bygoing is found after the poet has sung of Hygelac's thoughtful and open-handed queen, Hygd. He breaks off to put his hearers in mind of another who was far from such, the overweening Modthryth (lines 1931b-62). The 'Tale of Finn' in *Beowulf* (lines 1066b-1159) is an example of an episode. It is not simply a bygoing, for it is fitted into the main tale as the song that is sung in hall by Hrothgar's bard, after the slaying of Grendel.

---

[541] M Alexander, The Earliest English Poems, p.17.
[542] M Alexander, *The Earliest English Poems*, pp.18-19.

Then there are asides and 'alightings' (allusions), touching on highlights, on turning points, on startling or baleful moments. In *Waldere* there is the aside about Theodric the Ostrogoth, and a 'sideways word' on the sword 'Mimming'. One particular kind of alighting is that which touches on things set to happen in coming days. So the *Beowulf* poet speaks of the day when the great hall of Heorot will be burned to the ground (see lines 81-85, 778-82), and of Hygelac's redeless (ill-advised) fame-faring into the lands of the Frisians and Franks, when he 'fell beneath his shield'.

The early English poet was also given to 'under-saying' (understatement). So in *Beowulf* the hero says that it was not given to Dæghrefn (a warrior of the Franks) to hand to his overlord the breastplate of the fallen Hygelac – for the good reason that Beowulf slew the Frank with his bare hands (lines 2503-4).

The early English poet also had a true love of making moral points, of setting forth folk-wisdom, of underlining something good or evil. He had a rich store of sayings to draw on, each shorn of padding and striking to the heart of a thing. In the so-called gnomic verse there are many such sayings: 'Idle hands are leisure enough for the gamester when he throws the dice ... Weary shall he be who runs against the wind ... Guile goes with foul play, skill with what is fitting.'[543]

The lyric refrain is found in Old English songcraft, though not often. It is key to the poem *Deor* with its six-fold, 'That passed away; so may this!'. Another case is, 'Our fate is forked' (Alexander's wording) which comes twice in *Wulf and Eadwacer*.

The poet made use of riddling, of the enigmatic, of the 'two-sided' (ambiguous) word. Such a word might have meanings which lay on its 'borders', or only a little beneath the 'outwardness' of the word. The hearers in hall seemed to take it as rare for things to be as they seemed, so that more often than otherwise they must be 'unknotted.' A case of two-sidedness is the word 'wrecca' (modern English 'wretch'). The Old English word can mean someone who has been driven from his homeland by an overthrower or an incomer, or who has been caught up in a feud that might not be wholly of his making. But it can also fit that man who has brought outlawry upon himself by his own wild deeds. When the word is used of Hengest what are we to understand by it? And when we are straightway told that he was a 'guest' (another two-sided word – it could also mean, 'stranger' or 'foe'), how are we to take that? (see *Beowulf* lines 1137-38) Bliss notes, ruefully, that we can admire and enjoy the many-sidedness when we know the matter, but when that matter is in truth the thing we are trying to fathom, it makes understanding so much harder to reach.[544]

Let us look at some of the tales that, like enough, were part of the 'stock' of the Anglo-Saxon poet: Offa of Angeln, Heoden and Hild, Welund, and Waldere.

---

543 Maxims I C, lines 46-51, in LJ Rodrigues, *Anglo-Saxon Verse Charms, Maxims & Heroic Legends*, p.123.

544 A Bliss, *Finn and Hengest*, p.65.

# Tales from the northern folkdoms

## *Offa of Angeln*

In English kinlore Offa of Angeln was the forefather of the kings of English Mercia, the eighth name back from Penda, the seventh century pagan warrior-king. He is twelfth before that other Offa who was king of Mercia, AD 757-796, and Bretwalda ('Britain-wielder', or high king). The first Offa must have lived in the latter half of the fourth century AD. *Widsith*, lines 35-44, tells how the youthful Offa set 'with single sword' the boundary between the Angles and the Myrgings. Something of the background to this bound-setting comes to light in the writings of the medieval Danish historian Saxo Grammaticus (c.1150-c.1220). The tale seems to be something as follows.

Freawine was lord of the Waernas, and under-king to Wærmund of Angeln, Offa's father. This Freawine was slain by Eadgils, the war-like king of the neighbouring Myrgings. His sons Cedd and Wiga, bent on revenge, set off for the Myrging land and came upon Eadgils alone in the weald. Cedd fought with him while Wiga looked on, but when Cedd was hard pressed and like to be slain, Wiga stepped in and slew Eadgils. The brothers were welcomed as heroes when they first came home, but then tales began to be heard of how, trothless, their onset had been two-against-one. Offa was linked to the brothers in some way, either as brother-in-law or, perhaps more likely, foster brother, and he felt himself to be caught up in their shame. Time went by and king Wærmund grew old. He was then challenged by Meaca, who seems to have been king of the Myrgings under an overlord of the whole Swæfe (Suebi) confederation. The youthful Offa, who had hitherto been dumb, spoke out, saying he would fight both the Myrging lord and a Myrging champion together. So would he undo the shame of Cedd and Wiga. Wærmund brought out his old sword, 'Screp', and with it Offa slew the two Myrgings in the fight on the island of Fifeldor, at the mouth of the Eider. So was the Angle-Myrging boundary fixed at Fifeldor.

One other tale is told of Offa. In *Beowulf* lines 1931-62 the poet alights on it in passing. Modthryth, a princess fair, but fraught, had been wont to bring death upon any man in hall who dared to glance at her. But Offa wed and tamed her, so that she became a great and gracious queen.

## *Heoden and Hild*

Several versions of this tale have come down to us. In the Icelandic of Snorri Sturluson (AD 1179-1241) Hild is borne away by Hethin (Heoden) by main strength. Her father Hogni (Hagena) goes after him, and their two warbands fight. At the end of the day those warriors who have fallen are turned to stone, only to be woken during the night by the craft of Hild. So the fight goes on from day to day, and shall until Doomsday.

In the Middle High German version of the tale (dating from about the same time as Snorri), Hagena, king in Ireland, hangs all word-bearers sent to ask for his daughter, Hild. Heoden, who has been told by his leading men that it is fitting he should wed, asks the bard Heorrenda whether there is any way he might win Hild. The answer given is that the thing can be done only with the help of Wada. This Wada (Wade in Middle English) seems to have been a sea-giant of great strength, and he was both feared and revered among the folkdoms settled on the shores of the Baltic and the North Sea. To those he looked on with liking he was a helper in time of need. He had a wonder-boat, 'Guingelot', which bore him swiftly where there was work for him to do.[545] In her book *Spellcraft*, Kathleen Herbert has Wada as the mankinding ('personification') of the sea currents, and a fish-herd and game-warden of the sea-beasts.[546]

Wada is called, and he fares forth to Ireland with Heorrenda. They come as merchants, saying they have been banned from their homeland. At the king's hall Heorrenda sings, and folk are filled with gladness and wonder at his songcraft. Afterwards, Hild has him to her bower to sing to her. There he casts aside the merchant guise and woos Hild on behalf of his lord. Hild says that she is willing to run away with him. The 'merchants' then tell Hagena that the ban upon them has been lifted, and they are going home. Down on the shore they find a way to part Hild from her father and mother, and carry her off to their ship. They reach home, and Heoden and Hild are wed. But Hagena comes soon after. In the fight that follows Hagena wounds Heoden, but he is wounded in turn, and hard pressed, by Wada. Hild asks Heorrenda to step in, and he parts the two fighters. Wada, by his leechcraft, then heals both men. Hagena, seeing that his daughter is well-wed, gives his blessing and goes home.

In the version of the Danish historian, Saxo Grammaticus, Hithinus (Heoden) and Höginus (Hagena) are sworn brethren, and Höginus gives Hithinus his daughter, Hilda. But he later believes a false tale that Hithinus has betrayed his daughter. They fight three times, and the third time they wound each other unto death.

In his book on the Old English poem *Widsith* RW Chambers brings out the point that the alightings on this tale in *Widsith*, and in another Old English poem *Deor*, are older, by hundreds of years, than any of the versions that have come down to us. He holds that these alightings tend to back the Middle High German version. (Though he thinks Saxo's setting of the tale among the islands and near-islands ('peninsulas') of the Baltic is more likely than a North Sea setting.[547]) *Widsith* seems to link Wada with Hagena and Heoden, naming them together (lines 21-22). Wada is also said to be of the Halsings. *Deor* underlines the wonderful songcraft of Heorrenda. In Chambers' view the likely features of the Anglian story are: the wooing of Hild by

---

[545] See RW Chambers, Widsith: a study in Old English heroic legend, pp.95-100.

[546] K Herbert, *Spellcraft*, p.238.

[547] RW Chambers, Widsith: a study in Old English heroic legend, pp.105, 108-9.

the songcraft of Heorrenda, the help given by Wada, and the fall of Hagena and perhaps Heoden as well. The grief of strife between sworn brethren (as portrayed by Saxo) was also likely part of the Anglian tale.

## Welund

Welund may have been a man, but it seems more likely that he was an elf-smith. He was taken by his foe, king Niðhad, who crippled him – cutting the tendons in his legs, so that he might not get away. Welund was then made to work for the king. But Welund was avenged in full. First, he slew the two sons of Niðhad, and made cups from their skulls, gems from their eyes, and brooches from their teeth. Then when the king's daughter, Beaduhild, came to his smithy with a ring to be mended, he made her drowsy with beer, and afterwards seduced her. (She bore him a son, Widia.) Meanwhile Welund's brother Egil snared birds, and made a feather coat for him, with which he flew away.

Welund is pictured on the front panel of the Franks casket, working in his smithy, a beheaded body on the ground. He is passing the beer to Beaduhild. There is another woman standing beside the king's daughter. She may be her maid, or perhaps Welund's swan-maiden wife. On the right of the scene Egil is busy catching birds.

## Waldere

Versions of the Waldere tale have come down to us in Old English, German, Latin and Polish, and in the Norse *Thidrek's Saga*. In Old English we have only two fragments of a manuscript of the poem *Waldere*, dated by its script to about AD 1000. The Latin verse *Waltharius* was written by a monk of St Gall, Ekkehard I, about AD 930. Here is an outline of the story.

Attila, king of the Huns, made war in the West. The Franks, Burgundians and Aquitanians bowed under his yoke, and gave hostages. Gibicho, king of the Franks, gave a warrior named Hagano as hostage (his own son was then only a bairn at the breast). Heriricus, king of the Burgundians, gave his daughter Hiltgunt, and Alphere, king of Aquitaine, gave his son Waltharius. (Waltharius and Hiltgunt were betrothed to one another.) Waltharius and Hagano fought side by side in Attila's wars, and became as brothers. In time Waltharius rose to leadership in Attila's host. A good many years went by, then the Frankish king Gibicho died, and his son Guntharius became king. He stopped paying the tribute money to the Huns, and Hagano, most likely fearing the outcome for a hostage, fled back to his own land. Attila did not want to lose Waltharius as well, and Queen Ospirin put it to him that they might bind him to them through wedlock with a Hunnish princess. But Waltharius and Hiltgunt had already made plans to flee. Back from yet more great deeds of war Waltharius had Attila, Ospirin and the Hunnish lords come to a feast. Hiltgunt, meantime, gathered treasure and stowed it in two chests. Whilst the Huns slept off their drink, the lovers fled on one horse. After forty days they reached the Rhine, where a gift to the ferryman of some wondrous fish somehow found its way to

Guntharius. He knew at once that Waltharius must be back, and he smelt plunder. He set out to find the lovers, taking eleven followers, and also a most unwilling Hagano. They came upon the lovers camped in a narrow cleft in the Vosges mountains. Waltharius was ready to share the treasure with Guntharius, but the king wished for the whole, and he sent his men to the onset. Because the cleft was so narrow they could only come at Waltharius one at a time, and he slew them one by one. He wielded two swords in the fighting, one of them being the high-famed 'Mimming' that had belonged to the wonder-smith Welund. (We are not told how Waltharius came by it.) All this time Hagano stood aside, but when his own nephew was slain by Waltharius he at last came forward in the onset against his former shield-brother. Hagano and Guntharius waited until Waltharius came out into the open, and then fell upon him. In the fight Guntharius lost a leg, Waltharius his right hand, and Hagano an eye and some of his teeth. After this they were willing to end the fight, and Hiltgunt bound up their wounds. Waltharius and Hiltgunt reached home, where they were wed, and Waltharius was king for thirty years.

In the Old English version, Gibicho is Gifeca and Guntharius is Guthhere. Waltharius is Waldere, Hiltgunt is Hildegyth, and Hagano is Hagen(a). Kathleen Herbert points out that the three hostages came from the three great Germanic folkdoms set up in what had been Roman Gaul, the Visigoths, the Franks, and the Burgundians.[548] Waldere of Aquitaine must be a Visigoth. (The Visigoths built a great kingdom in Aquitaine and Spain in the fifth century AD.) The kindreds of the other two hostages must be turned about. Germanic tale, along with Old English songcraft, is at one in naming Gifeca and Guthhere as Burgundians, not Franks. We must then take Hildegyth to be a Frankish princess.

The chronology of the tale does not perhaps wholly fit together. The flight of Waldere and Hildegyth would have to have taken place before AD 437 when the Burgundians suffered a crushing defeat at the hands of the Huns, and king Gundahari (Guthhere) was slain. At that time Attila shared the kingship of the Huns with his brother Bleda. It was not until 445 that he became king alone, following the death of his brother (perhaps murdered by him).

---

[548] K Herbert, *Spellcraft*, p.269.

# The Finnsburg Fragment

The *Finnsburg Fragment* has been named a 'lay' (what the early English called a 'leoð'), a song to be sung by a bard at a feast. Our only knowledge of the *Fragment* comes from the work of George Hickes (1642-1715). Hickes was a 'non-juror', that is, one of those clergymen of the Church of England who would not swear an oath to William III. He had given his oath to James II, the king overthrown in the 'Bloodless Revolution' of 1688, and believed that he could not now lawfully give it to another. Hickes spent much of the following years gathering grammatical and literary matter about the languages of northern Europe. His work was published at Oxford in 1705 as *Linguarum veterum. Septentrionalium Thesaurus Grammatico-Criticus et Archæologicus*. Among the matter which Hickes found was forty-eight lines of Old English verse, which he said he came across on a single leaf in a book of 'Semi-Saxon' homilies in Lambeth Palace Library. This leaf has not been seen since, so Hickes' work cannot be checked. (It has been suggested that he might have taken the leaf out of the Library and given it into the hands of his printer for him to work on.) Where other work by Hickes can be checked against Old English poems that are still around it becomes clear that Hickes made mistakes. (He was living in hiding at times, which hardly helped.) Anyway, it cannot be said that we have a clear, sound text of the *Fragment*, for there are a number of places where Hickes' work needs emending.

The poem opens (part way through a sentence) with men looking out from their hall. It is the middle of the night, but something has roused them and they catch the glint of weapons in the moonlight. They hardly have time to ready themselves before there is a deadly onset against the hall. The men holding the hall number sixty. Their leader is Hnæf, and several of his followers are named: Sigeferth (a chief of the Secgan) and Eaha who hold one door, Ordlaf, Guthlaf and Hengest who hold the other. As the onset is about to begin Guthhere urges one of the attackers, Garulf son of Guthlaf, not to risk so precious a life in the first onset. Garulf pays no heed, but calls out, asking who holds the door? Sigeferth answers that it is he. The fighting begins and Garulf is the first to fall. Through five days the fighting goes on, and not one of the defenders falls. Thus these warriors render payment in full for all the bright mead that Hnæf has given them in the past. At last a wounded warrior turns away, his mail-coat riven through, his helmet pierced. Then the folk's 'herd' (that is, 'shield' or 'protector') asks how can the other warriors endure their wounds?

If the *Fragment* was all we had, there would be little hope of understanding this tale. It would be like seeking to make out a picture with only a few pieces of jigsaw. But the *Fragment* is not all we have. There are two other sources to draw on, the *Beowulf* epic, and the poem *Widsith*. In the first part of *Beowulf* we are told of the monster, Grendel, of his night raids on king Hrothgar's hall of Heorot, of his rending and slaying good men. Then the hero Beowulf comes and grapples with him. The monster flees, fatally wounded, his life-blood ebbing away. Afterwards the king gives a feast in the hall and hands out gifts, and bids his bard sing to the gathering. The tale taken up by the bard is that of a fight at the hall of Finnsburg. He tells of the death of Hnæf, of the sorrow of the lady Hildeburh, of the untroth of the Jutes. Finn, the lord of that hall, loses so many men he cannot win the fight. There is a truce between him and Hengest, and afterward the body of Hnæf is laid on a funeral pyre with that of his sister-son (nephew). Hengest broods through the winter over what has been done. In the spring he, with the Danes, wreaks wrath on Finn and Finnsburg.

The poem *Widsith* is a 'who's who' of Germanic folkdoms, rulers and heroes from the third to fifth centuries AD, set within the framework of the poet's forth-faring with a lady Ealhhild to the hall of Eormenric the Goth. We are not given any more of the Finnsburg tale, but the poem names some who were part of that story (lines 20-35).

It is worth noting that most of the North Sea folkdoms had a stake in the Finnsburg tale, so that 'we are attempting to unravel the echoes of a largely historical tale right in the centre of the intricacies of "North Sea" history of the fifth and sixth centuries'.[549] And for the English the tale will have a special place if it can be shown that the Hengest of the *Chronicle* was one and the same man with the Hengest of the poetry. Alan Bliss thinks that this can be shown. He urges that the 'two' bearers of the name Hengest lived at the same time, and had adventures in the same waters. One was a Jute, or at least a leader of Jutes, and was looked upon as the forebear of the kings of the Jutish kingdom of Kent. The other was a leading figure in a tale in which the name 'Eotena'/'Eotenum' is significant – and this name is most likely to be taken as referring to Jutes. Bliss notes, 'It is not forcing the evidence, but following its most obvious leading to identify the two Hengests, and believe that we have preserved two traditions of different adventures in the life-history of one famous adventurer'.[550]

Another thread is found in a passage in MS Cotton Vespasian D iv (fol. 139v) discovered by Dr Rudolf Imelmann. This gives a short list of Germanic heroes still known in English tradition, after the Norman Conquest. The names are Hrothwulf and Hunlaf(ing), Unwine and Widia, Horsa and Hengest, Waltef and Hama. JRR Tolkien showed that there are four names here which do not belong. Unwine and Widia are wrongly separated from Hama, and all three belong to Gothic story. Waltef is a Norman Conquest-era hero. If we take out these four, we are left with Hrothwulf, Hunlaf, Hengest and Horsa. Hunlaf(ing) is associated with Hengest in the *Episode*, and Horsa with the Hengest who came to Britain. Here is good supporting evidence for identifying the 'two' Hengests. If there really were two, surely a writer of that time would have said something.

---

549 A Bliss, *Finn and Hengest*, p.37.
550 A Bliss, p.67.

There are a few further matters, little in themselves perhaps, which yet help strengthen the belief that true history underlies the Finnsburg tale. The simple uncompounded names (Hoc, Finn, Hnæf, and so on) fit well with the fifth century, and early place-name evidence in England.[551] The funeral by burning (of Hnæf and his sister-son, see *Beowulf* lines 1114-5) marks this as a pre-Christian, heathen tale. And Gustav Binz points out that men and places bearing names linked to the Finn story are found in Essex, and the old 'Ytena-land' of Hampshire (though not, oddly, in Kent).[552]

## *The Fragment and the Episode – seeking answers*

Although there are only 48 lines of poetry in the *Finnsburg Fragment*, they leave us with some unanswered questions. First, is it indeed Hnæf who leads one side in the fight? Line 40 clearly speaks of Hnæf being repaid for his mead by the war-worthiness of his men. But the opening of the *Fragment* is not wholly clear. What we have is '[hor]nas byrnað næfre', that is, 'the horns (gables) are never burning?' It can be seen from lines 3 and 4 that someone has spotted flickering light outside, and he asks, is this the dawn? a dragon? surely the gables are never burning? In today's English we do use the word 'never' in this way (as in 'you're never going out in this rain?') But it seems that there is no case of this usage in Old English. Moreover, if this is 'never' at the end of the line, then it is emphatic, and that, says Bliss, is 'odd'.[553] Furthermore, line 2 is somewhat short and awkward as it stands. Altogether there is wide agreement that we take the 'næfre' at the end of line 1 as the first of Hickes's mistakes, emend it to 'Hnæf' and set it at the beginning of the next line. This then reads, 'Then Hnæf, the king young in war, answered …'

Next, we need to understand the role of Guthlaf. With Ordlaf and Hengest he holds one of the two doorways of the hall. But among those who make the onset on the hall (and the first to be slain) is Garulf son of Guthlaf. So is this a case of a son fighting on one side, while his father fights for the other? Or were their two Guthlafs? Or, again, has Hickes got someone's name wrong? The first of these three answers might be right. We know from the record of the Fight at Merton (*Anglo-Saxon Chronicle* 755) that in each warband there were men with kindred who fought for the other side. Yet to have, as in the *Fragment*, a father on one side, his son on the other, would still be something to be remarked, a noteworthy thread in a tale of tangled troth. One would look for some word from the poet, but there is none. As to there being two Guthlafs, again this might be so, but one would look to the poet to make the matter plain. There are two Godrics in the poem *The Battle of Maldon*, and the poet makes it clear who is who by naming their fathers (lines 186, 320). He also

---

551 A Bliss, p.63.

552 RW Chambers, *Widsith: a study in Old English heroic legend*, p.67n (where, however, no details of actual examples are given).

553 A Bliss, p.83.

clearly says of the second Godric (who seeks to strengthen his fellow warriors as they face the end) that this is not the Godric who earlier left the field of battle (line 325). Thus, a mistake in the copying or printing of one of the Guthlafs in the *Fragment* seems the most likely answer. Bliss thinks that 'Guðulf' (a good Germanic name) would, on palæographical grounds, be a sound emendation of the name of Garulf's father. [554]

Third, right at the end of the *Fragment*, a wounded warrior turns away. Is he one of those in the onset, or one of the withstanders (defenders)? And another matter, bound up with this: who is 'the folk's herd' who asks how the wounds of the others can be borne? Is it Finn, wondering at the strength of the defence? Or is it Hnæf, concerned for his men as he sees one of them so badly wounded? Bliss thinks the warrior is one of those in the onset, and that the folk's herd/ shield is, therefore, Finn. He thinks it less likely that Hnæf would feel wonder at the strength of the defence. However, Bliss acknowledges that we cannot be sure, either way.[555]

There are two other matters about which we would dearly like answers. First, what lies at the root of the hatred which is the cause of the onset? (There is no answer to be had from within the *Fragment* itself, so for now we must leave this on one side.) And then, what is it that makes the life of Garulf so precious in the eyes of Guthhere? Again, there is no answer to be had from within the *Fragment*, but there may be a clue in the poem *Widsith*. In line 26, right before the name of Finn Folkwalding in line 27, *Widsith* names one Gefwulf of the 'Ytum' (Jutes?). Bliss thinks it may well be that Garulf and Gefwulf are one. He thinks that Gefwulf is more likely to be the true name, for *Widsith* is a better authority than Hickes' *Fragment*. If so, and if Garulf/ Gefwulf was the Jutish king (the last, indeed of the line) then we would have the glimmer of an answer. But we must leave the matter there for the now.

We next turn to the *Episode* (lines 1066-1159 of the *Beowulf* poem). In Hrothgar's hall, after Beowulf has slain the monster, Grendel, the king's bard takes up a tale before the gathering. The tale is of a sudden woe that befalls Finn and his followers, and of the fall of Hnæf of the Scylding house, a hero of the Half-Danes. We are told that Hildeburh, Hoc's daughter, had no cause to praise the troth of the 'Eotan'. In the morning following the 'shield-play' she finds she has lost both son and brother. As for Finn he has lost so many men, he cannot go on with the fight against Hengest. And so a truce is agreed. The Danes shall be given another hall, to be shared with the Eotan, and whenever Folk-wielder's son shall give gifts to his Frisians, he will give as much to Hengest's warriors. Finn swears that their serving the slayer of their lord shall not be held against them, since necessity is laid upon them. And if any Frisian does bring the matter up, then the sword shall settle it. A funeral pyre is made, and Hildeburh has the body of her son laid beside that of his uncle. As the fire

[554] A Bliss, p.33.

[555] A Bliss, *Finn and Hengest*, pp.89-90.

swallows up the slain, Hildeburh makes her lament. Hengest now settles down with Finn. He is not happy, and he thinks of home, but the winter storms mean there can be no seafaring. In the spring his thoughts turn to wrath-wreaking (vengeance), and when Hunlaf's son lays the sword 'Hildeleoma' (whose edges were known to the Eotan) in his lap, he does not say nay. Guthlaf and Oslaf cross the sea to their Dane-land kinsfolk, speak of their grief and lay the blame on Finn. This leads to renewed fighting, and Finn in his turn is slain. After this the Scylding warriors take the lady Hildeburh, together with all the booty they can lay hands on, and go again to the land of the Danes.

The first thing to be settled is, do the *Fragment* and the *Episode* refer to the same matter? It would seem so. In the *Fragment* we have part of the tale of a night onset against a hall, and in the *Episode* it seems clear that we have an account of the aftermath. We also have a clearer 'who's who'. The fighting in the *Fragment* is at Finnsburg, and in the *Episode* we have Finn, the son of one who bears the name, or title, of 'Folk-wielder'. We have Hnæf again. He is said to be of the Scylding house, and his warriors are Scyldings. These are also called Danes, and Hnæf is a hero of the 'Half-Danes'. He is uncle to the son of Hildeburh, daughter of Hoc. So we may take it that Hnæf and Hildeburh are brother and sister, the children of Hoc. And we have Hengest again, and learn that leadership of the Danes fell to him after the death of Hnæf. If there are two tales here, then there are two Hnæfs and two Hengests, and another Guthlaf, all caught up in two separate fights that yet seem truly much alike. It does seem well-nigh certain that the underlying story is one tale.

But although we now know more about the fight at Finnsburg, there are also yet more knotty matters unanswered. Hnæf is hero of the 'Half-Danes'. So is he of mixed blood? And is there a link with Healfdene Scylding, the father of king Hrothgar in *Beowulf*? Who are the 'Eotan' whose troth Hildeburh has no cause to praise, and whose side are they on? And on whose side did her son fight (and fall)? What is the nature of the truce between Finn and Hengest? What is the meaning of the laying of the sword 'Hildeleoma' in Hengest's lap? What are the links, if any, between the Guthlaf and Ordlaf of the *Fragment*, and the Guthlaf, Oslaf and Hunlaf of the *Episode*? Can we gain any light on the two unanswered matters from the *Fragment*? – the root of the underlying hatred, and the role of Garulf/ Gefwulf? Are there trothless Eotan at the heart of the matter?

Alan Bliss takes a long look at the name 'Half-Dane'.[556] He believes that the name is a nickname or surname, that it does mean what it implies (that is, someone who is half-Danish), but that someone might gain the name through kindred links, without it being literally true for him. He suggests that it was first the surname of Hoc the father of Hnæf, and that it came to Healfdene Scylding through a marriage link – that of his father (whose true name is now lost) with a daughter of Hoc. Healfdene may then be seen as a bit of an outsider, a 'colonial', so to speak, who made good in the time when

---

[556] A Bliss, *Finn and Hengest*, pp.37-45.

the Danes were spreading outwards from their homeland in southern Sweden into the Cimbric peninsula and the islands. If the guess is right then Healfdene stood in that most-valued of kindred ties as 'sister-son' to Hnæf, and also to Hildeburh.

The name 'Eotan' is 'translated' as 'Jutes', though it could also be taken as the Old English word for giants or trolls. So in the poem *Beowulf*, in an aside about the exiled Danish king Heremod (lines 898-915) that king is betrayed among the 'eotenum' (line 902). Some take this betrayal as happening in the land of the Jutes, but others see it as a betrayal among the giants. However, the warfare in the *Fragment* and the *Episode* (whether that warfare is historical or legendary), is clearly warfare among men, not monsters. So we may take the Eotan here as indeed Jutes. And we may note, at this point, that the spelling 'Jute' is a book form. Bede Latinised the old Northumbrian 'Juta' (singular), 'Juti' (plural). These forms represent Germanic *Iutiz < *Eutiz. The Anglian forms would have been 'Iote', 'Iotan' (later 'Eote', 'Eotan', whence the genitive plural 'Eot(e)na' – the most familiar forms in epic poetry). In West Saxon the forms would be , 'Yte', 'Ytan' (genitive plural 'Ytena'). In *Widsith* we have 'Ytum'.[557]

What of the untroth of the Eotan that brought such sorrow upon Hildeburh? We can really do no more than guess, but there may be a slight lead as we think about the historical background of the time. The Frisians were perhaps the first power along the southern rim of the North Sea at this time. The Danes were beginning to spread westwards, and were perhaps starting to encroach on the Frisian 'sphere of influence'. The Eotan were a small folk in the middle. Perhaps the two 'great powers' had been meddling in Eotan affairs and, as so often happens when this is the case, the Eotan became a 'house sundered' – between those who 'bowed the neck' to a forceful neighbour (in this case the Danes) and those who were 'stiff-necked'. And, again as so often happens, these two groups of the one folkdom may have come to hate each other more than they hated outsiders. There may, then, have been Eotan on both sides in the fight at Finnsburg – Eotan who had thrown in their lot with the Danes, and others who had gone into exile among the Frisians. As for Garulf/ Gefwulf, we might guess that he was the last of the old kingly line of the Eotan, and the leader of the exiled Eotan. Perhaps with his death there died the last hope of a free Eotan folkdom in the old homeland of the Cimbric peninsula.

Next, there is the matter of Hildeburh's son who fell at Finnsburg. It is not clear whether he fought alongside his father's folk in the onset against the hall, or whether he was inside the hall, with his mother's brother, Hnæf, and fought shoulder to shoulder with him in the withstanding. But if he had met his death taking part in the onset, it would seem most likely that Finn would have taken on himself the matter of his burial, and this is not what happened. It is Hildeburh who has her dead son laid beside her brother, on the funeral pyre. Now the blood tie between a man and his sister's son was a very close one in the Anglo-Saxon

---

[557] A Bliss, p.61.

world, and it could well be that Hildeburh's son had been fostered by Hnæf. If so, and he had come of warrior age (at about 14 to 15 years), then the bringing of this son back to his home, could well be the reason why Hnæf is at Finnsburg. Bearing in mind the sister-son tie, and the thought that for some years Hnæf may have stood in the place of father and teacher, we can well understand that the lad might be inside the hall, and choose to stand by Hnæf.

Can we give this son of Finn and Hildeburh a name? The name of Finn himself has found its way into the kinship rolls of the Anglo-Saxon kings, as given in the *Chronicle* annals for 547 (the Northumbrian line) and 855 (the Wessex line). Back beyond Woden, we have, in some manuscripts of the *Chronicle*, Frealaf who is son of Frithuwulf, son of Finn, son of Godwulf, son of Geat. In other manuscripts the name of Frithuwulf is not given. In the *Historia Brittonum*, we have the line Frealaf, son of Fredulf, son of Finn, son of Folcwald. (This, by the way, suggests that 'Folk-wielder' was a title borne by Finn's father, Godwulf, a title which then passed to Finn.) Bliss suggests that the fame of Finn was such that later kings wanted him added to their kinship rolls. He was then fitted, along with the name of his father and of those who came after him, into what had once been a straightforward mythical line of Woden – Frea – Geat. If so, is it Frithuwulf who is the son of Finn, or is it Frealaf? When Frithuwulf's name is given he is always next to Finn. So Bliss suggests that he is the son who died at Finnsburg, and the Frealaf who carries on the line was perhaps a younger brother, rather than being the son of Frithuwulf. Like enough he was but a child at the time of the Frisian Slaughter.

With the truce between Finn and Hengest, and the latter's soul-searching through the long winter months, we come to the true meat and marrow of the Finnsburg tale. The Anglo-Saxon poets had a deep awareness of life's tangles, of men and women torn two ways. A man was part of that network of 'oughts', things that he owed to his lord, to his forebears, to his friends, his wife, his guests. What he owed to one, however, might go against what he owed to another. He must wrestle with these intanglings. They might perhaps untangle themselves in the end, or by ill-fate bring upon the man his undoing. Or, again, a man might seem to cut through the intanglings (he might slay his foe, or give a daughter in wedlock to the son of that foe) only for the grievances to fester and break out again, with another slaying, perhaps, and the embittering of the lives of his children and children's children.

It seems clear enough that Hengest was the number two in Hnæf's warband, and that leadership fell to him after Hnæf was slain. By the 'laws' of heroic society there should have been no truce with Finn. Hengest, with those of the sixty who were yet alive, was bound to seek vengeance for Hnæf, or die in the seeking. But perhaps it was not that straightforward. (We can rule out fight-weariness, for that would have seemed a lame get-out in the old Germanic world.) So let us go back to those words at the beginning of the *Episode*: 'No cause, indeed, had Hildeburh to praise the Jutish troth.' We have guessed that the Jutes were at the bottom of this tangle at Finnsburg, and that Finn's Jutes nursed a bitter hatred against Hnæf's Jutes, and against Hengest above all. We might then take it that it was Finn's Jutes, along with some of their Frisian comrades in arms, who started this fight. There was surely no reason why Finn himself would make an onset against his own hall, where his son slept, and where his wife's brother was his guest. Finn, then, would have been awoken by the clash of weapons, found that his men's blood was up and that he could not hold them back. He would have seen that some of his men were already slain, and so found himself drawn into the fighting. Then when the fighting was broken off, some five days later, and Finn and Hengest met face to face, Hengest would have had to acknowledge that it was not by Finn's will that Hnæf had fallen. And so he took oath to be Finn's man. After this, through the idle winter months, Hengest had time enough to think over what had happened. Hnæf was dead. Finn had not willed that death, but those who wrought the deed answered to Finn. It was Finn who must be made to pay, but (and here was the new twist in this tale) Hengest was now Finn's man. He had sworn troth to him. So Hengest brooded over it all, and was torn two ways – until Hunlaf's son laid the sword 'Hildeleoma' in his lap.

The laying of 'Hildeleoma' (that is, 'battle-bright') in Hengest's lap was clearly a deed fraught with meaning. We have seen (in thinking about Anglo-Saxon weapons and warfare) that a famed sword had a stored up 'life' or 'force'. The battles in which it had dealt out death, the warriors who had wielded it, the oaths sworn upon its keen edges, the feuds it had stirred or settled – all these were still part of the ongoing 'life' of the weapon. This 'Hildeleoma' was truly a famed sword, its edges known among the Jutes. And that saying is most truly 'two-edged' and surely meant to be so. The gathering in Hrothgar's hall would have seen what lay behind this, and relished such keen-edged wording. But we have to guess. Were the edges of this sword known among the Jutes because it was a Jutish sword and had wrought great deeds for them? Or had their forebears faced it in battle, and had cause to rue it? Perhaps both these things were so. If the Jutes were a folk asundered, perhaps the sword had wrought *for* some Jutes – say in the hands of Hoc and Hnæf as they took one side in Jutish infighting – and against others, such as the house of Garulf/ Gefwulf. As to the laying of the sword in Hengest's lap it seems most likely that this was both a giving of troth and a challenge. In Hnæf's mixed warband, where Hengest the Jute was the number two, Hunlaf's son is perhaps the first among the Danes. Now with Hnæf's sword he says to Hengest, 'We are with you, we are yours, if you will do what you must do – avenge our slain lord.'

So who is Hunlaf's son? And what may be the links between the Guthlaf, Oslaf and Hunlaf of the *Episode* and the Guthlaf and Ordlaf of the *Fragment*? It may be that Oslaf and Ordlaf were one and the same man. Bliss notes that in Old English sources the first parts of names may vary (through shortcomings of memory, and/or manuscript miscopying) while the first letter, and the latter half of the name, stay the same. Thus we read of Ordbeorht/ Osbeorht, Bishop of Selsey, and of Ordgar/ Osgar, Abbot of Abingdon. In the case of Ordlaf/ Oslaf Bliss thinks Ordlaf is most likely the right spelling.[558] As to 'Hunlaf's son' (line 1143) Bliss makes the point that in the *Episode*, the poet is given to speaking of a character in one place, giving him his own name, then speaking of him next in a round-about way (though he does not do this with a new character). Thus Hrothgar is 'Healfdene's helper in battle' (line 1064). Hildeburh is named in line 1071, and is then referred to as 'Hoc's daughter' in line 1076. Finn is named in lines 1068, 1081, and is then 'Folk-wielder's son' in line 1089. Bliss suggests that the poet has done things in a slightly different way in lines 1143-8, for once using the round-about term first, having in mind that he is about to name the one he means. In line 1148 Guthlaf and Oslaf (Ordlaf) are named, and Bliss takes Ordlaf to be the elder, the 'Hunlaf's son' who lays the sword in Hengest's lap.[559]

Lastly, is there any clue to where Finnsburg was? Morris suggests the Leeuwarden area of the Netherlands. Early cruciform brooches have been found in graves there, of a type also found in Jutish and Anglian graves in Schleswig and Denmark, but which are not found in early Anglo-Saxon graves in England. (The earliest cruciform brooches found there are of the next typological stage.) He suggests a date in the period 390-430, and nearer 430 (since the Leeuwarden burials also include brooch types found in Britain).[560]

---

[558] A Bliss, *Finn and Hengest*, p.31.

[559] A Bliss, p.79.

[560] J Morris, General Editor, *Arthurian Sources*, Volume 4, Places and Peoples, and Saxon Archaeology, p.32.

# The picture of Hengest in the *Finnsburg Fragment* and the *Episode*

What picture of Hengest do we get from the *Finnsburg Fragment* and the *Episode*? Bliss thinks that he is almost certainly the 'wrecca' of the *Episode* line 1137. This word 'wrecca' is the root of today's English 'wretch', but to the Anglo-Saxons it meant an exile, even an outlaw. (The word is also applied to Cain, the Devil, and the fallen angels.) In Old English songcraft it is used of men driven from their homeland by usurpers, invaders, feuds, or their own wild deeds, and throwing in their lot with the warband of some famed leader. Thus the word can also come to mean an adventurer, or hero.

Hengest may well have been an exile, living among the Danes. The Jutes and the Danes were neighbours, and perhaps natural foes, and each (Danes on one side, Jutes on the other), may have given refuge to each other's exiles.[561] Thus we may see Hengest as a masterless man, making his way in the world by his sword. He seems to have been a bold and daring warrior. He was, on the whole, a man true to his word, though if one should cheat him, he would be ready to cheat in turn. The character of the Hengest of the Finnsburg tale would seem to fit with the Hengest of Kentish tradition. At the time of his coming into Kent he probably led a mixed warband of Jutes from Jutland, 'Frisian' Jutes (that is, Jutes who had migrated to Frisia) and Frisians who were fleeing the Sea-Danes. There may also have been Ripuarian Franks from the lower Rhine in his warband.[562] He was perhaps one who, at key moments in his life had felt cornered into taking the wrong way. He came to distrust others and to look for the worst in them. In the end he himself became grasping and untrustworthy.

## *Hengest's saga*

In the poems of Part three we have sought to piece together the adventures of Hengest the Jute. (The *Finnsburg Fragment* forms lines 294b to 341a in the re-made poem, 'The Slaughter in Frisia'.) Here follows a prose version of the two poems.

Finn 'Folk-wielder' (about 400 to about 452), was the son of Godwulf 'Grasper'. This Godwulf had brought all the Frisian principalities under his hand, and built a kingdom that stretched from Rome's border on the Rhine, eastwards to the mouth of the Weser. The kingdom passed in time to his son, Finn, who built the great hall of Finnsburg, to make known his fame. Yet Finn was troubled in his mind as he watched the growing might of the Danish kingdom, first under Hoc Half-Dane, then under his son Hnæf. Hoc had overthrown the Jutish kingdom (until then a 'buffer'

---

561 A Bliss, p.59.

562 J Lindsay, *Arthur and his times*, p.198.

between Frisian and Dane) and he was helped in this by infighting between western and eastern Jutes. Guthulf, the Jutish lord, had at some time slain a war-leader of the eastern Jutes, one Sigebert. So it was that at the time of Guthulf's hosting against the Danes, the easterners would not move. Guthulf was overwhelmed in the battle, and the easterners then acknowledged Hoc's lordship. But those warriors of the western Jutes who yet lived took the young Gefwulf, Guthulf's son, and sought refuge with Finn and the Frisians. And they hoarded in their hearts a deep bitterness against their eastern brethren.

After the death of Hoc his son Hnæf followed the same warlike ways. Seeing this, Finn called together his elders and wisemen, that they might tell him what to do. There was among them one named Wulfrith, a wily man, the only eastern Jute who had left with the westerners and come to Finnsburg. In his faring through the North Sea world he had been at the hall of Hoc Half-Dane, and had seen Hoc's winsome daughter, Hildeburh. Now, said Wulfrith, if Finn should wed her, and have a son by her, that son might bind the Danish kingdom to the Frisian. The plan went down well with Finn and his elders, and Finn straightway sent word-bearers, with gifts for Hnæf. And the Dane liked the plan, too. He saw it as a means of ensuring that Finn kept his Jutes in check. And might not a son of Hildeburh (sister-son to himself) bind the Frisian folkdom to the Danish? Hildeburh also was willing, for she thought she might weave peace between the two kingdoms.

Hildeburh and Finn were wed, perhaps about 435, and in the following year the lady gave birth to a son, Frithuwulf. When he was weaned he was sent as foster-son to Hildeburh's brother, Hnæf. There he stayed until, at fifteen, he came to war-years. Then, with summer over and the onset of winter not far away, Hnæf took Frithuwulf, with sixty warriors (Danes, Jutes, and others) and sailed to Frisia. They were warmly welcomed by Finn. This was about 451.

Frisians, Jutes and Danes sat together in hall. But between them there were thoughts of wrongs unrighted, and there was the strong drink that stirs strife. Bitter words were spoken against the Danes, and even more against the eastern Jutes, first among them Hnæf's right-hand man, Hengest. Finn saw that he must keep the two sides apart. He told Hnæf that the hall of Finnsburg should be given over to the Danes and their friends for that night, and he would take his own men to another hall. He also bade his son Frithuwulf stay with Hnæf, for he thought his Jutish followers would not dare to fall upon his guests, if so they threatened the life of his own son.

Some while after midnight Hnæf was awakened by Hengest. He went with him to those who kept watch at the door, and as they looked out they saw flickering lights where the wandering moon shone down upon the fortress. Then Hnæf guessed these were the mail-shirts, sword-blades, and bright helms of bitter foes. He at once bade his sleeping warriors awake, take their own mail-shirts and weapons, and hold the doors against their foes. So began a bitter night-battle, and the first to fall, as he took part in the onset, was Gefwulf, last of the old kingly line of the Jutes.

Hnæf's sixty warriors fought fiercely through five days and nights, but one by one the leading warriors were cut down, and then Hnæf himself fell. The Danes began to falter, but the young Frithuwulf put new heart into them, showing them the way by his words and his war-deeds. At last he felt the death-blow, and he lay down to die beside his mother's brother. Finn, meanwhile, had lost many men, and this was a warring he had never sought. So when peace was mooted he was quick to offer open-handed terms. Those Danes who were yet alive should be given another hall. Let them live apart with their Jutish friends, and when it came to the giving of gifts, they would be given as much as his own men. And if any Frisian or Jute in Finn's following should seek to stir up strife again, mocking the Danes because they had clasped hands with the slayer of their lord, then that man should be put to death. On these terms Hengest (to whom leadership had fallen after the death of Hnæf) swore binding oaths to Finn. The bodies of Hnæf and Frithuwulf were laid side by side on the funeral pyre (with others who had fallen) as Hildeburh sang a grievous lament.

That winter Hildeburh gave birth to another son, Frealaf, and through that winter and spring (about 451-2) Hengest brooded over what had been done. His lord was slain and unavenged, and though it had not been by Finn's will, yet it was wrought by Finn's men. But he, Hengest, had bound himself to Finn with strong oaths, for there had seemed nothing else to be done. As Hengest grieved over these things, the Dane Ordlaf son of Hunlaf laid in his lap 'Hildeleoma', Hnæf's blade, and then Hengest was in two minds no more. He saw that evil must be repaid.

In the spring Ordlaf came before Finn and told him he would sail back to Dane-land with those of their following who were yet alive. Hengest would abide at Finnsburg. If there should be any hint of war about Finn's halls, let him send word and (quoth Ordlaf) the Danes would hasten back over sea. (In the outcome the words were deep, and two-edged. The Danes would indeed come back – to bring war on Finn.) The Frisian, seemingly unaware of what was meant, sent the Danes away with his blessing. As soon as Ordlaf reached home, he called together the leading men among the Danes, told how Hnæf and Frithuwulf had fallen in that night onset, and challenged them: were their brethren to lie unavenged? The Danes were filled with wrath, and a great war-host gathered and sailed for Frisia.

Finnsburg was strongly built, and the Frisians did not fear the coming of the Danes. Yet, as they fought, the hall behind them was set alight, and that by the hand of Hengest! In grief and wrath Finn rushed upon him, but was felled by his hand. After the overthrow of the fortress the Danes and their friends heaped up a great hoard of the treasure they found there. When Hengest had made sure of his half, he sailed away, having made Frisia too hot to hold him. The Danes went back to their homeland, taking with them the lady Hildeburh, now bereft of brother, son, and husband. As she was going the lady sang a song of deep woe for the hall of Finnsburg and those it had known.

After Finnsburg Hengest and his war-band (with the crafty Wulfrith now among them) roamed the North Sea, making a living by warring and reaving. And then one day they fell in with word-bearers from Britain, on the lookout for likely men to recruit as fighters. The outcome was that Hengest and his men crossed to Thanet, and met with Vortigern and his Council (about 453). Vortigern was leader of the British/ Pelagian/ pagan party against the Roman party led by the house of Aurelius. He had gained the upper hand in the Council after the appeal for help from Aëtius had fallen on deaf ears (446). This Vortigern was a crafty political player. In open meeting he led the Council in agreeing terms with Hengest for 'federate' services in fighting the Picts, but afterwards, in his own bower, he raised with Hengest the matter of the threat to his position from the Aurelians.

After Hengest and his men had fought off the Picts, Vortigern stalled on the matter of reward, and urged Hengest to bring more fighters from his homeland to help Vortigern against the Roman party. Then would Vortigern give Thanet to Hengest, as had been promised. In his heart Hengest was wroth, but he would bide his time. He brought over more of his own folk, among them his daughter Hrothwyn. Wulfrith now counseled Hengest to bind the slippery Vortigern to him by forging a marriage alliance between the king's son, Vortimer, and the lady Hrothwyn. With this in mind Hengest invited Vortigern and some of his leading men to a feast. But at the feast it was Vortigern, not Vortimer, who was captivated by Hrothwyn. He asked Hengest to name the bride-wealth for her. The Jute said he would take nothing less than the whole kingdom of Kent, both the west and the east, and Vortigern agreed. The lady Hrothwyn was given to him, and Vortigern had Gwyrangon, king of Kent, slain by stealth. This was about 455.

There was outrage in Britain at the murder of Gwyrangon. Vortigern was overthrown, and his son Vortimer was made 'Britain-land's Shield'. Two British war-hosts now set out against the Jutes in Kent. One marched down the great Roman road (Watling Street), and the other followed an ancient downland trackway (since called the Pilgrims' Way). The northern host was thrown back at the line of the Darent. They thought to hold the Cray, but were taken in the rear, and they fled back to London. Meanwhile the southern host met the Jutes at Aylesford on the Medway. At first they were driven back, but a charge of the horse-lords (cavalry) turned the day, and at nightfall the two sides, both badly mauled, drew apart. Horsa the brother of Hengest, and Catigern, brother of Vortimer, were among the dead. The Eotan bore the body of Horsa downstream, to bury him on a headland.

Britons and Jutes now agreed to make peace. The Britons gave up East Kent to the Jutes who, in their turn, let go of the West. The lady Hrothwyn was sent back to her father's house. Yet there was plenty of scope for trouble. For the Britons there was the bitterness of Gwyrangon's death, and the loss of lands in the East. For the Jutes there was the lure of the West's woodland wealth. For both there was the matter of the blood of Aylesford unavenged. Cross-border raiding ended with Gwyrangon's kin lured into a snare and killed. This so angered Vortimer that he bade Hengest come to his hall and give account of himself. When the latter would not, Vortimer mustered a great war-host, and they swept right through Kent, reaching the shore over against Thanet. The Jutes fled to the island, though Wipped won lasting fame fighting to the death. Afterwards, Vortimer sold the captured womenfolk and children into Roman slavery.

A wearying siege followed, with the Jutes penned up in Thanet and the Britons lacking the warships to get across to the island. Then Vortimer sickened through a festering arrow-wound. While he was laid up, the lady Hrothwyn came to see him. She offered him a draught that would heal him, if only he would give himself to her. But Vortimer would have none of her. When he died the third day thereafter, many believed that it was Hrothwyn's doing, and they named her the 'witch-whore'.

Now the Jutish host sailed away, and the Britons headed home believing the war was won. Half the host hastened to London with Vortimer's body, but half lingered heedlessly. So were they taken in a dawn onset, hard by Rochester, as the Jutes (who had not sailed far) landed at the mouth of the Medway.

In the upheaval following the death of Vortimer, Vortigern wormed his way back into power by gift (bribe) and guile. He then sent word to Hengest that they should make a lasting peace – and he wanted Hrothwyn back. Let the elders from each side come together, leaving their weapons behind in token of troth. Wulfrith urged Hengest not to trust Vortigern's word, for he was surely plotting an ambush. Hengest more than half believed him, and he bade his elders hide, each man, a 'seax' (short sword) under his shirt. At the feast a British bard sang the Song of Branwen, a tale in which a British host went a-warring in Ireland, and only seven came back alive. Hengest, already on edge, read into the Briton's words an urging on his fellows to bring the same fate on the Jutes. Then Vortigern put forward his terms of peace. He was brimming with self-assurance. Aëtius, who he had long feared, had been murdered in 454. Rome itself had been sacked by the Vandals in 455, and there seemed little likelihood that any other Roman would arise to fill the place of Aëtius. So Vortigern offered Hengest East Kent for his life-time, after which it would pass to the son that Hrothwyn should bear to Vortigern. Hengest was greatly angered at this latest untroth and bade his men draw their knives. In the slaughter that followed Vortigern alone was spared, and he was made to promise three kingdoms, to ransom his life.

Fate now began to catch up with the players in this drama. In the following year (about 474) Ambrosius and Uther of the house of Aurelius landed from Brittany. Nearly all men forsook Vortigern, and he fled northwards. As he rode through the night during a thunderstorm he was thrown from his horse and killed. Over the next few years the tide of war between Britons and Saxons ebbed and flowed. New British mounted forces made inroads, stirring Hengest to make a thrust into British lands. But he was too self-assured and heedless. He was caught unawares in a dawn onset and was dealt his death thrust (about 488). As he lay dying he looked back ruefully over his life, and he acknowledged he had wrought much evil. He grieved most of all over the fight at Finnsburg and his 'wyrd' so warped.

Among the 'threads' of this tale are: 'wyrd', wrath-wreaking (vengeance), the worth of defeated valour, and strife between two 'oughts'.

## Wyrd

There are many references to 'wyrd' (or doom). Among examples in the poem, *The Slaughter in Frisia*, we are told that Guthulf followed his wyrd-way (line 21). Hagena 'forsook not his wyrd', but went to his death (lines 50-1). The night of the onset on Finnsburg was doom-laden (line 275). If a man was reckless his doom would dawn before its day (line 354). Sigeferth threatened Gefwulf saying 'the fate you'd foist on me shall fall on you!' (lines 317-20). The Danes held out life to Eomær the shoreward, saying 'A life undoomed from wrath is wrested!' (line 631). Death-dealing darts seek the doomed (line 643), and a man falls by fated spear (line 647). In the poem, *The Stallion*, the rune-shafts thrown by Wulfrith may seem to fall at random, but in truth they are 'fate-bidden' (line 126). We are told that to a man in his youth his fate seems far-off, but it works unseen and, on a sudden, o'erleaps his life (lines 716-8). In the end it is God who works out man's wyrd (lines 5, 785).

## Wrath-wreaking

The Germanic stress on wrath-wreaking is seen in two lines of the first poem: 'For evil wrought I must evil render' (*The Slaughter in Frisia*, 512), and 'For blood shed unrightly full fee must be found (*The Slaughter in Frisia*, 707).

## The worth of defeated valour

The Germanic appreciation of the worth of defeated valour is seen in the holding of the hall by a mere sixty Danes and Jutes, and (on the other side) Eomær's dogged defence of the way through the salt marsh (*The Slaughter in Frisia*, 634ff).

## Strife between two 'oughts'

This is seen most clearly as Hengest wrestles with the knowledge that he ought to wreak wrath for Hnæf's death, but also that he ought to keep troth with Finn (who had not willed Hnæf's death, but was lord to those who slew him). This is the heart of the tale (*The Slaughter in Frisia*, 483-7, 500-512). Finn, too, must have gone through deep waters, as he thought of his own men slain and unavenged, but thought also of the shamed hospitality of Finnsburg.

## An aside on Christian undertones and other 'threads' of the tale

Henry Mayr-Harting notes that the poem *Beowulf* 'is suffused with Christian allusions, phrases and ways of thought'.[563] This is not to say that there is any underlying Christian message, but the word-shaper is aware of God, the 'Wielder

---

[563] H Mayr-Harting, *The Coming of Christianity*, p.235.

of glory' (*Beowulf*, line 17) behind the things that happen. It was he who sent the young child Beow, born to Scyld (lines 12-13). The shoreward sent Beowulf and his friends on their way to Heorot with the prayer that the Father All-wielder would watch over their undertakings (lines 316-7). Hrothgar told Beowulf that God could easily put an end to Grendel's raids (lines 478-9). Indeed, it was the King of Glory who had sent Beowulf to guard the hall of Heorot against the monster (lines 665-7). And Beowulf, for his part, trusted in the favour of the 'Measurer of fate', that is God (line 670). As he lay down to await the coming of Grendel, Beowulf spoke surely of the wise God, the holy Lord who would award glory as he saw fit (lines 685-7). And so it goes on.

The remade tale of Hengest which follows here, has likewise been given – ever so lightly – Christian undertones.

First, the unfailing pattern of the seasons (*The Slaughter in Frisia*, line 96) and the signs of spring after the dreariness of winter are marks of 'God's tried troth' (*The Slaughter in Frisia*, 491-3), the fulfilling once more of the promise he made after the Great Flood that seedtime and harvest, summer and winter, would not cease (Genesis 8:22).

Next, Finnsburg's hall and its feasting may be seen as a foretaste of the heavenly hall where God's folk shall feast together (*The Slaughter in Frisia*, 161).

Third, the death of Hnæf and Frithuwulf together is named in words like those used of Saul and Jonathan, see 2 Samuel 1:23 (*The Slaughter in Frisia*, 459).

Fourth, Hildeburh found her heathen faith wanting in her time of most need (*The Slaughter in Frisia*, 803-7), and there is perhaps a hint of unspoken longing for the true God. The faithful shore-ward, Eomær, prays with dying breath (*The Slaughter in Frisia*, 666-8) to 'All-Father'. This is the chief god, Woden, though it was a title which would later be taken up by Christian missionaries and applied to the God of the Bible.

Fifth, in telling of the landing of Hengest and Horsa in Thanet (*The Stallion*, lines 159-61) the poet makes reference to St Augustine and his forty missionary companions who, as 'war-smiths' of Christ, would also land on Thanet, to begin the work of bringing the light of the gospel to the pagan English (Bede, *HE*, I.25). The 'ring-mail of right' and 'shields wrought of truth' recall the picture of the 'armour of God' in Ephesians 6:13-17.

Sixth, Vortigern likens the 400 or so years of the Romans in Britain to the Egyptian bondage of Israel, see Genesis 15:13, Exodus 12:41 (*The Stallion*, 197, 199).

Seventh, as the treachery of Vortigern unfolds, and Hengest begins to think of paying him back, the latter is referred to as the 'rod of God's wrath' (*The Stallion*, 247), the role once given to Assyria as the 'rod' of God's judgement (see Isaiah 10:5).

Eighth, at the fight on the Medway, as the British horse thunder down the slopes to the river the waters draw back (*The Stallion*, 447) in a faint echo of the waters of the Red Sea parting before the host of Israel (Exodus 14:21-22).

Ninth, at the height of his success Vortimer takes Jutish women and children captive. He cannot but acknowledge how fair they are, and his words recall those of Saint Gregory when, some 150 or so years later, he saw English lads in the thrall markets of Rome. They seemed goodly to him, fair of face and with curly hair.[564] Gregory was moved to wish that the English might come to faith in Christ. But Vortimer sees these Jutish folk as a snare, like the women of Midian who led Israel astray (Numbers 25). So Vortimer has the captive women and children sold into thralldom. (This trade went on for a long time to come, hence the fair-haired lads for sale in Rome in Gregory's day.) Many a time in history God has brought good from evil. One of the most striking cases was the sale of Joseph into thralldom, by the hand of his own brothers, and his going down into Egypt. The brothers meant it for evil, but God (who was behind these happenings all along) meant it for good, sending Joseph ahead, so that many might be saved alive from famine (see Genesis 50:20). Now the poem alludes to the way in which God will again bring good from evil. He will one day move Gregory to send Augustine and his fellows to England bringing the good news of life and light through faith in Christ (see *The Stallion*, 567-87).

[564] See *The Life of St Gregory* by a monk of Whitby, quoted in RW Chambers, *England before the Norman Conquest*, p.106.

# The Slaughter in Frisia

'Tis meet in man that he mind this wonder,
how God, great-hearted, heaps gifts, unstinting,
yet man, unmindful, his Maker grieves.
His heart, grown high, heeds not his wyrd.
Then fiend from hell with hate-filled dart
fells man with fever, or death's stroke is dealt
in spear-storm's din, or sea-mare sinks,
in wild waves' grasp to Deep's dark hall.
Whose then the wealth-hoard? And God weighs all,
finds right deeds unwrought, the wrong wrought too well.
Thus with Finn Folkwielder, Godwulf's first strength.
In manhood's morn, the gift-stool grasping,
wide lands he won, wrought him a mead-hall
by restless sea-rim, reared up her roof-trees.
Stag's head, set high, outglared his foes.
"Fair stands great Finnsburg" (that Folk-lord quoth),
"nonesuch in northland, makes known my might."
(The hand that held the hissing brand
was not yet come to weapon-years.)
Bitter the breasts, baleful the words,
when Godric's son followed his wyrd-way.
(Hoc hewed his helm). "Where were East-folk
in lord's most need?" And West-folk fled
to Frisia's hall, took Finn as folklord,
while eastern Eotan clasped hands with Hoc
(little their love for Sigebert's slayer).

Forth fared the Half-Dane, his life-thread frayed.
Then Scyldings' son the war-blade wielded,
out-fought Danes' foes, made folkdoms fear.
And Finn Folkwielder bade his elders
ring the rede-hall, render wisdom.
Some said, War! others, Wile! 'till one thrust through –
Wulfrith Witfast. His word they heeded!
"Far have I fared through many folklands.
With Swedes I sat, with grim Spear-Danes,
with Heathobards in hall. Sword-edge was hardened
in war-play with Wends (wives were made widows).

Geat-lord gave gladly for riddles unbound.
No slack-hand was Hrethel – he rendered rightly.
Huns harrowed Guthhere, Burgundian lord.
Though dear his life's light, he longed for death.
With Gifthas I sat, with Wulfings, Goths.
Ruthless Eormenric rendered richly,
gave gold to gleemen (wolfish his heart!)
Mead-horn in hall I shared with Halsings,
wintered with Rugians, bold island folk.
Heoden loved Hild, Hagena's daughter,
by word-craft won her – Heorrenda's weaving –
bore off the maiden, fled far o'er sea.
Hagena, hard following, dealt death on the strand,
forsook not his wyrd, fell at the slaughter field
by Wada's hand. With Saxons I sat,
with Secgs and Swordmen, and Langobardi.
Among Hetware – ravening reavers –
rede I rendered, won rings of strength.
Among Werns, war-mongers, I dwelt many days.
Meat and mead-horn I shared with Myrgings.
Eomer of Angeln, famed father's son,
gave gifts gladly. Alewih the Dane
thrust through the shield-wall, felled foes in swathes,
deadly his sword-dints. In high-hearted deeds
he did not outdo Offa the Angle.
For Offa, in youth, yearned for war-fame.
Foremost on Fifeldor, one sword his weapon,
no yard he yielded, laid Myrgings low,
marked there the marchland. To Hoc's hall I came,
drank down the mead-horn held by king's daughter.
Hildeburh her name, by heaven blessed,
winsome, winning, a fair frith-weaver,
a wife most worthy – would folk-lord wed.
The bairn she would bear, two kingdoms might bind."

Words so witful made wise the hearers!
The war-like Dane would wage no war
'gainst sister-son! Finn Folkwielder
sent lords to Dane-land, with rich gifts laden,
red gold, elf-wrought, rings of wonder.

Warm was Hnaef's welcome.    At once he saw the gain
(and longingly he looked    on lordly gold).
With Frisian folk-lord    bound in troth-bonds,
his Eotan war-smiths    no strife might stir
Hildeburh the winsome    was not unwilling.
Weal would she work,    strife-thoughts unweave.

Swift over swan-riding    swept Frisian sail,
bearing lady of Dane-land    to lofty hall.
There Finn Folkwielder    gave word and wife-gift.
After quickening in womb    the queen gave birth,
brought forth a son    ('Frithuwulf' she named him),
and he being weaned    was led to her lord.
Then Finn Folkwielder    called foremost lords,
and bade them bear    the child beloved
to Dane-lord's land.    Let mother-brother
watch and ward him,    teach him war and troth.

Hnæf held in heart    his sister-son,
tireless he taught him    lore and life-way,
word-weaving, war-craft,    hardship and hunting.

By All-Wielder's word    came sowing and harvest.
Fifteen winters fled,    bore Frithuwulf on
to manhood's morn.    Then Dane-lord quoth
(heart-ache hiding),    "Summer is nigh ended,
boughs heavy with haws,    rich hoard for fowls,
the harvest brought home.    Dark-clad swallows
south-way have sought.    Anon shines forth
the first full moon of winter;    grass wan, be-rimed,
cold mist in morn,    spiders spin their webs.
Woodlands now withered,    await winter's dread blast.
Where seething seas    the headlands storm,
no song-craft is heard    save gannets' call,
mocking of sea-mews,    the great erne's scream.
Fitting we fare    to father's homeland,
the swan-road riding,    sea-strife mocking."

Far-striving longships,    with stern-browed oarsmen,
seeking the sea-roads    where war-fame is won.
Right hard rowed Ordlaf –    bold Hunlaf's son –

with Guthlaf his brother,   lords of the Danes.
Shoulder by shoulder   unshirking sat Sigeferth,
of Secg folk sprung,   spear-lord unfearing.
At the rueing of Ravensburh   wrathfully he wreaked.
Old wrongs he righted,   new ones were wrought.
Folk-meeting found ill,   rendered him 'wretch'.
He shook out his shirt,   fared forth in wrath.
Eawa, Eofor's son,   bent back to the work,
with Wiglaf Wolf's-bane   and Horsa the Eote.

Hard by the helmsman   the Hengest, sharp-eyed,
scanned hoar waves heaving,   white spray hissing.
Sleek 'mares', snorting,   rode the wild waves,
with throbbing, thrilling   of thrustful sides,
'till from the masthead   came loud hail of look-out:
"Ahead stretches strand   where wind sweeps the dunes.
Here is the hearthland   the Frisians name 'home'! "
Landwards they led   their high-stemmed longships.
Shouting, laughing,   shipmen leapt forth.

The shore-ward, sharp-eyed,   saw bright helms shining,
fell weapons flicker   in west-wending sun.
Thrust heels into horse sides,   through high dunes threading,
fared forth on shore,   shaking ash-spear,
greeted farcomers gravely.   "Sea-lords," quoth he,
"Through long winters warding   this windswept shore,
never 'till now   beheld I such ships,
queenly sea-mares,   quelling the wave-strife,

nor such war-lords,    in grim gear girt,
who boldly, unbidden,    set foot on shore.
Finn Folkwielder,    the lord of these lands,
bade me ward and watch    for Hildeburh's kin,
war -crafty men,    bringing hither king's son.
Before you fare further    say whence you come."

Fearless, the folk-king    his word-hoard unbound,
"Hnæf is my name,    of Half-Dane's kin,
Finn's queen is our sister,    this youth her son,
Weapons he wields,    to manhood he's won."
The shore-ward, gladsome,    sprang from the saddle.
Knightly he knelt    to folk-lord's son.
Then leapt to his feet,    warmly in hand-grasp
the Half-Dane held,    with quick heart quoth:
"Eomær my name,    your way-leader now,
to high-halled Finnsburg,    red-glowing with gold.
Warely your war-boats    my men shall ward."

Stern-browed strivers    fared from the strand,
shoulder to shoulder,    shaking ash spears.
The Sea-lord's sixty,    Danes and Eotan.
Even-gloom gath'ring,    they gained the hall
where heroes were housed,    foretasting heaven's hearth.

The shore-ward halted,    his war-horse wheeled.
"Alack I must leave you,    again watch the shore.
May heaven's high blessing    the mead-sharing hallow."

By stone-way striding   came sea-worn band.
Firelight flickered,   glinted on war-shields
stacked at the threshold,   with ash-spears in thicket.
Eanmund the steward   gave wayfarers welcome.
“Long looked-for your coming,   Shield of the Danes,
long-waited the ‘frith-child’,   Hildeburh’s son,
long-readied the mead   that binds Frisian and Dane.”

Finn, glad-hearted,   took Hnæf in his arms,
then grasped his son,   Frithuwulf the Fair.
Hearth-thanes heeded   his hastening word,
brought forth the boards.   At queen’s quickening,
stepped forth the maidens,   mead-horns bearing.

Seldom sleeps sword   when one’s lord lies slain,
when wrongs are unrighted,   wrath-thirst unquenched.
When fell foes down ale   strong drink stirs strife.
Eotan shield-wielders   the newcomers eyed,
saw weapons won   by untroth in war.
These glared at the guests,   in under-speech growled,
“Where fathers framed halls   these Sea-Danes now feast,
from fields they furrowed   fill byres to the roof,
drink draughts from wells   our forebears delved.
The blades they bear   our war-smiths worked.
When Guthulf wended   his last war-way,
on fated field   Sea-Danes dealt death.
Now in our midst   sit the slayers’ sons!”
Brows grew blacker,   beholding the Hengest.

Danes they loved little, the Hengest loved least,
no man in the marchlands more hated than he.
"What whore bore this wretch (no Eote he in truth),
from fatherland's foes taking gifts of gold?"

Now out from the shadows, sleek rat slinking,
swart-coated reaver, bent on plunder,
snatched meat under mead-bench, fled back to his mate.
For one Eotan lord, swift theft watching,
thoughts were shaped sharply, word-hoard unlocked:
"Rats reave readily at churl's rude hearth.
And now, behold, in king's hall they come!"
(Was this wry-speaking of lordly and lowly,
or word-wounding more woeful than blows?)
Then quoth another (a high Frisian lord),
"Soothly thou sayest. From dung-heaps they dart,
then strut by the benches like king's guests in hall.
Yet, fear-filled, they flee, if finger threatens!
Rats should be ridden from hearth and hall"
Stony the stares, as still-ly they sat.
Hnæf's shoulders shook, wrath shadowed his brow.
Sea Danes looked on, waiting the war-word.
But Hengest, steel-hearted, chose not to hear,
laid hand on Hnæf's arm, drank deep from mead-horn.

Up rose queen Hildeburh (great now with child).
Heavy her heart, but winsome her words,
frith would she weave, woo men from strife.
(Yet woe must waylay our earth-won bliss.)
To Dane-land's lord the horn she handed,
bade him drink deeply, drain the sweet draught.
Among the mead benches, queenly, wending,
to high and low spoke weal-weaving words.
Thus Hildeburh strove strongly, strife to unweave,
then left the high hall, went back to her bower.

Now must Finn, folk-lord, choose words of weight,
bind men bent on war – Frisians, Eotan –
hot-heads each one. Quoth he to the Sea-lord,
"Long would I linger in hall's light and laughter,
send round the mead-horn, share in song-craft.

Yet wist I well    way-weary you are.
'Tis meet you rest    'till morning light.
This hearth and hall,    I gladly lend.
Hearth-friends shall house them    in hall full nigh.
'Hall-ward' I name you,    watch well this house!"
And Frisia's folk-lord    spoke thus with his son:
"No hardship I hold it,    Frithuwulf, dear son,
that you wend this while    with foster-father.
I bid you bide here."    (So were hot-heads bound,
the fight forestalled –    lest Finn's son they fell.)
Thus Finn, with his war-host,    withdrew from the hall.
Swiftly the night    swallowed their tread.

Hengest drained mead-horn,    thrust back the board,
to threshold leapt lightly    lingered in doorway.
As ears delved the darkness    he heard doom's call,
harsh screech of night-hawk,    naming men for death.
Grimly he grasped    the great door's bar,
hefted it high,    set it in hold,
bade spearmen bide,    grimly he spake:
"Wolf-hearts, ravening,    rend the redeless.
Yet with deeds of daring    the undoomed win free
So be wakeful, watching,    ware-eyed as owls!"
Hnæf watched in wonder,    thought furrowed his brow.
"By muchness of mead.    mind-strength is marred.
Words stirring war-strife    in red-dawn are rued.
Finn is my brother,    a war-lord of worth.
Not soon would he waylay    a guest in hall."
Hengest stood fast,    sword shifting in sheath –
hardly he held back    that blood-thirsting blade!
Eyes glinting, grim-like,    he growled these words:
"Folkwielder I fear not,    he havens no harm.
Yet others are with him,    with hate-hoard in heart,
guest-worth they weigh not,    unweal they weave.
You heard their words –    'rats to be ridden'.
Am I not a Eote?    What's heart-writ I read.
Among all the folkdoms    set by these seas,
where is the war-band,    finding forefathers' foes,
would war-play forgo,    leave wrath unwreaked?"

Hnæf, by the hearth,    unsheathed 'Hildeleoma'.
Grimly he greeted    keen blade of kindred –
the sweat-stained hilt    forefathers had held.
Bright wrath-wreaker    in firelight flickered,
life-quencher quickened    'gainst Daneland's foes.
Witless the war-lord    who feared not its bite!

Hoarding his heart-strength,    Hnæf laid down
in sea-weathered sark,    sword held in hand,
in doom-laden night.    War-smiths kept ward,
(weary their watching)    the moon wandering
in brooding clouds,    no life a-stir.

The Hengest came,    shook Hnæf awake,
bade rest begone.    By opened window
Ordlaf stood fast,    with Guthlaf his brother.
Eyes delved the dark,    where light flickered fleetly,
ears sought the sound,    of reavers' stealth.
Quoth Ordlaf outright    (bitter his speech),
"Whence this whisp'ring    wending so thiefly?
Wherefore this glinting,    gleaming through dark?
Dares the new day    to dawn forth by night?"
Shield-friend laughed softly,    shaped well his answer,
"A dragon of dread    in gold delighting,
with greed-lit eyes,    fire-breath a-flicker,
wends the night-winds    hunts down the hoard."
Guthlaf glowered,    grim-lipped, he growled,
"Some house-ward, unwitting    left hearth unwatched.
Fire, hoarse with hunger,    thrusts down the hall.
See! Roof-beams writhe,    horned gables burning!"
Then Hnæf held forth,    the king young in war,
"No east-born day is this,    nor dragon flying here,
nor of this hall    are horns now burning.
Here foes are afoot,    and gore-fowls sing,
grey-hoods howl,    and war-spears rasp,
shield answers shaft.    Now shines the moon,
by cloud-ways wending;    now woes are astir,
and this folk's hoarded hate    shall end in bitter strife.
But awake now,    my warriors,
hold lindens in hand,    your hearts keep fast

at the fore of the fray,    fightsome in mind!"
Many a thane, gold-laden,    rose and girt on his sword;
then doorwards strode    those lordly war-smiths,
Sigeferth and Eawa,    drawing forth their swords,
and to the other door    Ordlaf and Guthlaf,
with Hengest himself    hard at their heels.
Guthhere without    would hold back Gefwulf,
that he, though geared for war,    should not set life at risk
in that first onfall    at hall's fraught doors,
where one, war-hardened,    would quickly take it.
But he, daring-minded,    called openly
above war-talk of weapons,    asked who held the door.
"Sigeferth is my name", quoth one,    "I am a Secgan lord,
foot-loose, far-known,    not few the blows I've borne
in much hard harrying.    And here 'tis foredeemed
the fate you'd foist on me    shall fall on you!"

Then was there in hall,    the roar of slaughter.
Bold hands bore    the strong shield-boards,
'bone-helms' burst,    the hall-floor throbbed,
'till in the fight    fell Gefwulf,
ere-est of all    those earth-dwellers,
Guthulf's son,    good men about him,
the bodies of the brave.    The raven wheeled,
swart and sallow-brown.    Sword's flame gleamed
as if all Finnsburg    were a-fired.
I have heard of none so worthy    in all men's warrings –
sixty weapon-wielders    bearing well their arms –
nor heard I of youths    for white mead giving
such yield as these youths    gave to Hnæf.

Through five days they fought,    yet none there fell;
worthy shield-friends    held fast the door.
Then a war-smith, wounded,    staggered away,
said his mail-shirt    was sheared right through,
his battle-gear a-gape,    war-helm far gone.
Then the folkland's shield    straightway asked him
how war-smiths yet lasted,    their wounds outlived,
or which of the youths    yet forstood the foe,
as bone-breaking blows    battered linden boards,

and gore-crows croaked,  craving men's flesh,
and grey-hoods howled,  death's dread huntsmen.
And folkland's lord  spake thus, grimly:
"Who shall fathom  such depth of hatred?
Shield-friends shrink not!  Shut fast the doors!
In war-shirts, link-wrought,  be strength-clad, steadfast.
Let hearts dwell on high deeds  the forefathers won."
And, without, wise Guthhere  grieved for the wilful –
Gefwulf, high-hearted,  of high kindred come,
hope of his hearthland,  last of kings' line:
"Sharp death, surely,  shadows the heedless.
His doom has dawned  before its day.
Life held lightly  is lost for naught;
high fame in death  is dearly bought,
son of your fathers  with no son to follow."

The forefathers have sung  the famed deeds of old,
of Welund, Waldere,  Offa and Wada.
Wielding Welund's fell blade  (fire-forged, war-hardened)
Waldere handed hammer blows  to helmed foe-men,
when Guthhere, hoard-hungry,  scorned heaped ring-wealth,
wrought unrightly  to wrest treasure untold
from the hero's hand.  Then spake fair Hildegyth,
unlocked her word-hoard,  "Now is dawned that day,
dear lord, Ælfhere's son,  to win, of two things, one –
your life-hoard for-lost,  or name-worth living ever.
Fear not fell-play –  sword shall not falter,
a doughty blade, I deem  trothful to the true.
Guthhere, greed-gripped,  shall rue its thirst for blood."
(By that dread blade  Guthhere's death drew nigh.
Hagen's hand alone  held back his doom.)

Meaca the Myrging  mocked Angeln's lord,
bade him bow the knee,  bring wealth, heaped high,
or win woe-filled death.  Then Offa, lord's last-born
(his worth light-weighed)  found speech unspelled,
bade Myrging lord  mark well his word:
"On Fifeldor, sea-bound,  at Eider's mouth,
fare forth with war-gear,  shield-friend at hand.
My strength in strife,  outmatching your might,

shall right the wrong    my kinsfolk wrought,
when two slew one,    laid Eadgils low.
For folkdom I'll fight,    though death-thrust I find."
On sea-tossed strand,    the Myrging stepped,
helm-grim, heart-high,    haughty his words.
Offa stood steadfast,    gripped stern elder-blade.
Swift the sword-swoop    as Offa struck once,
cleft clean through Meaca    (no helm might hinder).
His fellow faltered,    then doom befell him.

Heoden wooed Hild –    love's song stirred her.
They sailed the swan-way,    reaped Hagena's wrath.
In sword-strife on strand    deadly the stroke-play.
They neared death's gates,    though yet undoomed.
Wada, stern wave-lord,    stood fast in the way.

There is no time to tell    of Hwala and Hrathra,
of Eomær the elder    of Frithugar, Freawine,
of the maiden Maethhild    and Geat's boundless love.
All won fair fame    (our fathers have told us)
yet none fought more fell-ly    than Hnæf's helmed host.

Once more through the hall    the spear-storm raged,
when war-worth is won    and doomed men die,
linden shields are shattered,    and ring-coats shorn.
Eawa and Ælfhere    feared not the fight.
Deathless in dying,    they live on in song.
Full-oft in fight    'Hildeleoma', elf-wrought
had rent wrought mail,    halved haughty helms,
and never 'till now    its name forsaken.
Now weary, unwary,    the Sea-Danes' lord
left breast unwarded,    and foe's fell blade
sheared through his shirt.    Sword slipped from his grasp,
as war-strength waned.    He yielded his life.
Foreboding filled hearts,    Danes faltered, fell back.
Then Frithuwulf, grief-struck,    fought back his tears,
called to the host    that had drunk Hnæf's mead:
"Now high talk in hall    shall be weighed in war.
We swore to our lord    to wield 'gainst war-lords
the gear he gave,    the swords, the helms
we bear this night.    Our troth he trusted.
Do now the deeds    then woven in words.
A man may not linger    when his lord lies dead."
The housecarls heeded,    they hewed like woodsmen,
one last gift to grasp –    to lie with their lord.
No man might thwart doom    in war's wild uproar.
Eotan earl, grim-helmed,    found out that youth
who yearned to lie    with the lord he loved,
dealt the death he sought,    sheared through his ring-mail.
Hnæf, Frithuwulf,    one-hearted in life,
at new day's dawning,    they slept in death.
Alack for that dawn    alighting on death!
Alack for the sun    glowering, blood-red!
Alack for the morn wind    sighing, sorrowing!
Alack for the high hall    'whelmed in woe!
No more the hearth-friends    sharing the horn.
Of Finn's famed war-band    few were unscathed.
No way to war longer,    the Danes yet forstood him.
Weary this warring    that never he sought.
When men spoke frith,    fairly he answered,
Let Hengest, as host-lord,    set hands in his,
then folklord would find    a hall for the mighty,

for Dane-lords and friends.        He would give at the gift-stool
to each man his meed,        rings of red gold.
Then Hengest in hall        laid sword-hand in host's,
gave life-binding oaths        to be Finn's man.
And Finn Folkwielder        swore oath for oath
that frith now forged        no foe should sunder.
Should Frisian war-lord,        with tongue, spite-sharpened,
stir minds to strife,        speak of wrath unwreaked,
his doom should be dealt        by sword's death-thrust.

Sea-Danes, sorrowing        heaped high the wood-stack.
'Shield' of the Scyldings        they set in the midst,
with iron-hard war-helm        (boar-crest unbowed),
mail-sark all marred.        Stepped forth fair Hildeburh
grief-songs she sang,        groaned under breath:
"The man that is mighty        in the morn of his days,
is soon swept away,        shorn of his strength.
Though he linger a little,        the life-fire dims,
death binds the boldest        and bears him away.
Alack, my brother,        alack beloved son,
in life and in death        you were not sundered!"
The song was stilled,        Hildeburh sighed,
Straightway came others,        ferried the fallen.
Fire-brands flickering,        licked at the wood-stack.
Woodsmoke, wind-born,        billowed drearly,
fire gorged greedily        gulped down its prey.
Red fire, roaring,        o'erwhelmed the weeping,
sank down sullenly,        smouldered, unsated.

Winter's first full moon        stepped coldly forth.
Wild winds swept bare        the wealdland's boughs.
Sun strove strengthless.        Nights numb with cold,
field and furrow        ash-strewn with frost,
still meres blackened,        in ice-hard hold,
as winter, wolf-hearted        gripped all in his grasp.
By sea-strand's swirling        lone call of sea-mew,
with whaup's call mingled        and great erne's wailing.
Wind whipped the billows,        waves reared and roared.
No high-prowed sea-mare        might ride that wrath.
In drear winter depths        came that day of toil –

a-bed lay Hildeburh,    by birth-pangs bowed.
To folkland's lord    she bore a man-child,
in lap she laid him,    her 'son of grief'.
Then Finn's sister swore    she would mother this son.
Frealaf she named him,    Folkwielder's heir.

Through brooding nights,    through storm-dark days,
the Hengest sat stone-like,    with dark thoughts strove,
of wrongs unrighted,    of blood unwreaked,
Not of Finn's forging,    that foul-play in hall.
Yet his were the war-lords    broke troth by night.
How weary the wending    of winter days,
under Yulemonths' snows,    with north wind sighing
by eaves and eye-doors,    gnawing men's bones!
Wild wood's grey reavers    waylay the gates.
Then winter wanes,    by God's tried troth.
Gladly men greet    the first signs of summer:
snow's hold slackens,    swirling of melt-water,
fields become fens,    rough play of winds,
woods roar and writhe,    with lengthening days,
homing of house-swallows,    swooping, darting,
showers in the sunlight,    sweet smell of earth.
Men yearn for the sea-roads,    and salt-winds' sighing.

As Hengest sat stonily,    came Hunlaf's son,
laid in the lap    'Hildeleoma', battle-light,
bright wonder-blade,    heir-loom of elder days,
whose edges, elf-wrought,    Eotan well knew.
Once only it wilted,    when Hnæf's doom dawned.
Now thrusting, throbbing,    for foes' death it thirsted.
The Hengest stirred,    two-minded no more.
The lord that he loved    lay dead in the grave.
Though bound to the slayer    in oath-bonds unsought,
wrath he would wreak.    He unlocked his word-hoard:
"The fast-friend I loved    is slain in untroth,
and Finn is lord    to those laid him low.
For evil wrought    I must evil render."

Ordlaf ætheling,    Hunlaf's bold son,
stood before Folk-lord,    weighed out his words:
"Sea-lords we are,    o'er wide seas wending.

Hearts are yet havened where hearth-land bore us.
Homeward we hasten, in Dane-land delighting.
The Hengest, our brother, shall here abide.
Surely his sword's edge king's foes shall fear!
If war is wakened, word he shall send us
of strife a-stirring. We'll hasten on ship-board.
O'er seas swift sailing, to foes deal death."
Folk-ward, unwary, his blessing bestowed.

Glittering, gleaming, mail-shirts o'er leather,
headstrong, hardy in high-crested helms,
wielding war-spears – Danelanders wending,
shoulder to shoulder, down wind-whipped strand,
where sea-mares snorted, wave-strife awaiting.
Hard by on headland grim-browed shore-ward
sat his steed still-ly, ash-spear held high.
Keen watch he had kept, warded their war-boats,
from ill-will of winter, from surging of storm-waves.
Fain would he fall on these friends made foes,
Yet sharpness of shame quelled the wrath he would wreak.
It was Frisians, alack, who dealt death to their guests.
From shore's clasp freed, their keel cleft the waves.
Mast soared skywards, sails outbillowing.
Wind and wave quickened weald-born limbs,
and ship's swan-breast thrust swirling seas,
quivering, questing, quelling waves' onrush,
with sea-strength's roar, and sighing of shrouds,
with shuddering, shivering, 'till eyes, far-seeking,
lit on loved shore, on headlands held dear.
On raced the sea-mare, reared up on the strand.
In haste came hythe-ward, hailed the home-comers.
Long had he looked forth, scanned the sky-rim,
for folkland's Shield and famed hearth-friends.
He ran out the ropes, bound sea-mare fast
'gainst seething seas, then searched the benches
for Hnæf's loved brow – heart misgave him.
Forth fared wordsmen through land's four fourths,
by weald and waste, through wild and fen,
to farm and fold and high-towered fastness,
bade Dane-land's lords to Hunlaf's hall.

Hither came high lords,   matchless in worth,
with witfast redesmen,   wondrous in rune-craft,
with hoar-headed elders,   warded the folk-hoard,
weighed times and tokens,   delved deep for truth.
Hither came word-wise,   weavers of songs,
and far-famed war-lords,   fearless in spear-strife.
Hither came huntsmen   high-hearted, hardy,
wise in woodcraft,   knew deer and den.
Ordlaf, stern-faced,   stilled that throng
with hand upheld,   then told his tale
of Finnsburg's hall,   and faring fated,
how Eotan lords,   with hearts hate-gripped
and speech spite-filled   stirred up old wrongs,
how Frisians followed,   and troth was trampled.
They stormed the steading,   slew Hnæf in hall.
Frithuwulf fought on,   was felled in turn.
His tale full told,   Ordlaf spake thus:
"Lords of the Sea-Danes,   weigh well my words!
Shall our fathers' sons,   dealt death unrightly,
lie ever in earth-bed,   their slayers unslain?
If wrath is not wrought   for blood that is shed,
who for us shall wreak wrath   when our doom is dealt?
Surely fell foes   would fear us no more."
Great was the wrath wrought   'gainst Eotan untroth!
Word-bearers wended   through all that folkland,
bade men leave their plough-shares,   and unsheath the swords.
Each homestead, heeding,   made haste to hosting.

Sea-strand darkened   by a thousand shields,
thicket of fell-spears –   death-bearing darts.
Keen-edged swords   slept yet in sheaths
(fitting that foes   should fear their wakening!)
Stout linden boards   on strong shoulders borne
by high-helmed warriors,   stern-faced as death.
Sails shook and shivered,   longed for the sea-ways.
Mighty the hosting   of the Dane-land folk!

From high-helmed foreland,   shore-ward held watch –
Eomær, Eadwine's son,   first among Frisians.
Through winter's blast,   and summer's ease,

he watched unwearied –    his only songs
the sea-grass stirring,    the surging waves,
full-throated outburst    of red-shanked wader,
bubbling song of whaup,    sea-mews' lone call.
Through ten years twice-told    he'd held these shores,
yet never beheld he    a sea-host so mighty.
Osfrith, onlooking,    well loved that lord,
feared he would lose him    (he held life lightly),
urged him ride hard    for heedless Finnsburg,
that Frisians might ready    for foes' dread onset.
No wary word    would Eomær hear.
"My watch and ward    I give to no other.
Not death I fear,    but shamed life's lingering."
Straightway he called    Siward the Saxon,
bade him ride hard    for Finnsburg's hall,
bid men bar the gates,    gird on their gear."
Loath was the hostage    these words to heed.
"Here in the shield-wall,    shouldered with you,
rightly I stand.    How should I live,
if my lord lies slain?"    Then quoth Eomær,
"Short-lived the sundering!    Though death find us first,
hard shall it follow    to Finnsburg's hold."
Osfrith, foreboding,    drew forth bold blade –
stirred from its sleep,    it glittered in sunlight.
Ecgbald stood ready,    bitter his spear-tip!
Thrythwulf, unthrifty    in dealing out death,
welcomed foes' onset.    Winebeald, unwavering,
weighed the war-axe    fingered the blade.
Ealhmund, in earnest,    loosed hawk dear-held,
swiftly it swooped    from hand to holt.
(After the war-play,    after doom fulfilled,
that spear-hawk, trothfast,    found out her lord,
mourned frame much-marred,    kept sleepless watch.)

Up from the strand    came Ordlaf striding
"Eomær, Eadwine's son,    give ear to my word!
To Finn our reckoning    is rightly rendered
for guests he greeted    with grievous gifts.
Eomær, hear us!    This host do not hinder.

A life undoomed    from wrath is wrested!"
Then earl gave answer,    bold words brought forth,
"Sea-lords, fame-seeking,    my word is set!
Here at the threshold    of loved hearthland
I stand this day    at lord's behest.
No foe shall fare    forth from this shore
save by blood-soaked sarks    of folkland's sons."

Sea-wolves thrust forward,    sought battle-fame –
war-shouts shattering,    rending the ears,
spear shafts throbbing    on stout linden boards,
red-blades rasping,    roused from their sheaths,
sharp arrows speeding,    swift and sure,
death-dealing darts    seeking the doomed.
Ecgbald, sister-son,    foremost of æthelings,
first now to fall,    by fell sword for-hewn.
Osfrith sprang forward,    the slayer he slew,
before he was felled    by fated spear.
Winebeald, Ealhmund    heaped high their foes,
'till, sword-arms wearied,    they fell, side by side –
fast friends in hall,    fast-bound in death.
In war-play Thrythwulf    thrust, and thrived,
he sold not his life    'till sword-thirst was sated.
The shield-wall shrank,    shorn of its strength.
Then spoke Eomær    (shook his ash-spear),
"Heart-strength is hardened,    thought the keener,
mind-strength undimmed,    as our might dwindles.
Here lie my friends,    thanes all for-hewn,
laid low in the dust.    No rest shall he reap
who now flees the fight,    from war-play wends.
Too long I have lived –    my last home lies here."
Then war-hardy lord,    thrust into throng,
wrought there ruefully,    'till keen-eyed spearman
sent swift flying dart,    unlocked his life-hoard.
Then strength was sapped,    sword fell lifeless.
Yet once more he willed    words from his hoard,
"All-Father, hear me!    Fast troth have I kept,
Keep troth with me    at my faring-forth.
In heaven's halls    may I sit at your board."

Mighty the hosting    of the Dane-land folk!
High hedge of spears    glittering in sunlight,
stout linden boards    on strong shoulders borne
by dark-helmed shield-lords,    grim-faced as death,
to Finnsburg for-gathered,    fast shut against them,
swart ravens wheeling,    grey-hoods howling,
thirsting, eyeing    the march of doomed men.
Mad rush of sea-wolves,    with wrath to wreak,
ash-shafts crashing    on broad-rimmed shields,
arrows whining,    with spite speeding,
sharp spears screeching,    stout boards splintering,
shield-lords shouting,    mail-sarks gleaming.
Fastness of Frisians    feared little that onset.
Her stout oak stakes    scorned the spear-strokes,
her gates frowned grimly,    threw back the Danes.
Grievous the groans    of men gripped by death,
sorrowing, sundered    from hearth and home.
(Ordlaf must mourn,    he moaned for Guthlaf.)
Frisians, high-hearted,    full-throated, roared:
"Foes' doom is dealt,    they falter, they flee!" –
yet soon they would rue    their nightfall at noon.
Shield-lord, sharp-minded,    smelt bitter burning,
heard rasping, rending    of ravening fire,
turning, looked on    drear smoke billowing,
fire's dread fingers    roof-thatch clawing.
roof-trees, life-lorn,    in fell flames falling,
the hall beloved,    in death throes writhing.
And at the burning    stood high-helmed Hengest!
With breast nigh bursting,    with tears grief-born,
through thick of fighting    Finn thrust forward,
by dark wrath driven,    death unheeding.
Hengest grasped 'Battle-light'    Hnæf's bright blade –
for foe's blood thirsting,    for lord's life a reckoning –
spake thus with Finn,    loved lord's slayer:
"Yours the war-smiths    waylaid the unwary,
the guests given you,    who trusted your troth.
Like fell foes they wrought –    grievous their blows –
by shame unshaken,    in the shadows of night.
For blood shed unrightly    full fee must be found."
Down swept the sword-arm,    bringing swift death,

thrust through the mail-sark,     life blood unlocked.
At Finnsburg's fair hall,     high-built for fame,
where maidens bore mead     among mighty lords,
and word-smiths sang     the high deeds of old,
and hearth-friends feasted,     forgot winter's woes –
in hall loved in life     Finn lay down in death.

Once more the war-host     of Dane-land folk,
ringed round the fortress,     roared their wrath,
like wild waves crashing     on stone-bound shore.
Great gates faltered,     stout bars groaned.
Tall towered-walls     shuddered, shook,
by fell foes beset     without, within.
Then the lack-willed     fled the fastness,
forsook their troth,     forgot the gifts
given in hall     by hearth-land's lord –
Finn Folkwielder,     the open-handed.
They left the war-play,     sought the wild wood,
sheltering boughs     shielded lives now shamed.
More than were meet     wended that way.
Wulfric, Wulf's son,     fled not the fight.
Three famed fighters     fell by his sword,
ere last of life-breath     left his soul-house.
Sigestan shirked not,     though shaft was shivered.
Deadly the dints     he dealt out to Danes,
stood fast with Freagar,     in stark war-play,
shoulder by shoulder     'till strength ebbed away –
last of the hearth-friends     for-hewn at Finn's side.
From gate to garth     the Sea-Danes delved,
brought forth the wealth-hoard,     heaped in hall
great gold arm rings,     glowing in firelight,
dark gold, dwarf-wrought     in the depths of the earth,
bear-skins and beaver,     and kingly cloaks,
sword-blades, bitter-edged,     rune-writ, threatening,
sheaths, gem-studded,     delighting the eye,
great horns of aurochs,     rimmed round with silver,
ring-mail, close-wrought,     death-thrust defying,
great bows of yew,     taut strings throbbing,
shafts straight and true,     slender goose feathers,
arrow heads steel-blue,     sharp as winter wind,

shoulder-clasps, fire-red,   brooches, buckles –
writhing beasts, richly-wrought –   wonder work of smiths.
No dragon of dread   e'er held such hoard!
Eotan and Sea-Danes   heaped up their halves.
Straightway, the Hengest   shipped his wealth-share,
fared forth from that shore   to fish elsewhere.
(There were wars enough   where wealth might be won.)
With him fared Wulfrith   (the Britons would rue it).

Dane-land's hosting   left blackened Finnsburg –
smouldering, smoking –   sought the sea-ways,
bore Hildeburh with them,   Hoc's fair daughter,
bereft of brother,   of son and husband,
comely maiden,   forsaken, forlorn.
(Meet it is in man   that he mind this word:
'Wrath unresting   spawns rightless deeds.')

Now Hildeburh, heart-harrowed,   took up this song:
"Woe, woe, woe of mine!   Sorrow upon sorrow!
Grief heaped on grief!   How shall I bear it?
Frithuwulf, for you I sorrow.   Wherefore wyrd so warped?
For Hnæf, fair brother,   our father's first strength,
for you I yearn,   and my heart is heavy.
Witless the war-lord   who feared not your might!
From the death of doomed foe   your sword turned not back.
Hnæf and Frithuwulf,   most fair and beloved,
you swooped on the prey   swifter than spear-hawk.

Folkland's strong shield,    Finn great-hearted,
wondrous your love,    weaving my weal.
For you I sorrow,    dear homeland's lord.
How foul the deed,    and him who dealt it!
Eotan, unruthful,    reckless in wrath,
bitter their blades,    spite-filled their spears,
they hoard harm like wealth.    Woe to the ill-willed
who work not the weal    given them to weave!

"Finnsburg, so dark tonight,    no lamp, no light!
Finnsburg, so cold tonight,    no red glow of fire!
Finnsburg lies still tonight,    no roar of flame.
Finnsburg forlorn tonight,    no laughter, no song.
Finnsburg is lone tonight,    no hand to keep it.
Finnsburg is shorn tonight,    bereft of her Shield.
While her lord lived,    no beam need bar her doors!

"Finnsburg! the harpers    are heard in you no more.
The wonder-craft of smith    is wrought in you no more.
The wilsome word-play    is woven in you no more.
The comely maidens,    lithely as the deer,
bearing bright mead-horns,    are seen in you no more.
The wall-brands blazing,    light-hearted youths,
beloved faces, fire-lit,    gladden hearts no more.
How lonely stands the hall,    once full-warriored,
her high-horned gables,    her roof-trees, rendered dust!
Her shield-gates shattered,    her gold grown dim!

"From hearth-land hither    I came full-handed,
to homeland hie me,    heart-sick, empty.
Winter, untimely,    has withered my spring.
Why should life linger,    cling to the hopelorn?
Though death flee from me,    his drear house I'll seek.
Freya, fraught lady,    I feared you for naught!
A queen quick-grasping,    gift-thirst ne'er quenched.
Mean-handed your meed,    unminding my troth,
your handmaid unhelped    in her most need.
A shield of shadow    I'll trust no more."
Forlorn lies Finnsburg,    its gates a-gape,
mute mounds, shapeless,    dark under night's helm.
All earth-fame fades,    finds its even-tide.

## Notes

1-10. Wisdom sayings were very much part of Old English writing, and the poem opens with a little homily on man's heedlessness. God may be good to a man, yet man takes it lightly, becomes over-mighty, and does not ponder the wyrd (doom) that awaits him.

12. **gift-stool**: The bonds between a Dark Age chieftain and his followers were kept strong through the giving of gifts – weapons, for example, and brooches, clasps, arm rings and the like, made from precious metals. (See the giving of gifts by Hrothgar, in *Beowulf* lines 80-81.) The king or chieftain sat on the 'gift-stool' in hall, to give out the gifts, and this became another word for a royal throne.

15. **Stag's head set high**: Antlers fastened to the apex of the hall, and perhaps totemic (see the reference to 'horns' in line 1 of the *Finnesburg Fragment.*

18-19. **The hand that held the hissing brand ...** In the way of Anglo-Saxon writers the poet adds a foreboding word. The great hall of Finnsburg would be burned to the ground one day, when the deed-doer (Hengest) had come to weapon-years.

20-26. It was the way of the Anglo-Saxon poet to speak aside in words few and dark. The hearers of his own day, with wits about them, would grasp his meaning. But readers today are too often lost for lack of background knowledge. Here the poet, having spoken of Finnsburg, goes back to earlier happenings among the Eotena (Jutes). He reminds his hearers that when Godric's son (the Jutish king, Guthulf, father of the Gefwulf of the poem) went a-warring against the Danes the eastern Jutes did not stir. This was because they yet harboured wrath over the death of one of their own, Sigebert, slain by Guthulf. The king fell in battle with Hoc Half-Dane, and this was seen as fated to happen (he '**followed his wyrd-way**'). Those western Jutes who were left took flight to Frisia, and they in turn harboured wrath against the eastern Jutes who, as they saw it, had left their lord in the lurch.

27-28. **the Half-Dane**, that is, Hoc, king of the Danes.

**life-thread**: A reference to the unfolding of history, and of the lives of men and women, in terms of the 'weaving' of wyrd or destiny. The fraying, loosening, or breaking of the life-thread therefore spelt death.

The **Scyldings' son** is Hnæf, son of Hoc. The kingly house of the Danes were named from their forebear Scyld, great-grandfather of the Hrothgar of the *Beowulf* poem.

33. **Wulfrith Witfast** is pictured in the tale as the only one of the eastern Eotan who sailed with the western folk to the Frisian lands.

34. **Far have I fared ...** In the way of the *Widsith* poet Wulfrith tells of his faring through the folkdoms of the southern Baltic and northern Germany. As he names the folkdoms he has known a strange pattern comes out. It seems that he wins a welcome from one folk, then fares onward and finds a welcome with another who are their sworn foes. After dwelling among the Spear-Danes he goes to the Heathobards (lines

35-6). He then goes from the Huns to the Burgundians (line 40), from the Halsings to the Rugians (lines 45-6), and from the Myrgings to the Angles (lines 57-8).

35. **Swedes**: In the fifth century AD the Swedes occupied only the middle belt of modern Sweden, around Lakes Vänern and Vättern.

35. **Spear-Danes**: The Danes are first known in southern Sweden and Seeland. By AD 500 they had moved into northern Jutland.

36. **Heathobards**: This Germanic folk were long-time foes of the Danes.

37. **Wends**: The Veneti of Tacitus (*Germania* 46). They dwelt east of the middle Vistula. 'Wends' seems to have been the name given to these Slavomic neighbours by the Germans (Chambers, p.209).

38. **Geat-lord**: The Geats lived south of the central lakes of Sweden.

39. **Hrethel**: Fifth century AD king of the Geats. His daughter was mother of the hero, Beowulf, who rid the great hall named 'Heorot' of the monster, Grendel.

40. **Huns harrowed Guthhere, Burgundian lord**: The Huns first appeared in Europe (perhaps from central Asia) in the fourth century AD. Under the leadership of Attila (AD 406-453) they built a powerful empire in east and central Europe, but it quickly fell apart after Attila's death.

The Burgundians are first recorded as an Eastern Germanic tribe, neighbours of the Goths and the Gepidae. By the end of the third century AD they had migrated westwards and, from across the Rhine, they began to threaten Gaul.

42. **Gifthas ... Wulfings ... Goths**:

The Gifthas were an East Germanic folk.

The Wulfings dwelt on the Baltic coast, with the Goths as their neighbours to the south. In the fourth century AD the latter occupied the plains north of the Black Sea, between the Sea of Azov and the Danube.

43. **Eormenric**: king of the Ostrogoths, renowned for his greed and trothlessness. According to the historian Ammianus Marcellinus he committed suicide in AD 375 as his kingdom was being overrun by the Huns.

45. **Halsings**: The Halsings probably lived on the lower Trave, and were near neighbours of the Angles. Chambers (*Widsith*, p.194) says they were probably of 'Anglo-Frisian' stock.

46. **Rugians**: The Island-Rugians seem to have dwelt on the islands and peninsulas at the mouth of the Vistula, and possibly along the Baltic coast as far west as the Oder. They migrated southwards to what is now Austria, in the mid-fifth century AD.

47-52. **Heoden loved Hild ... Heorrenda**: See under 'Tales of the northern folkdoms' above.

52. **Saxons**: The Saxons dwelt between the Weser and the Elbe before migrating to Britain in the fifth/sixth centuries AD.

53. **Secgs and Swordmen, and Langobardi**: The Secgs are ruled by Sæferth in *Widsith*, the Sigeferth named here. Next to nothing is known about them, but from the context we may take it that they lived somewhere along the southern shores of the Baltic. It has been suggested that the Swordmen are the Suardones of Tacitus (*Germania* 40), a folk related to the Angles. However, the identification is not proven (see Chambers, p.210). The ancient home of the Langobardi (Lombards) seems to have been between the Elbe and the south-west shores of the Baltic.

54. **Hetware**: The Hatuarii of classical sources, a Frankish folk dwelling between the mouth of the Rhine and the Zuider Zee. Later they moved further up the Rhine, to the neighbourhood of Cleves. Here, in AD 521, they were attacked by Hygelac the Geat, but they defeated and killed him.

56. **Werns**: The Varini of Tacitus, who says that they (with the Angles) were among seven Germanic tribes who shared a common worship of Nerthus, or Mother Earth (*Germania* 40). The Werns dwelt in Schleswig, between the Danes to the north and the Angles to the South.

57. **Myrgings**: Probably dwelt between the Eider and the Elbe.

58. **Eomer of Angeln**: He is named the son of Offa in *Beowulf* lines 1957-60. He was in fact the grandson, his father being Angeltheow son of Offa.

59. **Alewih the Dane**: Apart from the brief reference in *Widsith* lines 36-38, Alewih is wholly unknown.

62, 64. **Offa the Angle … Fifeldor**: According to Saxo Grammaticus the fight took place on the island of Fifeldor at the mouth of the Eider river.

69. **frith-weaver**: In her book *Peace-Weavers and Shield-Maidens* Kathleen Herbert explains the part played by women in holding society together through 'weaving' peace. As in everyday life they were spinners and weavers ('spinsters', 'websters'), so in a deeper sense they wove peace in the community. In particular, a high-born woman might be given in wedlock to bring peace between two kindreds or dynasties that would otherwise be at enmity. Here her work was bound up with the greatest weaving of all, the weaving of Wyrd or destiny (Herbert, p.16).

80. **his** (that is, Finn's) **Eotan war-smiths**: meaning those Eotan warriors who fled west to Frisia after Hoc Half-Dane slew their lord.

96. **by All-Wielder's word**: the pattern of sowing, summer, harvest and winter witness to the faithfulness of God, who gave his word that while the earth remains these things shall not cease (Genesis 8:22).

103. **the first full moon of winter**: 'Winterfylleth' (October) was the time when the first full moon of the winter was seen.

115-6. **Secg folk ... Sigeferth**: See note to line 53.

117. **At the rueing of Ravensburh**: see on lines 20-26. Again the poet speaks aside, and darkly, of things well enough known to his hearers (in this case, a bitter fight), but now long-forgotten.

119. **wretch**: that is, outlaw.

161. **foretasting heaven's hearth**: The life of the warrior beyond death is pictured in terms of the feast in hall, but on a more glorious scale. There is perhaps some likeness here to the Christian celebration of holy communion as a foretaste of the banquet of the Messiah and his folk in heaven.

170. **frith-child**: that is, the 'peace-child' who (it was hoped) would bind Frisians and Danes together.

196. **swart-coated reaver**: that is, the black rat. Oliver Rackham (*History of the Countryside*, pp.46-7) writes that the black rat is now thought to be a native of South India. It spread into Mediterranean lands by late Classical times, and thence to Germany and Britain by the 3rd century AD. The black rat carries bubonic plague, and it is plausible that the pestilence which swept across Europe in the 540s, in the time of the emperor Justinian, was this disease.

208. **Rats should be ridden**: that is, got rid of.

243-4. **doom's call/Harsh screech of night-hawk**: the nightjar. According to traditional belief, the call of the nightjar, heard after dark, was a foretelling of death.

267, 269. **'Hildeleoma ... sweat-stained hilt**: 'Hildeleoma' (that is, 'battle-light') is clearly a sword handed down within the kindred. The reference to the 'sweat-stained hilt' may suggest a belief that something of the being of the forebears was actually passed to that hilt, as it was handled in battle.

307. **doorwards**: that is, towards the door.

311. **Guthhere**: not the same man as Guthhere the Burgundian (line 40).

332-3. **nor heard I of youths**: the young men of Hnæf's war-band had drunk his mead, and they now repay him as they sell their lives dearly.

359. **Welund, Waldere, Offa and Wada**: See 'Tales from the northern folkdoms' above. Welund and Beadohild are named in the poem *Deor* (lines 1-13) among those whose great sorrows passed in the end.

362. **when Guthhere, hoard-hungry**: not the Guthhere of this poem, but Guntharius the Frank, the grasping king of the tale of Waldere.

373. **Meaca the Myrging**: see under 'Offa of Angeln' in 'Tales from the northern folkdoms' above.

395. **Hwala and Hrathra**: far distant forebears of the kingly house of Wessex. Nothing is known about them.

396. **Eomær the elder**: 'Eomær' means 'famous horse'. Perhaps he was named 'the elder' so that there would not be confusion with Eomær, grandson of Offa of Angeln. Nothing whatever is known about him.

396. **Frithugar, Freawine**: Nothing is known of Frithugar, but his son Freawine is the king of the Waernas slain by Eadgils (see under 'Offa of Angeln' in 'Tales from the northern folkdoms' above). He would therefore have lived about the mid-fourth century AD (GJ Copley, *The conquest of Wessex in the sixth century*, p.135).

397. **Mæthhild … Geat**: There is a brief reference to Geat's boundless love for Maethhild in *Deor* lines 14-17. There is nothing else known for certain. However, Kemp Malone identified the pair with the Gaute/Gauti and Magnhild in a Scandinavian ballad, a tale with some parallels to the Orpheus story. Magnhild sorrows because she is to drown, and no one can escape their fate. She is duly drowned, but is brought back to life by the harp-playing of Gaute. (See Kathleen Herbert, *Spellcraft*, pp.278-82.)

438, 442. **set hands in his ... laid sword-hand in host's**: When a warrior swore troth with his lord he placed his hands together, enclosed within his lord's hands.

450. **Scyldings**: see note on line 28.

459. **in life and in death you were not sundered!** compare 2 Samuel 1:23.

467. **Winter's first full moon**: see note on line 103.

491. **Wild wood's grey reavers**: wolves. These might hover around the dwellings of men in the hungry time of midwinter.

492. **by God's tried troth**: a hint of God's word, given after the Great Flood, that seedtime and harvest, summer and winter, would not cease (Genesis 8:22).

501. **Laid in the lap 'Hildeleoma', battle-light**: A clear challenge to Hengest to avenge the slaying of his lord. The incident is referred to in *Beowulf*, lines 1142-5.

503. **Eotan well knew**: Either because it had once been theirs, or because it had slain many of them.

512. **For evil wrought**: A blunt setting-forth of the ancient Germanic code of revenge.

521. **We'll hasten on ship-board**: Ordlaf promises that the Danes will come back if they hear any word of war in the land of the Frisians. But his words are two-edged. The Danes will indeed come back – to *bring* war, and to help Hengest wreak vengeance for the death of Hnæf.

538. **weald-born**: that is, made of timber from the weald or forest.

556. **rune-craft**: In ancient northern mythology Woden won knowledge of the runes as he hung for nine days and nights on the great World Tree (the ash 'Yggdrasill' in Norse mythology), pierced with a spear. The runic letters became vehicles for

magical power, used (by those who understood them) for divination, for protective spells, and the like.

595. **full-throated outburst of red-shanked wader**: the cry of the redshank is variously described as 'ringing', 'clamorous', 'explosive'.

666. **All-Father**: that is, Woden, the chief god of the ancient Germanic pantheon.

689. **their nightfall at noon**: that is, their untimely deaths.

743. **aurochs**: The wild ancestor of European domestic cattle. It is unlikely that it was found in Britain beyond the Bronze Age, but it survived in wildwood areas of continental Europe until the seventeenth century. (The last animals died out in Jaktorowa Forest, in Poland, in 1627, see O Rackham, *History of the Countryside*, p.33.) The Anglo-Saxons knew of the aurochs, and called the runic letter *ur* (equivalent of U) after it. Two large drinking vessels made from aurochs horns were among the kingly treasures of the Sutton Hoo ship burial (RLS Bruce-Mitford, *The Sutton Hoo Ship Burial*, p.29).

755. **the Britons would rue it**: the rede-crafty Wulfrith would play a key part in the outwitting of Vortigern, and in Hengest's wresting of the kingdom of Kent from the British.

787. **no beam need bar her doors!** that is, so long as Finn lived his strength and skill in war were enough to ensure the security of Finnsburg.

803. **Freya**: see note on Frija/Freya in 'Anglo-Saxon heathenism' above.

# 'The Stallion'

How warped man's ways – who knows their working?
Gainful, guileful grasping unrightly,
no wolf of the wildlands more wily, unruthful,
Let man who is death-bound mark well this word:
"High heaven's King has wrought man's wyrd
(both witful and wareless work but his will).
He renders rightly, reckoning the deed."

Swirling of storm-waves, roaring, striving,
seething of salt-spray, hissing, spiteful,
as Hengest 'Lack-lord' wandered the whale-mere,
with sea-wolves benumbed, winter-wearied.
No hall their home, no hearth-warmed bliss,
no bright mead glittering, gladdening the lips.
No songs of strife-deeds stirring the heart,
only sea-fowl following, ill foreboding.
The Hengest, storm heeding, sought haven for sea-mares.
Sleek keels slipped in where once Roman prows
set down strong anchors, below fair fortress
and high-towered lighthouse, now standing unlit.
Here, at the inn hearth, Eotan sought ease:
the Hengest, with Horsa, and 'Hrofi' the Ganger,
Ceolmund and Ciorra, Gythla and Ægel,
Wulfrith 'Witfast' and Wipped 'Spear's son'.
The Hengest, mead-glad, spoke thus with his friends:
"The world's wrath-riven – a war-lord's delight.
The Huns' host is smarting, they hoard up their hate.
They've sworn to their swords blood thirst to slake.
The Franks seek folkdom where Romans once trod.
There's little of love 'twixt Gothland and Rome.
Too often troth's trampled, now swords have their say.
Over Middle-earth Sea the Vandals, unhindered,
send sea-hosts scouring, snatching at will,
wresting the riches from soft-living Rome.
Here's wealth-hoards awaiting, high fame to win –
only, which war to choose? 'Twixt two minds I strive!"

Hard by the hearth,    lords out of Britain
leaned close to listen,    then unlocked the word-hoard:
"Now weaving of wyrd,    twines your way with ours!
The weapons you wield    are thirsty for war.
Our lord seeks for such    to strengthen his hand.
Rich his rewards    for men of right-worth.
E'en now we fare forth,    fell war-lords to seek."
"Fell lords you've found,"    (the Hengest spake forth),
"Tell out your tale –    the name of your lord,
the wide lands he wields,    the wars he would wage."
The Britons gave answer    (drank down the mead),
"Fairest of folklands    our fathers found,
a sea-strong fortress,    where men reap riches.
Yet riches bring reavers,    as honey draws bees.
Scots scour from Erin,    Picts out the north,
sleek sea-mares of Saxons    slink through the fens.
But to fearless war-lords,    who shall fend off such foes,
there's bright mead and gold,    broad lands to till.
Our lord's open-handed    (Vortigern his name)
In Britain-land's Council    he's held high by all."
Shading his eyes,    the Hengest made answer:
"We've heard of this Britain,    sea-stranded land,
how headlands cling hardly    at earth's dread rim,
in the outmost sea.    Mists drift drearly,
winds sigh wearily,    and upheaving waves
thrash and thunder    'gainst land's threshold.
'Tis a land, we're told,    where lone erne wails,
where wild cats spit,    and grey wolves prowl,
a worn and withered land    of wizened thorns,
of moors and meres –    a land for ents and elves!"
The Britons laughed long,    "A tall tale you've heard!
Over farthest firth    past Prydyn's forehead,
lie lands bleak and bare,    fast-bound in ice.
But Britain is blest,    her smooth swelling hills,
like a mother's breasts,    to sons give suck,
Britain! 'Tis richly girt    with heather, gorse,
berried slopes, plunging burns,    mossy banks, teeming fish.
Well-watered the meads,    where mills grind grain,

wide the weald-lands, wood-leas for swine,
horns' hoarse bellowing, drives on the hounds.
Deep in darkness men delve in mines,
bring forth bright gold. In high-famed halls,
are songs wonder-woven, maidens, shy-eyed, comely!"
Riches for reaping! (so thought the reavers)
"Your words are well-heard", quoth Hengest, rising,
"By morrow's mid day, our mind we'll make known."

Sunlight alighting on lapping waters,
found Eotan earls at sea-mare's stern.
Right rede they sought of Wulfrith Witfast.
"Speak now," quoth Hengest. "Through far lands you've fared,
found out men's hearts. Tell us of Vortigern,
his gift-giving, his troth. Tell us of Britain-land,
its wealth and its wars." Wulfrith, much-wintered,
was never hot-hearted, nor hasty in speech.
His mind-sight matched his keen-edged blade.
He weighed well the whither and wherefore of things,
far-seeing, fore-thoughtful, spoke ever fitly.
Wryly he wrought words half-mocking:
"No word-weaver I, to match these Welsh.
Like poets, like lovers, they told their tale,
of Britons' folkland, a fastness, wave-bound.
Right fair her havens! Wide her wealdlands.
Yet Britons' 'house' is house asundered.
Some rue Rome's going, would raise a war-host,
fare forth through Gaul, throw back Rome's foes.
Others, right glad, would step in Rome's shoes,
themselves shear the sheep. Some are steadfast,
follow forefathers' gods. Others name Christ,
the new god of Rome. Those of the lowlands
fear men from the hills, hold them uncouth.
Those of the uplands scorn soft-living south.
As for that fox, two-tongued Vortigern,
it were well you go warely, keep by your war-gear!"
"So whither our warring?" the Hengest asked.
"Seek fame and folkland midst Britons' folly,

or wend elsewhither?     Render your rede!"
The Witfast thought long,     then unlocked his hoard.
"Winter-wearied,     fowls I have followed,
I've watched their wheeling,     unwoven warnings.
All tell one tale!     From far and nigh
fowls come to feast     on fated war-smiths –
the sleek, swart raven,     the sallow kite –
with wolf of the weald.     For in Britons' land
spears quicken and quiver     as war is let loose."
Then forth from his breast     the Witfast thrust
a fell fistful     of arrows, black-shafted.

Wulfrith, far-seeing,     arms outreaching,
uttered words unearthly,     a tongue unknown,
Men clasped their cloaks,     as fear froze their hearts.
The Witfast wielded     his fraught hand-hoard,
threw it forth,     to fall, fate-bidden.
Stealthy, he stooped,     hands stole forth,
as sightless he sought     the first rune-shaft,
held it high.     "Here is 'uruz' –
great-horned aurochs,     awesome in onset,
as horse-lords of Britain.     Eotan war-craft
shall outmatch their might,     make them an offering
to Freyr the fair."     He stooped again,
held high a rune,     quoth, "Here is 'othala',

the hearth-land, the homeland,     hearts' true longing.
From Britons' wrath,     you'll wrench a kingdom,
clasp it, cleave to it."     Again he stooped:
" 'Ehwas', the horse,     your 'brother' beast!
His coming now     adds weight to words
of might outmatched,     of heroes' home.
Once more he stooped,     found dread 'ear', fourfold.
"Now in the ash-storm     men must strive
four times in fight,     face death's dread sting,
and from the last,     foes flee like fire.
The grave shall grasp     both friend and foe,
as death is dealt     to whom 'tis deemed."
" 'Lagu'! " cried Wulfrith,     as one last word
the rune-wit won,     unhoarded things hidden.
"Here's word of Vortigern,     unsteady as water.
The 'waves' he would ride     shall swamp his 'ship',
his deeds, his undoing,     his wiles outwitted!
He's snatched in snare     his hand has shaped.
'Tis all wyrd-writ –     all say the same!"

High-prowed keels,     crunching the foreshore,
war-wolves of Hengest     heaving their sea-mares
above swirling surf.     Sunlight on water,
unstill brightness,     little stream chattering,
banks rose-bright –     'Hipwell' they named her.
(On a day foredeemed,     Christ's war-smiths would come
in 'ring-mail' of right,     with 'shields' wrought of truth,
would throw down Foe's holds     in High Father's name.)

To Cantware's hall,     to Council of Britain,
from kingdom's far corners     word-bearers were come.
First, from far north,     one told of Picts
reaving through Rheged.     Another brought word
of Deiran untroth,     another of sleek craft
threading Trent-waters,     of Icel angling for prey.
"Wherever we turn,"     the High Lord growled,
"Foes foul the nest."     "Not foes alone!"
spake one from the West,     " 'Tis Briton 'gainst Briton.

We tear our own throats,    and thieve from friends."
Men wrangled, wrath-hearted,    'till breath ran out.
"Enough!" quoth Vortigern.    "Let's make fast the 'door',
then root through the 'house',    and rid it of rot.
The shield-hosts of Britain    shall stand by Rheged,
shoulder to shoulder,    shore up the Wall.
Here's Hengest, sea-stallion,    with sea-mares' sons.
We'll buy their swords    with Thanet land."

The lamps burned low    in dim inner room,
as high king with Hengest    held long night-speech.
"Now tell your tale,"    quoth Vortigern,
"of Franks and Frisians,    and Saxon lords.
Where now the Hun hoards,    and where Rome's hosts?
Whither their war-fleets,    their store-wains, their horse?"
Then Hengest gave answer,    unlocked his word-hoard,
"No war-keels of Rome    cleave northern seas.
Their strength's gone south,    where Vandals, sea-wolves,
thrusting, thronging,    threaten their doors."
With narrowed eye,    the king went on.
"Britain's ringed round    by reavers without,
yet worse for our weal    are the snakes within.
Well says that by-word,    'Fear more the one
havened in house,    than thousand without.'
And foremost I fear    the Aurelian house,
more Roman than Rome,    to Aëtius tied.
They yearn for the yoke    of thralldom again.
Through four hundred years    Rome's reaped our wealth,
taken whelps for their war-hosts,    daughters for whores.
We went not to 'Egypt',    they brought it to us!"
He drank down his wine,    went on again,
"Here's work, then, for war-smiths,    and wealth to reap.
Thrust northwards hard,    and thresh these Picts,
let them rue their raiding.    Yet rend them not –
a fearful Rheged    keeps faith with us."

Through summer of strife,    by the Roman wall,
hovering like hawks,    Eotan war-host

harried the hunters.    Picts heading south
they left unhindered,    then waylaid their homing,
when cumbered with kine    (and kept half their worth!)
At summer's setting    Picts sought their hills,
while Hengest with Horsa,    their 'harvest' full-won,
came into Kent-land,    sought from the king
the meed that was meet –    fair Thanet's isle.
In high rede-hall,    Britain-land's elders
gathered in folk-moot.    The king spake thus:
"Hengest's sea-hounds    our foes have hunted,
harried them, howling,    to their northern holes.
The far door's fastened,    the near door's ajar.
Frank lords are thrustful,    threaten our hearths,
sea-scouring Saxons    search ever for prey.
It is right I render    to Hengest's hounds
the meat, and mead,    and clothing sworn,
with hide of land    to build a hall.
With this (no more)    we'll hold them in hand.
Then Hengest shall hie    to Eotan homes,
bring hither more hounds    to shield our shores."
"Weigh this warely,"    a redesman warned,
"Whether 'tis witting,    having wolves to the fold –
wolves become watch-hounds,    yet wolfish in heart!"
"Your word is well-spoken,    but 'tis they must beware.
My hand shall be heavy,    should hearts play foul!"

“A hide for a hall – you swore us Thanet!”
(Thus spake Hengest in that inmost bower.)
The king quoth coolly (hard gleamed his eye),
“Thanet land we swore, not the land of Thanet.
Now heed me, Hengest! That land you yearn
shall yet be yours. You have heard me speak
of Rome’s fast friends, the Aurelian house.
They heap their hopes on stern Aëtius
who, in Rome’s rule, rides ever higher –
his son’s betrothed to High King’s daughter.
Hear now my word. Send home to Eote-land,
bring hither a host of war-hardened men.
Then Thanet’s your meed. But if you’re war-weary
gold shall be given you. We’ll seek another.”
(Right well would he rue that mean-hearted meed.
By hand of Hengest (rod of God’s wrath)
for hire he’d withheld life-hoard he’d lose.)

Hengest, wrath-hearted, kept thought-hoard hid.
(Little the loss to him who speaks least!)
A fraught war-blade that war-lord wielded,
hilt wrought with runes – ‘The raven’s friend’ –
dark stained with sweat, from forebears’ striving,
keen edge, elf-wrought, unmarred by spells.
The strife it stirred, with shed blood settled.
Of sword-sworn oaths it brooked no breach,
swift death it dealt, where men played foul!
“Beware!” quoth Wulfrith, when Hengest sought rede.
“Rightful your wrath, yet unright the time
to wield that weapon – let blade sleep yet.
To our folkland far send forth a word,
bring hither a host to hold these shores.
A high hall rear, then to our hearth
let come the King, with all his kin,
shoulder to shoulder share meat and mead.
Bring hither your daughter and bind that king
by wedlock woven – the lady Hrothwyn
and high king’s whelp.” And thus ’twas done
(a bitter sowing from which sprang grief!)

Hengest, with Horsa, sat down in hall
with high-settled Vortigern, his son at his side,
and Wulfrith Witfast , with Caradawg Two-speech.
Forth fared the maidens with horns of fine mead,
fair Hrothwyn first (fraught she as Freya),
lissom, lithe-like as the linden.
Bright-braided tresses ringed queenly throat,
strand upon strand, swirling, falling,
softly settling on curving shoulders.
Smooth brow, clear, and smouldering eyes,
alive, alight as new day's dawn,
daring, darting, dancing, teasing,
now dark and deep, in long-lashed shade,
now burning, flaming. Full-formed her teeth
'twixt laughsome lips, a shower of white
ringed round with red (as reddest foxgloves).
So slight her waist, so smooth her arms,
white as the snowdrop at winter's end.
Winsome she, and wondrous, all womanly –
bewitching, bewildering, beguiling, undoing!
To the King came Hrothwyn, held out the cup,
willed him good weal (so Caradawg told him)
and so passed on. She wended the mead-boards,
the while the King the lady followed
with reaving eyes and restless thirst.
The Hengest marked it, minded, mulled it.
Likewise the maiden saw, yet loathed him.
(She loathed not the son. Vortimer, she weened,
was war-lord of worth, a maiden's longing.
Would her fair brow might stir *his* heart!)
The King spake thus in Hengest's ear:
"Now would I bind us in stronger bonds.
To hearth and high-seat your daughter I'd have.
Name your bride-wealth – to half my kingdom!"
The Hengest stalled (and stirred the 'fire'!)
told love-sick king, "Among our folk,
The folkdom's father may not say 'yea'.
High Eotan lords must render rede
at morrow's meet. Then shall you hear."

Sat Hengest in hall,   with Eotan lords,
with Horsa and 'Hrofi',   strong hounds of war,
with Wipped 'Spear's son',   with Wiga, Wulfrith,
Godmær and Gythla,   and black-browed 'Raven',
Beornfrith and Beornmund,   of famed father sprung,
Ceolmund and Ceolla,   and Ciorra 'Deed-doer'.
"I thought to snare the son"   (quoth Hengest, wryly),
"but snared the King himself!   What word shall we give?"
All minds were one –   for Hrothwyn's hand
the king must give   Cantware's folkland,
with western lands,   e'en to the weald.

Lightly lies the bride price   unlocked from other's wealth!
The Vortigern sent word   (Wulfrith standing by),
called Gwyrangon,   Cantware's lord,
laid words against him,   and lodged him in hold
'till doom was deemed.   Came the door-ward,
third night thence,   handed him a pouch,
and left without a word.   Within were foodstuffs –
a gift from friends! –   fresh barley cakes,
burnt grain in bag,   some beans and leeks and nuts.
And lodged among the leeks   a little scroll,
wherein was rudely writ   (as by one unlearn'd):
"Hard is my head,   hammered, finely filed.
I thrust in my beak,   draw back the bolt.
Strong chests, iron-bound,   I open with ease.
Hall doors fly back,   that owners thought sure.
My lord lays hold   of treasures fast-held,
and sets them free.   Find me if you can!"
Gwyrangon, fevered,   fingered through that pouch,
found buried in the bag   a key and folded scroll!
"In holt hard by" (he read)   "lie friends a-hidden,
with swift-footed steeds.   Take heart, and live –
your doom's not nigh!"   In dead of night,
unhindered, Gwyrangon   slipped from that hold,
sought holt hard by.   At dawn next day
they found his lifeless frame,   felled by one foul thrust.

Great wrath arose through Britain-land.
Gwyrangon's death had shamed her sons.
Swift steeds bore word, sped through all the land.
They called the Council, where three hundred spoke as one.
Their king unkingly should be king no more.
At his own high hall, with his Saxon whore,
by Hafren's flood, there let him dwell.
Vortimer they named 'Britain-land's Shield'.
(Bitter was Hrothwyn's broth with her many-wintered lord!)

In early summer days, when earth awakes,
war-hosts fare forth, for fame – and death!
So, from London-burh went two hosts of Britons,
as two 'claws' clutching – to crush the Eotan foe!
One marched forth, full-hearted, with war-horns' fury,
by Roman stone-road sought the Bridge Fort.
Another host held south sought the Way of Dyfnwal,
(that wise and worthful king wayfarers' friend,
of whom the fathers tell, who marked and measured
highways and hollow-ways, horse-ways and foot-ways,
by ford and fastness faring through the land.)

Woe to the wareless at the Oak-wood River,
threading the waters where Wulfrith's host,
hidden in holt, awaited their onset.
Eotan arrows, eager for evil,
scored and scathed the linden shields –
shattered, splintered them, then sheared through sarks,
found out the fated, loosed the life-flood.
And then the spear-storm breaking on war-boards,
in death's throat thrusting those who might not live.
Britons fled the field, thought to hold the Crei.
Wulfruth Wolf-wit outwitted them once more,
leading his half-host by woodland ways,
taking Britons behind, breaching their walls.
Hearts faltered, failed – they fled to London-burh.

Broad shields of Britain (Vortimer, Catigern)
closed with the foe at the Medeway fords –
Hengest's strong host, spear-tips glittering,
Spear-shafts on shields, harsh shouts of men,
bow strings strumming, stirring from sleep,
quickening, quivering (hateful that harp-song),
sleek ravens swooping, soaring, screaming,
grey-hoods howling, at woodland's eaves.
Vortimer, lordly, rode round the host.
"Brood of Britain-land," (spake that bold lord),
" 'Tis meet we mind how the Most High
sundered the sons of men, made seventy from one,
set fast the bounds, of each folkland.
And 'tis meet we mind how long our fathers groaned,
in thrall among Greeks, no land to name their own;
how they fared forth (famed Brutus at their head)
through forty years, not knowing whither,
wandered wide seas – their 'wilderness' –
led by the Lord's angel to the land beloved.
Again, 'tis meet we mind how the Most High
thrust down before them those 'sons of Anak'
(o'erthrew their fastness, made of it a heap).
And shall these Saxons, these sons of Ammon,
throw us to the waves, once more to wander?
Shall heathen heels foul the Lord's own land?
Keep troth with God, and he'll keep troth with you!"

Forth to the fords came Eotan word-smith.
Bidden by Hengest he spake haughty words:
"Britons, why fight us, make food for ravens?
Hope not for help from your northern host.
Their doom was dealt at Darent's flood.
Better buy life than bide the storm!
Give up bright gold, gems elf-wrought.
Yield to our yoke, and mercy is yours."
Grim-helmed Vortimer (great was his wrath),
gripped the war-spear, growled these words:
"Storm of ash-spears, O sea-reaver's son,

with whirlwind of arrows    and bitter sword-play,
these your winnings!"    Vortimer rose up,
shook free from sheath    sword famed in song,
bade Britons stand    in stern shieldwall.
Came war-lords in wedge-shape    (as Woden laid down),
spear-thicket thronging,    thrusting the shieldwall.
Ceolla, 'Helm Cleaver',    loved clash of spear,
above words of love    from fairest lips.
One shame he most dreaded –    to reach his grave unscathed
(*that* were the greatest grief!)    Wordsmiths shall weigh his deeds.
Ceolmund! Deadly his blows,    dealing sorrow.
While this world lasts    his war-fame shall live.
Ciorra, 'Deed-doer',    stern-faced in death,
The doom to him handed,    he grasped without fear.
The slaughter of sea-hounds    was not slack that day.
Yet for each one felled,    two more stepped forth.
Shoulder to shoulder,    Britons unshirking,
must now yield ground    to weight of shields.
Then Vortimer held high    his great war-spear,
waved on the mighty,    called forth the thunder
of horse-lords' hooves.    Glad-hearted was Catigern
seeing spear tip's gleam,    spake thus with his lords:
"Here is high fame    for those that hate ease!
'Tis meet we mind, this day,    our words in hall,
make deeds of words,    wrest war-fame from our foes.
Let the fearful flee,    forgo his share of fame.
He is worth no weal    that can bide no woe.
Friends are sore beset –    death hard on heels.
Our lives for theirs!    we'll live on in song!"
Throbbing, thundering,    thrusting all before,
horse-lords, harrowers,    hurtled down the slope,
rushed the Medeway –    its waters drew back.
Shieldwall shivered,    buckled, broke,
ash-shafts shattered.    Some fled the field –
witting, yet unwarlike,    they saved wretched lives.

Horsa, with hearth-friends, yet held his ground,
an 'island' beset by swirling horse.
Catigern wheeled, gripped well his weapons,
bore down on battle, like fire-bolt of thunder.
Godmær, grim-helmed, thrust spear-butt in ground,
held fast the head, 'gainst oncoming horse,
thrust through its breast – the steed fell, thrashing.
Catigern leapt clear, caught up his sword,
with one stroke shattered Horsa's shield-board.
Another sheared and shredded mail-sark.
A third delved deep, thrust death upon him.
Sea-wolves, wrath-roused ringed round Catigern –
bitter their blades. More bitter still
that Briton's blows. Of battle lords
he halved the helms, 'till downed at last,
of Godmær's hand (his most-famed thrust).

Weary the wending sun, westering, burning
as fire at the forge. The light fading,
grey-coats slunk from shadows, sleek ravens alighted,
to feed their fill, as bloodied hosts fell back.
Vortimer sought long for Catigern,
and came at last where death had laid him,
looked on, a-longing. "Not less fair" (sighed he)
"Are heaven's halls by your home-coming.
Yet sore bereft, my brother, are Britain's breasts
where you sucked, won strength. Swift your battle-ride,
helm of our horse-lords! High-hearted your deeds!"

With heavy hearts    Eotan sea-hounds
bore Horsa's body    to their waiting boat,
slowly, sadly,    slipped down the flood.
On the third day, thence    came thronging host
where sea winds sweep    the headland's brow.
Here they piled the wood,    set rowing bench and oar
(steeped with Horsa's sweat),    his sword of wondrous hilt,
his great boar-helm,    his shirt of mail
(bright still, though breached),    his broken linden board.
(Through these once thrilled    the throbbing life.)
And in their midst    they laid their lord,
with burning brands    stirred bright the fire.
Wood-reek, sullen, rose,    and woman bent with years,
of wizened arm and step,    wailed forth the woe-filled song.
They heaped high the barrow    o'er lord they loved,
that ships, wave-striving,    might see where he kept watch.
Then twelve horse-lords,    hardy sons of war,
rode stern war-steeds    around that heap.
Sorrowing they sang    the song of high deeds –
the fame fore-writ –    that Horsa wrought.
Among folkdom's foes    his sword was feared.

After the strife-storm    at Medeway fords,
Briton and Eotan    forged frith betwixt them.
Hengest swore troth    with Britain-land's Shield.
Britons yielded    Cantware's folkland,
while Eotan loosed    the western weald –
half the bride-wealth    for Hrothwyn's hand
(and she was sent home    to father's house).

'Time weighs man's troth,    tries well his worth'
Yet how shall troth hold    where trust's still-born?
Great the grieving    of Gwyrangon's sons,
for a father loved,    most foully slain.
And great the grieving    over rich lands lost.
Men were mindful, too,    of Medeway's fords,
of wrath unwreaked    for friends bereft of life,
who'd shared the shieldwall.    When (asked Britons)
would Eotan doom    pay for Eotan deeds?

When (asked Eotan)    would Britons' wrongs
come home to roost?    In these dark waters
Wulfrith stirred    and Hrothwyn fished.
One year, and the next,    the marchlands smouldered.
Britons threaded ford-ways,    fired fields and thorps,
drove off the kine.    Eotan eyes, meantime,
looked with longing    on wealden wealth,
at summer's setting    drove swine to feed.
So was wrath reared    until that day when,
drawn on by guile,    Gwyrangon's sons
were snatched in snare,    undone by Saxon craft,
their life-hoard lost    in some lonely dell.
Word winged to Vortimer    of Eotan warring.
Then Britain's Strong Shield    straightway sent word,
bade Hengest to hall,    to yield the slayers.
After Hengest's 'nay',    word sped forth again.

Mighty the hosting    of the Britain-land folk!
As storm-waves of winter,    hurl at the headland,
clawing, clutching    cliff-strength shaking –
thrown back, thwarted,    then thrusting again –
so was the oncoming    of Britain-land's host.
Medeway o'erleaping,    through Cantland thrusting,
they hemmed in the host    of the Eotan lords,
by wind-swept shore    and winding creek,
at the Written Stone,    by the Gallic sea.
The shieldwall shivered,    hearts were shaken.
The lack-willed fled,    like sheep, wolf-driven!
Striving, shoving,    they shouldered war-boats,
heaved and hauled them,    to water's edge,
clambered, clutching,    oars out-thrusting.
Wave-steeds, shamed,    shipped the fearful
to Thanet's shore,    all fame forgone.
One that was war-wise    did not waver,
Wipped, Hwita's son.    In whatever land
tidings were told    of swords unsheathed,
thither he sped –    war was his love.
Steadfast he stood,    sold ground dearly.

He dealt hard dints –    each one brought death.
"No foothold here    for foe", quoth he.
"While weapons play    I'll not forsake them!
This ground I'll grasp    'till it grips me!"
Bows were busy,    bitter, waspish.
Swift-swooping dart,    shearing the wind,
fist-flung of Briton,    flew fast and true,
ripped through ring-mail,    strong sark unwrought,
of Hwita's son.    He welcomed death:
"Heart-strength is hardened    as hand-strength ebbs.
Willingly I wend.    Give now my name
to strand I've straddled,    my last stronghold."

War-blades grew weary,    sun sank westwards.
Where life yet lingered    the leech-crafty worked,
death's hold held off,    mended the marred.
By Cantland's shore    stood Eotan women –
fearful, forlorn,    with children clinging,
helpless, herded,    in Britons' hands.
Hither rode Vortimer,    on high-stepping steed,
halted, wondered,    unlocked his hoard:
"How fair of frame    these Eotan folk!
Like God's chosen    these children here,
eyes of heaven's hue,    curled hair like gold.
Comely the women,    slender, swan-breasted.
Even so, I'm thinking,    were Midian's maids,
who wove their wiles,    bewitched the witless,
yoked them to their gods.    Swift was the wrath!"
He stayed, two-minded,    then frowned and said,
"Oft and again    these Saxons, unrueing,
the hapless from hearth    to sorrow have sold.
As they have dealt    to them be done.
Bind them in bonds,    to havens bear them.
Seek there the buyers,    from Gaul and Rome,
who trade in souls.    Sell these as thralls."
(From doom he dealt –    bereft of ruth –
would God wrest good,    bring light and life.)

Weary the warring,   through many weeks,
Eotan islanded,   Britons without ships.
Vortimer lay a-bed,   by black shaft felled,
brow a-burning   limbs a-shiver.
With soundless steps   came woman wending
where shield-lord lay.   He looked up dully,
and there beheld   the lady Hrothwyn!

Fair was she as Freya   (and fraught besides),
eyes burning bright,   eager to beguile him,
and bind him to her.   Quoth she, a-sighing,
“Greatly I grieve,   seeing folkland’s fairest
laid low by fever.   Now hear me, lord!
A draught I’ve drawn,   to quench death’s sting.
I hold you in my hand.   Love me and live,
as I live and burn   with love for you!”
“Lady, it may not be,   I love another.”
Beneath her breath,   the elf-maid laughed.
“And is this ‘other’   fairer e’en than I?
Loves she as I love –   with bold, wild love?
Will she yield you all,   fare forth with you,
whither and wherever,   wend even to the Darkness?”
Vortimer, though fevered,   shuddered at these words.
Sternly he spake:   “With Freya’s child
I may not match –   I am Christ’s man.”
Hrothwyn drew back.   “These words,” she mocked,
“are witling’s words.   Elf-shot you are.
Here is the draught,”   (she held forth a flask).

"Naught else can save you.    Unless to me you yield,
your life is lorn."    "Begone, witch-maid!
Naught have you I need.    I know the Lord of life.
Here and hereafter    he holds me safe
in the hollow of his hand –    I have his word."
The lady clenched her fists    clapped close her ears,
hate gleamed in glaring eye    as she fled the camp.
Watchmen shivered,    clasped well their cloaks,
sought to shield their souls    'gainst bitter glance.
The third day thence,    Vortimer was dead.
In under-breath    men darkly whispered
'twas witch-whore's deed,    by spells soul-bought.

Eotan ship-host    sought the sea-ways.
Britons blithely    watched their going.
From shore he shielded    their lord they shouldered –
though he bade them    build his barrow
on headland's height,    to watch and ward.
Wherefore the need    now shore was won?
Heedless their homing,    unwarlike their watch,
with wains slow-wending,    weighted with spoil.
Eotan with east wind    eased in their ships,
crept to the shore,    under night's cloak.
At new day's dawning    war woke the witless.
Some fought fell-ly,    most fled like fire.

Heart-searching in halls    of Britain-land's lords.
Their Shield was shattered,    who'd lead the host?
Not slow was Vortigern    to grasp the hour.
By gift and guile    he wormed his way
to Council, kingship,    to overwieldship.
He soon sped word,    bade Hengest come
with Eotan elders,    ride to the rede-moot.
Frith they would forge    between their folkdoms.
(And the king would have    his Saxon wife.)
"Let no man wield weapon,"    (thus the king's word)
"Hands without war-gear,    hearts without wiles!"
Wulfrith, Rune-wise,    ready-witted,

in every good    he unearthed guile.
Aside he spoke    in Hengest's ear:
"Fair the word, foul the deed    of Britain's king!
He'll have his men    to watch our way.
Mark well my word,    go not unweaponed."
Hengest heeded,    called his elders,
bade each have hidden    hard-edged seax.

Meat in the hall,    the mead-horn shared,
while Briton wove words    won from the harp,
sang of the Mighty    who once walked the land,
sang the sorrows    of Branwen fair,
sang of the starling    she reared and taught,
and the word of woe,    sent by its wing.
Then Bran the Blest    brought war to Erin.
Wondrous that war-host !    Seven only came home!
("How's this?" thought Hengest,    "A hidden word?
Is this the doom    they deem for us?")
Haughty the hall-speech    of hearts mead-drunk.
Eotan song-lords    sang of war-worth.
Whose strength (they asked)    had striven with Picts,
wrested the land    from ruthless reavers?
" 'Twas wolf 'gainst wolf,"    one answered, mocking.
"Ship-thieves I saw,    shut up in Thanet.
Water, not war-craft,    won them their lives.
By witchcraft, not war-skill,    our Shield was shattered."
"Enough!" quoth Vortigern,    "leave talk so light.
We are here in hall    folk-frith to forge."
Mood-glad that king,    mellowed by mead.
The foes once feared,    were nigh forgotten.
Aëtius, Shield-lord,    strong arm of Rome,
was slain in his blood    by High King's word.
Aurelius' sons    were a threat far off.
Let them fret and frown    in 'little Britain'!
"Hengest, hearken!    For Hrothwyn my wife,
I yield Cantware-land,    as far as Medeway's fords.
In after days    let Hrothwyn's son
(whom she shall bear me)    hold all that land."

His brow wrath-written, Hengest wrought hard words,
"For Hrothwyn's hand whole land you gave,
from western Weald to Saxon Shore.
When troth's undone, swords will have their say!"
The king called out, "Since deal was cut
our foes are fallen. We fear no more.
Threadbare your threats. If you would thrive –
keep doom from door, live out your days –
heed words of wit, wake not your woe.
Take gladly what I give – or leave with naught!"
'Tis true, thought Hengest, the home-way's watched.
I dare not let these Britons live.
Their life for ours! He leapt up on his feet.
Bellowed, "Brothers! let loose the seax,
the forsworn slaughter ere they slay us!"
Rasping of unsheathed blades, groans of the dying,
shouting, swearing of men, fight-frenzied,
hounds a-howling, as Eotan, Frisian
fell on their foes. Britons, weaponless,
sheep for slaughter, in life found death.
Some, war-witful, sold lives dearly.
One, oak-limbed, heaved high a mead-bench,
whirled it, hurled it, on doomed heads heaped it,
dealt death in dying. His name's not told.
(Unfitting, I'm thinking, it should be forgot.)
Dead heaped in hall – Britain's first men.
Vortigern, alone, bought life forsworn,
with three fair kingdoms (Hengest named the price).

Wondrous the weaving of threads wyrd-wrought!
To one of youth-years wyrd seems far off.
Then, unlooked for, it o'erleaps his life!
So with that Vortigern. At new year's dawning,
he sat in hall, his lords about him.
Then doors thrust open – a wordsman, breathless!
"From ship havens hasting, I have ridden, unresting.
Swift as the spear-hawk swoop Aurelius' sons.
Men heed their call, flock to the hosting."

The redesmen rose,     left one by one.
At even-fall     that Vortigern fled,
storm-wrack gathering     as he rode far north.
Wind roared in wrath,     the rain lashed down,
with din of thunder     and darts of lightning.

Mare, fear-driven,     fled through the night.
Fire-spear striking,     she reared up, screaming.
Her rider, thrown off,     stirred never again!

Wulfrith the Wily,     long Woden's man,
won sharp war-wit     of that god's hand.
But Grima's gifts,     are ever two-edged.
A day is dealt     when loan's called in.
Wulfrith had word     of war on the marches,
of wains heaped high,     wealth for the taking!
Forth fared the Witfast,     on horse, fleet-footed.
Hard at his heels     were war-tried men,
(eyes glittered with greed),     to reave the reavers.
And there, unlooked for,     by Wulfrith's side,
a plunging war-horse,     thunder-hoofed,
a great grey beast,     and one astride him,
helmed and hooded,     heavy-shouldered – taller he
by head and breast     than other men.
Wolf-skin cloak drawn     close about him,
hunching forward,     striving, thrusting.

On sudden turning –   one eye glaring!
Wulfrith knew him,   and gasped in fear!
"Wherefore, Woden,   ride you with us?
Bide yet a while,   and one more feast
we'll spread before you."   No word spake Woden,
eye, hood-shrouded,   showed no ruth.
Grim spear gripping,   he leaned across,
the death-thrust dealt   to Wulfrith Witfast.

And now, naught fearing,   Britons came again –
the host of the horse-lords   swooping like hawks.
Hengest, high-hearted,   struck hard, far westwards.
He went unwarely,   and riders ringed his camp.
In swift dawn onset,   the Hengest was dealt
his dread death-thrust,   it delved his heart.
With shieldwall shrinking,   he grimly spoke:
"My ship's found shoals   where'er I've steered.
Much of evil   have I wrought, yet
when first I came   to weapon years,
wielded the war-blade,   I was not minded so.
Alack for those lords   who shared the mead-hall.
The Witfast swore   they meant our death,
and so I slew them.   I would it were not so.
Vortigern! Alack that wyrd   made me his man!
Hrothwyn I sold!   Bitter the sowing!
Alack that wyrd so warped   drew me to meet
with Wulfrith Witfast.   Deep runes he read,
man's cunning kenned.   Good he knew not.
Finn Folkwielder   I thrust from life,
and Finnsburg I fired   (my own hand held the brand).
Unfitting that death.   Woe be on those
whose wrath unresting   stirred up that strife!
Would I had fallen   in Finnsburg's fight,
wreaking wrath for Hnæf,   beloved shield-friend.
Nowhere have I found troth.   The gods, it seems,
are shorn of strength."   And so he died.
Let man who is death-bound   mark well this word:
"High heaven's King   has wrought man's wyrd."

## Notes

**The Stallion**, that is, Hengest ('Stallion' being the meaning of his name').

1-7. As in the first song, the poet begins with some wisdom writing. Man gives himself to evil. He should rather remember the judgment of God, and not forget that the High King of heaven has wrought man's wyrd.

10. **Hengest 'Lack-lord'**: Hengest is a lordless man, an outlaw.

15. **sea-fowl ... ill foreboding**: the Anglo-Saxons, along with other folk of long ago, saw birds as almost 'otherworldly'. Their movements were watched for omens of things to come. The erne (eagle) was one such, and its 'name' (which has been followed back to deep roots in Indo-European speech) was really no name at all (it simply meant 'the Bird') the true name being taboo. The nightjar was believed to forewarn of death, and the Storm Petrel was seen as warning of bad weather.

16. **sea-mares**: a poetic name for longships.

17-19. **where once Roman prows set down strong anchors ... lighthouse**: the place referred to is Boulogne, first called Gesoriacum, then Bononia. It was the main port for sea traffic between Gaul and Britain, and there was a lighthouse there, as at Dover. The Romans built a fort/naval base at Boulogne as part of the Saxon Shore sea defence network.

21. **'Hrofi' the Ganger**: taken to be a tall Eotan warrior, nicknamed 'Hrofi' (roof), one too tall and heavy for any horse to bear, so that he must go everywhere on foot. Bede tells us that Rochester was known to the English as 'Hrofaescastrae' (*HE* II.3). The Romano-Celtic name was 'Durobrivae', and Alcock suggests this was clipped to D'robriw in Primitive Welsh and heard by the early English as something like 'Hrofri'. They then assimilated this to the English word 'hrof' (L Alcock, *Arthur's Britain*, pp.194-5).

22. **Ceolmund and Ciorra, Gythla and Ægel**: most of the names given to the Eotan warriors in the poem have been taken from east Kentish place-names. Chilham, near Canterbury, is likely 'Ciolla's ham' (Ciolla's homestead or estate), Ciolla being a shortened form of Ceolmund. Charing, near Ashford, is 'Ciorra's place.' (Ciorra is a Kentish form of 'Ceorra'.) Gillingham is the 'ham of Gylla's folk' with Gylla perhaps based on the name Gythla. Aylesford, near Maidstone, is 'Ægel's ford', which may be another name for the 'Ægelesþrep' of *Anglo-Saxon Chronicle* 455.

23. **Wipped**: the English thane whose death in battle is recorded in the *Chronicle* record for 465. According to the entry the battle site was named, from him, 'Wippedesfleot'.

26-33. **The Huns' host**: The Huns are still licking their wounds after the great battle of the Catalaunian Fields in AD 451. Hengest sees the Franks as on the look-out for openings to broaden their borders. The ship-hosts of the Vandals are raiding the west Mediterranean from North Africa. (For the historical background to this passage, see 'In time of "the breaking of nations" ' above.)

58-9. **How headlands cling hardly**: A reference to the old geography which has the lands where men dwell ringed about by the great Ocean. Britain is seen as on the edge of the world of men, by that 'outmost sea'.

67. **Prydyn's forehead**: Pictland, in the far north of Scotland.

88. **much-wintered**: The Anglo-Saxons reckoned the years of a man's life by the number of winters he had seen. And it was from the lessons learned through life that man gained wisdom. Thus 'no man grows wise without he have his share of winters' (*The Wanderer*, lines 64-5).

94. **Welsh**: This is the Anglo-Saxon 'wealh' meaning 'foreigner' (but also 'thrall').

113. **fowls I have followed**: See note on line 15.

128ff. **the first rune-shaft**: for the runes, and their use in augury, see 'The runes' under 'Anglo-Saxon heathenism' above. Gildas refers to 'the barbarians' seeking omens before they came to Britain, see *DEB* 23.3. Here, Wulfrith throws down the rune-shafts, then gropes for them 'sightless'. (He either simply closes his eyes, or he is in some kind of trance.) He picks up those shafts his hands find and reads them. The first letter he finds is 'uruz', representing the great aurochs, or wild ox. Wulfrith understands this in terms of the awesome power of the aurochs, and also its role as a sacrificial animal to be offered to the Germanic god, Freyr. 'Othala', the next letter found, is thought to be linked to the word 'ethel', homeland. The letter 'ehwas' represented the horse, an animal of high worth, sometimes seen as sacred. The names Hengest ('stallion') and Horsa ('horse') may suggest beliefs about 'kinship' with notable animals. Such ideas are found in ancient paganism. For example, among the smaller tribes of Iron Age Britain we find the Bibroci (the 'beaver men'), the Gabrantovices (the 'goat-fighters') and the Brannovices (the 'raven-fighters'). Wulfrith refers to the horse as Hengest's 'brother beast' (line 138). The might of the Britons shall be outmatched, and a home for Eotan heroes won (line 140). Next there is the runic 'ear'. There were two words spelt 'ear' in Old English. One meant 'ear of corn' and the other 'ocean'. Neither of these meanings fits with 'ear' in the *Rune Poem*. It is said there that '*Ear* is hateful to every man, when the flesh, the pale corpse, surely begins to cool, to choose the earth as a bed-fellow; flowers disappear, joys depart, pledges fail' (ASPR, VI, p.30, lines 90-4, cited in GR Owen, *Rites and Religions of the Anglo-Saxons*, p.58). This rune seems to be linked with death and the grave, and Wulfrith takes the four 'ear' rune-shafts as meaning there will be four bloody battles. The last letter picked up by Wulfrith is 'lagu' which represents water. Wulfrith takes it as speaking of Vortigern's unsteadiness and untrustworthiness, and of the way in which he is overwhelmed as he plays with things he does not understand.

158. The name 'Ebbsfleet' probably comes from 'Hēopwelles flēot', that is, 'the river Hēopwell'. This in turn means 'stream where hips grew' (E Ekwall, *The Concise Oxford Dictionary of English Place-names*, p.159.)

159-61. **Christ's war-smiths**: The reference is to St Augustine and his forty missionary companions who, as soldiers of Christ, landed somewhere on Thanet (Bede, *HE*, I.25). The 'ring-mail of right' and 'shields wrought of truth' recall the picture of the 'armour of God' in Ephesians 6:13-17. These lines here are in the manner of a later Christian addition to an original poem. The Christian scribe sees the hand of God in the later coming of his servants, by the same way as Hengest and his war-band, to undo the heathenism the latter brought. The 'Foe' is Satan.

162. **To Cantware's hall**: The large Roman theatre in Canterbury long served as the assembly place of the Cantware (Nicholas Brooks, in S Bassett, editor, *The Origins of Anglo-Saxon Kingdoms*, p.68).

165. **Rheged**: this British kingdom of the fifth to seventh centuries lay around the Solway Firth, and included Carlisle, Annan, and the Eden valley.

166. **of Deiran untroth**: *Historia Brittonum* 61 tells us of one, Soemil, who 'first separated Deira from Bernicia'. (Deira was, roughly, what is now the East Riding of Yorkshire.) The meaning seems to be that Soemil (perhaps a leader of *laeti*) broke free from the authority of the post-Roman rulers of this corner of Britannia Secunda. The *Historia* gives a kinship list showing Soemil as the great-great-great-grandfather of Ælle, who was king of Deira 568-598. If Soemil was truly a historical figure, then we must suppose that he lived from about AD 420 to 470. Soemil is not named in the *Chronicle*'s kinship list (*Chronicle*, 560), but he has the right first letter to his name (there are five names beginning with 'S' in the 560 annal).

167. **Icel angling for prey**: Icel is said to have been the forebear of the Mercian kingly house, the 'Iclingas'. In the Mercian kinship list he is the great-grandson of Offa of Angeln, and he would thus have been in the prime of life in about the 460s. (But counting back from Penda, who was king of Mercia from about 626-655, would give a date for Icel around 500. Perhaps one or two names have dropped out of the lists.) Icel may have been the leader of Angles moving west out of East Anglia.

173. **"Let's make fast the 'door' ...** Vortigern's proposal is that, first, Hadrian's Wall (line 176) must be secured again, and then barbarian incursions can be mopped up afterwards.

177. **sea-stallion**: a reference to the meaning of Hengest's name ('stallion').

194. **the Aurelian house**: the reference is to Ambrosius Aurelianus, and to Uther (Eutherius?) the legendary father of Arthur.

195. **Aëtius**: Roman general, the strongman who strove for more than twenty years to hold the Western Empire together. His greatest test came in 451 when he halted Attila's warring in Gaul at the great battle of the Catalaunian Fields.

197, 199: **four hundred years ... Egypt**: Vortigern likens the roughly four hundred years of Roman rule in Britain, to the four hundred-year bondage of the Israelites in Egypt.

198. **Taken whelps for their war-hosts**: young Britons drafted into the Roman armies.

223. **hide of land**: The 'hide' was an Anglo-Saxon land measurement. It was a holding that was enough to support a household.

239-241. **stern Aëtius ... rises ever higher**: In 453, two years after the battle of the Catalaunian Fields, Aëtius secured the betrothal of Placidia, daughter of the emperor Valentian III, to his son Gaudentius.

247. **rod of God's wrath**: a Christian scribe sees Hengest filling the role once given to Assyria as the 'rod' of God's judgment (see Isaiah 10:5). In the poem this judgement overtakes a sinful king, and a ruling class whose rivalry has been tearing the folkdom asunder.

251-7: **Hengest wielded ... 'The raven's friend'**: for swords and their 'life' or 'force', see under 'The warcraft of the Heroic age' above. Hengest's sword is 'The raven's friend' because the many men it slays are food for the raven.

268. **high king's whelp**: Vortimer.

272. **Caradawg Two-speech**: that is, 'interpreter' – the Ceretic named in *Historia Brittonum* 37.

274. **Freya**: see note on Frija/Freya in 'Anglo-Saxon heathenism' above.

303. **to half my kingdom**: In the *Historia Brittonum* Vortigern asks Hengest for the hand of Hrothwyn, saying 'Ask of me what you will, even to the half of my kingdom' (*HB* 37). It seems this was long a proverbial way of speaking, when someone meant to be open-handed. Thus it is found in the Bible in the stories of Ahasuerus and Esther (Esther 5:3, 6) and Herod Antipas and Salome (Mark 6:23). The offer was not to be taken prosaically!

311-4. **Wiga**: here are more names drawn from place-names, mostly in east Kent. Wingham, near Canterbury, is the 'ham (homestead, estate) of Wiga's folk.' Godmersham, between Canterbury and Ashford, is 'Godmær's ham.' Barfreston, between Canterbury and Dover, is 'Beornfrith's tun (homestead, town)'. Bermondsey, Surrey is 'Beornmund's island'. (We may picture Beornmund adventuring on his own account after a spell in Hengest's war-band.) Chillenden, between Canterbury and Deal, is 'Ciolla's valley or pasture' (Ciolla being a Kentish form of 'Ceolla'.). For Ceolmund, Ciorra, Gythla and Ægel, see note on line 22. 'The Raven' (line 312) is the nickname of an otherwise unnamed warrior.

322. **Gwyrangon**: according to the *Historia Brittonum* Vortigern the high king gave Gwyrangon's kingdom of Kent to Hengest as bride wealth for Hengest's daughter. He also gave Gwyrangon into the hands of the Jutes (*HB* 37).

331-6. **Hard is my head**: these lines draw on the riddle of the key, number 91 in *The Exeter Book Riddles*.

358. **Roman stone-road**: Watling Street, from London to Richborough.

358. **Bridge Fort**: Rochester. The Romano-British name for the town was Durobrivae, 'the Fort at the Bridges'. This might mean that there were two bridges over the Medway here, but it is thought more likely that the reference is to a number of spans or stages of one bridge.

360-4. **the Way of Dyfnwal**: Dyfnwal Moel Mut is a figure of medieval Welsh legend. In Geoffrey of Monmouth's work of legendary history, *Historia Regum Britanniae* ('Histories of the Kings of Britain'), he is named 'Dunwallo Molmutius'.) According to Geoffrey he and his son Belinus built the four arms of two great stone roads across Britain, one road from Cornwall to Caithness, and the other from Menevia (St David's) to Southampton. He laid on these roads the same holiness as rivers and places of worship, and set them under the king's shielding. Dyfnwal was also a great measurer. He determined the length of Britain first from Blathaon Head (perhaps 'the headland of the wolves') in Prydyn (that is, Pictland) to Penwith (Penwith Point between Land's End and Mousehole) in Cornwall, and found it to be 900 miles. Blathaon may be either John o' Groats or Dunnet Head. From there to Land's End is in truth 860 miles. Then Dunwallo/Dyfnwal measured the way from Crigyll in Anglesey to Sarre in Kent. Crigyll is now only a sheltered bay, and Sarre, likewise, a small settlement, but they were perhaps significant ports at one time. Dyfnwal measured the length of this way as 500 miles, though the true distance is only about 330 miles. Dyfnwal's measuring was based on the grain of barley: there were three lengths of barley corn to an inch, three inches in a handbreadth, three handbreadths in a foot, three feet in a step, three steps in a leap, three leaps in a 'land' or ridge. A thousand lands/ridges made a mile. In the poem Dyfnwal is taken to be the builder of the old trackway now known as The Pilgrims' Way. If Dyfnwal is based on a historical figure he might perhaps have lived about 400 BC.

365. **at the Oak-wood River**: the river Darent, a British river-name meaning 'the river where oaks are common'.

374. **clear Crei**: the river Cray. This is a another British river-name meaning 'fresh, clean'.

382. **Spear-shafts on shields**: spear-shafts beaten rhythmically on the rims of the warriors' shields.

389-91. **how the Most High/ Sundered the sons of men**: Vortimer refers to part of a truly old poem in the Old Testament. This tells how, at the beginning of the history of mankind, God sundered the sons of men and fixed the bounds of the folkdoms 'according to the number of the sons of God' (Deuteronomy 32:8). The 'sons of God' commonly refers to angels in the Old Testament. The meaning seems to be that from the one race of men God made the seventy folkdoms listed in Genesis 10, entrusting each one to the oversight of a guardian prince-angel. (There are references to such 'princes' in Daniel 10:13, 20-21 which speak of the princes of Persia and of Greece, and of the archangel Michael who is prince of the folk of Israel.)

394. **in thrall ... famed Brutus at their head**: in his *Historia Regum Britanniae* Geoffrey of Monmouth tells the tale of Brutus the son of Silvius, son of Ascanius, son of Aeneas the Trojan. When out hunting with his father he unwittingly slays him with an arrow, and so must needs flee the land of Italy. He comes to Greece, where he finds other Trojans living in thralldom to king Pandrasus. He is chosen to be

leader in a war of deliverance, and he takes king Pandrasus in a daring night onset upon the Greek camp. To ransom his life the king agrees that the Trojans may have ships and leave his kingdom. He also agrees to give Brutus his daughter Ignoge as wife. The Trojans sail westwards through the Mediterranean. When they come to the shores of the Tyrrhene Sea, they find there other afterkin (descendants) of the Trojans, led by the mighty Corineus, and these join them. The Trojans come at last to an island in the ocean, where giants are the only dwellers. They begin to settle there, and when the giants fall on them they slay them after a hard battle. The island is named Britain after Brutus. Other twelfth century versions of early British history are based on Geoffrey of Monmouth. In the middle of the century Wace wrote his *Roman de Brut* in Norman French, and about 1190 Layamon wrote his *Brut* in Old English. The name 'Brut' came to mean a chronicle of British history. A Middle Welsh version of Geoffrey is called the *Brut y Brenhinedd* ('Brut of the Kings'), and another work following on from that is called the *Brut y Tywysogion* ('Brut of the Princes').

395-7. **Through forty years, not knowing whither**: Vortimer makes the wanderings of the Britons' Trojan forebears alike with the wanderings of Israel, who were forty years in the wilderness. There is also a likening made to the forthfaring of Abraham who, heeding God's call, went forth from Ur 'not knowing where he was to go' (Hebrews 11:8).

399. **'sons of Anak'**: the sons of Anak were giants who dwelt in the land of Canaan (Numbers 13:33). They were driven out by Caleb, one of the heroes of the conquest (Joshua 15:14).

401. **these Saxons, these sons of Ammon**: the Ammonites were relentless foes of God's folk in Old Testament times.

405ff. **Forth to the fords came Eotan word-smith**: compare *The battle of Maldon*, lines 25ff. where a word-bearer of the Viking raiders comes forth to urge Bryhtnoth and his Saxon host to buy peace and life with gold.

420. **wedge-shape (as Woden laid down)**: in the warfare of the age (among the Romans, the Germans and, later, the Vikings), the wedge-shaped battle line was the standard way of breaching a shieldwall. Again, see 'The warcraft of the Heroic Age', above. Among the Vikings the secret of the wedge formation was thought to have been the gift of Odin/Woden (Ellis Davidson, *Gods and Myths of Northern Europe* p.49, Underwood, *Anglo-Saxon Weapons and Warfare*, p.132).

447. **its waters drew back**: the poet perhaps likens the parting of the Medway to the parting of the Red Sea before the host of Israel (Exodus 14:21-22).

483ff. **rowing bench and oar**: these lines draw on a view of man's life wherein things that have been close to him, handled by him and steeped with his sweat, become in some way part of his being. Among such would be the rowing bench where he sat, his oar, his sword-hilt, his spear and shield.

494ff. **Then twelve horse-lords**: compare *Beowulf* lines 3169-70.

539. **the Written Stone**: in the *Historia Brittonum* the third battle between Britons and Saxons is fought 'by the Inscribed Stone on the shore of the Gallic Sea' (*HB* 44). This may be the great Roman arch of marble that once stood at Richborough.

562-3. **Give now my name to strand I've straddled**: Wipped would have the place where he made his last stand named after him. This was the 'Wippedesfleot' of *Anglo-Saxon Chronicle* 465.

572-4. **How fair of frame these Eotan folk!**: Vortimer's words are like to those of Saint Gregory when, some 150 or so years later, he saw English youths in the thrall markets of Rome. They seemed goodly to him, fair of face and with curly hair. (See *The Life of S Gregory* by a monk of Whitby, quoted in RW Chambers *England before the Norman Conquest* p.106). The writer here sees both a likeness and a contrast. Gregory was moved to wish that the English might come to faith in Christ. Vortimer sees these youths (and women) only as a snare. (See further on lines 586-7.)

576. **Midian's maids**: see Numbers 25.

586-7. **From doom he dealt ... would God wrest good**: Vortimer had the captive women and children sold into thralldom, part of a trade which had gone on for a long time, and would go on yet for centuries. But when the right time was come God would use the deed to bring good from evil, as Augustine and his fellow missionaries were sent to England by Pope Gregory in 596/7.

604. **elf-maid**: as an elven maid – passing fair, yet fraught. See note on 'Otherworld beings' above, and also K Herbert *Looking for the Lost Gods of England*, pp. 39-40.

608. **the Darkness**: the Underworld.

613. **Elf-shot**: wounded unto death by an elven arrow.

626. **soul-bought**: that is, it is darkly whispered that Hrothwyn has bought from the Evil One the power of weaving spells, but at the price of her own soul.

630. **Though he bade them build his barrow**: the *Historia Brittonum* says that the dying Vortimer bade his men set his tomb by the shore, at the port from which the Saxons had fled away. If they did so then their foes would never again dwell in the land. However, the Britons did not heed this word (*HB* 44).

638. **most fled like fire**: the *Chronicle* says that in 473 Hengest and Æsc (Oisc) fought with the Britons and won great spoil, 'and the Welsh fled from the English like fire.'

645. **with Eotan elders**: the *Historia Brittonum* tells the tale of the meeting of the elders, and the trothlessness of Hengest in *HB* 44-45.

660-5. **Branwen**: the Welsh story of Branwen daughter of Llyr is one of the tales gathered in *The Mabinogion*. Matholwch king of Ireland sails to Britain, seeking friendship and the hand of Branwen in wedlock. Her brother Bran the Blest (king over the Islands of the Mighty), with the council, agrees to bestow the maiden and a great wedding feast is held. But Efnisien, Branwen's half-brother, is the great strife-stirrer, and he is ill-pleased. He cripples Matholwch's horses. A peace is patched up, and Matholwch and his men go back to Ireland, taking Branwen with them. For a year all is well, then the men of Ireland start to grumble about the affront to their lord. Matholwch sends Branwen to work as a kitchen wench. To stop the news getting back to Britain he bans ships from going there, and impounds any that come from Britain. Then Branwen rears a starling, teaches it how it may know her brother, and sends it to Britain with a letter hidden under the root of its wings. Bran the Blest is greatly grieved and he brings a great host to Ireland. The Britons win the war at the last, and slaughter the Irish, but only seven are left alive to sail back to Britain.

680-1. **Aëtius, Shield-lord**: Aëtius had secured the betrothal of the emperor's daughter to his own son (see lines 239-41). The emperor believed that Aëtius wanted to see his son on the throne. With the Huns no longer a threat Valentinian let his jealousy get the better of him, and he had Aëtius murdered (454). He was then murdered in turn, the following year, by two officers of Aëtius.

682. **Aurelius' sons**: see note on line 194.

683. **little Britain**: Brittany, where Ambrosius and Uther took refuge after the murder of their brother Constans.

690. **Saxon Shore**: the coastlands of south-east Britain, threatened by Saxon raids. The Romans built a line of forts guarding naval bases at key inlets. Eastern Kent, with forts at Reculver and Richborough (at either end of the Wantsum Channel), was part of the Saxon Shore sea defence network.

715. **three fair kingdoms**: the *Historia Brittonum* says that after the slaughter of his council Vortigern ransomed his life by making over Essex, Sussex, and Middlesex to Hengest (*HB* 46).

723. **Aurelius' sons**: see note on line 194.

733ff. **Wulfrith the Wily, long Woden's man**: in his *Gesta Danorum* the Danish historian Saxo Grammaticus (c.1150 – c.1220) tells how Woden slew Harald Wartooth, king of the Danes, whom he had once favoured. The same fate now comes to Wulfrith. The lesson is clear: the friendship of the god is fraught, two-edged.

735. **Grima**: a by-name for Woden which may have arisen from the belief that he often went about in disguise. ('Grima' is an Old English word for a mask or helmet.)

758. **the host of the horse-lords**: a horsed, fast-moving field army, such as may have turned the tide of war in the Britons' favour, for a while in the second half of the fifth century. These may be the underlying truth at the root of the later tales of Arthur and his mounted knights. The *Historia Brittonum* outlines the military career of Arthur, who fought alongside the kings of the Britons and was their leader in battle (*HB* 56). As far as one can tell (the battle sites are hard to pin down) the wars ranged through the length and breadth of the land. This would fit in with the picture of a horsed field-army going to each threatened point in turn.

# Further matter

## *Wordhoard*

| | |
|---|---|
| ætheling | prince |
| afterkin | descendants |
| alighting | allusion |
| anon | at once |
| ash-shaft | spear |
| ash-storm | battle |
| bairn | baby, child |
| baleful | threatening |
| be-rimed | frosted |
| beset | besiege |
| blithe | happy |
| blitheless | unhappy |
| blitheness | happiness |
| board | table, or shield |
| bower | chamber |
| bygoing | digression |
| by-word | proverb |
| death-bound | subject to death |
| death-fast | held by death |
| deed-thoughts | thoughts that spawn deeds |
| dint | blow |
| doom-dealer | one by whom fate overtakes another |
| ent | giant |
| ere-est | first, foremost |
| erne | eagle |
| even-dim | dusk |
| even-gloom | dusk |
| eye-door | window |
| fallow | pale yellow |
| fame-faring | adventuring |
| farcomer | stranger |
| far-kin | distant kin |
| far-wending | travelling far |
| faring forth | setting out, departure |
| fastness | stronghold |
| fell-ly | fiercely |

| | |
|---|---|
| fire-spear | lightning strike |
| folkdom | nation |
| folk-frith | peace between nations |
| folk-hoard | traditions, histories |
| folk-king | the king as embodiment of his folk |
| folkland | motherland |
| folk-lord | king |
| folk-ward | guardian of the folk, king |
| for-gathered | gathered |
| for-hewn | cut down, slain |
| for-lost | utterly lost |
| fore-deemed | predestined |
| forstand | stand firm |
| forth-way | way, road |
| frith | peace |
| frith-child | child of a marriage binding former foes |
| frith-weaver | peacemaker |
| frith-words | words of peace |
| gainful | hungry for gain |
| gift-stool | throne |
| grey-coat | wolf |
| grey reaver | wolf |
| grief-hoard | stored up grief |
| hall-ward | guardian of a hall |
| hand-meet | hand-to-hand fighting |
| hard-way | Roman (stone) road |
| hate-hoard | stored up hatred, resentment |
| havened | anchored |
| heart-blighted | bitter, resentful |
| hearth-friend | warrior who has shared hearth and hall |
| heart-hidden | concealed in the heart |
| hearth-land | motherland |
| hearthwards | homewards |
| heart-writ | 'written' on the heart |
| high-hearted | bold, fearless |
| high-seat | throne |
| high-settle | throne |
| hoar | frosty |
| hoar-headed | white-haired, old |
| hold | stronghold |

| | |
|---|---|
| holt | wood, copse |
| hopelorn | without hope |
| hot-handed | fierce |
| housecarl | member of a personal war-band or bodyguard |
| house-swallow | house martin |
| house-ward | servant, caretaker |
| kinlord | head of one's kindred or tribe |
| kinlore, kinship roll | genealogy |
| lack-willed | lacking staying-power |
| leechcraft | medical skill |
| leech-crafty | having medical skills |
| life-hoard | the years of one's life |
| life-lorn | weary of life, bereft of life |
| life-thread | 'thread' of life |
| likeword | synonym |
| linden board / shield | shield made of lime wood |
| linden-play | battle |
| lithely | graceful(ly) |
| lore-lord | keeper of the traditions of the kin group |
| lorn | lost |
| mail-sark | mail-shirt |
| mankinding | personification |
| many-wintered | aged |
| marchland | border land |
| mead | drink made from honey and water |
| mead-glad | elated after drinking well |
| meed | reward |
| meed-worth | deserving of reward |
| meet | fitting, right |
| mere | pool, lake, marsh |
| misdeem | misunderstand |
| mood-glad | joyful, well-satisfied |
| mother-brother | maternal uncle |
| night-hawk | nightjar |
| oak-wrought steed | ship |
| onblowing | inspiration |
| one-hearted | united |
| ongoingness | continuity |
| onset(ter) | attack(er) |
| onsudden | on a sudden |

| | |
|---|---|
| outfalling | sequence |
| out-thrusting | projecting |
| overcoming | victory |
| overwieldship | the power wielded by a high king |
| reave | rob |
| reaver | robber, pirate |
| reaving | robbery, piracy |
| recking | weighing up |
| reckless | not reckoning danger |
| rede | advice, counsel |
| rede-hall | council chamber |
| redeless | ill-advised, ill-judged, naïve |
| rede-moot | gathering of elders in council |
| redesman | counsellor |
| red shanked wader | redshank |
| ridden | got rid of |
| rightless | wholly in the wrong |
| rime | tell |
| ring-coat, ring-mail | chain-mail |
| roof-tree | upright beam in a wooden hall |
| rune-wise | wisdom gained through the reading of rune letters |
| rune-wit | one having the skill of reading runes |
| rune-writ | foreseen in the reading of rune letters |
| ruth | pity, mercy |
| ruthful | merciful |
| sark | shirt |
| 'sea-hawk' | sea-rover's ship |
| sea-hound | sailor, sea-warrior |
| sea-mare | ship |
| sea-mew | gull |
| sea-strife | storm at sea |
| sea-wolf | seafaring warrior |
| seax | short sword |
| shield-friend | companion in war |
| shield-host | army |
| shield-lord | warrior |
| shieldwall | battle-line |
| shift | tactic |
| shore-ward | coast guard |
| sideways word | allusion |

| | |
|---|---|
| sister-son | nephew |
| sky-rim | horizon |
| songcraft | the art of song-making, poetry |
| soothly | truly |
| soul-house | body |
| sound-likeness | alliteration |
| spear-storm | battle |
| spear-strife | battle, war-making |
| 'stand' | stanza |
| still-ly | not moving |
| stone-bound | rocky |
| stone-way | stone-flagged path |
| strife-deed | warlike deeds |
| strike hands | make a bargain |
| swan-riding | sea |
| swan-road | sea |
| swan-way | sea |
| swart | black |
| sword-strife | battle |
| thane | meaning varies from servant, to warrior or hero |
| thiefly | in an underhanded way |
| thorp | farm |
| thrall | slave |
| troth | good faith, faithfulness, trustworthiness |
| troth-bonds | solemn commitment |
| trothfast | faithful |
| trothless | treacherous |
| troth-tried | found faithful |
| two-sided (word) | ambiguous |
| two-speeched | bilingual |
| unblithe | joyless |
| under-saying | understatement |
| under-speech | talk under one's breath |
| unheeding | taking no notice |
| unminding | taking no notice of |
| unnigh | far |
| unrecking | reckless, heedless |
| unrightly | wrongly, treacherously |
| unrime | unravel, solve |
| unruth | no pity |

| | |
|---|---|
| unruthful | pitiless |
| unspelled | spell broken |
| untroth | treachery |
| unwarded | unguarded |
| unweal | unhappy state |
| unweighty | unregarded |
| unwitful | unwise |
| unwitting | careless, foolish |
| unwreaked | unavenged |
| unwrought | left undone |
| wain | wagon |
| war-board | shield |
| war-craft | skill in war |
| war-crafty | skilled in war |
| ward, warding | guard, guarding |
| wareful | wary |
| wareless | heedless, unwary |
| warely | warily |
| war-hardy | warlike |
| war-play | war, war-making |
| war-smith | man skilled in, or given to, war |
| war-strife | war |
| war-talk | the sound of weapon on weapon |
| war-wain | chariot |
| war-way | war path |
| war-weaver | warrior |
| war-wise | skilled in the use of weapons, and in war |
| war wood | weapon made of wood |
| war-word | word accepting, or provoking, war |
| war-worth | honour won in war |
| war-wright | man skilled in, or given to, war |
| wave-steed | ship |
| wave-strife | turbulent sea |
| way-leader | guide |
| way-weary | travel weary |
| way-wending | travelling |
| weal | well-being |
| weald | forest |
| weald-born | made of wood |
| wealth-hoard | treasure |

| | |
|---|---|
| weal-weaving | soothing, bringing about harmony |
| weal-words | harmonious words |
| weapon-years | old enough to bear arms in battle (commonly 15 years) |
| weight-stone | stone weight |
| westly | westwards |
| whale-mere | sea |
| whaup | curlew |
| whilen | sometimes |
| wide-handed | generous |
| wield, wielder | rule, ruler |
| wilsome | pleasant |
| winter years | old age (having seen many winters) |
| wist | know, knew |
| wit | know |
| witfast | sound in one's thinking |
| withstand(er) | defend(er) |
| witless | foolish |
| witling | fool |
| witly | wisely |
| wit-word | wise word |
| woe-weaving | trouble making |
| woe-written | doomed beforehand |
| wolf-heart | cruel heart |
| wood-craft | skilled in woodland ways and hunting |
| wood-leas | woodland glades, pastures |
| wood-wise | understanding trees and woodland |
| word-bearer | messenger, emissary |
| word-craft | skill in using words |
| word-hoard | power of speech |
| word-lord | messenger |
| word-play | riddles, puns and the like |
| wordsman | messenger |
| wordsmith | one skilled in using words |
| word-store | vocabulary |
| word-wealth | word-skill |
| word-weaver | one skilled in putting words together |
| word-weaving | the making of songs |
| word-wise | wisdom in using words |
| world-lore | knowledge of the world and its ways |
| worth-saying | weighing, or judging worth |

| | |
|---|---|
| worthful | worthy |
| wrath-riven | torn by anger or bitter disagreement |
| wrath-storm | outburst of anger |
| wrath-thirst | vengefulness |
| wrath-wreaker | avenger |
| wrath-wreaking | vengeance |
| wrath-wright | one who fosters revenge |
| wreak wrath | avenge |
| wretch | exile |
| wretch-folk | exiles |
| wyrd | doom, fate |
| wyrd-way | predestined path |
| wyrd-word | word about doom or fate |
| wyrd-writ | foreordained |
| Yulemonths | December and January (Ere-Yule and After-Yule) |

## *Folklist ('The Slaughter in Frisia')*

**Ælfhere** Danish warrior.

**Ecgbald** Frisian shore-ward.

**Ealhmund** Frisian shore-ward.

**Eanmund** steward of Finn's hall.

**Eawa** son of Eofor. Hickes has 'Eaha', a very rare name indeed (though 'Eahha' is found elsewhere). Bliss likes the emendation 'Eawa', a name found in Mercian kinship-lists. This name might be linked to that of the 'Eowa' folk, found in *Widsith*,line 26 (just before the Jutes and Finn are named).

**Eomær** son of Eadwine, warden of the Frisian Shore.

**Finn** Folkwielder, son of Godwulf. That Finn is set between Woden and Geat in Old English kinship lists (*Anglo-Saxon Chronicle*, 855) is most likely a mark of his great fame. (There is no real evidence of any Finn among the old gods.) In *Widsith*, line 27, Finn is called 'Folcwalding'. In the Finnsburg episode of *Beowulf* he is 'Folcwalda's son' (line 1089). 'Folcwalda/ Folcwalding' sounds less like a name, and more like a title for the head of some Frisian confederacy.

**Freagar** Frisian warrior who fought to the death in the second fight at Finnsburg.

**Frealaf** son of Finn (or grandson? – see next entry).

**Frithuwulf** son of Finn. Bliss suggests that Finn may have had two sons, one of whom was slain in the fight at Finnsburg, the other (younger) one growing up to carry on the kingly line. He further suggests that the younger son later came to be listed in the kinship roll as the son of his brother (something found in other kinship rolls). Bliss thinks Frithuwulf was the elder brother, since in the sources where he is named, he is always next to Finn (see Bliss, pp.45-50), and Frealaf the younger.

**Gefwulf**/Garulf, son of Guthulf. 'Garulf' is a key figure in the *Finnsburg Fragment*. Guthhere tries to hold him back (line 18), and there seems to be some strong reason why Garulf should not lightly risk his life. (He will not listen, and is killed, line 31.) Bliss suggests that this 'Garulf' is the Gefwulf of the Jutes in *Widsith* line 26, that he is last of a kingly line, and that the hopes of others besides Guthhere rested with him (see Bliss, pp.33-34).

**Godwulf** 'Grasper', father of Finn.

**Guthhere** is likely older than Gefwulf (who he tries in vain to hold back). He seems to be a leader, and may well be of the same high kindred as Gefwulf.

**Guthlaf** younger son of Hunlaf.

**Guthulf** (or Guthlaf, Guthulf), son of Godric, lord of the Eotena. In the *Fragment* lines 31-33, Garulf/Gefwulf is 'Guthlaf's son'. Is this the Guthlaf of line 16? If so, then father and son were fighting on opposite sides. Perhaps there were two Guthlafs at Finnsburg? Or is this another of Hickes' miswritings? Bliss thinks that if either of the first two thoughts were right, something would have been said, even in so short a fragment. (Guthlaf is a rare name, so it would be strange indeed to find two bearers of the name in this one incident.) Bliss would therefore take this 'Guthlaf' as a miswriting. But what has been miswritten? Bliss says 'Guthulf' is likely enough (see Bliss, pp.31-33).

**Hengest** the Eote (Jute), exile, and leader of a mingled war-band of Eotan, Frisians and others.

**Hildeburh** daughter of Hoc of the Danes, and wife of Finn Folkwielder.

**Hnæf Hocing**, Half-Dane. It seems clear (from the Finnsburg episode in *Beowulf*) that Hnæf and Hildeburh are brother and sister, and that Hildeburh is the older. (Her son fights alongside Hnæf.) Bliss suggests that at the time of the fight at Finnsburg Hnæf may have been about 25-30 years old, Hildeburh about 33 years, and her son (sister-son to Hnæf) about 15 years (Bliss, p.51). In the episode Hnæf is 'the Half-Danes' hero' (*Beowulf* line 1069). The Finnsburg tale, in which Danes overcome in the end after being grievously wronged by the Frisians, was surely a meaningful choice for a song in the Danish hall of Heorot.

**Hoc Half-Dane**, king of the Danes.

**Horsa the Eote**, brother of Hengest.

**Ordlaf**, elder son of Hunlaf. Ordlaf and his brother Guthlaf probably represent a more purely Danish element in Hnæf's rather mixed war-band. The tale of Hunlaf is lost. But he must have won such fame that his son could be known simply as Hunlafing. Bliss suggests that Hunlaf may possibly have been related to Healfdene, the father of the Hrothgar of the *Beowulf* poem (Bliss, p.79). Dr Rudolf Imelmann found the name 'Hunlaf(ing)' in a list of eight Germanic heroes, in the late MS Cotton Vespasian D iv (fol. 139v). It seems that in English tradition the Hunlaf warrior family were still remembered after the Norman Conquest (see Chambers, p.254, Bliss pp.76-77).

**Osfrith** Frisian shore-ward.

**Sigeferth** 'Unfearing', son of Sigemund. In the *Finnsburg Fragment* Sigeferth seems to be one of Hnæf's warriors. At the least he is among the defenders. He is of the Secgan folk, almost certainly the Secgs named in *Widsith*, lines 31, 63. In line 31 of that poem 'Sæferth' is named as ruler of the Secgs. The name is close to 'Sigeferth', and we may take it that the two were at least related, and could well be one and the same warrior. Sigeferth calls himself 'wrecca' (modern English 'wretch'), that is 'exile' or 'outlaw'. So he is not a Secgan lord with a following, but rather an exile and an adventurer.

**Sigestan** one of Finn's war-band, who fought to the death in the second fight at Finnsburg.

**Siward** the Saxon, hostage in Frisia, who served under Eomær, warden of the Frisian Shore.

**Thrythwulf** Frisian shore-ward.

**Wiglaf** 'Wolf's-bane', one of Hnæf's war-band.

**Winebeald**, Frisian shore-ward.

**Wulfric** son of Wulf. One of Finn's war-band, who fought to the death in the second fight at Finnsburg.

**Wulfrith** 'Witfast', Eotan warrior, Woden's man and a master of the runes. In the first poem, 'Of the Slaughter in Frisia', he is one of the Eotan exiles at the hall of Finn. In 'The Stallion' he has become Hengest's man.

## *Folklist ('The Stallion')*

**Ægel** Eotan warrior. He is taken to be the Ægel who gave his name to Aylesford, near Maidstone, which is perhaps the 'Ægelesþrep' where, according to the *Anglo-Saxon Chronicle*, Hengest and Horsa fought against king Vortigern (*Chronicle* 455).

**Beornfrith**, Eotan warrior.

**Beornmund**, Eotan warrior. The name is found in the place-name 'Bermondsey', which is 'Beornmund's island'.

**Caradawg** 'Two-speech', interpreter between Vortigern and Hrothwyn, at the feast in Hengest's hall.

**Catigern** son of Vortigern, who fights alongside his brother, Vortimer, at the battle on the Medway.

**Ceolla** 'Helm Cleaver', Eotan warrior, slain in the battle at Ægelesþrep.

**Ceolmund** Eotan warrior, slain at Ægelesþrep.

**Ciorra** 'Deed-doer', Eotan warrior slain at Ægelesþrep.

**Godmær** Eotan warrior who, at the Medway battle, bring's down Catigern's horse, and afterwards slays the rider ('his most-famed thrust').

**Gythla** Eotan warrior.

**Hengest** 'Lack-lord'. After the slaying and avenging of his lord, Hnæf the Dane, the lordless Hengest took service with Vortigern and wrested Kent from the Britons. His name means 'stallion'.

**Horsa** ('horse') brother of Hengest.

**Hrofi** 'Unhorse', too tall and heavy for any horse to bear.

**Hrothwyn** daughter of Hengest, given in wedlock to king Vortigern.

**Vortigern** high king of the Britons.

**Vortimer** son of Vortigern. Named 'Britain-land's Shield' after the overthrow of his father by the Council.

**Wiga** Eotan lord.

**Wipped** son of Hwita, 'Spear's son', Eotan warrior who fought to the death at the battle by the Written Stone. In *Anglo-Saxon Chronicle* 465 the place of the battle is named 'Wippedesfleot'.

**Wulfrith** 'Witfast', also called 'Wolf-wit', the Wily, 'Rede-wit', 'Rune-wise'. He is a strife-stirrer, a crafty man who (by Woden's help) sees what is written in the runes. He is, besides, no mean warrior.

## *The House of Finn and Hnæf*

- Godwulf 'Grasper'
  - Finn Folkwielder m Hildeburh
    - Frithwulf
    - Frealaf
      - Freawine
- Hoc Half-Dane
  - Hildeburh (m Finn Folkwielder)
  - Hnæf Hocing
  - daughter m Beowulf the Dane
    - Healfdane Scylding
      - Hrothgar

## *The Eotena*

- Godric
  - Guthulf
    - Gefwulf

- Woden
  - Wehta
    - Witta
      - Wihtgils
        - Hengest
          - Oisc
            - Octa
              - Eormenric
                - Athelberht
        - Hors(a)

## *Places*

**'Bridge Fort'** Rochester.

**Cantland** Kent.

**Cantware's hall** 'Cantware' is the Anglo-Saxon equivalent of 'Cantiaci', the British tribe who dwelt in Kent/ Cantium (probably meaning 'the corner land'). This meeting-place may have been in the old Roman theatre of Durovernum/Canterbury.

**Cantware-land** land of the Cantware, that is, Kent.

**Crei** River Cray, Kent.

**Darent** River Darent, Kent.

**Deira** post-Roman British (later Anglian) kingdom, roughly the East Riding of Yorkshire.

**Fifeldor** island at the mouth of the River Eider, Germany.

**Finnsburg** in the northern Netherlands, perhaps in the Leeuwarden area.

**Gallic Sea** English Channel.

**Hafren** River Severn.

**Hipwell** 'the stream where hips grow', later Hipwellsfleet, which is probably, though not certainly, Ebbsfleet. The *Chronicle* names the landing place as 'Heopwinesfleot' or 'Ypwinesfleot', close to, though not the same as, Yppelesfleot (Ebbsfleet).

**Horseford** Aylesford?

**Medeway** River Medway, Kent.

**Middle-earth Sea** Mediterranean Sea.

**Oakwood river** the Darent. This British river name ('Derventio/Derwent') comes from Britsh 'derva' meaning 'oak'. The sense is 'river where oaks were common'.

**Prydyn** old name for Britain; the Welsh came to use it of Pictland, the north of Scotland.

**Ravensburh** site unknown; 'Ravenswood' (*Beowulf* line 2925) was a forest in Sweden, where the Swedish king Ongenþeow slew Hæðcyn king of the Geats in battle.

**Rheged** post-Roman British kingdom, lying either side of the Solway Firth, embracing south-west Scotland and north-west England.

**Rome-land** the Roman empire.

**Rutupi port** Rutupiae, that is, Richborough.

**Weser** River in north-west Germany.

# Chronology

| The Roman world | Britain and the Germanic world (based on reasoned guesswork) |
|---|---|
| **350-75,** Franks penetrate northern Gaul. | c.**350-400**, Offa of Angeln. |
| **372**, Huns defeat the Alans. | |
| **375-8**, Huns defeat the Ostrogoths, then the Visigoths. | |
| **378**, defeat and death of the emperor Valens, fighting the Visigoths at Adrianople. | |
| **c.400-410**, the Huns enter Pannonia. | |
| **406**, December 31st, Suebi, Vandals and Alans cross the frozen Rhine and pour into Gaul. | **407-11**, Constantine III proclaimed emperor in Britain; he takes Roman troops from Britain in his bid for power. |
| **410**, Alaric and his Visigoths sack Rome; Alaric dies soon after. | **410**, Honorius in his 'Rescript' tells the Britons they must now look to their own defence. |
| **412-414** Alaric's brother-in-law Ataulf sets up a Visigoth kingdom in Gaul. | **c.400-452**, Finn Folkwielder. |
| | **c.415**, birth of Hengest. |
| **425-55**, Valentinian III emperor in the West, backed by Aëtius. | |
| **433-445**, Attila and Bleda joint rulers of the Huns (Attila sole ruler, 445-53). | **c.435**, flight of Waldere and Hildegyth from the court of Attila. |
| | **c.435**, wedding of Finn and Hildeburh. |
| | **c.436**, birth of Frithuwulf, son of Finn. |
| **437**, Burgundians defeated by the Huns. | **c.435/440**, birth of Healfdene (father of Hrothgar the Dane). |
| | **c.438**, birth of Hrothwyn. |
| | **c.440**, birth of Oisc. |

| | |
|---|---|
| **442,** Aëtius settles the Alans in the Loire region, the Burgundians in Savoy. | |
| | **c.446**, the Britons appeal in vain for help from Aëtius. |
| **450**, death of Clodian/Chlodion king of the Ripuarian Franks; his son Merovech seeks Roman help against his brother Gundebaud, who turns to the Huns. | **c.450**, Soemil 'first separated Deira from Bernicia' (*Historia Brittonum* 61). |
| **451**, Attila's demand (for marriage with Valentinian's sister, with half a kingdom) being refused, he invades Gaul with his Huns and allies; battle of the Catalaunian Fields. | **c.451,** the 'Frisian slaughter' at Finnsburg.<br>**c.452,** the Danish overthrow of Finnsburg. |
| **453**, death of Attila; Gepids, Ostrogoths throw off the Hunnish yoke. | **c.453**, Hengest and Horsa come to Kent at the invitation of Vortigern. |
| **454**, Aëtius murdered on the orders of Valentinian III (who is murdered in turn, 455). | |
| **455**, Rome sacked by the Vandals. | **c.455**, Vortigern/Hrothwyn marriage. |
| | **c.455-73**, Britons and Jutes war in Kent. |
| **464**, death of Aegidius, 'magister militum' in North Gaul. | **c.460s**, Icel founds the Mercian kingdom, perhaps leading a migration from East Anglia. |
| | **c.465/70**, birth of Hrothgar (nephew of Hnæf?). |
| **481-511**, Clovis king of the Franks; his growing power perhaps puts pressure on Saxons settled in Gaul. | **c.477** Ælle founds the kingdom of the South Saxons. |
| **486**, Clovis overthrows Syagrius and makes himself master of north Gaul. | **c.480**, Jutish settlements in Hampshire and the Isle of Wight. |
| | **c.488**, death of Hengest. |
| | **c.496**, victory of Britons under 'Arthur' at Mount Badon. |

**c.500/05**, Hrothgar becomes king of the Danes.

**c.510**, victory of Hygelac, king of the Geats, over the Swedes at Ravenswood.

**c.520/525**, Beowulf's visit to Heorot; ill-fated marriage alliance of the Danish princess Freawaru to the Heathobard Ingeld.

**c.525/30**, Hygelac rashly invades the territory of the Frisians and Franks, and meets his death.

# The Texts

## *The Finn episode from Beowulf*

Louis J Rodrigues, *Anglo-Saxon Verse Charms, Maxims & Heroic Legends*

Hrothgar's *scop*
upon the mead-benches should tell:
Finn's followers when sudden woe befell them,
Hnæf of the Scyldings, the Half-Danes' hero,
was fated to fall on the Frisian field.
No need had Hildeburh indeed to praise
the Jutes' good faith; blamesless, she was
deprived of her dear ones at the shield-play:
son and brother fell to their fate
wounded by spears; a sad woman that.
Not without reason did Hoc's daughter
mourn destiny's decree, when morning came
and she could see, beneath the sky,
the slaughter of kinsmen. Where once she held
most joy in the world, the war took all
Finn's *thanes*, save only a few,
so that he could not on the field
fight with Hengest at all
nor guard the survivors by stirring against
the prince's *thane*; but they offered in truce
to provide for them another place,
hall and high-seat, and half the rights
to share with the sons of the Jutes;
that Folcwalda's son, at the gift-giving,
every day should honour the Danes,
grant treasures to Hengest's troop,
even as much precious wealth
in plated gold as the Frisian's kin
would be glad to get in the beer-hall.
Then they confirmed on either side
the firm peace-compact. To Hengest, Finn swore
solemn oaths, declared, unfeigned, that those

surviving the fight, with his *witan's* advice,
he would hold in honour so that no man
by word or deed should break the truce,
nor for malice ever mention that,
lordless, their prince's slayer, they
followed, now need forced them to it.
If, with rash speech, a Frisian should
revive the reason for that hate
then sword's edge should settle it.
Funeral pyre prepared, piled gold raised
from hoard, the war-Scyldings' best
of heroes was made ready on the pyre.
At the fire were easily seen
blood-stained battle-shirt, golden boar-crest,
iron-hard swine, many an *ætheling*
weary with wounds; some in battle fell.
Then Hildeburh on Hnæf's bier bade
them yield her own son to the flames,
burn his body, place him on the fire,
at his uncle's shoulder. The woman mourned,
grieved, lamented loud. The warrior went up.
The greatest of death-fires to the welkin wound,
roared before the barrow. Heads dissolved,
wounds gaped wide, as blood sprang out,
body's hate-bites. Fire swallowed up –
greediest of spirits – those slain in war
on both sides; shaken was their strength.
 The warriors departed to their dwellings,
lacking friends, to look on Friesland's
homes and high-city. Hengest still stayed on
with Finn; through a winter, slaughter-stained,
all desolate, he dreamed about his land,
though over the wave he could not drive
his ring-prowed ship; storms stirred the sea,
strove with the wind; winter locked the waves
in icy bonds – until there came another year
to men's dwellings, as it still does,
ever biding its time,

glorious bright weather. Then was winter gone,
earth's lap fair, the exile eager to depart,
the guest from the dwellings; yet, vengeance for
his wrongs he thought on more than that sea-voyage –
how he might foment discord
to settle the sons of the Jutes.
So he did not decline his duty when
Hunlaf's son placed Battle-Bright,
the best of blades, upon his lap:
its edges were known to the Jutes.
Thus to the war-wild Finn in his turn, too,
cruel sword-evil came to his home,
when Guthlaf and Oslaf complained of grim onslaught
and sorrow subsequent to the sea-voyage,
blamed him for their woes; the breast cannot hold
a restless heart. Then was hall reddened
with bodies of foes, Finn slain,
the king with his men, and the queen taken.
The Scylding warriors bore to the ship
all the hall-trappings of the land's king,
whatsoever they could find at Finn's
of torques, precious gems. On the sea-track
they brought the lady back to the Danes,
led her to her people.

## *Gildas, De Excidio Britanniae*

Edited and translated by Michael Winterbottom, *Gildas, The Ruin of Britain and other works* (Chichester: Phillimore, 1978), pp.23-4, 26-8.

20.1 So the miserable remnants sent off a letter again, this time to the Roman commander Agitius [Aëtius?], in the following terms: 'To Agitius. thrice consul: the groans of the British'. Further on came this complaint: 'The barbarians push us back to the sea, the sea pushes us back to the barbarians; between these two kinds of death, we are either drowned or slaughtered'. But they got no help in return.

23.1 Then all the members of the council, together with the proud tyrant [Vortigern?], were struck blind; the guard – or rather the method of destruction – they devised for our land was that the ferocious Saxons (name not to be spoken!), hated by man and God, should be let into the island like wolves into the fold, to beat back the peoples of the north.

23.2 Nothing more destructive, nothing more bitter has ever befallen the land. How utter the blindness of their minds! How desperate and crass the stupidity! Of their own free will they invited under the same roof a people whom they feared worse than death even in their absence – 'the silly princes of Zoan', as has been said, 'giving foolish advice to Pharaoh'.

23.3 Then a pack of cubs burst forth from the lair of the barbarian lioness, coming in three 'keels' as they call warships in their language. The winds were favourable; favourable too the omens and auguries, which prophesied, according to a sure portent among them, that they would live for three hundred years in the land towards which their prows were directed, and that for half the time, a hundred and fifty years, they would repeatedly lay it waste. On the orders of the ill-fated tyrant, they first of all fixed their dreadful claws on the east side of the island , ostensibly to fight for our country, in fact to fight against it.

25.2 After a time, when the cruel plunderers had gone home, God gave strength to the survivors. Wretched people fled to them from all directions, as eagerly as bees to the beehive when a storm threatens, and begged whole-heartedly, 'burdening heaven with unnumbered prayers', that they should not be altogether destroyed.

25.3 Their leader was Ambrosius Aurelianus, a gentleman who, perhaps alone of the Romans, had survived the shock of this notable storm: certainly his parents, who had worn the purple, were slain in it. His descendants in our own day have become greatly inferior to their grandfaher's excellence. Under him, our people regained their strength, and challenged the victors to battle. The lord assented, and the battle went their way.

26.1 From then on victory went now to our countrymen, now to their enemies: so that in this people the Lord could make trial (as he tends to) of his latter-day Israel to see whether it loves him or not. This lasted right up to the year of the siege of Badon Hill, pretty well the last defeat of the villains, and certainly not the least. That was the year of my birth; as I know, one month of the forty-fourth year since then has already passed.

## *The Anglo-Saxon Chronicle*

Translated by GN Garmonsway (London: JM Dent & Sons, 1953), pp.12-14.

449. In this year Marcian and Valentinian obtained the kingdom and reigned seven winters. In their days Hengest and Horsa invited by Vortigern, king of the Britons, came to at a place which is called *Ypwinesfleot* [Ebbsfleet, Kent?] at first to help the Britons, but later they fought against them. The king ordered them to fight against the Picts, and so they did and had victory whereever they came. They then sent to Angel; ordered (them) to send them more aid and to be told of the worthlessness of the Britons and the excellence of the land. They then sent them more aid. These men came from three nations of Germany: from the Old Saxons, from the Angles, from the Jutes. From the Jutes came the people of Kent, and the Wihtware, that is, the race which now dwells in the Isle of Wight, and the kindred among the West Saxons which is still called the kindred of the Jutes. From the Old Saxons came the East Saxons and South Saxons and West Saxons. From Angel, which has stood waste ever since between the Jutes and the Saxons, came the East Angles, Middle Angles, Mercians, and all the Northumbrians. Their leaders were two brothers, Hengest and Horsa; they were sons of Wihtgils. Wihtgils was the son of Witta, the son of Wecta, the son of Woden; from this Woden sprang all our royal kindred, and that of the peoples dwelling south of the Humber.

455. In this year Hengest and Horsa fought against king Vortigern at a place which is called *Ægelesþrep* [Aylesford, Kent?], and his brother Horsa was slain. And after that Hengest succeeded to the kingdom and Æsc, his son.

456. In this year Hengest and Æsc fought against the Britons at a place which is called *Crecganford* [Crayford, Kent?], and there slew four companies; and the Britons then forsook Kent, and fled to London in great terror.

465. In this year Hengest and Æsc fought against the Welsh, near *Wippedesfleot*, and there slew twelve Welsh nobles; and one of their own thegns, whose name was Wipped, was slain there.

473. In this year Hengest and Æsc fought against the Welsh and captured innumerable spoils, and the Welsh fled from the English like fire.

## *Bede, The Ecclesiastical History of the English People*

Edited by Judith McClure and Roger Collins (Oxford: Oxford University Press, 2008)

Book I, chapter 15: In the year of our Lord 449 Marcian, forty-sixth from Augustus, became emperor with Valentinian and ruled for seven years. At that time the race of the Angles or Saxons, invited by Vortigern, came to Britain in three warships and by his command were granted a place of settlement in the eastern part of the island, ostensibly to fight on behalf of the country, but their real intention was to conquer it. First they fought against the enemy who attacked from the north and the Saxons won the victory. A report of this as well as of the fertility of the island and the slackness of the Britons reached their homes and at once a much larger fleet was sent over with a stronger band of warriors; this, added to the contingent already there, made an invincible army. The newcomers received from the Britons a grant of land in their midst, on condition that they fought against their foes for the peace and safety of the country, and for this the soldiers were also to receive pay.

They came from three very powerful Germanic tribes, the Saxons, Angles, and Jutes. The people of Kent and inhabitants of the Isle of Wight are of Jutish origin and also those opposite the Isle of Wight, that part of the kingdom of Wessex which is still today called the nation of the Jutes. From the Saxon country, that is, the district now known as Old Saxony, came the East Saxons, the South Saxons, and the West Saxons. Besides this, from the country of the Angles, that is, the land between the kingdoms of the Jutes and the Saxons, which is called *Angulus*, came the East Angles, the Middle Angles, the Mercians, and all the Northumbrian race (that is, those people who dwell north of the river Humber) as well as the other Anglian tribes. *Angulus* is said to have remained deserted from that day to this. Their first leaders are said to have been two brothers, Hengist and Horsa. Horsa was afterwards killed in battle by the Britons, and in the eastern part of Kent there is still a monument bearing his name.

## *Historia Brittonum*

Edited and translated by John Morris, *Nennius, British History and The Welsh Annals* (Chichester: Phillimore, 1980), pp. 26, 28, 31-2.

31. It came to pass that after this war between the British and the Romans, when their generals were killed, and after the killing of the tyrant Maximus and the end of the Roman empire in Britain, the British went in fear for forty years. Vortigern ruled in Britain, and during his rule in Britain he was under pressure, from fear of the Picts and the Irish, and of a Roman invasion, and, not least, from dread of Ambrosius. Then came three keels, driven into exile from Germany. In them were the brothers Horsa and Hengest, sons of Wihtgils, son of Witta; son of Wehta, son of Woden, son of Frealaf, son of Frithuwulf, son of Finn, son of Folkwielder, son of Geat, who said they were son of God; but he was not the God of gods, Amen, the God of Hosts, but one of the idols they worshipped. Vortigern welcomed them, and handed over to them the island that in their language is called Thanet, in British Ruoihm.

When Gratian ruled for the second time with Equitius, the Saxons were received by Vortigern, 347 years after the Passion of Christ.

37. But Hengest was an experienced man, shrewd and skilful. Sizing up the king's impotence, and the military weakness of his people, he held a council, and said to the British king 'We are few; if you wish, we can send home and invite warriors from the fighting men of our country, that the number who fight for you and your people may be larger.' The king ordered it to be done, and envoys were sent across the sea, and came back with sixteen keels, with picked warriors in them. In one of the keels came Hengest's daughter, a beautiful and very handsome girl. When the keels had arrived, Hengest held a banquet for Vortigern, and his men and his interpreter, whose name was Ceretic, and he told the girl to serve their wine and spirits. They all got exceedingly drunk. When they were drinking Satan entered into Vortigern's heart, and made him love the girl. Through his interpreter he asked her father for her hand, saying 'Ask of me what you will, even to the half of my kingdom.'

Hengest took counsel with the elders of Angeln, to decide what they should ask of the king for the girl, and they all agreed to ask for the country that in their language is called Canturguoralen, in ours Kent. So he granted it to them, although Gwyrangon was ruling in Kent, and did not know that his kingdom was being handed over to the heathens, and that he was himself given secretly into their power on his own. So the girl was given in marriage to Vortigern, and he slept with her, and loved her deeply.

43. Meanwhile, Vortigern's son Vortimer fought vigorously against Hengest and Horsa and their people, and expelled them as far as the aforesaid island called Thanet, and there three times shut them up and besieged them, attacking, threatening and terrifying them. So they sent envoys overseas to Germany to summon keels with a vast number of fighting men. And afterwards they used to fight against the kings of one nation, sometimes victoriously advancing their frontiers, sometimes being defeated and expelled.

44. Vortimer fought four keen battles against them. The first battle was on the river Darenth. The second battle was at the ford called Episford in their language, Rhyd yr afael in ours, and there fell Horsa, and also Vortigern's son Cateyrn. The third battle was fought in the open country by the Inscribed Stone on the shore of the Gallic Sea. The barbarians were beaten and he was victorious. They fled to their keels and were drowned as they clambered aboard them like women.

But Vortimer soon after died. Before he died he told his followers to set his tomb by the coast, in the port from which [the English] had departed, saying 'I entrust it to you. Wherever else they may hold a British port or may have settled, they will never again live in this land.' But they ignored his command and did not bury him where he had told them: for he is buried in Lincoln. But if they had kept his command, there is no doubt that they would have obtained whatever they wished through the prayers of saint Germanus.

45. But the barbarians returned in force, for Vortigern was their friend, because of his wife, and none was resolute to drive them out; for they occupied Britain not because of their strength, but because it was the will of God. Who can resist the will of God, even if he tries? The Lord did what He would, for He rules and governs all the nations.

So it came to pass that after the death of Vortimer, son of king Vortigern, and after the return of Hengest and his hosts, they instigated a treacherous plan, to trick Vortigern and his army. They sent envoys to ask for peace and to make a permanent treaty. Vortiern called a council of his elders to examine what they should do. Ultimately one opinion prevailed with all, that they should make peace. The envoys went back, and conference was convened, where the two sides, British and English, should meet, unarmed, to confirm the treaty.

46. But Hengest told all his followers to hide their daggers under their feet in their shoes, saying 'When I call out to you and say "*English, draw your knives*", take your daggers from your shoes and fall upon them, and stand firm against them. But do not kill the king; keep him alive, for my daughter's sake, whom I wedded to him, for it is better for us that he be ransomed from us.' So the conference assembled, and the English, friendly in their words, but wolfish in heart and deed, sat down, like allies, man beside man. Hengest cried out as he had said, and all the three hundred Elders of king Vortigern were murdered, and the king alone was taken and held prisoner. To save his life, he ceded several districts, namely Essex and Sussex, together with Middlesex and other districts that they chose and designated.

# Booklist


L Alcock, *Arthur's Britain* (Harmondsworth: Penguin, 1971, 1975)

M Alexander, editor, *Beowulf* (London: Penguin Books, 1995)

M Alexander, translator, *The Earliest English Poems* (Harmondsworth: Penguin Books, Second edition 1977, 1982)

JND Anderson, *A Lawyer among the Theologians* (London: Hodder and Stoughton, 1973)

M Ashley, *The Mammoth Book of British Kings and Queens* (London: Robinson Publishing, 1998)

M Ashton and C Lewis, editors, *The Medieval Landscape of Wessex* (Oxford: Oxbow Books, 1994)

Asser, *Life of King Alfred*, edited by Simon Keynes and Michael Lapidge (Harmondsworth: Penguin Books, 1983)

S Bassett, editor, *The Origins of Anglo-Saxon kingdoms* (London: Leicester University, Press 1989)

D Bebbington, *Patterns in history* (Leicester: Inter-Varsity Press, 1979)

Bede, *The Ecclesiastical History of the English People,* edited by Judith McClure and Roger Collins (Oxford: Oxford University Press, 2008)

P Bidwell, *Roman forts in Britain* (London: Batsford/English Heritage, 1997)

Alan Bliss, editor, *JRR Tolkien: Finn and Hengest* (London: Harper Collins, 1998)

R Bromwich, AOH Jarman, Brynley F Roberts, editors, *The Arthur of the Welsh* (Cardiff: University of Wales Press, 1991)

R Bromwich, editor, *Trioedd Ynys Prydein* (Cardiff: University of Wales Press, 2006)

Nicholas Brooks, *Anglo-Saxon Myths: State and Church 400-1066* (London: Hambledon Press, 2000)

HM Chadwick, *The Origin of the English Nation* (Cambridge: Cambridge University Press, 1907)

RW Chambers, *Widsith: a study in Old English heroic legend* (Cambridge: Cambridge University Press, 1912)

RW Chambers, *England before the Norman Conquest* (London: Longmans, Green, 1926)

Robert Claiborne, *English: Its life and times* (London: Bloomsbury, 1983, 1990, reprinted 1994)

AS Esmonde Cleary, *The Ending of Roman Britain* (London: Batsford, 1989)

RG Collingwood, *Roman Britain*, Oxford History of England (Oxford: Oxford University Press, Second edition 1937, reprinted 1963)

GJ Copley, *The conquest of Wessex in the sixth century* (London: Phoenix, 1954)

B Cunliffe, *Wessex to AD 1000* (London: Longman, 1993)

KR Dark, *Civitas to Kingdom: British Political Continuity 300-800* (London: Leicester University Press, 1994)

P Drewett, David Rudling and Mark Gardiner, *The South-east to AD 1000* (London: Longman, 1988)

E Ekwall, *The Concise Oxford Dictionary of English Place-names* (Oxford: Oxford University Press, fourth edition 1960)

Peter Ellis, editor, *Roman Wiltshire and after* (Devizes: Wiltshire Archaeological and Natural History Society, 2001)

PB Ellis, *Celt and Saxon* (London: Constable, 1993)

HR Ellis Davidson, *Gods and Myths of Northern Europe* (Harmondsworth: Penguin Books, 1964, 1982)

H Elton, *Warfare in Roman Europe, A.D. 350–425* Oxford Classical Monographs (Oxford: Clarendon Press, 1997)

SS Evans, *Lords of battle* (Woodbridge: Boydell Press, 1997)

A Everitt, *Continuity and Colonization: the evolution of Kentish settlement* (Leicester: Leicester University Press, 1986)

E Foord, *The Last Age of Roman Britain* (London: Harrap, 1925)

William O Frazer and Andrew Tyrrell, editors, *Social Identity in Early Medieval Britain* (London: Leicester University Press, 2000)

GN Garmonsway, editor, *Anglo-Saxon Chronicle* (London: JM Dent, 1953, 1962)

M Gelling, *The West Midlands in the Early Middle Ages* (Leicester: Leicester University Press, 1992)

M Gelling, *Place-Names in the Landscape* (London: Phoenix Press, 2000, reprint of 1984 edition)

Geoffrey of Monmouth, *Historia Regum Britanniae* (London: JM Dent, 1912, 1944)

Gildas, *De Excidio Britanniae*, edited by M Winterbottom (London: Phillimore, 1978)

M Grant, *The Fall of the Roman Empire* (revised edition 1990, reprinted London: Phoenix, 1997)

LV Grinsell, *The Archaeology of Wessex* (London: Methuen, 1958)

K Harrison, *The Framework of Anglo-Saxon history to A.D. 900* (Cambridge: Cambridge University Press, 1976, 2010)

J Haywood, *Dark Age Naval Power* (Hockwold-cum-Wilton: Anglo-Saxon Books, 1991)

K Herbert, *Looking for the Lost Gods of England* (Hockwold-cum-Wilton: Anglo-Saxon Books, 1994)

K Herbert, *Spellcraft* (Pinner: Anglo-Saxon Books, 1993)

NJ Higham, *The English Conquest* (Manchester: Manchester University Press, 1994)

C Hills, *Origins of the English* (London: Gerald Duckworth, 2003)

G Hindley, *A Brief History of the Anglo-Saxons* (London: Robinson, 2006)

John Hines, editor, *The Anglo-Saxons from the migration period to the eighth century: An ethnographic perspective*, Center for Interdisciplinary Research on Social Stress (Woodbridge: The Boydell Press, 1997):

W Pohl, 'Ethnic names and identities in the British Isles: A comparative perspective', pp.7-40.

Ian Wood, 'Before and after the migration to Britain', pp.41-64

Thomas Charles-Edwards, 'Anglo-Saxon kinship revisited', pp.171-210

Giorgio Ausenda, 'Current issues and future directions in the study of the early Anglo-Saxon period', pp.411-450.

M Holmes, *King Arthur, a military history* (London: Blandford Press, 1996)

D Hooke, *The Landscape of Anglo-Saxon England* (London: Leicester University Press, 1998)

Nicholas Howe, *Migration and Mythmaking in Anglo-Saxon England* (New Haven and London: Yale University Press, 1989; new edtion, University of Notre Dame Press, 2001).

T Beaumont James *Winchester* (London: Batsford/English Heritage 1997)

Eric John, *Reassessing Anglo-Saxon England* (Manchester: Manchester University Press, 1996)

Stephen Johnson, *Later Roman Britain* (London: Paladin, 1980, 1982)

B Jones and D Mattingly, *An Atlas of Roman Britain* (London: Guild Publishing, 1990)

Gwyn Jones, *Kings, Beasts and Heroes* (Oxford: Oxford University Press, 1972)

DP Kirby, *The Earliest English Kings* (Cambridge, 1991)

Scott M Langston, *Exodus Through the Centuries* (Oxford: Blackwell Publishing, 2006)

Michael Lapidge and David Dumville, *Gildas: New Approaches* (Woodbridge: Boydell Press, 1984)

H Last, 'The peoples of Northern Europe, The Getae and Dacians' in *The Cambridge Ancient History* Volume XI (London: Cambridge University Press, 1954)

CS Lewis, *Fern-seed and Elephants* (Glasgow: Fontana/Collins, 1975)

J Lindsay, *Arthur and his times* (London: Frederick Muller, 1958)

HR Loyn, *Anglo-Saxon England and the Norman Conquest* (Harlow: Longman, 1962)

M Lyle, *Canterbury* (London: Batsford/English Heritage, 1994)

W Manning, *Roman Wales* (Cardiff: University of Wales Press, 2001)

Henry Mayr-Harting, *The Coming of Christianity to Anglo-Saxon England* (London: Batsford, 1972, 1977)

HEL Mellersh, *Chronology of the Ancient World* (London: Book Club Associates, 1976)

AH Merrills, *History and Geography in Late Antiquity* (Cambridge: Cambridge University Press, 2005)

J Morris, editor, *Historia Brittonum* (London: Phillimore, 1980)

J Morris, *The Age of Arthur,* Vol.1 (Chichester: Phillimore, 1977)

J Morris, *Arthurian Period Sources*, Vol.4 Places and peoples, and Saxon archaeology (Chichester: Phillimore, 1995)

JNL Myres, *The English Settlements* (Oxford: Oxford University Press, 1986, 1989)

Francis Owen, *The Germanic People* (New York: Dorset Press, 1990)

RI Page, *Runes* (London: British Museum Press, 1987, 1995)

S Pollington, *The English Warrior* (Hockwold-cum-Wilton: Anglo-Saxon Books, 1996)

ALF Rivet and C Smith, *The place-names of Roman Britain* (London: Book Club Associates, 1979, 1981)

Louis J Rodrigues, *Anglo-Saxon Verse Charms, Maxims & Heroic Legends* (Pinner: Anglo-Saxon Books, 1993)

John Rowlands and others, editors, *Welsh Family History* (The Association of Family History Societies of Wales, 1993

P Salway, *Roman Britain*, Oxford History of England (Oxford: Oxford University Press, 1981, 1988)

PH Sawyer, *From Roman Britain to Norman England* (London: Methuen, 1978)

GO Sayles, *The Medieval Foundations of England* (London: Methuen, 1948, 1966)

T Severin, *The Brendan Voyage* (London: Arrow Books, 1978)

P Sims-Williams, *Ancient Celtic Place-Names in Europe and Asia Minor* (Oxford: Blackwell Publishing, 2006)

CA Snyder, *An Age of Tyrants* (Stroud: Sutton Publishing, 1998)

P Stafford, *The East Midlands in the Early Middle Ages* (Leicester: Leicester University Press, 1985)

EG Stanley, editor, *British Academy Papers on Anglo-Saxon England* (published for the British Academy at Oxford: Oxford University Press, 1990).

Doris Mary Stenton, editor, *Preparatory to Anglo-Saxon England* being the collected papers of Frank Merry Stenton (Oxford: Oxford University Press, 1970)

FM Stenton, *Anglo-Saxon England* (Oxford: Oxford University Press, Second edition 1947, reprinted 1967)

Tacitus, translated by H Mattingly, *The Agricola and The Germania* (Harmondsworth: Penguin Books, 1948)

C Thomas, *Celtic Britain* (London: Thames and Hudson, 1986)

C Thomas, *Christianity in Roman Britain to AD 500* (London: Batsford, 1981, 1993)

JRR Tolkien, *Tree and Leaf, Smith of Wootton Major, The Homecoming of Beorhtnoth Beorhthelm's Son* (London: Unwin Books, 1975)

Richard Underwood *Anglo-Saxon Weapons and Warfare* (Stroud: Tempus Publishing, 1999)

J Wacher, *The Towns of Roman Britain* (London: Book Club Associates, 1974)

JM Wallace-Hadrill, '*Bede's Ecclesiastical History of the English People: A Historical Commentary*, Oxford Medieval Texts (Oxford: Oxford University Press, 1988)

Leslie Webster and Janet Backhouse, editors, *The Making of England: Anglo-Saxon Art and Culture AD 600-900* (London: British Museum Press, 1991)

CL Wrenn and WF Bolton, editors, *Beowulf, With the Finnesburg Fragment* (Exeter: Exeter University Press, revised edition 1988)

B Yorke, *Kings and kingdoms of early Anglo-Saxon England* (London: Seaby, 1990)

B Yorke, *Wessex in the Early Middle Ages* (London: Leicester University Press. 1995)

# Articles in the Dictionary of National Biography

J Campbell, article on Bede, volume 4, pp.758-65.

François Kerlouégan, article on Gildas, volume 22, pp.223-25.

# Journal articles

D Anlezark, 'Sceaf, Japheth and the origins of the Anglo-Saxons', *Anglo-Saxon England*, Volume 31, December 2002, pp.13-46.

Charlotte Behr, 'The origins of kingship in early medieval Kent', in *Early Medieval Europe*, volume 9, part 1, 2000, pp.25-52.

Simon Esmonde Cleary, 'Approaches to the Differences between Late Romano-British and Early Anglo-Saxon Archaeology' in *Anglo-Saxon Studies in Archaeology and History* 6 (Oxford: Oxford University Committee for Archaeology, 1993), pp.57-63.

Jan Davidse, 'The Sense of History in the Works of the Venerable Bede', *Studi Medievali* 3rd series, xxiii (1983), pp.647-95

DN Dumville, 'The West Saxon Genealogical Regnal List and the chronology of Wessex', *Peritia*, Volume 4, 1985, pp.21-66

DN Dumville, 'Kingship, Genealogies and Regnal Lists', in PH Sawyer and IN Wood, editors, *Early Medieval Kingship* (The School of History, University of Leeds, 1977, pp.72-104).

Sarah Foot, 'Remembering, Forgetting and Inventing: Attitudes to the Past in England at the End of the First Viking Age', in *Transactions of the Royal Historical Society* Sixth Series, IX (Cambridge: Cambridge University Press, 1999), pp.185-200.

Adam Fox, 'Remembering the Past in Early Modern England: Oral and Written Tradition', in *Transactions of the Royal Historical Society* Sixth Series, IX (Cambridge: Cambridge University Press, 1999), pp.233-256.

Patrick J Geary, 'Land, Language, and Memory in Europe 700-1100', in *Transactions of the Royal Historical Society* Sixth Series, IX (Cambridge: Cambridge University Press, 1999), pp.169-184.

Margaret Gelling, 'Why Aren't We Speaking Welsh?' in *Anglo-Saxon Studies in Archaeology and History* 6 (Oxford: Oxford University Committee for Archaeology, 1993), pp.51-56.

Danny Gerrets, 'Evidence of Political Centralization in Westergo: the Excavations at Wijnaldum in a (supra-) Regional Perspective', in *Anglo-Saxon Studies in Archaeology and History* 10 (Oxford: Oxford University Committee for Archaeology, 1999), pp.119-126.

Anthonie Heidinga, 'The Frisian Achievement in the First Millennium AD', in *Anglo-Saxon Studies in Archaeology and History* 10 (Oxford: Oxford University Committee for Archaeology, 1999), pp.11-16.

John Hines, 'The Becoming of the English: Identity, Material culture and Language in Early Anglo-Saxon England' in *Anglo-Saxon Studies in Archaeology and History* 7 (Oxford: Oxford University Committee for Archaeology, 1994), pp.49-59

DJ James, '*Sorviodunum* – A Review of the Archaeological Evidence', *Wiltshire Archaelogical and Natural History Magazine*, volume 95, 2002

Harald Kleinschmidt, 'Bede and the Jutes: A critique of historiography', *NOWELE* 24, 1994

Otto S Knottnerus, 'The Wadden Sea Region: A Unique Cultural landscape' in *Wadden Sea Ecosystem* no.12, 2001.

MLW Laistner, 'Bede as a Classical and Patristic Scholar' *Transactions of the Royal Historical Society*, 16 (1933)

A Mawer, 'Animal and Personal Names in OE Place-names', *The Modern Language Review* Volume XIV, Number 3, July 1919, pp.233-44.

John McNamara, 'Bede's Role in Circulating Legend in the *Historia Ecclesiastica*' in *Anglo-Saxon Studies in Archaeology and History* 7 (Oxford: Oxford University Committee for Archaeology, 1994), pp.61-69.

John Musty and JED Stratton, 'A Saxon cemetery at Winterbourne Gunner, near Salisbury', *Wiltshire Archaelogical and Natural History Magazine*, 59, 1964

S Oppenheimer, 'Myths of British Ancestry', *Prospect* magazine, 127, 21/10/06

Christopher Scull, 'Archaeology, Early Anglo-Saxon Society and the Origins of Anglo-Saxon Kingdoms' in *Anglo-Saxon Studies in Archaeology and History* 6 (Oxford: Oxford University Committee for Archaeology, 1993), pp.65-82.

Christopher Scull, 'Social Archaeology and Anglo-Saxon Kingdom Origins', in *Anglo-Saxon Studies in Archaeology and History* 10 (Oxford: Oxford University Committee for Archaeology, 1999), pp.17-24.

Patrick Sims-Williams, 'The settlement of England in Bede and the *Chronicle*' in *Anglo-Saxon England*, 12 (1983), pp.1-41.

P. Sims-Williams, 'Gildas and the Anglo-Saxons', *Cambridge Medieval Celtic Studies*, 6 (1983), pp.1–30.

Richard Sowerby, 'Hengest and Horsa: the manipulation of history and myth from the *adventus Saxonum* to *Historia Brittonum*' in *Nottingham Medieval Studies*, Volume 51, 2007 (Brepols Publishers) pp.1-19.

Patricia M Thane, 'Oral History, Memory and Written Tradition: An introduction', in *Transactions of the Royal Historical Society* Sixth Series, IX (Cambridge: Cambridge University Press, 1999), pp.161-8.

Mark G Thomas, Michael PH Stumpf and Heinrich Härke: 'Evidence for an apartheid-like social structure in early Anglo-Saxon England', 2006 (see 'Proceedings of the Royal Society' website)

Alistair Thomson, 'Making the Most of Memories: The Empirical and Subjective Value of Oral History',in *Transactions of the Royal Historical Society* Sixth Series, IX (Cambridge: Cambridge University Press, 1999), pp.291-301.

JE Turville-Petre, 'Hengest and Horsa' in *Saga Book of the Viking Society*, 14 (1953-7), pp.273-290.

Damian J Tyler, 'Bede, the *Anglo-Saxon Chronicle*, and Early West Saxon Kingship', *Southern History*, volume 19, 1977.

GH Wheeler, 'The genealogy of the Early West Saxon Kings', *English Historical Review*, xxxvi, 1921, pp.161-2.

Alex Woolf, 'An Interpolation in the Text of Gildas's *De Excidio Britanniae*', *Peritia*, Volume 16, 2002, pp.161-167.

Barbara Yorke, 'Fact or Fiction? The written evidence for the fifth and sixth centuries AD', in *Anglo-Saxon Studies in Archaeology and History* 6 (Oxford: Oxford University Committee for Archaeology, 1993), pp.45-50.

Barbara Yorke, 'The Origins of Anglo-Saxon Kingdoms: The Contribution of Written Sources', in *Anglo-Saxon Studies in Archaeology and History* 10 (Oxford: Oxford University Committee for Archaeology, 1999), pp.25-29.

Barbara Yorke, 'Joint Kingship in Kent', in *Archaeolgia Cantiana*, volume 99, 1983.

## Some of our other title

Please see www.asbooks.co.uk for latest availability and prices

## First Steps in Old English

### An easy to follow language course for the beginner

**Stephen Pollington**

A complete and easy to use Old English language course that contains all the exercises and texts needed to learn Old English. This course has been designed to be of help to a wide range of students, from those who are teaching themselves at home, to undergraduates who are learning Old English as part of their English degree course. The author has adopted a step-by-step approach that enables students of differing abilities to advance at their own pace. The course includes practice and translation exercises, a glossary of the words used in the course, and many Old English texts, including the *Battle of Brunanburh* and *Battle of Maldon*.

£16-95 272 pages

## Old English Poems, Prose & Lessons 2 CDs

**read by Stephen Pollington**

These CDs contain lessons and texts from *First Steps in Old English.*

Tracks include: 1. Deor. 2. Beowulf – The Funeral of Scyld Scefing. 3. Engla Tocyme (The Arrival of the English). 4. Ines Domas. Two Extracts from the Laws of King Ine. 5. Deniga Hergung (The Danes' Harrying) Anglo-Saxon Chronicle Entry AD997. 6. Durham 7. The Ordeal (Be ðon ðe ordales weddigaþ) 8. Wið Dweorh (Against a Dwarf) 9. Wið Wennum (Against Wens) 10. Wið Wæterælfadle (Against Waterelf Sickness) 11. The Nine Herbs Charm 12. Læcedomas (Leechdoms) 13. Beowulf's Greeting 14. The Battle of Brunanburh 15. A Guide to Pronunciation.
And more than 30 other lessons and extracts of Old English verse and prose.

£15 2 CDs - Free Old English transcript from www.asbooks.co.uk.

## Learn Old English with Leofwin

**Matt Love**

This is a new approach to learning old English – as a *living language*. Leofwin and his family are your guides through six lively, entertaining, topic-based units. New vocabulary and grammar are presented in context, step by step, so that younger readers and non-language specialists can feel engaged rather than intimidated. The author has complemented the text with a wealth of illustrations. There are listening, speaking, reading and writing exercises throughout. Free soundtracks available on the Anglo-Saxon Books website.

£14.95 160 pages

## **Wordcraft**: Concise English/Old English Dictionary and Thesaurus

**Stephen Pollington**

This book provides Old English equivalents to the commoner modern words in both dictionary and thesaurus formats. The Thesaurus presents vocabulary relevant to a wide range of individual topics in alphabetical lists, thus making it easily accessible to those with specific areas of interest. Each thematic listing is encoded for cross-reference from the Dictionary. The two sections will be of invaluable assistance to students of the language, as well as to those with either a general or a specific interest in the Anglo-Saxon period.

£9.95 256 pages

## An Introduction to the Old English Language and its Literature

**Stephen Pollington**

The purpose of this general introduction to Old English is not to deal with the teaching of Old English but to dispel some misconceptions about the language and to give an outline of its structure and its literature. Some basic knowledge of these is essential to an understanding of the early period of English history and the present form of the language.

£5.95 48 pages

## Monasteriales Indicia

### The Anglo-Saxon Monastic Sign Language

**Edited with notes and translation by Debby Banham**

The *Monasteriales Indicia* is one of very few texts which let us see how evryday life was lived in monasteries in the early Middle Ages. Written in Old English and preserved in a manuscript of the mid-eleventh century, it consists of 127 signs used by Anglo-Saxon monks during the times when the Benedictine Rule forbade them to speak. These indicate the foods the monks ate, the clothes they wore, and the books they used in church and chapter, as well as the tools they used in their daily life, and persons they might meet both in the monastery and outside. The text is printed here with a parallel translation. The introduction gives a summary of the background, both historical and textual, as well as a brief look at the later evidence for monastic sign language in England.

£5.95 96 pages

## Anglo-Saxon Art, Myth & Material Culture from the 4th to 7th Century

**Stephen Pollington**

In all the metalwork and archaeological oddments we have from the Anglo-Saxon period, is there anything one could call 'art'? The contributors to this book believe that not only was there considerable artistry in the output of early Anglo-Saxon workshops, but that it was vigorous, complex and technically challenging.

The designs found on Anglo-Saxon artifacts is never mere ornament: in a society which used visual and verbal signals to demonstrate power, authority, status and ethnicity, no visual statement was ever empty of meaning. The aim of this work is to prompt a better understanding of Anglo-Saxon art and the society which produced it.

Stephen Pollington, Lindsay Kerr and Brett Hammond have assembled in these pages much information and many previously unpublished illustrations which show a wide variety of artifacts, designs and motifs. It is hoped that this will help bring about a wider knowledge and appreciation of Anglo-Saxon art.

£49 62 colour plates, 226 black & white illustrations

## The Battle of Maldon: Text and Translation

**Translated and edited by Bill Griffiths**

The Battle of Maldon was fought between the men of Essex and the Vikings in AD 991. The action was captured in an Anglo-Saxon poem whose vividness and heroic spirit has fascinated readers and scholars for generations. *The Battle of Maldon* includes the source text; edited text; parallel literal translation; verse translation; a review of 103 books and articles.

This edition has a helpful guide to Old English verse.

£5.95 96 pages

## Beowulf: Text and Translation

**Translated by John Porter**

The verse in which the story unfolds is, by common consent, the finest writing surviving in Old English, a text that all students of the language and many general readers will want to tackle in the original form. To aid understanding of the Old English, a literal word-by-word translation is printed opposite the edited text and provides a practical key to this Anglo-Saxon masterpiece.

£6.95 192 pages

## An Introduction to Early English Law

**Bill Griffiths**

Much of Anglo-Saxon life followed a traditional pattern, of custom, and of dependence on kin-groups for land, support and security. The Viking incursions of the ninth century and the reconquest of the north that followed both disturbed this pattern and led to a new emphasis on centralized power and law, with royal and ecclesiastical officials prominent as arbitrators and settlers of disputes. The diversity and development of early English law is sampled here by selecting several law-codes to be read in translation - that of Æthelbert of Kent, being the first to be issued in England, Alfred the Great's, the most clearly thought-out of all, and short codes from the reigns of Edmund and Æthelred the Unready.

£5.95 96 pages

## English Heroic Legends

**Kathleen Herbert**

The author has taken the skeletons of ancient Germanic legends about great kings, queens and heroes, and put flesh on them. Kathleen Herbert's extensive knowledge of the period is reflected in the wealth of detail she brings to these tales of adventure, passion, bloodshed and magic.

The book is in two parts. First are the stories that originate deep in the past, yet because they have not been hackneyed, they are still strange and enchanting. After that there is a selection of the source material, with information about where it can be found and some discussion about how it can be used.

£9-95 268 pages

## Peace-Weavers and Shield-Maidens: Women in Early English Society

**Kathleen Herbert**

The recorded history of the English people did not start in 1066 as popularly believed but one-thousand years earlier. The Roman historian Cornelius Tacitus noted in *Germania*, published in the year 98, that the English (Latin *Anglii*), who lived in the southern part of the Jutland peninsula, were members of an alliance of Goddess-worshippers. The author has taken that as an appropriate opening to an account of the earliest Englishwomen, the part they played in the making of England, what they did in peace and war, the impressions they left in Britain and on the continent, how they were recorded in the chronicles, how they come alive in heroic verse and riddles.

£5.95 64 pages

## Anglo-Saxon Runes

**John. M. Kemble**

Kemble's essay *On Anglo-Saxon Runes* first appeared in the journal *Archaeologia* for 1840; it draws on the work of Wilhelm Grimm, but breaks new ground for Anglo-Saxon studies in his survey of the Ruthwell Cross and the Cynewulf poems. It is an expression both of his own indomitable spirit and of the fascination and mystery of the Runes themselves, making one of the most attractive introductions to the topic. For this edition new notes have been supplied, which include translations of Latin and Old English material quoted in the text, to make this key work in the study of runes more accessible to the general reader.

£5.95 80 pages

## Looking for the Lost Gods of England

**Kathleen Herbert**

Kathleen Herbert sifts through the royal genealogies, charms, verse and other sources to find clues to the names and attributes of the Gods and Goddesses of the early English. The earliest account of English heathen practices reveals that they worshipped the Earth Mother and called her Nerthus. The tales, beliefs and traditions of that time are still with us in, for example, Sand able to stir our minds and imaginations.

£5.95 64 pages

## Rudiments of Runelore

**Stephen Pollington**

This book provides both a comprehensive introduction for those coming to the subject for the first time, and a handy and inexpensive reference work for those with some knowledge of the subject. The *Abecedarium Nordmannicum* and the English, Norwegian and Icelandic rune poems are included in their original and translated form. Also included is work on the three Brandon runic inscriptions and the Norfolk 'Tiw' runes.

£5.95 88 pages

## Anglo-Saxon FAQs

**Stephen Pollington**

125 questions and answers on a wide range of topics.

Are there any Anglo-Saxon jokes? Who was the Venerable Bede? Did the women wear make-up? What musical instruments did they have? How was food preserved? Did they have shops? Did their ships have sails? Why was Ethelred called 'Unready'? Did they have clocks? Did they celebrate Christmas? What are runes? What weapons and tactics did they use? Were there female warriors? What was the Synod of Whitby?

£9.95 128pages

## Tastes of Anglo-Saxon England

**Mary Savelli**

These easy to follow recipes will enable you to enjoy a mix of ingredients and flavours that were widely known in Anglo-Saxon England but are rarely experienced today. In addition to the 46 recipes, there is background information about households and cooking techniques.

£5.95 80 pages

## **Plain English** – A Wealth of Words

**Bryan Evans**

The message here is not that we should strive in a narrow-minded way to scorn and drive out all borrowed words – it is that, if we stop and think, we can probably find a plain English word for what we want to say. We will thus keep plain English alive and help it thrive. We have been given a great gift, let us wherever possible use it and keep it safe.

This wordbook outlines the story of English then it offers 'A hundred words to start you off' (*shorten* rather than *abbreviate*, *speed up* instead of *accelerate*, *drive home* rather than *emphasize*, and so on). In the main part of the book will be found over 10,000 English words that are still alive and well, then a list of some 3,600 borrowed words, with suggestions about English words we might use instead. It is hoped that this book will help readers think about the words they use, and in doing so speak and write more clearly.

£12.95 328 pages

## A Guide to Late Anglo-Saxon England
### From Alfred to Eadgar II 871–1074

**Donald Henson**

This guide has been prepared with the aim of providing the general readers with both an overview of the period and a wealth of background information. Facts and figures are presented in a way that makes this a useful reference handbook.

Contents include: The Origins of England; Physical Geography; Human Geography; English Society; Government and Politics; The Church; Language and Literature; Personal Names; Effects of the Norman Conquest. All of the kings from Alfred to Eadgar II are dealt with separately and there is a chronicle of events for each of their reigns. There are also maps, family trees and extensive appendices.

£9.95 6 maps, 3 family trees, 208 pages

## The English Elite in 1066 - Gone but not forgotten

**Donald Henson**

The people listed in this book formed the topmost section of the ruling elite in 1066. It includes all those who held office between the death of Eadward III (January 1066) and the abdication of Eadgar II (December 1066). There are 455 individuals in the main entries and these have been divided according to their office or position.

The following information is listed where available:

What is known of their life;
Their landed wealth;
The early sources in which information about the individual can be found
Modern references that give details about his or her life.

In addition to the biographical details, there is a wealth of background information about English society and government. A series of appendices provide detailed information about particular topics or groups of people.

£14.95 272 pages

## Tolkien's *Mythology for England*
### A Guide to Middle-Earth
**Edmund Wainwright**

Tolkien set out to create a mythology for England and the English but the popularity of his books and the recent films has spread across the English-speaking world and beyond.

You will find here an outline of Tolkien's life and work. The main part of the book consists of an alphabetical subject entry which will help you gain a greater understanding of Tolkien's Middle-Earth, the creatures that inhabit it, and the languages they spoke. It will also give an insight into a culture and way-of-life that extolled values which are as valid today as they were over 1,000 years ago.

This book focuses on *The Lord of the Rings* and shows how Tolkien's knowledge of Anglo-Saxon and Norse literature and history helped shape its plot and characters.

£9-95 hardback 128 pages

## The Origins of the Anglo-Saxons
**Donald Henson**

This book has three great strengths.

> First, it pulls together and summarises the whole range of evidence bearing on the subject, offering an up-to-date assessment: the book is, in other words, a highly efficient introduction to the subject. Second – perhaps reflecting Henson's position as a leading practitioner of public archaeology (he is currently Education and Outreach Co-ordinator for the Council for British Archaeology) – the book is refreshingly jargon free and accessible. Third, Henson is not afraid to offer strong, controversial interpretations. The Origins of the Anglo-Saxons can therefore be strongly recommended to those who want a detailed road-map of the evidence and debates for the migration period.
>
> *Current Archaeology*

£14.95 296 pages

## The Elder Gods – The Otherworld of Early England
**Stephen Pollington**

The purpose of the work is to bring together a range of evidence for pre-Christian beliefs and attitudes to the Otherworld drawn from archaeology, linguistics, literary studies and comparative mythology. The rich and varied English tradition influenced the worldview of the later mediaeval and Norse societies. Aspects of this tradition are with us still in the 21st century.

£29 70 illustrations 528 pages

## Anglo-Saxon Riddles
**Translated by John Porter**

Here you will find ingenious characters who speak their names in riddles, and meet a one-eyed garlic seller, a bookworm, an iceberg, an oyster, the sun and moon and a host of others from the everyday life and imagination of the Anglo-Saxons. Their sense of the awesome power of creation goes hand in hand with a frank delight in obscenity, a fascination with disguise and with the mysterious processes by which the natural world is turned to human use. This edition contains **all 95 riddles of the Exeter Book in both Old English and Modern English.**

£5.95 144 page

## Organisations

### Þa Engliscan Gesiðas (The English Companions)

Þa Engliscan Gesiðas is a historical and cultural society exclusively devoted to Anglo-Saxon history. The Fellowship publishes a quarterly journal, *Wiðowinde,* and has a website with regularly updated information and discussions. Local groups arrange their own meetings and attend lectures, exhibitions and events. Members are able to share their interest with like-minded people and learn more about the origins and growth of English culture, including language, literature, archaeology, anthropology, architecture, art, religion, mythology, folklore and material culture.

For further details see www.tha-engliscan-gesithas.org.uk or write to:

Membership Secretary, The English Companions, PO Box 62790, London, SW12 2BH

### Regia Anglorum

Regia Anglorum is an active group of enthusiasts who attempt to portray as accurately as possible the life and times of the people who lived in the British Isles around a thousand years ago. We investigate a wide range of crafts and have a Living History Exhibit that frequently erects some thirty tented period structures.

We have a thriving membership and 40 branches in the British Isles and United States - so there might be one near you. We especially welcome families with children.

www.regia.org *General information* eolder@regia.org *Membership* join@regia.org

### The Sutton Hoo Society

Our aims and objectives focus on promoting research and education relating to the Anglo Saxon Royal cemetery at Sutton Hoo, Suffolk in the UK. The Society publishes a newsletter SAXON twice a year, which keeps members up to date with society activities, carries resumes of lectures and visits, and reports progress on research and publication associated with the site. If you would like to join the Society please see website: www.suttonhoo.org

### Wuffing Education

Wuffing Education provides those interested in the history, archaeology, literature and culture of the Anglo-Saxons with the chance to meet experts and fellow enthusiasts for a whole day of in-depth seminars and discussions. Day Schools take place at the historic Tranmer House overlooking the burial mounds of Sutton Hoo in Suffolk.

For details of programme of events contact:-

Wuffing Education, 4 Hilly Fields, Woodbridge, Suffolk IP12 4DX
email education@wuffings.co.uk website www.wuffings.co.uk
Tel. 01394 383908 or 01728 688749

## Places to visit

### **Bede's World** at Jarrow

Bede's world tells the remarkable story of the life and times of the Venerable Bede, 673–735 AD. Visitors can explore the origins of early medieval Northumbria and Bede's life and achievements through his own writings and the excavations of the monasteries at Jarrow and other sites.

Location – 10 miles from Newcastle upon Tyne, off the A19 near the southern entrance to the River Tyne tunnel. Bus services 526 & 527

Bede's World, Church Bank, Jarrow, Tyne and Wear, NE32 3DY

Tel. 0191 489 2106; Fax: 0191 428 2361; website: www.bedesworld.co.uk

### **Sutton Hoo** near Woodbridge, Suffolk

Sutton Hoo is a group of low burial mounds overlooking the River Deben in south-east Suffolk. Excavations in 1939 brought to light the richest burial ever discovered in Britain – an Anglo-Saxon ship containing a magnificent treasure which has become one of the principal attractions of the British Museum. The mound from which the treasure was dug is thought to be the grave of Rædwald, an early English king who died in 624/5 AD.

This National Trust site has an excellent visitor centre, which includes a reconstruction of the burial chamber and its grave goods. Some original objects as well as replicas of the treasure are on display.

2 miles east of Woodbridge on B1083 Tel. 01394 389700

### West Stow Anglo-Saxon Village

An early Anglo-Saxon Settlement reconstructed on the site where it was excavated consisting of timber and thatch hall, houses and workshop. There is also a museum containing objects found during the excavation of the site. Open all year 10am (except Christmas) Last entrance summer 4pm; winter 3-30pm. Special provision for school parties. A teachers' resource pack is available. Costumed events are held on some weekends, especially Easter Sunday and August Bank Holiday Monday. Craft courses are organised.

For further details see www.weststow.org or contact:

The Visitor Centre, West Stow Country Park, Icklingham Road, West Stow,
Bury St Edmunds, Suffolk IP28 6HG Tel. 01284 728718